THE FOURTH
REVOLUTION

To Don
Can you believe this?
we came through this.
With best wishes.
Bill
1/06

THE FOURTH REVOLUTION

Transformations in American Society from the Sixties to the Present

ROBERT V. DANIELS

Routledge
Taylor & Francis Group

NEW YORK AND LONDON

Published in 2006 by
Routledge
Taylor & Francis Group
270 Madison Avenue
New York, NY 10016

Published in Great Britain by
Routledge
Taylor & Francis Group
2 Park Square
Milton Park, Abingdon
Oxon OX14 4RN

© 2006 by Taylor & Francis Group, LLC
Routledge is an imprint of Taylor & Francis Group

Printed in the United States of America on acid-free paper
10 9 8 7 6 5 4 3 2 1

International Standard Book Number-10: 0-415-91077-3 (Hardcover) 0-415-91078-1 (Softcover)
International Standard Book Number-13: 978-0-415-91077-4 (Hardcover) 978-0-415-91078-1 (Softcover)
Library of Congress Card Number 2005014298

Library of Congress Cataloging-in-Publication Data

Daniels, Robert Vincent.
 The fourth revolution : transformations in American society from the sixties to the present / Robert V. Daniels.
  p. cm.
 Includes bibliographical references and index.
 ISBN 0-415-91077-3 (hardback : alk. paper) -- ISBN 0-415-91078-1 (pbk. : alk. paper) 1. Social change--United States--History--20th century. 2. Social movements--United States--History--20th century. 3. Revolutions--United States--History. 4. United States--Social conditions--1945- I. Title

HN59.D36 2005
303.48'4'097309045--dc22   2005014298

Taylor & Francis Group
is the Academic Division of Informa plc.

Visit the Taylor & Francis Web site at
http://www.taylorandfrancis.com

and the Routledge Web site at
http://www.routledge-ny.com

Contents

Introduction:
A New Kind of Revolution

An antiwar demonstration is broken up by hard-hat construction workers. Blacks pillage and burn at the news that their leader who preached nonviolence has been assassinated. Women picket the Atlantic City Miss America contest and throw their underwear into a trash bin. Chinese youth seize their teachers and parade them with dunce caps on their heads. Students in Paris throw up barricades and battle the police with sticks and paving stones.

What do all these well-remembered episodes of the late 1960s have in common, and what do they tell us about the modern condition? They all exhibit violent, revolutionary emotions, even though none led to the forcible overthrow of a government. They all underscore how turbulent the recent past has been despite its material advances. But a concept has been lacking that can bring all these diverse symptoms of stress and conflict into a coherent picture of contemporary society and what it has been going through.

It is easy to say simply that our times are revolutionary, but this does not explain very much. Granted, the twentieth century was witness to more revolutionary violence than any epoch before it, perhaps more than all previous human history. But not all revolutionary change comes about by violence. In fact, after midcentury, with no more than localized fighting, the Western world and particularly the United States of America underwent a revolution in their ways of life and of the mind just as profound as any forcible governmental overturns of the past.

Many expressions of this new revolution are thoroughly familiar—the youth revolt, the civil rights movement in the United States, radical feminism, the sexual revolution. But the fundamental distinction between movements of this sort and the old legacy of revolutionary beliefs is not well understood by either the advocates or the opponents of a new social order. We hear of the "New Left" versus the "Old Left" or the "new liberalism" versus the "old liberalism," but no one seems sure where old values leave off and new ones take over. In fact, as I attempt to show in this book, the new kind of revolution is altogether different from those that preceded it, not only because it has gone on around governments more than through them but also because it is animated by a basically new set of issues and goals.

What are these new issues and goals, and why is this revolution the "fourth"? The Fourth Revolution came upon us in the aftermath of a centuries-long series of revolutionary upheavals that have defined modern civilization. It is a new experience of social disorder and value conflict, shared by the United States to one degree or another with most other industrialized countries. This is the social upheaval that welled up in the mid- and later 1960s, expanded and consolidated its influence through the seventies and eighties, and showed its face with renewed insistence in the nineties. Throughout, it has been distinguished by demands for radical change not so much in government and economy as in face-to-face human encounters, in the relations between races, sexes, ages, producers and nonproducers, teachers and students, the normal and the abnormal.

In this light, we can affirm that 1776 was not the last American Revolution. In the past hundred years, the United States has undergone not one but two more distinct revolutionary experiences—the New Deal era of the 1930s and the great Cultural Revolution of the sixties, if we can call it that. Though muted by comparison with the greatest revolutions in European history—the government was not violently overthrown in the recent American cases—these episodes nonetheless manifested the same laws of ebb and flow in the advance and recession of political and social change. America at the millennium was still feeling the pendulum swings set in motion by the last of these revolutionary challenges.

If the constellation of new social movements in the United States and elsewhere since the 1960s truly deserves to be called a revolution, what then were the three that preceded it? To answer this question and thereby to understand what the Fourth Revolution really means, and what is different about it, we need to take a long look back at the history of mankind's revolutionary struggles. We can view the whole of civilization in modern times as a transition by fits and starts, often violent, from traditional society to what we can still only very roughly delineate as modern society. Begun in Western Europe, this transformative process now operates worldwide. Its essence has been a struggle to overcome the power hierarchies and obligatory belief systems on which practically all traditional societies everywhere in the world have been based. Each stage of the transition has been exemplified by a particular revolution, driven by a particular kind of revolt against old hierarchies and authorities, and advancing most sharply in one particular country at a time.

* * *

Western Europe happened to be the locale where the transition from traditional to modern society first appeared, and it was in Western Europe that revolutionary events at the end of the Middle Ages marked the onset of that transition. At the explicit level, the first modern revolutionary upheavals were primarily religious movements, beginning with the German and Dutch Reformation of the sixteenth century and culminating in the English Revolution of the seventeenth. This initial wave of modern revolution was directed in the first instance against the hierarchical authority of certain people over other people in matters of religion, and thus to support the "priesthood of all believers." It was a fight for the freedom and responsibility of the individual conscience, but at the same time it was the prototype for succeeding struggles for freedom and equality in all other aspects of life.

Next, overlapping the religious revolt came the political kind of revolution, encompassing the wave of revolutionary upsurge in the Western world that perked in the French Revolution of 1789. These movements all aimed at overturning the old monarchical order and securing political freedom and equality in place of hereditary power and the privileges of noble blood. The American Revolution of 1776 was a key event in advancing the first two revolutionary sources of modern life, in religion and in government.

The third kind of revolution remains far less complete, and it is still a divisive factor in Western society as well as in the world at large. It was an economic struggle—a revolt against forms of privilege and inequality that were based not on religious status or noble birth but on the power of property owners over nonowners. Usually movements of this nature were bound up with the idea of socialism, though in America they were better known in the paler variants of populism, progressivism, and New Deal liberalism.

The great historic representative of the Third Revolution, obviously, was the Russian Revolution, together with the Communist movements that rose up in its wake around the world. But this does not mean that the aspirations of the economic revolution are confined to the parties known as Communist or that this kind of struggle is exclusively bound to the terror and totality of the Russian model. Throughout the Western world, with or without benefit of ideological guidance, movements have taken shape with the aim of counterbalancing the power of the owners of private capital, whether this objective be pursued through governmental restraints on business or the collective private action of trade unionism. In the United States, the anticapital movement surged up in nearly revolutionary terms in the era of the New Deal. Outside the West, capital has more often than not been identified with foreign ownership, so that movements of the Third Revolution commonly identified themselves with nationalism and anti-imperialism, and often linked up with the Soviet Union on that ground.

During the long sequence of modern revolutions, each successive upsurge of rebellious sentiment became focused in its most violent form in particular countries. The Netherlands and then England pursued the religious revolution, America and France embodied the political revolution, and Russia epitomized the economic revolution. Naturally, the issues were mixed in each case, and the successive forms of the revolutionary impulse were not confined to the countries where they took shape most clearly. Revolutions are international movements. Whatever their stripe, in whatever era, they have usually evoked both broad responses and stubborn reactions in other places, not just at home.

* * *

What, then, of the Fourth Revolution? This is a concept identifying the social protests that burst forth in many forms in the mid-twentieth century, all over the modern and modernizing world. The notion of the Fourth Revolution covers an array of movements primarily directed not against religious, political, or economic overlords but against relationships of power and inequality in direct personal relationships throughout society. The Fourth Revolution includes the rebellion of the young against the old and established; the rebellion of women against their traditionally inferior status; rebellions against racial domination and subordination, above all in the United States; and the revolt against meritocracy, that is, against the authority of officials and experts in all sectors of social organization, public or private. This last has been the special target of student movements around the world.

The Fourth Revolution strives for the ultimate in personal freedom and equality for all. A constellation of protests bracketed as the New Left, it is as distinct from the Old Left as the latter was from the liberals-turned-conservative who stayed in the tradition of the religious and political revolutions.

As we look back, the Fourth Revolution expresses everything that made the 1960s and the decades that followed different from the 1950s.

As I attempt to show, the concept of the Fourth Revolution has great power of clarification in the muddled and simplistic political discourse of our epoch, particularly in the United States. It illuminates the different meanings in both "liberalism" and "conservatism" and the political realignments prompted by them. It helps identify and put in context the various campaigns for equal rights and equal recognition, ranging from the handicapped to the homosexual, that are still going on in the new millennium.

Unlike its predecessors, the Fourth Revolution has usually proceeded as a series of broad and amorphous social movements, without the literal overthrow of governments or even abrupt electoral takeovers. However, there was one extraordinary episode where the Fourth Revolution and its social values were embodied in a violent political upheaval. This was the era of the Cultural Revolution in Mao Tse-tung's China in the 1960s, actually a late phase in a long and arduous revolutionary experience going back more than a half a century. In America and Western Europe, the Fourth Revolution scored its impact through events that were unmistakably revolutionary in flavor even though governmental authority remained nominally intact. The claims of this new movement as the ultimate pursuit of social justice could not be ignored, even though in America, in the manner of all revolutionary upheavals, the Fourth Revolution was challenged by counterrevolutionary reactions that called into question not only the newest revolutionary aspirations but the conquests of the first three revolutions as well.

* * *

As this picture of successive waves of continent-wide and ultimately worldwide change suggests, revolution has a broader meaning than the familiar historical image of mobs, barricades, guillotines, and the violent assault on constituted authority. A revolution is not a momentary event; on the contrary, it is a long process that extends over years and even decades in the country where it is centered. The process takes time, as the particular revolutionary aspirations of a given epoch crystallize in an escalating series of assaults against tradition. Typically the process proceeds from moderate reform to utopian extremism, before circumstances and exhaustion deliver the movement into the hands of pragmatists, opportunists, and sometimes of counterrevolutionaries. These people in turn try to synthesize some kind of postrevolutionary order, using elements of both the old and the new.

Part or all of a revolutionary process in a given country may transpire without more than marginal violence. What makes a movement revolutionary is the depth of its challenge to accepted values and the intensity of conflict that it stirs up. And if the movement is indeed revolutionary, it almost always goes through the characteristic series of ascending and descending stages that has marked all the great revolutions of history.

In most places the Fourth Revolution has taken the less violent, less literal form, marked by dramatic social struggles but without extending to violent governmental overthrow. This kind of conflict could be called a "semirevolution," where the movement of new values is able to transform or at least polarize the public psyche even though the institutions of government may not be seriously threatened by violent subversion. In many cases the advances of the Fourth Revolution are testimony to the efficacy of the philosophy of nonviolent protest. Nevertheless, just as in the classic, violent revolutions, the stage-by stage model of the revolutionary process still process model works for semirevolutions, to describe the swings of the political pendulum from early enthusiasm to subsequent radicalization and on to ultimate retreat and consolidation.

In the history of twentieth-century America, it is possible to discern three distinct semirevolutionary cycles of reform and reaction. The first two, the Progressive Era before World War I and the New Deal of the 1930s, were manifestations of the diluted American version of the economic revolution, the worldwide egalitarian struggle against the power of private property. President Lyndon Johnson introduced his "Great Society" program of the 1960s to revive this unfinished revolution. However, combined with the contentious issue of the Vietnam War, Johnson's Great Society initiatives quickly triggered rebellious forces of a very different sort. These were the social protests of the Fourth Revolution, expressed both at the level of national policy and in the localized violence of the student movement and the movement for racial equality.

In all these instances of semirevolutionary change, as in episodes of semirevolution that could be cited in Europe (e.g., the British Labour government of 1945–51, or the student revolts of 1968), the forces for change peaked and faltered in the face of resistance to their revolutionary aims. In each instance, conforming to the process model of the revolution, the rebel surge gave way to pragmatic consolidation and sometimes to outright counterrevolutionary leadership that hoped to roll back all the changes brought in by the semirevolution. The United States went through such periods of reaction after both world wars and again in a muted way in the 1970s and 1980s. Recognizing the postrevolutionary character of these eras helps to explain the frustration of reformers in times like these.

* * *

The objective of this book, in essence, is to explain the recent political experience of the United States and analogous movements elsewhere by analyzing them in the historical framework of revolutionary change and counterrevolutionary resistance. It is directed to anyone who feels a sense of concern or perplexity about the present state of modern civilization and is interested in the implications that the history of revolutionary crisis in different times and places may have for us today. No solutions are offered, and no partisanship is intended; the sole aim is to understand a little better where the world has come from, as the basis for choosing the steps that might take us where we wish to go.

An opening look at political debate in the United States shows the confusion that has enveloped all political categories and alignments as the Fourth Revolution and the "culture wars" unfolded. Then the book turns to the concept of revolution as an expression of modernization, explains the sequence of four kinds of revolution, and lays out the revolutionary process as a pattern in nonviolent as well as violent change. This framework is followed by an exposition of the first three revolutions in the history of the United States.

After this ground-work the book turns directly to the Fourth Revolution, in global terms and in the American setting of the Great Society and the upheavals of the 1960s. The Fourth Revolution in the United States is then detailed in successive of chapters on the civil rights movement, the student movement and the youth rebellion, and feminism and the sexual revolution. Then come accounts of the aftermath of revolution, as counterrevolution mounted its resistance at the same time that the revolutionary impetus pushed into diverse parts of the body social. The next-to-last chapter is the actual summing up and conclusion, while the final chapter discusses the possible emergence of an altogether new revolutionary development, a Fifth Revolution, rooted in the most extreme elements of the Fourth but going on to an even more radical agenda that calls into question some of the most fundamental propositions of modern civilization.

As explained further in the Addendum to Chapter 10, certain terminology has changed in the course of the Fourth Revolution itself. The practice here is to employ the designations in use at the time of the events being described—thus, "black" instead of "African-American," "American Indian" instead of "Native American," and so forth.

CHAPTER 1

The Terms of Revolutionary Debate

For decades the Western world and above all the United States of America have been in the throes of a new revolution, not a massively violent and bloody one, to be sure, but a revolution nonetheless. It has not been a revolution of the kind familiar in history, where crowds mount the barricades, troops seize government buildings, and royal heads roll; it has not changed the physical face of life or destroyed public institutions. Nevertheless, this Revolution of the Sixties, as it is often identified, was a real one, more so than many Americans realized who saw it only as juvenile wrongheadedness or negativistic exhibitionism. The revolution touched many parts of the world, but few areas—save the violence-ridden Far East—so deeply and none so permanently as the United States. In the phrase of *Washington Post* writer E.J. Dionne, it set off a "cultural civil war" that is still going on.[1]

This revolution was not the kind that history normally depicts, of coups and terror and dictatorship. Nor was it a revolution in the tradition of the past three centuries, a movement to depose the ruling classes in the name of constitutional government or collective economy. Instead, it has proceeded, not always quietly but without any general insurrection, as a sea change in the prevailing way of life and thought. While it stayed within narrow confines politically, the Revolution of the Sixties struck deep in the dimensions of human relations and psychology. It has been a revolution of values, the kind of revolution religious reformers have always called for, though not necessarily what they expected—a revolution in the human heart.

This new revolution was not permitted to run smoothly ahead; instead, it suffered intervals of counterrevolutionary rollback. Just as in the classical revolutions of history, aftershocks of disillusion and reaction that shook American political and intellectual life. Yet the new revolution has not relented in principle, and its expressions—above all, the "culture wars"—have continued and even revived right down to the present. The question remains open as to its potential advance onward into the future.

But for all the turmoil and soul-searching that this revolutionary tide has provoked, it has won very little understanding in depth, either in the United States or overseas. The University of Virginia sociologist James Hunter attributed the trouble to "hostility rooted in different systems of moral understanding" and bemoaned "the absence of conceptual categories or analytical tools for understanding cultural conflict."[2] Millions of people who came to maturity during the 1960s can testify that they "didn't know what hit us," all the while that the Western world thought it was successfully standing off revolution in the guise of the Communist Bloc and the ideology of Marxism–Leninism. The West simply lacked any mental categories by which it could comprehend the new revolution that it was experiencing internally, or even clearly describe and debate it.

This dimness marks the United States above all, though it is the country most shaken in the present era by the struggle of revolution and counterrevolution. Americans do not think with a sense of historical process but view the world more in terms that are moral and emotional, and at the same time simplistic, encapsulated in slogans and analogies. Though presidential campaigns, ought theoretically to highlight public concerns and remedies, the level of insight they achieve has been dropping ever downward. History, for the disputants, is a series of reassuring guideposts, often mythologized, as a substitute for defining their real principles.

Revolutionary Cycles in America

While Europe has had more familiarity with revolution in recent times, the American tradition is that of one "good" revolution, the Revolution of 1776, that was long supposed to have put the nation's values and institutions in place for all time. This tradition has made it even harder for many Americans to recognize the new revolution for what it is, as a profound internal transformation and not some diabolical subversion instigated from who knows where. Nor has this revolution been the first great social crisis experienced by the nation since its independence. The Civil War era was both revolutionary and counterrevolutionary, and it was marked by one of the worst ordeals of internal violence ever experienced by any country.

The New Deal era, following the crisis of the Great Depression, was another time of struggle over basic principles, though like the revolution of the 1960s and after, it did not descend into systemic as opposed to episodic violence.

Distinct cycles of reform and reaction have run regularly through American history in the past century and a half, as Arthur Schlesinger pointed out in his well-known essay on this theme.[3] They have tended to peak about every thirty years, in other words once in a generation, as potential leaders nourished on reform in one era come into positions of influence after an interval of retrenchment and turn the country toward change again, for a while. In recent decades, presidential campaigns focused the ups and downs of the cycle precisely into a thirty-two-year period, with high points of reform and protest in 1936 and 1968, and troughs of nostalgia in 1952 and 1984.

These cycles in American politics do not just repeat the same old debates, however. New issues have been infused into them, while the country has grown and changed and experienced new stresses and new problems. What distinguished the reformist peak of the 1930s (and the Progressive Era thirty years before) from previous turns of the political revolving door was the surge in controversy over economic issues and competing class interests. Struggles of this sort were secondary in America's eighteenth-century revolution, though the familiar thesis of the Progressive historian Charles A. Beard would hold that the years of constitution-making were a time of postrevolutionary reaction aiming to make sure that the economic interests of the elite would not be put in jeopardy by a runaway democracy.[4]

Since the late nineteenth century, economic issues have reared up with each repeat of the political cycle. In the 1960s, however, debate took a new turn, as a new set of political principles, reflecting the new revolution we are trying to define, became the driving force in national change. Toward the millennium, the sentiments of the new revolution still loomed large as the cycle seemed to rise again.

The unique feature of the present epoch in American life is the overlapping presence of two unfinished revolutionary agendas, both likely to recur with the political cycle, sometimes reinforcing each other and sometimes competing. The older, economic agenda, having lost much of its constituency and excitement, remains far from complete, while the newer, social agenda presses on aggressively but also with the sense that it is still distant from full realization. Much of the public, confused and frustrated, turns away from politics except when an unconventional personality like H. Ross Perot declares war on the whole system.

Liberalisms and Conservatisms

People in the United States today no longer understand what they are arguing about. Debate still proceeds along the political spectrum—liberal and conservative, Left and Right—but the old terms no longer show through meaningfully in the haze of new problems and new challenges that are but dimly grasped even by the activists who represent them. The commentator Mickey Kaus found American liberalism hopelessly confused about the goals of politics: "The house of liberalism needs more than repairing, remodeling, or even thorough renovation. We need to rip the house down and build it anew on a more secure foundation."[5] E.J. Dionne extended the indictment to both of "the dominant ideologies of American politics. … Liberalism and conservatism *prevent* the nation from settling the questions that most trouble it."[6] As the cultural historian Christopher Lasch observed, "Old political ideologies have exhausted their capacity either to explain events or to inspire men and women to constructive action."[7]

Despite this evidence of confusion, polemics still wax violent over the heresies that each side presumes are festering under the banners of the other camp. The words *liberal* and *conservative* remain active in our language, and if they are not analyzed for all their diverse implications they will continue to be used for purposes of political obfuscation. So the first requirement for understanding the revolutionary world of our time is to look to the forms of language that shape political responses to this world and cleanse them of the contradictions and misunderstandings that events have piled up in contemporary thinking.

The familiar terms of *liberalism* and *conservatism* together convey several sets of meanings that are not often distinguished. Their most general meaning is relational: Where does one stand on the political spectrum in relation to innovation and tradition? The liberal advocates whatever form of change in public life is being debated in a given epoch, and the conservative resists it, while the radical would forge ahead violently and the reactionary wants to turn the clock back, perhaps also by force. In this sense, people are liberal or conservative not by virtue of the particular view they hold but depending on whether those views are ahead of the times or behind them.

Beyond these basic meanings, there is a series of historical pairings of liberalism and conservatism that express support or opposition to particular programs of change in particular epochs. As people who have experienced America's transition from the 1950s to the 1970s will immediately understand, a viewpoint that is radical in one era can reduce to merely liberal in the next, and ultimately conservative, as it is incorporated into the status quo and defended by opponents of further change against new generations of liberals and radicals. Looking back over two centuries of American history, with a parallel glance at Europe, one can see the progression of political and social thought through three distinct sets of liberal–conservative polarities. These are, roughly speaking, the political, the economic, and the social.

The distinction between the political and economic meanings of liberalism and conservatism has been developed at great length by a host of writers, to contrast the classical political liberalism of the nineteenth century and with the Progressive–New Deal economic liberalism of the twentieth. In this vein, the conservative philosopher Robert Heineman distinguished "classical liberalism" and the newer "reform liberalism."[8] The liberal J.G. Merquior recognized the same distinction as "classical liberalism" and "social liberalism."[9]

Political liberalism, based on constitutional government, individual rights, the separation of church and state, laissez-faire economics, and the independence of subject nations, emerged in the eighteenth century in the wake of the English Revolution and under the beneficent glow of the Age of Enlightenment. This was the classical liberalism anchored in the thought of Thomas Jefferson, Tom Paine, and Adam Smith, that, as Louis Hartz showed in his classic work,[10] permeated the American psyche. The new United States inherited almost nothing of the old European conservatism of absolute monarchy, legal class privilege, state churches, and mercantilist regulation of the economy. This was the America that so impressed de Tocqueville. "The immigrants who fixed themselves on the shores of America in the beginning of the seventeenth century," he wrote in *Democracy in America,* "severed the democratic principle from all the principles which repressed it in the old communities of Europe."[11]

Eliminating what remained of the old conservatism, the American Revolution affirmed classical liberalism as the context for all subsequent political life and debate. In Britain too, by the time the old Whig and Tory parties took on the names Liberal and Conservative, respectively, in the middle of the nineteenth century, parliamentary government and capitalist enterprise were firmly established, and politics revolved around classical liberalism; party differences were to be found mainly in nuances such as free trade and extension of the suffrage. On the European Continent, by contrast, classical liberalism had to fight its way through one revolutionary battle after another against monarchism and the survivals of feudalism, from 1789 until the last third of the nineteenth century, before liberal principles more or less prevailed west of the Russian border.

This victory of liberalism in continental Europe was not general, secure, or permanent. In the past century, everywhere in Central and Eastern

Europe, classical liberalism fell back in the face of twin onslaughts of by the radical Left of Communism and the radical Right of Fascism and Nazism. The term *liberal* survives today in Western Europe only as the designation of those political movements, usually small, that resist both the controlled economy of the socialists and the clericalism of the Christian Democrats. Only the British Conservative Party, notwithstanding its name, is a significant embodiment of the classical liberal philosophy. The British Liberals, reduced to minor party status by the rise of socialism and the Labour Party, endure today merely as one element (along with Labour's former right wing) in the watered-down reformism of the Liberal-Democratic Party.

Marxists used to describe classical liberalism as the ideology of the bourgeoisie as it waged class war against feudal landowners and absolute monarchies in the name of economic freedom and the legal equality of individuals. There is much truth in this characterization, considering that Marx formulated his theory of class struggle and the ideological "superstructure" justifying the interests of the ruling class just when the business class was coming into its own in Europe. But in America, the Revolution of 1776 bequeathed classical liberalism as the frame of reference shared by practically everyone. This liberalism was not a class ideology but a national faith.

The second liberal–conservative polarity, of much more recent vintage, revolves around economic rather than political issues. It took shape during the nineteenth century in reaction to problems generated by industrial capitalism that had never been addressed by classical liberalism. In Europe the quest for economic reform found its embodiment in the Social-Democratic or Labor parties, along with more radical elements who rallied to the cause of Soviet-style Communism after the Russian Revolution. In America, challenges to the economic order of classical liberalism emerged mainly within the existing two-party structure of politics, in the form of Progressivism at the turn of the century and New Deal liberalism in the 1930s.

Liberalism in this new sense was directed toward structural economic change, to remedy the perceived evils of the competitive capitalist struggle and, as President Franklin Roosevelt said, to put human rights ahead of property rights. The new liberalism embraced the Welfare State, supported trade unionism, attacked the power of corporate monopoly (by nationalization in Europe, by trust-busting and regulation in America), addressed income inequalities by progressive taxation, and endeavored to stabilize the economy by recourse to the Keynesian fiscal balance wheel.

The conservative term in this new debate was a defense of the nineteenth-century system of free-market economics and limited government, letting the devil take the hindmost according to the justice of Social Darwinism. In other words, the new conservatives in the economic sense were the old classical liberals. In America, there was no other philosophical position for defenders of the economic status quo to fall back on, although in Europe between the wars economic conservatism all too often degenerated into the Fascist and Nazi backlash against political liberalism as well. Meanwhile, economic liberalism was often upstaged by the radicalism of the Communist International.

Neither New Deal liberalism nor European Social Democracy can be as neatly analyzed in class terms as was classical liberalism in Europe. To be sure, enlisting the bulk of the industrial working class (that is, in countries where the workers were not captured by the Communists), these parallel movements of reform did partake of the class struggle of the proletariat against the capitalists. But for New Deal liberalism or Social Democracy to gain the opportunity to rule, they had to win over substantial numbers of farmers and middle-class elements in some sort of populist coalition against the power of concentrated wealth. The historian Alonzo Hamby has asserted, perhaps a bit overconfidently, "The New Deal made collectivist democratic liberalism the norm in American politics," a norm that "won gradual, reluctant acceptance from a conservative opposition forced toward it by the imperatives of acquiring and keeping political power."[12] A broadly perceived commonality of economic interest in collective bargaining, full employment, stabilizing of markets and competition, social insurance, and consumer protection was the foundation for the political success of liberalism in the economic sense.

This economic liberalism of the New Deal era in America was never fully implemented, diverted and frustrated as it was first by the nation's preoccupation with World War II and then by the conservative reaction in the popular mood for the following decade and a half. Mid-twentieth-century America settled into an equilibrium of half-fulfilled New Dealism in thought as well as action, beyond which in the Cold War era it was difficult to make further progress. Note, for instance, the nation's inability ever since the 1940s to complete the social insurance system with a universal health care component; its reluctance to enact a guarantee of full employment; the decline of trade unionism; the lapse in antitrust enforcement; and the failure to expand public enterprise on the model of the Tennessee Valley Authority. The Cold War permitted patriotism to be enlisted in the service of economic conservatism, with the suggestion that liberalism meant socialism and that socialism led inexorably to communism.

Liberals, thrown intellectually and politically on the defensive, could neither complete nor rethink their agenda.

The Social Revolution and the Crisis of Liberalism

The postwar era was unhinged in the 1960s by the intrusion of a totally new liberal–conservative face-off, the Fourth Revolution, in fact. Opinion was polarized again, but on new lines, around a social rather than economic issues. The occasion for this new eruption of discord was the political opening afforded by John Kennedy's "New Frontier" and Lyndon Johnson's "Great Society," movements ostensibly taking the Roosevelt New Deal as their point of departure. But the struggles that ensued at many levels of American life in the 1960s and early 1970s moved into a new dimension, only vaguely addressed by the old economic liberalism, which was a contest not over property rights and economic power but over social and cultural values, and for equal rights of participation in the established power structure. This struggle was manifested in the black civil rights movement and the movement for women's rights, culminating in the institutionalizing of affirmative action, attacks on extra-legal segregation, and de facto quota policies to offset past discrimination in education and employment. The struggle was further embodied in the educational revolution to democratize access and standards and to eradicate signs of "elitism." And it was shockingly exhibited, to paraphrase the Chinese slogan of that era, in the Great Middle-Class Cultural Revolution of midcentury youth as they discovered hair, sex, drugs, rock music, and the titillation of defiant behavior.

The supreme commandment of the new social liberalism was "Thou shalt not discriminate," a principle carried to unprecedented lengths in movements for equal treatment of the physically handicapped, the mentally ill, the sexually unconventional, and the legally delinquent. Integration, affirmative action, mass education with eased standards, and the proportionate representation of all kinds of disfavored groups in the existing pyramids of political and economic power became the new subjects of confrontation, fought over on battlegrounds ranging from the streets to the courtrooms.

Needless to say, these novel social and attitudinal developments were highly unsettling to many, adult Americans, whatever their alignment on the old economic issues. Everyone imbued with the puritan and patriarchal tradition reacted in horror, particularly over the specter of loose sex and the drugs and permissiveness that were presumed to induce such behavior. Social conflict took a form more generational than class. Even the old radical Left, those few in America as well as the many in Europe, generally felt a deep antipathy toward the New Left. People who for one reason or another resisted the new social liberalism took on the label "conservative" and the slogan of "traditional values," even though they may have been liberal on the old economic agenda. Such were the Neo-Conservatives and Reagan Democrats, the intellectual and working-class contingents whose switch exactly paralleled the way unyielding devotees of classical political liberalism had taken up the conservative position and label in response to economic liberalism.

Confusion over the terms of debate in American political life has been systematically exploited ever since the Nixon–McGovern presidential campaign of 1972. Rightly or wrongly, George McGovern was tagged with the liberal label in its new social meaning, and he went down to an unprecedented defeat as the wave of postrevolutionary reaction against the social innovations of the sixties swept millions of traditionally Democratic voters, liberal in the old economic terms, into the Republican presidential column. Thanks to the confusion of terms, Democratic candidates and presidents have been unable to sustain the old liberalism unburdened by the new. Michael Dukakis, in his 1988 presidential campaign, was the first to experience this liability acutely when he inadvertently identified himself with the "L-word."[13]

Republican candidates and their political consultants from Ronald Reagan to the present have sensed that the most immediate understanding of the word *liberal* in the mind of the American public is the liberal position on the new social issues, especially in its boldest variants. Accordingly, GOP politicians have systematically exploited fear of crime, covert racism, and antipathy to radical feminism and homosexual rights, all mobilized by the code words *mainstream, family,* and *traditional values.* The old economic liberalism of fairness, positive government, and the priority of social justice over Big Money, a platform that still might have evoked real enthusiasm, has been burdened down by the new social overtones of liberalism. In the perceptions of the swing voter, liberalism cannot escape the taint of cultural subversion. But at least until 1994 this rule did not apply so markedly to congressional elections, where Democratic majorities were still won on the basis of the old economically liberal benefits, sometimes relabeled "populism" or "progressivism." "The public-opinion polls seem to suggest," wrote the commentator Robert Kuttner during the Reagan era, "that the Democrats need to move right on social and perhaps defense issues, but left on economics."[14] American voters in the majority are social conservatives when they think about the general principles that come up in national campaigns, but contrary to the right-leaning "New Democrats," they are economic liberals when it comes to the concrete, pork-barrel matters of local campaigns.

One major element in the new conservative mood did involve a break from the old economic liberalism, and had much to do with the loosening of the New Deal coalition. The Johnsonian Great Society, directed in full faith at completing the work of the New Deal, found that those primarily in need of its ministrations were the underclass of minorities, the unemployed, and the unemployable, casualties of social injustice or social breakdown. These elements of the "Bottom Out-of-Sight" class, as the critic Paul Fussell termed it,[15] were the primary beneficiaries of welfare, Medicaid, food stamps, and social services. It was in their name that Legal Aid and the Office of Economic Opportunity commenced a novel incursion into the power structure of neighborhood and small-town America.

Because the standing achievements of the New Deal, plus the advances of the private sector in such areas as pensions and health insurance, plus the boom of the 1960s, provided well for most of the employed wage-and-salary-earning middle and working class, the accomplishments of the Great Society had the altogether unexpected effect of driving a sharp wedge into the American social structure at a very sensitive point. Below it were the underclass minorities who benefited from the government's new forms of largesse; above was the large majority who, according to their ability or their tax breaks, paid for those "social programs" (code words that average taxpayers understood as paying with money for somebody else's irresponsibility). Thus, simultaneously with the generational conflict of the Cultural Revolution, the 1960s saw the emergence of what can legitimately be called a new class struggle, involving social attitudes as well as economic interests. In place of the classic class struggle between workers and the owners of capital, it was a struggle, however unfortunate one may find it, of the working majority against the troublesome and unproductive (and disproportionately black) minority on the bottom. This was the animosity that culminated in the primitive welfare reform law of 1996.

A clarion call for what the economist John Kenneth Galbraith called a "revolt against the poor"[16] was California's "Proposition 13," launching the Great Taxpayer Revolt of the late 1970s and early 1980s. Articulate liberalism had by then so lost touch with its broader economic roots that it could reply only by arguing the unfairness of cutbacks affecting the destitute; little or nothing was said about the benefits that a well-funded government might bring to the middle class. No wonder the Republicans could hold the presidency for twelve years, and then win it back at the millennium, with a program to slash federal taxes, giving financial relief to the rich and psychological relief to everyone else who felt exploited for the benefit of the undeserving underclass.

Philosophies of Human Nature

Beneath all the successive lineups of liberal and conservative positions there are certain absolute and timeless philosophical assumptions about human nature and the human potential. On the liberal side are the optimists, the Rousseauians, who see men and women as naturally good, and improvable as well if only they are released from oppression or see their social conditions corrected. The pessimistic, conservative side, the Burkeans, see people as naturally undependable, sinful, or, worse, creatures who need a firm framework of tradition and institutions to guide them. Human-nature liberals have tended to the philosophy of social determinism: evils are caused by circumstances. Conservatives stress individual choice and responsibility, guided by social sanctions. If someone is poor, or neurotic, or criminal, it is the fault of the social environment, according to the liberal. It is consequently society's obligation to nurture the wayward individual and straighten out its own broader failings. For the conservative, deviant subjects have only themselves or their genes to blame and are properly constrained by circumstances or by the police power of the state.

As modern society has grown more affluent and more tolerant, philosophical liberalism has flourished, whereas times of adversity bring on the opposite. In America, according to Robert Heineman, "With the exception of the pre-Civil War South and the Puritans, conservative assumptions, which emphasize tradition, limited human capacity, and the need for controlling human passions, simply have not been seen as playing an important political role," though he believes the public has always been more conservative than its leaders.[17] At any rate, as individuals grow older, more mature—or more tired—they tend to slide from liberal to conservative attitudes in the basic philosophical sense, turning toward authority and standards and rejecting freewheeling liberal relativism.

The old classical liberals of the eighteenth and nineteenth centuries were, of course, optimists. Their conservative counterparts held the pessimistic view of mankind and warned of the destabilizing effects on the masses of the weakening of authority and untoward social change. Edmund Burke, patron saint of present-day conservatives, was an anomaly for his time, steeped as he was in the British constitutional system and sympathetic to the American Revolution, yet fearful that disruptions of tradition could unleash the worst in human nature in the manner of revolutionary France. Sometimes he has been called a "liberal conservative."[18]

When the new economic liberalism began to emerge a century after Rousseau and Burke, classical liberals found themselves going the way of the pessimists, arguing now that any tinkering with the competitive spur of the market would destroy incentives and responsibility and put an end to prosperity. New Deal liberals and European Social-Democrats, on the other hand, ascribing most misery and deviance to the economic system, picked up the banner of the optimistic philosophy. In the most recent stage, the optimistic view has been taken over by the social liberals, in the conviction that discrimination and unequal opportunity or collective historic wrongs lie at the root of poverty and crime. Hence affirmative action, deinstitutionalization, compassionate criminology, and prison furloughs. Those diverse elements who are ranged on the conservative side of the social question, even many among the Old Left and New Deal liberals, find themselves driven to pessimistic conclusions about the neglect of individual responsibility, effort, and competence. Commanding the political high ground in the United States since the 1970s, pessimistic conservatives draw overwhelming support from the public when they cry for law and order (as long as it does not extend to gun control) and berate the bleeding hearts in the judiciary and the correctional system for coddling criminals. Practically everyone now doubts the effectiveness of further social reform under the aegis of government.

The new philosophical pessimism evoked by the excesses and short-comings of Great Society liberalism was the common denominator of the Neo-Conservatives of the Irving Kristol–Nathan Glazer school.[19] These often improbable cases of conversion to an ostensibly stand-pat outlook were mostly relics of the New Deal tradition or the Old Left. They were driven to Burkean premises about man and society by the antics of the New Left, reverse discrimination, educational anarchy, and the preoccupation of the Welfare State with the underclass. By the 1980s they found themselves under the same Reaganite revival tent with New Right evangelicals, and have remained there with Bush the Younger.

Nationalism, Religion, and the Environment

As though this map of today's disputed philosophical terrain were not complicated enough, with the distinctions of liberalism and conservatism as relational, political, economic, social, and philosophical, there are other intense feelings on the American political scene that since the sixties have constantly been hooked onto the liberal–conservative dichotomy. These issues include some of the most heated questions confronting the American electorate: national defense, the natural environment, and the role of religion in public life.

Nationalism is one of those forces that moves around on the liberal–conservative spectrum depending on time and circumstances. Classical liberalism believed in the right of each people to a free national existence, in opposition to dynastic empires. In Europe, by the late nineteenth century, nationalism was captured by the conservatives and the empire-builders (and inherited by the Fascists and Nazis), while the Marxists were saying that the workers had no fatherland. In the third world in the twentieth century, by contrast, nationalism again became revolutionary.

In the United States, since 1917, nationalism has been more often linked with conservative viewpoints. During World War I, patriotism was invoked to silence radicals, if not liberals. In the Cold War era, identification of the free enterprise ideal with resistance to the Russians helped put a damper on any further progress of New Deal liberalism. Then came the eruption of the 1960s, when the new wave of social liberalism coincided with the civil rights movement and the Vietnam War. Opposition to this most debatable of America's belligerent involvements set off a confrontation of nationalism and antinationalism more heated than ever before witnessed in the United States. As Frances Fitzgerald showed in her graphic study of high-school textbooks,[20] ripples of antinationalism spread swiftly through the entire understanding of the American heritage, popular as well as academic, turning American history from a saga of saints and heroes to a litany of national and racial crimes. More recently, black, feminist, and Native American advocates, taking issue with the whole triumphalist view of the American past, have even challenged the traditional verities of Western civilization—but of this, more later.

Meanwhile, social conservatives resisted the mood of national shame. Until the fading of the Soviet threat, they seized every opportunity offered by Communist misbehavior to rehabilitate the spirit of American national honor and military strength. Some public figures of impeccable New Deal credentials accepted the conservative designation primarily because they feared the Soviet threat or resented Soviet treatment of dissidents and minorities, and therefore made common cause with more traditional conservatives in the rehabilitation of an activist American foreign policy. This was the school of Neo-Conservatives led by Senator Henry Jackson and the sociologist and future senator Daniel Patrick Moynihan, who mobilized in the early 1970s as the Committee for a Democratic Majority but lost many of their troops to Reagan in 1980. The collapse of Communism removed foreign policy for the time being from the field of polarized political contention in the United States, though Islamist terrorism stepped into that vacuum after the attacks of September 11, 2001. A few Americans on the far right, typified by the commentator and sometime presidential aspirant Patrick Buchanan, have revived the conservative kind of American nationalism that opposes any sort of foreign involvement not affecting the vital interests of the nation.

Even more difficult to make sense of in relation to the liberal–conservative spectrum is the area of environmental, resource, and energy issues that have arisen since the 1960s to command a large share of the nation's political attention. Logically those who shudder at the developer's bulldozer and nuclear power-plant failures should be classified as conservative, while those who still believe in better living through chemistry—that is, the blessings of technological progress—should be counted as the liberals. In fact the conventional labeling is the opposite. Those who call themselves conservatives hail the prospects of unlimited economic growth, and the self-styled liberals worry about pollution and historic preservation and other consequences of the growth that the industrialized world has already achieved.

Again the problem is to distinguish the relativistic and substantive meanings of the liberal and conservative labels. While an environmentalist is a conservative in the literal sense of the term, it is economic liberalism and its readiness to regulate the private businessman that incline people to the environmentalist view, and social liberalism happens to coincide with it most of the time as well. Some of the most radical manifestations of political protest in recent years have been directed against business endeavors threatening the natural habitat of endangered species or indigenous peoples. Conversely, nuclear-power advocates could be called liberals if not radicals in the relative sense because they endorse social and economic change, but they have usually come to this viewpoint as economic conservatives (i.e., nineteenth-century laissez-faire liberals) who assume that private business can do no wrong.

A third emotional issue intruding itself on the cluttered political spectrum in the United States is religion, primarily in the form of resurgent Protestant fundamentalism. As with environmental questions, there is no inherent connection of religious doctrine with liberalism or conservatism in their various concrete manifestations—and certainly not in the economic respect. Nevertheless, the new evangelical politics has ardently embraced the conservative label. The reason is simple enough: fundamentalism crystallized into a major political force in reacting against social liberalism and particularly against the sexual aspects of the latter, as witness campaigns against legal abortion, the Equal Rights Amendment, and gay rights. Moreover, the politics of religious conservatism reflects (though it does not always articulate them) the skeptical premises about human nature underlying conservatism in the philosophical sense.

A further link, more emotional than logical, has connected resurgent religious conservatism with American nationalism. The relationship is not new; Americans in the majority have long held to the religious assumption that they are God's chosen nation. Confrontation with officially atheist

Russia in the cold war merely underscored the affiliation of religion and patriotism. The evangelical refrain was Puritan morality, free enterprise, and military superiority.

Revolution, Reaction and the Future

In politics as in physics, every action has an equal and opposite reaction, or nearly so. Every revolution, every deep reform movement, is followed by a conservative reaction, with its content depending on the specific liberal–conservative agenda of the particular epoch. The revolutionary era that opened in Europe in 1789 gave way to monarchist reaction during the first half of the nineteenth century. The Populist and Progressive era in American history was followed by the laissez-faire normalcy of the 1920s, spiced by fear of the Russian Revolution. The New Deal revolution gave way to the reaction of the 1950s, descending at its worst to McCarthyism. In the same way, the near revolution of the sixties in social relations generated its own backlash, manifested politically in the electoral reactions of 1968, 1980, and 1994, and national polarization since 2000. Political scientists and pundits have scrambled to explain these shifts by the tactics and strategy of momentary leadership, though the basic national cleavages of urban versus rural, coasts versus middle, North versus South, "blue" versus "red" states are not new.[21]

The spirit of post-sixties reaction in America is particularly striking in the political mobilization of religious fundamentalism, railing against "liberal humanism" and the gender revolution in particular. Curiously, the religious reaction to social liberalism not only rejects that realm but also goes out of its way to repudiate economic liberalism in favor of unabashed free enterprise. On the other hand, endeavoring to invoke governmental authority in matters of faith and morals—symbolized by the school prayer issue—religious conservatives call into question the separation of politics and religion in the heritage of classical liberalism in America. The journalist Thomas Frank has dramatized the political power of this new alliance of old verities in his insightful and compelling book *What's the Matter with Kansas?*[22] Some classical liberals who were conservatives on economics —Barry Goldwater comes to mind, as well as the philosophical novelist Ayn Rand—stood their ground against these excesses of the New Right. They were the consistent libertarians.

Does the American future, politically and philosophically, belong to conservatism, or does liberalism in any sense of the word have a chance? The answer depends on which meaning one has in mind. The political heritage of classical liberalism still seems to be secure, reinforced by public distrust of government, and despite the authoritarian predilections of

Bush Republicans and the Religious Right. By contrast, the economic liberalism embodied in the post–New Deal compromise is splintered and apologetic. Meanwhile, social liberalism is vigorously engaged with its critics, particularly on those issues—welfare, crime, affirmative action, and so on—where it divides the underclass from the middle majority. But no one these days expresses much confidence in the liberal philosophy of mankind's perfectibility through improved institutions.

Is America destined, then, to be set back to the 1950s? Will it be confined to a post–Great Society compromise of equal access to an unequal social pyramid? Or is there some political future for a revival of liberal change, perhaps harking back to the unfinished economic business of the New Deal? Could a majority constituency ever be found again for faith in the improvability of humanity's lot? At times, economic frustration may prompt a growing number of citizens once again to accept governmental interventionism despite their misgivings, but it may equally lead them to blame the government for all their woes. In any case, little is likely to be accomplished in these confused times unless we can sort out the real issues that unite or divide us and debate new solutions without the burden of outworn political labels that confuse more than they contribute.

CHAPTER 2

A Revolutionary World

The poverty of political discourse in the United States today is evidence enough of the need for new perspectives and new analysis of our present condition. We need to turn to history, not for isolated lessons and parallels but to develop new tools of interpretation and to provide a long-term context for understanding our contemporary perplexities. This is what I propose to work out by applying to the contemporary United States the perspective of revolutionary change, and in particular the concept of the Fourth Revolution.

The Revolutionary Process

Revolution nowadays is commonly thought to be a destructive intrusion into the natural course of history. This is a shortsighted illusion that ignores the tremendous historical transformation separating traditional society—the Middle Ages in Europe and more recent analogues in other parts of the world—from modern society. In fact, the whole modern world and the entire modern way of life are products of a revolutionary past. All of the greatest changes of recent centuries have radiated around the world from a series of revolutionary centers, like waves made by some giant boulders cast by the gods on Olympus into the sea of humanity every century or so. If these upheavals had not taken place, it is impossible to conceive of modern belief, modern science, modern government, modern principles of equality and legality, modern mass society.

It is not enough, however, to recognize that we are living in a "revolutionary" age, that "the times they are a-changin'." The concept of revolution has a very definite meaning and offers specific explanatory powers as applied to our current circumstances. I attempt here to set forth a pattern or model of revolution as a characteristic process of change that is basic to understanding modern history. Even though revolutions are usually painful and costly, and are seemingly cruel or irrational afflictions when viewed close up, they represent a fundamental force, the "locomotives of history," as Marx called them, driving progress and evolution in the human condition.

Revolutions are processes of transformation rooted in the deepest nature of modern society. Contrary to the common supposition that attributes them to heroic or demented leaders and their philosophies or their plots, such movements arise and proceed for the most part independently of anyone's deliberate will and expectations, even of those who suppose that they are leading these convulsions. Revolutions are historical earthquakes, violent tremors set off when pressures building up along society's fault lines overcome the bonds of stability and expose humanity to frightening conflicts. Prerevolutionary tension is discernable, at least in retrospect, in a country's intellectual life, as new values give confidence to the discontented and undermine the old rulers' belief in themselves. The actual trigger of revolutionary events may come quite accidentally, as a financial crisis, an economic downturn, or a military misadventure. Often resolute leadership can contain or postpone the effects of such crises, but at other critical times incompetent and vacillating leadership invites the collapse of the Old Regime.

But this is only the beginning. A revolution has to be understood not just as a momentary event but as an extended process, that is, as a chain of events and situations where each link leads to the next in a recognizable way as governments break down and reemerge, and basic social values and relationships are transformed. Furthermore, the process of revolution tends to follow a characteristic pattern, not in absolute detail, of course, but in general outline. The best-known proposition of such a pattern of the revolutionary process was that conceived by the late Crane Brinton: a medical model of revolution as a "fever."[1]

Brinton's model tracks the experience of revolution through a series of stages analogous to the progress of a disease. Brought on by some previous weakness or infection in society, the malady appears first in a moderate, nonthreatening form, then takes a turn for the worse and rises to the acute pitch of its extremist or radical phase. After this crisis the illness subsides. The social body, like a convalescing individual, then returns to its old self, not unaffected but not wholly changed either, and perhaps stronger for the experience.

Major revolutions do indeed exhibit a distinctive series of stages more or less corresponding to the medical image, with some modifications and additions. They begin with a moderate phase: the rule of the Long Parliament in England when it challenged King Charles I and defeated him in civil war between 1640 and 1647; the rule of the Estates General and the Legislative Assembly in France between 1789 and 1792; the rule of the Provisional Government in Russia between the February and October revolutions of 1917. Then, whether step-by-step or all at once, the moderates are displaced by extremists: Cromwell and his army in England in the years 1647 to 1649, executing the King and establishing a republic; Robespierre and the Jacobins in France of 1792 to 1794, accomplishing the same in a reign of terror; Lenin and his Bolsheviks, imposing their dictatorship in the October Revolution of 1917 and dispatching the Tsar and the Imperial family the following year. Typically the extremist phase generates sects of ultra-revolutionaries, utopian idealists whose hopes and expectations go beyond the people in power and foreshadow the next revolutionary epoch, but these purists are always suppressed by the mainstream revolutionaries. Finally comes retrenchment, the Thermidorean Reaction, so called from the events of the French Revolution after the extremist dictator Robespierre lost his head on the ninth day of Thermidor, Year II, according to the revolutionary calendar, or July 27, 1794. The Thermidorean Reaction permits the nation to return to more normal conditions of life. Analogous events in England and Russia were not punctuated as dramatically as in France, but they are still fairly clear: Cromwell's dismissal of the "Parliament of the Saints" with their Puritan utopianism in 1653, and Lenin's introduction of the semicapitalist New Economic Policy in 1921.

To the three stages that Brinton describes, a fourth should be added, following or overlapping the retreat from revolutionary purity. This is the phase of postrevolutionary dictatorship, a regime constructed by an opportunistic strongman who is able to combine the practical features of the new regime with what cannot be suppressed of the old, in a new synthesis of personal power. In England, Cromwell himself was assuming the postrevolutionary role of a military dictator, when it was interrupted by his death in 1657. Napoleon Bonaparte played the part in France, from which the term "Bonapartism" has often been drawn for this phase. The corresponding figure in Russia was, obviously, Joseph Stalin.

If the postrevolutionary dictatorship then falters or, as in France, is overthrown by foreign enemies, a counterrevolution or even a literal restoration of the old monarchy may take place. However, these are steps backwards more in form than in substance: both Charles II in England in 1660 and Louis XVIII in France in 1815 had to accept semiconstitutional governments that had more in common with the early phase of the revolution than with the Old Regime. Moreover, in both these cases the ambiguity was resolved a few years later by a coup that avowedly reinstated the principles of the revolutionary moderates—the "Glorious Revolution" of 1688 in England and the "July Revolution" of 1830 in France. As for Russia, the model of successive revolutionary phases illuminates the movements of retrenchment and postrevolutionary dictatorship that proceeded beneath the surface continuity of the Communist regime—the New Economic Policy of 1921–28, the "Stalin Revolution" of the late 1920s and early 1930s, and the "Great Retreat" from revolutionary experiment in the mid- and later 1930s.[2] Even in the Russian case, postrevolutionary dictatorship ultimately came to an end, under Mikhail Gorbachev and Boris Yeltsin, in what might be termed a "moderate revolutionary revival."[3]

The process approach attempts to treat revolution as a natural phenomenon, driven through its successive stages by deep-seated social forces. In this perspective, revolutions are not really made by revolutionaries, even though revolutionary leaders and parties of various stripes always try to put themselves at the head of the process at each stage. Said Napoleon, in exile on St. Helena, "A revolution cannot be made or stopped."[4] Revolution in its fullest expression is the working out of a deep crisis in the life of a society, when the irresistible force of social evolution collides with the immovable object of traditional institutions.

Driving Forces of Revolution

Is there some vast but identifiable force for change underlying the long and tormented history of revolutions? Such an explanation can readily be found in the global process of social transformation that for lack of a more concrete, agreed-on designation is generally termed "modernization." To be sure, it has of late become fashionable among historians to quibble about this idea, and strictly speaking "modernization" means only bringing things up to date, whatever and whenever that may be. But as a broad historical concept the term has come to denote the prolonged, complex, and uneven process of change from traditional society to the features that distinguish our contemporary existence.

In the deeper sense modernization covers the transformation in recent centuries from a way of life that was hierarchical, religious, and largely rural and illiterate, one based on hand labor and animal power, to a way of life that is egalitarian in the legal respect, secular, largely urban and educated, and based on industry and technology. Modernization dissolves old community, friendship, and class relations and puts a premium on individual competence and achievement. It is "a process of increasing complexity in human affairs," moving toward "inquiry and questioning" and "a special kind of hope," in the words of the political scientist David Apter.[5] Sometimes modernization is equated with industrialization, but in a fully modernized economy the agrarian sector can be nearly as high tech as the urban–industrial sector; "technicization" might be a more apt term to cover both areas. By generating new social groups with new interests, who embrace new ideas and make new demands, modernization inexorably corrodes the old order, like a commercial development that guts the spirit of a historic town. Modernization can no more be resisted than the tides that King Canute commanded to roll back.

Modernization happened to begin in Western Europe, as early as the fifteenth century, and it happened to be led by the West—Western Europe and North America—until the twentieth century, when Asia started to catch up. This does not necessarily imply that there is something peculiarly "Western" about modernization, or that the West enjoys some sort of innate superiority for having initiated it. Traditional societies around the world, including medieval Europe, have had more in common with each other than any have had with the modern condition. Nevertheless, for better or worse, modernization is perceived in other parts of the world as "Westernization"; that is, as an alien way of life offered or imposed by the West upon other civilizations, even though it is in fact a global experience that has transformed Western society as much as any other, if perhaps more gradually. Identification with the West does not by itself explain what modernization is or its revolutionary impact, but the Western angle does give the process a sharper edge in places where it seems to come from outside.

The connection between modernization and revolution is one of the most obvious features of modern history, though surprisingly many theorists of modernization overlook its revolutionary implications. The eminent political scientist Samuel Huntington was an exception, when he linked "social mobilization" and "social frustration" with "political instability."[6] "Revolution," he asserted, "is the ultimate expression of the modernizing outlook."[7] The sociologist Theda Skocpol was more specific: "All modern social revolutions ... must be seen as closely related in their causes and accomplishments to the internationally uneven spread of capitalist economic development and nation-state formation on a world scale."[8]

Pressure for revolutionary change—the historical earthquake—typically accumulates as society modernizes while government tries to stand pat and defend the old order. Growing urban and mercantile elements in society—that is, the middle class, very broadly understood—provided the motive force for revolution from the sixteenth century to the eighteenth. By the late nineteenth and early twentieth centuries it was the new industrial workforce, the "proletariat" of Marxism. Sometimes revolution was triggered by modernizing efforts of the old government, aiming to centralize and rationalize its powers and its finances. King Charles I and Louis XV's chief minister Robert Turgot come to mind, not to mention the British government in the decade preceding the American Revolution.

The history of the classic revolutions, with the striking correspondences that emerge through all the differences of time and place and personality and ideology, suggests that there are certain universal qualities in the nature of human society that govern the way it will respond to severe stress. Modernization and disruptive social change stimulate caustic intellectual disaffection long before an actual revolution breaks out. In an actual crisis the parties of change tend at first to be cautious and legalistic. Then, as the reflexes of obedience to authority dissolve, pent-up grievances and more radical hopes activate the public and provide the platform on which extremists can climb to power. But the excesses of fanaticism undermine support for the revolution, and its leaders must ride the downward wave or be spilled by it. Finally, the need and opportunity for someone to repair the bonds and loyalties of a torn society offer the chance to some charismatic leader to impose his own manias in the name of order, whether revolutionary or counterrevolutionary or the two in succession. This is all a complicated and empirical way of describing how the pendulum of political change swings after a revolutionary crisis gives it that initial push.

Recognizing these back and forth movements is more than a key to understanding revolution. It clarifies how any major social change takes place, not only in revolution where it stands out more clearly but also in less violent situations where a society manages to respond to some stress or disturbance without an overt collapse of its governmental institutions.

Generated as it is by modernization, a given revolution necessarily embodies whatever forms of social change have matured at the moment when it breaks out. But matters go further. In the extremist phase of a revolution, the swing of the political pendulum, pushed by accumulated dissatisfaction with the Old Regime, carries the country in question temporarily beyond what its people are prepared to sustain permanently. This revolutionary overreaching is what sets the stage for the retrenchment phase and postrevolutionary consolidation. All revolutions, in the later stages of the process, betray their original devotees, except for those—sometimes even leaders—who are adaptable enough to change their spots to fit in with the times of retreat.

Nevertheless, retrenchment, postrevolutionary dictatorship, counter-revolution, and monarchical restoration cannot ignore the degree of change that really has taken place in the revolutionary country, change that rules out permanent return to the status quo ante. It is the force of social change already achieved but insufficiently accommodated under a postrevolutionary dictatorship or restored monarchy that ultimately propels the moderate revolutionary revival, or that may even set up a new revolutionary cycle (as in France from the Revolution of 1848 to the Paris Commune of 1871). Revolution is thus a cumbersome and agonizing series of events in the course of which a social system adapts to the dictates of the modernization process.

Nations, Classes, Values

The revolutionary experience is not confined to any one country at a time. All the great revolutions have been international in the issues they raise and in their impact on their neighbors. They always arouse both sympathy and antipathy. Sympathizers invite the revolutionary country to help them replicate the revolution, and enemies plot intervention to stifle the force of revolutionary example. But usually a revolution is slow to spread internationally. It moves only by fits and starts, because the country where it has first broken out is the place where the conflict between the Old Regime and the aspirations of that revolution was most acute. Other governments, in zones of diminishing revolutionary tension, are able successfully to resist the revolutionary movement, as Western Europe staved off the Communist challenge following World War I. The exception is when the initial revolutionary power can mobilize overweening military resources, as the French Revolution did, to expand its influence in the form of a temporary revolutionary imperialism.

Thanks to the influence of Marxism, it is common to think of revolution above all as the manifestation of class struggle. There was the bourgeoisie fighting the feudal aristocracy, as in the French Revolution, and then the proletariat against the bourgeoisie, as in revolutions from 1848 to 1917. The class approach undeniably has some truth to it, within limits, though revisionist historians dispute its simplicity. In any case, the class principle does not work very well to account for the ups and downs of the revolutionary process or to explain revolutions earlier than the French and later than the Russian. We need a broader conception of the stakes in revolution, one that takes account of psychology as well as economics. Such an approach would consider the issues in revolution as matters of broad values or principles of human relationships, not just the purely economic interests of particular classes or social strata. It would also take account of the generational factor in revolution. Revolutionaries, not surprisingly, are mainly young men, particularly those who throw their enthusiasm into revolutionary extremism to achieve whatever may be the goals of the times.

If revolutions are viewed as struggles over clusters of social values that emerge in the course of the modernization process, a richer panorama of revolutionary transformation opens up. Modernization generates revolution, but it generates different kinds of revolutions, contesting different sets of values, at successive stages in the modernizing process, and in countries further and further removed from the original West European center of the modernizing transformation. In consequence, we have seen in history a distinct sequence of revolutions—religious, political, economic, social—driven by different value conflicts in successive epochs and centered in a different country each time. Each major revolution evinced a struggle for a particular domain of freedom and equality that came into focus as traditional society was step by step being rejected.

The successive value conflicts of the four revolutions, bridging the long passage from traditional to modern society, were all defiant reactions against unequal power and prestige. No one can tell me what to do, says the revolutionary, just because he thinks he is nearer to God, or because he is higher born, or because he is richer, or because he is a white male or an educated expert. In other words, a series of traditional standards governing the status and prerogatives of individuals has one by one been overthrown—anointment by the Lord, parentage and hereditary right, private property, social and economic function. Prior to the First and Second revolutions, society was managed as theocracy and aristocracy. Those upheavals then enabled the ambitious man lacking noble birth to get ahead by getting rich; that is, in a secular plutocracy. The Third Revolution enabled the able man without wealth to get ahead, on the basis of meritocracy and credentials, or simply by membership in a revolutionary organization. The Fourth Revolution proposes that anybody, with or without special ability, should be able to get ahead, thanks to group entitlements.

Naturally the beneficiaries of one kind of revolution are suspicious of the next one, and they often turn up among its most intransigent enemies. Each social order—whether traditional societies or subsequent systems created by revolution—is convinced that protesters within its ranks are subversive. Enemies of the first, religious revolution persecute lapses from the correct faith; enemies of the second revolution, the democratic, disdain all those upstart elements of low birth; enemies of the economic revolution put down those who have not worked hard or speculated successfully to accumulate wealth; enemies of the fourth revolution resent those who claim equality by group right instead of individual qualifications.

Such animosities underlie the backswing that occurs in the course of each revolution. At times, accumulated hostility toward new change may break out in a violent form of counterrevolution, a revolution of the Right, so to speak. This kind of reaction, generically recognized as fascism, may exhibit many of the features of the classic revolution, including the role of violence and a sequence of distinct stages. The revolution of the Right repudiates the values not only of the revolution but also of all previous revolts against tradition. The revolution of the Right strives in one guise or another to return to a neomedievalist paternalism, defying the realities of modernized society.

Not much different, is the Moslem fundamentalist revolution exemplified by the Ayatollah Khomeini's Iran after 1979, couched in anti-Western terms but resembling the Western Right in its rejection of modern values in everything from religious toleration to the status of women.

Revolution without Overthrow

Each of the great worldwide explosions of revolutionary change has received its main impetus from the violent process of revolution in a particular country. But further revolutionary influences a field a society may feel without the actual overthrow of the government. This is particularly true in countries—Britain, for example—that have already experienced deep transformations of their institutions during previous revolutionary epochs. Thanks to the easing of some of their old rigidities, they remain more adaptable to the issues of a new revolutionary age, without breaking down as societies with more brittle structures might.

Thus situations may arise where a country experiences the deep conflicts of revolutionary values challenging the status quo but does not actually undergo the violent collapse of its political institutions. In these episodes it is nonetheless possible to see how a country's response to a revolutionary challenge swings from moderate liberalism to extremist radicalism and back through some sort of retrenchment to a postrevolutionary synthesis. Here, as in the more literal revolutions, the expectations of public opinion shift very quickly to and fro, much faster than the sentiments of private opinion among the "silent majority." Change may be focused in radical and violent movements in certain segments of society—among particular classes, regions, ideological or ethnic groupings, or institutions such as universities or labor organizations—without driving the society's central institutions of government through all the corresponding phases of radical disruption.

The notion of the semirevolution is a way of analyzing nonviolent but still deep and angry struggles for change, making it possible to apply to them the concept of the revolutionary process and the sequence of revolutionary values. It helps make clear how the successive forms of revolution have marked American history, and it is indispensable for comprehending how the Fourth Revolution has played out.

* * *

Even in their damped-down, semirevolution form, revolutions are more than passing convulsions or fevers. They release and solidify new conceptions of human life in society: new mythologies, if you will. Their legacy of new ideological premises is both enduring and cumulative, offering new forms of authority and faith, for better or worse, to replace the hoary principles of traditional society. Long after a revolution is over, its principles continue to serve as reference points for successor regimes to legitimize themselves and their policies. Eventually the values of a given revolution become the conservative rationale for a new status quo. Then a new revolution will erupt somewhere else in the world and challenge old revolutionary lands to confront new forms of change.

Three Revolutions in America

The clichés are correct about the United States. It is a country formed in revolution and built from revolutionary traditions. Compared to other countries torn and shaped by revolution, America has for all practical purposes no prerevolutionary past. But in the past hundred years, the nation has been pushed and challenged in ways it does not really understand, by new currents of revolutionary aspiration that did not exist when the nation was born.

While the American national mythology rightly identifies the country with revolution, it fails to recognize that this identification goes only so far. America has been built on the premises of the First and Second revolutions. This is why it has always been difficult for those Americans who call themselves conservatives and feel the instincts of philosophical conservatism to find a firm basis for their views in the national past. Instead, they fall back on classical liberalism as their alternative to twentieth-century economic and social liberalism. Conversely, liberals in the contemporary sense have to stretch the national tradition to accommodate their leanings toward the Third or Fourth revolutions. The nation incorporates as foundations of its historical identity the revolution for religious freedom (and more broadly, the freedom to think) and the revolution for political freedom (including national independence). But America has never fully come to terms with the Third Revolution, the economic one, and it has been periodically torn and divided in recent decades by the Fourth Revolution of social equality. These limits in the country's sympathies explain how it can be so revolutionary in its self-image and its rhetoric, and at the same time take consistently counterrevolutionary positions against the new forms of revolution that have erupted both at home and abroad in the twentieth century.

The English Background and the First Revolution

The American nation was founded by revolutionaries—at any rate, revolutionaries played a prominent part in the early settlement of the English North American colonies. Seventeenth-century migrants to New England were conspicuously protagonists of the First Revolution in the Mother Country, adherents of religious dissent who left before their revolution actually broke out at home in the 1640s. They vocally sympathized with the Puritan parliamentarians. Governor William Bradford of Plymouth Colony wrote joyfully in 1646, "The tyrannous Bishops are ejected ... and all their superstitions discarded and returned to Rome from whence they came, and the monuments of idolatry rooted out of the land. And the proud and profane supporters and cruel defenders of these ... marvelously overthrown."[1] Meanwhile the civil struggle in England drew in the kind of dissidents who might otherwise have continued to emigrate. A student of the "Great Migration" noted, "Why travel 3,000 miles to create a new society when one could now remake the world at home?"[2] In colonial society, despite the setback that the Brave New World suffered in England with the Restoration of 1660, the psychology and values of the First Revolution remained embedded. That foundation was reactivated by the mid-eighteenth-century religious revival, the "Great Awakening." This movement, according to a modern-day student of religion in politics, generated "millennial expectations that caused people to regard breaking free of England and founding a new republic not simply as a political experiment, but as part of God's great new work on earth."[3]

In the English Revolution, representative political institutions emerged simultaneously with individualist Protestantism as a key axis of struggle. The First Revolution thus shaded into the Second as the king and parliament faced off. This political aspiration was directly reflected in the creation of parallel revolutionary governments in the several colonies. These elective institutions survived the Restoration of 1660 with minimal deference to the principle of monarchical authority, thus anticipating the Glorious Revolution of 1688 and the Moderate Revolutionary Revival in England. In both the religious and political respects, the colonies enthroned the victory of the Puritan Revolution just when it was being turned back and compromised at home. This difference, as much as purely separatist impulses, set the stage for the American Revolution of the eighteenth century.

The Revolutionary Process in America

Writers on the American Revolution divide between the claim that it was especially virtuous among revolutions and the insistence that it was, in the words of the former Librarian of Congress, "hardly a revolution at all."[4] The British historian Denis Brogan explained the contradiction: "The special circumstances of the American situation made it possible to restrict the application of the profoundly revolutionary premises announced to a candid world."[5]

True, there was no Robespierre or Lenin-style terror in America, and no out-and-out postrevolutionary dictatorship. The uppermost urge among American revolutionaries was not the overturn of the social order but the separation from foreign rule and the establishment of an independent national identity. Yet there was plenty of violence of an internal, civil war sort along with the armed struggle against the British Crown, as the historian Carl Becker observed in his famous aphorism distinguishing the questions of "home rule" and "who should rule at home."[6] The priority of national independence over domestic change, together with the war fought to this end, dampened down the potential for more extreme revolution everywhere in the colonies. Nevertheless, the revolution confirmed a great leap in political psychology, from a society of deference to the upper orders as it was inherited from England, to the society of aggressive, egalitarian individualism described by Alexis de Tocqueville half a century later. "If we measure the radicalism by the amount of social change that actually took place," wrote the historian Gordon Wood, "by transformations in the relationships that bound people to each other—then the American Revolution was not conservative at all; on the contrary: it was as radical and as revolutionary as any in history."[7]

Eighteenth century American society, invigorated by the commerce and urban trades of early stage of modernization, was experiencing a distinctive prerevolutionary "cramp," imposed in this case by British rule, more annoying than repressive, yet arbitrary in its relations with the self-assertive yet unrepresented colonies. Intellectually, revolution was prepared by the European Enlightenment, the same philosophies of liberty and equality, of rationalism and representative government, anchored in the works of Locke, Montesquieu, Rousseau, and many others, that fed the French Revolution after giving the American Founding Fathers the bulk of their ideological nourishment. The economic component in this thinking was the antimercantilist, free-market doctrine of Adam Smith and his French contemporaries, the Physiocrats, views that reinforced the Americans' grievances over British trade restrictions. Along with these ideals was the sense of violated tradition, so important in the English Revolution, regarding the principles of representative government and the Puritan ethic.[8] "The commonwealth radicalism of seventeenth-century England continued to flow to the colonists," observed Bernard Bailyn, the leading authority on American revolutionary thought.[9]

If revolutions must begin with some triggering event that unstops the springs of pent-up political tension, it is usually war or financial crisis. For America, the initial signal was the French and Indian War (the Seven Years' War in Europe), which fueled the colonists' sense of self-reliance while leaving the British government in financial straits that it resolved to remedy in part by imposing more realistic exactions on its colonial subjects. These moves precipitated the Stamp Act crisis of 1765, and launched what amounted to a moderate revolution in the colonies, under the slogan of "no taxation without representation." The immediate result was America's breakthrough to a national political consciousness, along with Britain's de facto acknowledgment of colonial home rule in legislative matters.[10] Nonetheless, confrontation continued and colonial resistance stiffened, thanks in part to deliberate political agitation by figures such as Sam Adams. "America must finally work out her own salvation," Adams asserted in 1772, with overtones of outright independence.[11]

The moderate phase of the American Revolution was consummated in 1774, in the aftermath of the Boston tea crisis, by the formation of the Continental Congress, a proto-government of the united colonies. As a revolutionary organ the congress corresponded to the English Long Parliament or the French Estates General, affirming defiance of any British authority as by a foreign imposition.[12] Simultaneously, royal authority was repudiated in every colonial capital save British-occupied Boston. Simply by these decisions the colonial legislatures and their armed militias became institutions of revolutionary power. Wrote the conservative New York aristocrat Gouveneur Morris, "These sheep, simple as they are, cannot be gulled as heretofore. In short, there is no ruling them."[13]

War came in 1775 as an anticlimax, so far had political mobilization in the colonies gone. To be sure, the war radicalized the revolution in its national sense by evoking the explicit aim of independence. At the same time, it provoked what amounted to civil war between Patriots and Loyalists, a schism that cut across all social strata like the polarization of English society by the Long Parliament's defiance of King Charles I in 1642. In both cases the cleavage was primarily psychological, between those who loyally identified with authority and those driven by rebellion's self-assertion. In America the people who stood by the crown tended to come from either the top or from the bottom of society; that is, those enjoying deference and those who were willing to proffer it, or as one expert on the Loyalists saw them, "people who felt weak and threatened

... more afraid of America than they were of Britain."[14] As the premier social historian of the revolution J. Franklin Jameson argued, the price these Loyalists paid for their choice was statistically equal to or even more severe than the impact of the French Revolution, in terms of confiscation of landed property and forced emigration, if not in actual bloodletting.[15] In sum, the civil struggle accompanying the revolution had much to do with sorting out the individualist and antiauthoritarian values in the familiar American character.

In two of the colonies the revolutionary process went forward to a distinct extremist phase. These were New York and Pennsylvania, the jurisdictions experiencing the sharpest social tensions, in contrast to relatively democratic New England and the secure slaveholding aristocracies of the South. Loyalism had its strongest political base in these middle colonies, among the mercantile oligarchies, and here social conflict drove the revolution through the full sequence of phases.

In New York, where the conservative local leadership dragged its feet over resistance to Britain, what amounted to a revolutionary workers' party known as the "Committee of Mechanics" took shape in 1774.[16] By the following year, this movement had achieved what Lenin later called "dual power," as the legal government was confronted by its revolutionary challengers. The latter illegally organized New York's participation in the Continental Congress. Then came the news of Lexington and Concord, the American equivalent of the Storming of the Bastille. As Carl Becker described its impact in New York, "For nearly a week the city was ruled by the mob.... The arsenal was forced open, and about six hundred muskets distributed among the most active citizens, who formed themselves into voluntary corps and assumed the government of the city."[17] Anti-British moderates in the old government hastened to attach themselves to the radicals, and they joined in suppressing Loyalist counterrevolutionaries. This coalition was about to give way to a more radical takeover, when the entire revolutionary phenomenon in New York City was liquidated by British occupation in August 1776. That in turn ensured the local triumph of counterrevolution.[18]

Pennsylvania, like New York, had become a scene of open political hostility, with a religious edge, between the Episcopalian and Quaker oligarchy on one hand and the unrepresented or underrepresented multitude on the other. "Nowhere else," according to Gordon Wood, "was there more social antagonism expressed during the Revolution," and consequently "of all the states in the Revolution it saw the most abrupt and complete shift in political power."[19] As in New York, the democratic elements in Pennsylvania had created a form of dual power by organizing, early in 1775, a Provincial Convention, "clearly an extralegal body," as a specialist on these events described it, "used to supervise the conduct of the lawful Assembly."[20] This was exactly the role initially undertaken by the Petrograd Soviet in relation to the Russian Provisional Government in 1917.

As in New York, the "shot heard round the world" in April 1775 galvanized the revolution in Pennsylvania. The militia provided the democrats with their organization, like the army in the English Revolution and the National Guard in France. Like the revolutionary Russian army of 1917, the citizen-soldiers of revolutionary Pennsylvania rejected military discipline and demanded the right to elect their own officers.[21] Egalitarian and independence sentiment took form around the antimonarchical theme of Tom Paine's eloquent pamphlet *Common Sense,* published in January 1776. "Of more worth is one honest man to society, and in the sight of God," Paine wrote, "than all the crowned ruffians that ever lived."[22] Even the conservative John Adams conceded, "There is no good government but what is republican."[23] Backed both by their own militia and by the Continental Congress holding forth in Philadelphia, the radical minority in the official Pennsylvania Assembly managed to alter the anti-independence instructions of the colony's delegates to the congress. Then the radicals walked out of the assembly, denying it a quorum and consigning it to the ash heap of history. In its place an extralegal constitutional convention, elected by universal male suffrage without any property qualification for the vote,[24] adopted a constitution that was a model of eighteenth-century popular sovereignty, with a unicameral legislature supreme over a subordinate collective executive.[25]

Unlike New York, the brief British occupation of Pennsylvania's capital city of Philadelphia in 1777 and 1778 only stiffened the democratic movement in that colony. By 1779 inflation was feeding the beginnings of an even more radical stage of events, marked by riots and attempts at price control—exactly as in the French Revolution. The revolutionary government eliminated the last vestiges of legal inequality, confiscated all properties that anyone had inherited from Pennsylvania's founder William Penn, and abolished slavery. By twentieth-century standards, of course, these moves were not very radical; they reflected the eighteenth-century quest for a panacea in political democratization that did not come to grips with the economic basis of inequality.

Then the Thermidorean Reaction took hold in Pennsylvania, though it was still a change by ballot, not bullet. Conservatives prevailed electorially in the 1780s, endorsed the new federal constitution disliked by the democrats, and secured a new state constitution modeled on the federal, with a bicameral legislature and a strong executive to curb the whims of the mob. Thus ended the process of revolution in the most revolutionary colony. It did not extend to a bloody convulsion, but nevertheless it exhibited in recognizable degree the characteristic swings and stages of the revolutionary experience.

America and the Revolutionary Tradition

In most places, the American Revolution never went beyond its moderate stage. Violence there was, a war against British overlordship as well as against American opponents of independence, but practically no force was needed to overturn established local authority. Most colonial governments simply voted British suzerainty away, as colonies turned into states, while more ambitious quests to realize the democratic ideal were confined to a few local instances. Thus, apart from the struggle for independence, the American Revolution was only a semirevolution. It was a model of how restrained a revolution might be in the use of force and yet have major social and psychological effects.

Nationally, the revolution wound down as it did in Pennsylvania, sliding gradually into Thermidorean retrenchment and consolidation with the end of the Revolutionary War. The federal constitution was a reflection of this mood, aiming, according to the Charles Beard school of interpretation, to forestall democratic threats to property owners.[26] To this end, it worked. As events right up to the present have shown, the Constitution was a status quo framework that made it very difficult for anyone to use government to change society.

The Revolution left a country divided between the "factions" that the Federalist Papers deplored, but the revolutionary experience was the common point of departure of both the Federalist and Anti-Federalist parties. That tradition could only be played up, in the manner of the Jeffersonian Republicans, or played down as the Hamiltonian Federalists preferred. Thus an ongoing polarity was set up between positions that we would now call "liberal" and "conservative" in the relative sense, while the common philosophical context was classical liberalism in the doctrinal sense. The Jeffersonian Revolution, when Thomas Jefferson defeated John Adams in 1800, might then be viewed as the moderate revolutionary revival in America, changing the emphasis within the framework of classical liberalism and harking back to the populist aspect of the revolution against oligarchic privilege.

The American Revolution was the initial impetus for all those pendulum swings, the cycles of reformism and consolidation, that have marked U.S. political history ever since. In every generation the democratic implications of the Revolution have been reactivated, beginning with the Jeffersonian Revolution and continuing in the 1820s and early 1830s with the Jacksonian Revolution that confirmed the America of the common man (white and male, that is) depicted by Tocqueville. The post–Civil War Reconstruction era represented another such democratizing swing, attempting to perfect the Second Revolution in America by extending it to the black race. Unfortunately, the abandonment of Reconstruction in the 1870s, as the pendulum swung back in that particular cycle, left the Southern states far from consummation of the Second Revolution, with newly freed blacks still disfranchised and destitute. Laid down here was the basis for one of the key forces in the Fourth Revolution in America a century later, the black civil rights movement.

Meanwhile, in the Populist–Progressive era of the 1890s and 1900s, the political pendulum received a new kind of push. Economic issues emerged all around the industrialized and industrializing world to challenge the monopoly capitalism that was flourishing in the political climate of classical liberalism. This was the beginning of the Third Revolution in America and worldwide.

In its own time and for a hundred years afterward, the American Revolution was a benchmark for politics around the globe. Bernard Bailyn wrote, "The interest in American constitutionalism was intense throughout the Atlantic world in the revolutionary years, and in the generations that followed it remained deeply embedded in the awareness of political leaders, publicists, and intellectuals."[27] The "American myth" appeared to validate the critical philosophies of the Age of Enlightenment, by showing, in the words of the historian R.R. Palmer, "that ideas of the rights of man and the social contract, of liberty and equality, of responsible citizenship and popular sovereignty, of religious freedom, freedom of thought and speech, separation of powers and deliberately contrived written constitutions, need not remain in the realm of speculation, among the writers of books, but could be made the actual fabric of public life among real people, in this world, now."[28] Thus, for much of the world the victory of revolution in America raised up the ideal of democratic and nationalist revolution that was to transform the political physiognomy of regions from Latin America to Eastern Europe. Up until the opening of the twentieth century, no other country had fully caught up with the radicalism of the American Revolution. Even to this day, in the public psychology of democratic individualism, no other land has surpassed the American example.

Limits to the American Revolution

For all its radicalism in its own time, the American Revolution had its limits, limits that have been highlighted by new revolutionary challenges to the status quo in the twentieth century. There was only a marginal glimmer of the new kind of revolutionary protest, the economic, that began to crystallize in the industrialized world a century later. The nearest thing to armed class struggle in the eighteenth century was the series of uprisings by aggrieved farmers, including Shay's Rebellion in Massachusetts in 1786 over debt fore-closures, and the antitax Whiskey Rebellion in Western Pennsylvania in 1794, both of which were easily brought under control by the forces of order.

There was no hint in the Second Revolution in America of what was to come in the Fourth. The American Revolution offered nothing for the political and legal status of women, the half of society left out of most democratic considerations until the end of the following century. And its most glaring inconsistency was its toleration of slavery, although it did encourage that practice to be banned in the Northern colonies where it was economically inconsequential. Commented the historian Edmund S. Morgan, "It is perhaps the greatest irony of a revolution fought in the name of freedom that the men who carried it out were able to unite against British oppression because they had so completely and success-fully oppressed the largest segment of their own laboring population."[29]

Even so, the American Founding Fathers left a legacy of principle, enshrined in the Declaration of Independence, the Constitution, and the Bill of Rights, that contained a weapon for revolutions as yet undreamed of. In justification of their claims for independence and the evenhanded rule of law, the founders enunciated doctrines of equality that, taken literally, could support all of the claims of the Fourth Revolution. This extended not only to race and gender. Joseph Ellis, author of *Founding Brothers,* pointed out that it was John Adam's language in the Massachu-setts Constitution of 1779, including for "all people ... the right of enjoy-ing and defending their lives and liberties," that underlay that state's Supreme Court decision in February 2004 affirming the right of same-sex marriage.[30] The same reasoning holds for the separation of church and state, pressed logically by legal challenges in the 1960s and 1970s, even though it was called into question by counterrevolutionary currents there-after. What the Founders may have meant is debatable; what they said is there in black and white. As Ellis noted, it does not matter whether Jeffer-son and Adams in their own time foresaw or advocated socially radical propositions; the point is that to legitimate their own revolution they for-mulated principles whose force could not be escaped when new claims for revolutionary change arose in the centuries that followed.

The Second and the Third Revolution

The Third Revolution of economics was a very different experience from the Second Revolution of politics. First of all, it found the United States a vastly larger and more complex society that had been totally transformed by the industrial revolution. Heavily dependent on national markets and employment in the new industries, people were ever more vulnerable, as the Depression demonstrated, to economic forces beyond their control.

Nonetheless there remained major impediments to any revolutionary reordering of American thinking. Unlike the revolution of 1775, which preceded the frightening excesses of the political kind of revolution in France, the revolution against the power of private property was waged in America in the ominous shadow of the Russian Revolution, and it never transcended that fact. Furthermore, it had to contend with the deeply rooted individualist and antigovernmental presumptions in American political culture that had been driven home by the religious and political revolutions. This outlook continues even now to grip the popular mind despite its discrepancy with actual capitalist industrialism. It is always hard to introduce new revolutionary principles into a country that has inherited the successes of an earlier revolution.

Just as the Second Revolution of politics was prepared by the eighteenth-century philosophy of the Enlightenment, the Third Revolution of economics had its intellectual foundation in the rich and variegated history of nineteenth-century socialist thought, of which Marxism was the most influential though by no means exclusive current. While Marx's ideological heirs split over whether the capitalism could be overthrown through democratic evolution (in other words, in a semirevolution) or whether it required a violent uprising, practical steps to curb the power of private property were taken in Europe with the emergence of organized labor movements and Social-Democratic parties. Their equivalent in the United States was the Progressive movement of the 1890s and 1900s, followed by New Deal liberalism in the 1930s.

The Third Revolution in America

The United States was an unreceptive locale for the economic revolution. Ironically, this "American exceptionalism" resulted from the success of the political revolution in the United States, implanting its constitutional and democratic principles more firmly in the national psyche than anywhere else in the world. American tradition was a bulwark against both antiproperty experiments in economics and antidemocratic regression in politics. Even today, after the nation's experience with a series of frustrated semi-revolutions in economics, the American ideology of limited government and the primacy of private business still prevails, no matter how it may contradict reality, impede the public's best interests, and leave the egalitarian promise of the Second Revolution a mere legalistic shell.

The Third Revolution was carried forward in America by the country's distinctive generational cycle of political reformism, responding to the ever-widening discrepancy between modern economic reality and eighteenth-century theory. Thus the first wave of protest and reform directed at unequal economic power welled up in the Progressive movement, a generation after Reconstruction had attempted to cap off the Second Revolution with political equality for the former slaves. In the course of World War I and its aftermath, a typical midcycle phase of reaction set in. This lasted until the Great Depression, coinciding with another wave of generational restlessness, launched the New Deal, the high-water mark of economic revolution in the United States. Then, once again, war and its sequelae ushered in a period of reaction, until the next generational era of protest matured.

This time, in the 1960s, different objectives took over, as the unfinished agenda of the Third Revolution motivating Lyndon Johnson's "Great Society" was overridden by the distinctly new social issues of the Fourth Revolution. Reaction in the wake of these profound new challenges of race, age, and gender accumulated in the 1970s and 1980s and surged past the millennium. But more recently it has collided with a new cyclical upswing of the mood of protest aiming to reinvigorate and advance the causes of the Fourth Revolution. Thanks to this unusual conjuncture, the American psyche has been torn as never before by fundamental conflicts of unfulfilled revolutionary and counterrevolutionary impulses, the "culture wars."

In America, as in Western Europe, the economic revolution remained within the framework of a stable governmental structure, in contrast to the total revolution that carried socialism forward in Russia. Like the original American Revolution, the economic revolution had no true extremist climax in a forcible seizure of power, dictatorship, or terror. It was spread out over several generational cycles, and it depended very much on political leadership and the effect of unforeseeable disruptions such as wars and depressions. Nevertheless, in each cycle it still evinced the sequential pattern of the classic revolutionary process, going from the moderate to the more radical and back to conservative reaction. Each time, the public mood, governed by the national cycle, might allow one big push; then support would soften and resistance would harden, for another generation.

The Third Revolution in America bears directly on our understanding of the Fourth Revolution. Obviously it established the point of departure for the latter, both in the economic changes it accomplished and in the social aspirations it left unresolved. As a model of the semirevolutionary form of change, especially in the New Deal era, it helps explain the manner in which the Fourth Revolution proceeded. It primes us to recognize the depth of that new experience that has wrenched the nation over a prolonged period of time even though it left the country's political institutions formally intact.

The New Deal

The Progressive movement of the 1890s and 1900s was the first generational cycle of the economic revolution in America. It was a time of great passion but limited achievement, falling victim to a typical postrevolutionary reaction after its last gasp in the early Wilson years. With Warren Harding's "normalcy" the counterrevolution set in, and during the boom years of the 1920s under Republican hegemony the country reaffirmed its reluctance to go anywhere beyond the established verities of the Second Revolution.

It was not long, of course, before a new turn came in the American political cycle. The Depression, triggering financial panic and catastrophic unemployment, stirred desperate demands for action to save the nation and ensured the election of Franklin Roosevelt in 1932. This time the ground was better prepared to move the economic revolution forward, thanks to the background of successful experiment in the Progressive era, the intellectual capital of reformist theory built up during that time, and admiration, misplaced or not, for the perceived achievements of the anti-capitalist revolution in Russia. Moreover, by galvanizing industrial labor into an assertive force for change, the conditions of the Depression ensured more militant action from below to push fundamental reform in the economic system.

Roosevelt's initial intentions were scarcely radical. He had promised in his acceptance of the Democratic nomination in July 1932 to cut taxes, balance the budget, and "eliminate unnecessary functions of government," even as he was proposing massive public works and financial reforms to avert the danger of "unreasoning radicalism."[31] With such a naive beginning, it is not surprising that the emerging agenda of the New Deal was as much spontaneous and reactive as it was thought out beforehand. Its initial sponsors had only the vaguest idea of the revolutionary lengths their expedients could reach, and some of Roosevelt's early New Deal lieutenants —his "brains trust" leader Raymond Moley, Hugh Johnson of the ill-fated NRA (National Recovery Administration)—abandoned ship along the way. Yet Roosevelt's charismatic leadership, half idealist, half pragmatic, was crucial to the course of semirevolution that the nation managed to steer in these years of adversity, in contrast to the dismal conservatism that gripped Britain or the vicious totalitarianism that seized hold of Germany. John Maynard Keynes called the early New Deal "reasoned experiment within the framework of the existing social system," to avoid "leaving orthodoxy and revolution to fight it out."[32]

To this end, Roosevelt made the executive branch of government the engine of far-reaching change. Under his vigorous guidance, Congress passed most of the key New Deal legislation very quickly—on agriculture, banking, public works employment—in general, programs of regulation and compensation to correct for the vagaries of the free market. The revolution escalated in the congressional elections of 1934, when the Democrats broke precedent by actually gaining in the off year, thereby shedding their dependence on southern conservatives and pushing the president faster to the left.[33]

Roosevelt's early nemesis was the judicial branch of government. Dominated by appointees of the Republican administrations of the 1920s, the Supreme Court reasoned from what FDR called their "private social philosophy" of laissez-faire government,[34] and struck down the initial Depression-fighting measures of the New Deal, notably the NRA and the Agricultural Adjustment Act. The columnist Max Lerner saw the legal problem as "squaring … democratic forms with capitalist power," and observed, "The Supreme Court has acted as the final barricade against the assaults of democratic majorities."[35] Its actions were a far cry from the spearhead role that the judiciary and new constitutional interpretation would play a generation later in the Fourth Revolution. Roosevelt's response was his ill-fated plan to expand the Court with more liberal members—widely denounced as a dictatorial power-grab but actually no more radical than the ploy of Liberal prime minister Lloyd George to defang the British House of Lords in 1911 by threatening to create new Peers. In the event, though he was set back in the arena of public opinion, Roosevelt had his way with the Court without enlarging it, thanks to conservative retirements.

While Progressive principles such as trust-busting and workplace protections, were revived and pushed in the New Deal, much more was accomplished in putting in place the principles of the Welfare State, paralleling earlier innovations in Germany and Scandinavia and anticipating the "cradle to the grave" security principles of the British Labour Party as articulated by Sir William Beveridge. The Welfare State became the core of the "Second New Deal," after Roosevelt, balked by adamant judicial and business resistance and prodded by right-wing populist extremists such as Senator Huey Long and the radio evangelist Father Charles Coughlin, decided in mid-1935 to ratchet up the agenda of his revolution.[36] The longest-lasting New Deal achievement and the keystone of the Welfare State in America, the Social Security Act to encourage was passed at this point, along with the Wagner Labor Relations Act to encourage collective bargaining. Social Security was supposed to be accompanied by national health insurance, but this step, repeatedly attempted in later years, was never able to progress against the tide until the partial successes of the Johnson administration.[37]

The most radical impact of the New Deal was felt outside the formal walls of government, as the Roosevelt program inspired forces for revolutionary change in society at large. Central here was the upsurge and radicalization of the labor movement, facilitated crucially by the passage of the Wagner Act in 1935. Aided by its new legal rights of organization and collective bargaining, labor was stirred into unprecedented activism by the coal miners' fiery president John L. Lewis, bane of the comfortable bourgeoisie, when he broke from the stodgier AFL in 1935, to form the Committee for Industrial Organization, the CIO (subsequently remained Congress of Industrial Organizations), to push the concept of industrial unionism. Demonizing J.P. Morgan and the nation's financial elite, Lewis warned of a coming struggle over "whether the working population of this country shall have a voice in determining their destiny or whether they shall serve as indentured servants for a financial and economic dictatorship."[38] In the two years that followed, the country experienced a surge of trade-union militancy and violence, as the CIO's drive to organize basic industries collided with the traditional antiunion attitudes of corporate capitalism abetted by the individualist mystique in small-town America and in the South generally.[39]

More than any other sector of American society, the union movement displayed the classic dynamics of the revolutionary process, as it moved from piecemeal bargaining to radical defiance of the old industrial order. The great sit-down strikes and riots of 1937 represented the nearest approach in the United States to an extremist phase in the Third Revolution. Union organization accomplished a long-term power shift: as Lewis's biographer Robert Zeiger described it, it "brought an industrial working class into national economic and political arenas on a potent and long-term basis," thereby adding a permanent new weight to the equilibrium of social forces in America.[40] A decade and a half later, John Kenneth Galbraith was able to represent the unions as one of the three great balancing elements of "countervailing power" in the American economy, along with government and corporate business.[41]

Among the components of the Third Revolution, the labor movement of the 1930s was the closest paradigm for the broader and more diverse movements of social change that later appeared in America in the course of the Fourth Revolution. Like the radical movements yet to come in the 1960s, the labor movement represented a struggle outside of government, aided and encouraged by governmental actions, to be sure, but carrying the principles of its revolution further than the political process would have gone by itself. It was "an industrial insurgency from below," in the words of the labor historian Steve Fraser.[42] The labor movement included all the factional positions characteristic of the revolutionary political spectrum and exhibited the same progression from moderation to extremism and on to pragmatic retrenchment that characterizes the revolutionary process in general. All these features contribute to a model for understanding the spontaneous social movements of the Fourth Revolution that erupted on the American scene a generation later.

Extremism in the Third Revolution

On the political margins there was no dearth of candidates in the New Deal era for the extremist role. On the right there was a host of demagogic leaders and groups, of whom Senator Long and Father Coughlin were only the noisiest, all aping European fascism in their appeal to the angry, marginalized individual.[43] On the left was the whole gamut of European-style radical organizations, ranging from the Socialist Party (by this time quite moderate, under the leadership of Norman Thomas) to Trotskyists and Anarchists. However, the element that soon claimed the central place in American radicalism was the Communist Party–USA.

Originating in the split in the Socialist Party over whether to endorse the Bolshevik Revolution, the American Communists lived a semiunderground, sectarian existence during the 1920s while ever-tightening Soviet control pulled them toward conspiratorial tactics and revolutionary dogmatism. Their Stalinist leader William Z. Foster polled just a hundred thousand votes for president in 1932 while Norman Thomas was scoring nearly a million on the Socialist ticket, out of a total of forty million votes cast.

Until the mid-1930s, the Communists remained a radical fringe group, denouncing the New Deal as "fascist." Then came the counterrevolution in Soviet foreign policy, when Moscow, driven by fear of the Berlin–Rome–Tokyo axis, issued new directives for all Communist parties to pose as reformists and work with any democratic elements in "popular front" coalitions. The new party line, legitimizing collaboration with the New Deal and the labor movement, ironically brought the American Communists their greatest success and influence, not as revolutionaries but as antifascists and activists within the framework of the moderate semirevolution.[44] John L. Lewis, despite his anti-Communist record, took advantage of this turn to make pragmatic use of Communists as effective organizers in the CIO.[45] All this was taking place just when the political cycle in Russia had plunged to the depths of postrevolutionary totalitarianism.

The Soviet link became a serious embarrassment to the Communists with Stalin's purge trials and then with the Nazi–Soviet pact on the eve of

World War II. Though the Moscow connection again gave the CP-USA some misguided credence during the war, it ultimately destroyed the Communist component of the Third Revolution in America and embarrassed every other critic of the capitalist system. Postwar allegations of links to Soviet intelligence hastened the debacle, along with the Truman administration's loyalty and security programs of 1947 and its prosecution of the Communist Party for preaching the overthrow of the government (a theoretical crime in which the party had not indulged since the early 1930s). After the Communists' last-ditch attempt at popular front tactics with Henry Wallace's Progressive Party candidacy in 1948—when the national mood was already distinctly Thermidorean—the party shriveled in the political winds of the Cold War (in contrast to continued Communist strength as the main political opposition in France and Italy). Former party members, if not caught up in anti-Communist purges in the government or the private sector, lay low and withdrew from political activism.[46] More broadly, in the Cold War era, the association of economic reform with Communism or socialism (the two hardly being distinguished in frightened conservative minds) brought down on the Third Revolution all the emotions of patriotism and fear that the confrontation with the Soviets aroused. This was a disability that the Fourth Revolution did not suffer from: international politics in the era of the Vietnam War did not inhibit the revolution but fed it.

On the governmental plane, there was obviously no true extremist phase in the American version of the Third Revolution, no dictatorship, no terror, even though many of Roosevelt's enemies painted him in those shades. The broadest opposition to Roosevelt came over his perceived attempts to extend executive authority—in his Court Packing Plan, in his abortive "purge" of uncooperative Democratic senators in 1938, and above all in his decision to run for a third term in 1940. There were, to be sure, major shifts of power and influence within the American constitutional structure, from the legislative branch to the executive, and from the states to the federal government. Enemies of the New Deal looked on these changes as violations of the spirit if not the letter of the Constitution, and they still condemn them to this day. But the New Deal was never more than a semirevolution, and it cannot be compared with the agonies of a full-blown revolutionary experience.

Culmination and Exhaustion of the Third Revolution

The New Deal maintained its forward motion for scarcely half a decade. In part it became a victim of its own success: having eased the pain of economic crisis, the Roosevelt administration was rewarded with rising resistance to its agenda. Thus, the New Deal demonstrated that a semirevolution in any given generational epoch has only one real chance to score its gains; the rest is a rear-guard action. "Opportunities were open, possibilities were present in the spring of 1933," asserted Roosevelt's biographer Kenneth Davis, "that would not come again within the lifetime of anyone then alive."[47] Opposition to the New Deal program was concentrated in regional subcultures, the South and the rural or small-town North, wedded as they were to the political individualism and property rights of the Second Revolution while they adamantly opposed the redistribution of economic power central to the Third Revolution, not to mention the social principles of the Fourth Revolution when its time came.

Roosevelt's triumphal reelection in 1936 was the high point of the New Deal as a semirevolution. In his acceptance of renomination, the now radicalized president denounced "economic royalists" who had subjected the American people to "economic tyranny" and drew an explicit parallel with the revolution of 1775: "Our allegiance to American institutions requires the overthrow of this kind of power."[48] By 1937, however, the New Deal encountered a series of obstacles and began to lose its momentum. Economic recovery was set back by the recession of late 1937, brought on as Keynesian theory would predict when Roosevelt tried to balance his budget and cut back the federal fiscal stimulus. The last important piece of New Deal legislation was the Fair Labor Standards Act of 1938, passed barely five years after the Roosevelt administration took office, and then only with difficulty. In the off-year congressional elections of November 1938, the reformers lost their working majority to the coalition of Republicans and conservative southern Democrats (unscathed by Roosevelt's attempted purge) that dominated the national legislative branch most of the time until the South's conversion to Republicanism late in the century.

The year 1938 was thus the tipping point in the trajectory of the Third Revolution, the beginning of the Thermidorean Reaction in this cycle of American politics. Like a classic revolution when it overreaches, the semirevolution of the New Deal had gone beyond what the balance of social forces in the country was ready to sustain for any length of time. As foreign crises and then war came to preempt the attention of the Roosevelt administration, the Thermidorean mood took over even in the executive branch. As Roosevelt himself said, "Dr. New Deal" had to yield precedence to "Dr. Win-the-War."

Historian David Kennedy wrote: "The New Deal had been a walking corpse since at least 1938." Off-year congressional elections confirmed the conservative tide, when the Republicans nearly won the House of Representatives in 1942 and took control in 1946. "Congress moved swiftly, to lay the New Deal finally in its grave, and then to drive a stake through its heart."[49] When the war ended, private business was positioned to recover its economic, political, and social dominance more securely than ever.

The Managerial Revolution

In the Marxian paradigm, revolutions are directly linked with class struggles. This proposition is more or less true for some cases of revolution, notably France and Russia, but it fails in others, including the English and American revolutions where elements of all classes were ranged on both sides in cleavages that were more psychological than economic. Furthermore, it is not the downtrodden masses who rise through revolution to become the new ruling class (even though some of their sons may). The peasants did not displace the European aristocracies in the Second Revolution—it was the business class, the bourgeoisie, who prevailed. Similarly, in the Third Revolution in Russia the proletarians failed to become the rulers, being put back in their place by the political and managerial bureaucracy.

In its semirevolutionary forms as well as in the cataclysmic Russian case, the Third Revolution coincided with the pervasive trend in modern society toward a more complex, organized, and hierarchical structure of life and work. Thanks to this evolution, even in nominally capitalist countries, property ownership yielded at least in part to managerial skill and professional expertise—both based on formal education—as determinants of individual status and influence. The pure bourgeoisie, drawing its power from entrepreneurship and capital accumulation, found itself partly displaced and partly transformed, as a new class structure crystallized in advanced industrial societies. This phenomenon has been variously described and labeled by people as diverse as Adolf Berle and Gardiner Means, writing on the upstaging of owners by corporate managers; the former Trotskyist James Burnham, writing on the bureaucratic parallels among Communism, fascism, and the New Deal, and the one-time vice president of Communist Yugoslavia Milovan Djilas, writing on the "new class," the bureaucracy that emerged from the so-called proletarian revolution.

The trend was already apparent in the United States back in the Progressive era, at least retrospectively, as a victory for the new middle class of professionals and managers and as a giant step toward the bureaucratization of society. The British historian Alan Dawley called the resulting synthesis "managerial liberalism," a government–corporate alliance reigning de facto between the Progressive era and the New Deal and returning to hold sway in the nation's economic life ever since World War II.[51] However, the advent of managerialism and the "new class" was not necessarily as evil as it seemed to Jeffersonian nostalgics. In the spirit of Progressivism prevailing throughout the first half of the twentieth century, the civil service bureaucracy was animated by an ethic of public service that in the perspective of the millennium seems quaint if not beyond belief. "The New Dealers," wrote William Leuchtenburg, "felt themselves part of a broadly humanistic movement to make man's life on earth more tolerable, a movement that might someday even achieve a cooperative commonwealth."[52] The contrast with both the public-be-damned attitude of unregenerate capitalism and the biology-based particularism marking the advanced stage of the Fourth Revolution was emblematic of the principles distinguishing these successive revolutionary impulses.

Enemies of the New Deal faulted it—and continue today to fault its legacy—for "elitism" and "social engineering" that presumed to dictate to the populace what was best for them. This contention ignores other forms of social engineering; for example, the system-building accomplished by the Founding Fathers pursuant to the principles of the Second Revolution or the vast changes imposed by the rise of the corporate economy, nominally private and politically unaccountable but cumulatively epoch-making in its impact on everyday life. The question is not whether social engineering will occur but under whose control and to what ends. In particular, the social engineering associated with a nonviolent revolution, unlike the fanaticism and power-building of a total revolutionary upheaval or the blindness of market-driven evolution, can proceed both gradually and rationally, legislatively rather than apocalyptically, as long as it enjoys political support.

Critics on the left have disparaged the New Deal because it aimed only to "save capitalism" by timely reforms.[53] In fact this was exactly what Roosevelt claimed credit for, though the capitalists never appreciated his help.[54] Kenneth Davis maintained that two years were lost in the incoherent reflexes of the "First New Deal," before Roosevelt developed a more deliberate vision of social change.[55] Nevertheless, lasting shifts in the American power structure did take place. "On a very wide front and in the truest possible sense," Joseph Alsop wrote, "Franklin Delano Roosevelt included the excluded."[56]

Intentionally or not, Roosevelt bequeathed to the country a new institutional and policy synthesis, and gave a new meaning to the term "liberal." As historian Alan Brinkley observed, this was not someone who believed in overturning capitalism but a leader who was "committed to using the state to compensate for capitalism's inevitable flaws."[57] By the same token, these New Deal accomplishments redefined conservatism as the rejection of any such governmental intervention in the pyramid of private power sanctified by the market.

The Aftermath of the Third Revolution

The New Deal era left much unfinished business, in its own agenda as well in other directions of social change that became the mission of the Fourth Revolution. Balked in midcourse by conservative opposition, and attenuated by the war, the New Deal achieved little in the direction of the classic European Left ideal of socialized enterprise and economic planning, and it left society not much more equalized economically than before, though thanks to the economic stimulats of the war almost every level of the population found itself better off. Perhaps the greatest social impact of the New Deal, achieved by a combination of actions inside and outside government, was in the status of industrial labor, becoming politically respectable as its members were absorbed into an expanded middle class. In this respect the New Deal succeeded so well that it undermined the constituency for any further aggressive reform in the economic realm, much as the French peasants abandoned the revolutionary cause once they got title to their land.

The weakness in the New Deal legacy was to focus more on Welfare State income redistribution than on socialistic power redistribution. When the Welfare State emphasis was carried forward to the Great Society of the 1960s, it could easily be perceived as mere subsidizing of an unproductive underclass. Meanwhile, the New Deal did little specifically to improve the status of women and racial minorities, except as a side effect of the war effort. The Social Security system presumed, "under the sway of Victorian family-wage ideology," according to one feminist writer,[58] that women would still spend most of their lives as homemakers. In racial matters the Roosevelt administration hesitated to do much for fear of alienating southern political support for its economic program—and even that proved transitory. The unions were also tainted with racism and patriarchalism, which did not endear them later on to the partisans of the Fourth Revolution. But another generation was still to pass before these issues came to the forefront of the nation's political concerns.

Postwar America conformed to the typical postrevolutionary trend toward Thermidorean consolidation and conservative counterrevolution. President Harry Truman was a Thermidorean by his own admission: he complained of "crackpots and the lunatic fringe" around Roosevelt and told his then aide Clark Clifford, "I want to keep my feet on the ground. ... The American people have been through a lot of experiments and they want a rest from experiments."[59] Yet a Thermidorean is not a counterrevolutionary: Truman fought to hold existing New Deal achievements against attempts to turn the clock back. He tried unsuccessfully to veto the Taft–Hartley labor relations act of 1947 with its obstacles to further labor organization (allowing the South to remain an antiunion attraction undercutting labor standards elsewhere). He even endorsed the concept of civil rights for blacks in the 1948 Democratic platform, only to provoke the Dixiecrat presidential candidacy of Strom Thurmond that almost cost Truman his reelection. And he tried to round out parts of the New Deal program with initiatives for full employment and national health insurance, only to be balked by the conservative coalition in Congress.

As the Cold War set in, liberalism of the economic sort, associated with socialism and hence in the popular mind linked with the Communist menace, came under a cloud from which it did not escape until its aims were at the point of being preempted by the new social issues. The Soviet threat served to divide or deter potential supporters of the economic revolution in the same way that fear and hatred of Napoleon and the French set back the principles of the political revolution in early nineteenth-century Europe. Until the end of the 1950s, a climate of intolerant nationalistic conformity—of which McCarthyism was only the most egregious manifestation—inhibited serious social criticism. Historians looked for consensus rather than conflict in the nation's past. Meanwhile, de facto centralization of the economy and the militarization of governmental priorities carried over from war to cold war.[60] All this, under President Dwight Eisenhower's benign paternalism, represented the pale American analogue of a postrevolutionary dictatorship. Then, in the 1960s, thrust up by a new turn in the generational cycle, came what initially appeared to be a "moderate revolutionary revival" in the process of the Third Revolution, on the model of the Jeffersonian Revolution of 1800 that consolidated the principles of the Second Revolution. Reality proved to be more complicated. What began as an effort under presidents Kennedy and Johnson to revive the spirit of the New Deal quickly turned into a different kind of upheaval driven by the new goals and struggles of the Fourth Revolution.

CHAPTER 4

The Great Society and the Trajectory
of the Fourth Revolution

A generation was to pass, after the battles of the 1930s and 1940s to equalize economic power and provide a safety net for all, before new revolutionary energy erupted in America and Western Europe. Initially, this
Revolution of the Sixties was identified in most minds with the contests of
the previous epoch, as Left versus Right or conservative versus liberal. But
it soon became clear that the new struggles were bringing to the political
arena fundamentally different issues, in a new domain of revolutionary
confrontation. The Fourth Revolution had arrived, opening up the fight
for equality in the social sphere and challenging old forms of dominance
and submission based on race, gender, and age and expertise.

In the wide range of its driving forces, aims, and achievements, the
Fourth Revolution was more complex than any of its antecedents,
especially in America. Propelled by so many interrelated forces of protest
struggling for their particular goals of social equality, the Fourth Revolution has been the focus of contention in American public life for more
than a generation. Despite the diversity among its elements, however, the
Fourth Revolution in America needs to be viewed as a single historical
experience.

This chapter begins that inquiry by focusing on the role of government
under the Kennedy and Johnson administrations. Then, in the three chapters that follow, the main social components of the Fourth Revolution—
the quest for racial equality, the youth revolt and the cultural revolution,

and the campaign for women's rights and opportunities—are detailed as they emerged and played out their dynamics in the 1960s and early 1970s. Subsequent chapters bring these movements together as they worked out their ultimate implications up to the present, and as they have contended at the same time with persistent forces of counterrevolution.

Thanks to the Second Revolution's heritage, the Fourth Revolution in America was contained within the nation's constitutional framework, as was the Third Revolution of economic equalization. Nevertheless, the Fourth Revolution conformed to the familiar pattern of the revolutionary process, as moderate reform led on to radical defiance, followed by division, disillusionment, and reaction. Moreover, like earlier movements for change, the various elements of social protest making up the Fourth Revolution were borne along by the distinctive generational cycle of protest that has surged up in the United States every thirty years or so.

Like all previous kinds of revolution, the Fourth Revolution also has been an international phenomenon. To be sure, it was not driven by one dominant center of revolutionary extremism, such as France and Russia had been in their respective revolutionary heydays. But if any country could be singled out as the focus of the Fourth Revolution, it would be the United States, as the French commentator Jean-François Revel suggested. "Today in America a new revolution is rising," Revel maintained, "a total affirmation of liberty for all in place of archaic prohibitions."[1]

From the Third Revolution to the Fourth

Just as the Third Revolution was the defining worldwide movement of the first half of the twentieth century, so did the Fourth Revolution put its stamp on the character of the century's second half. But in the United States the two movements were so close in time and terminology that public discourse about them, as we have noted, was hopelessly confused. Both the Third and Fourth revolutions in their American variants have been called "liberal," and consequently the differences between them, felt but not distinctly articulated by people who might often have sympathized with one but not the other, have rarely been made fully explicit.

Simply put, the Fourth Revolution picked up where the Third left off. It attacked perceived injustices and inequalities that the Third Revolution had not addressed, in relationships based on race, gender, and age and expertise. As did earlier revolutions, the Fourth Revolution incorporated into its mainstream some of the more utopian, fringe ideas generated by its predecessor, for example, antibureaucratic and antimanagerial sentiments resembling demands of the Ultra-Left in the Russian Revolution.

At the same time, the Fourth Revolution in its American manifestation failed to deal consistently with the unfinished economic agenda of the Third Revolution. To be sure, the principal governmental impetus in the upheaval of the sixties, President Lyndon Johnson's Great Society program, was intended to revive the spirit of Roosevelt's New Deal and broaden the benefits of the Welfare State. Here, as often before, the critical questions and proposals formulated by democratic socialists—in this case, Michael Harrington's exposé of poverty in *The Other America*—galvanized the efforts of liberal reformists right up to the presidential level.[2] On the other hand, the prime nongovernmental component of the Third Revolution, the labor movement, was notably absent from the Fourth, while the national mass media, reluctant to accept the Third Revolution, were openly sympathetic to the Fourth a generation later. Thus the Fourth Revolution leapfrogged over the inert body of the Third, so to speak, to press its own agenda of social equality even where the cause of economic equity had lapsed.

There was a curious unspoken confluence in America between the conservative defenders of Second Revolution laissez-faire economics and the radical promoters of Fourth Revolution social equality. Both forces rallied around the philosophy of constitutional rights, though their emphases may have been different; both were inclined to see the government as the enemy. Overrunning the limits of President Johnson's Great Society, the Fourth Revolution cut itself loose from the steadier kind of governmental sponsorship that the Third Revolution had in the New Deal. Apart from the moderate phase of the civil rights movement under Martin Luther King Jr. it had no distinct leadership even in its separate components. Where the revolution of the eighteenth century had extolled the legislative branch of government, and where the economic revolution had looked primarily to the executive branch, the Fourth Revolution found its main governmental support in the judicial branch, now playing an unaccustomed vanguard role in enforcing constitutionally new conceptions of equal rights.

The Fourth Revolution bit more deeply into the cultural body of the American nation than anything the country had ever encountered before. The youthful counterculture defied traditional social norms and values to an extent beyond any revolutionary precedent. Old moralism was rejected in favor of a culture of liberation; religion was displaced by psychology as the lodestone of belief and the arena of ethical judgment. The sense of shame evaporated, and standards of language and taste in public discourse and entertainment took a nosedive, abetted by court decisions that swept away most forms of censorship and liability for libel. Culturally, the nation sank to the egalitarian level of the lowest common denominator.

Resistance to the Fourth Revolution was most deeply entrenched in the same region, the South, that had dragged its feet on the Third; this hostility extended not only to equality for blacks[3] but also to women's rights and the cultural revolution in the large. However, opposition to the Fourth Revolution was not confined to the South. Nationwide, it aroused the deepest emotions, not only against the new social rights but also against the incomplete economic legacy of the Third Revolution (now often identified with the beneficiaries of the Fourth), and even against the religious and intellectual freedoms of the First Revolution. These responses showed how reaction against a new kind of revolution could spill over into a rejection of the whole history of previous revolutionary achievements. The Fourth Revolution truly set off an era of culture wars in America.

Origins of the Fourth Revolution

The Fourth Revolution in America did not begin in any dramatic national crisis such as depression or war, though war in the shape of the conflict in Vietnam entered in as a crucial accelerator of the process. No single cause can be adduced for all the currents in which the Fourth Revolution was expressed, either in the United States or around the world. There were, of course, broad trends in contemporary society that underlay the new restiveness—galloping urbanization and suburbanization, social mobility and a dissolving sense of community, rising educational standards and the advance of mass communications, the bureaucratization of public life and the commercialization of private life and the homogenization of both. Military and civilian mobilization in World War II, shaking up relationships and routines throughout American society, accelerated all these developments. But broad factors such as these do not offer much understanding of why the Fourth Revolution should have burst forth when it did and in the way it did.

True, the generational cycle in American politics, along with sheer boredom with the fifties, made a new upswing of the reform spirit likely in the sixties. Children of 1930s leftists—the "red diaper babies"—were initially prominent in New Left activism. But generational considerations in themselves do not explain why the distinctive new social demands of the Fourth Revolution took command and crowded out renewed commitment to the Third Revolution.

While the generational cycle may have contributed to revolutionary readiness, the direct origins of the Fourth Revolution have to be sought in the circumstances affecting each particular element of the new upheaval. Setting the stage for the black revolution, as Nicholas Lemann pointed out, was the huge migration of blacks during and after World War II from the rural South to the inner cities, northern as well as southern.[4] The youth revolution reflected the massive demographic impact of the post–World War II baby boom. Women's equality and the sexual revolution were encouraged by a variety of developments, ranging from the birth control pill to employment opportunities in an economy depending less on manual labor and more on office and service occupations. The demands of an increasingly hierarchical and merit-oriented society posed a tempting target for an antiexpert reaction that had something implicitly in common with right-wing anti-intellectual populism.

Intellectual preparation of the Fourth Revolution is easier to identify. The literary and entertainment movements of the "Beat Generation" of the 1950s, concentrated in California, went so far as "a total rejection of the whole society ... the business civilization," in the words of their chronicler Lawrence Lipton.[5] Writers such as Allen Ginsburg and Jack Kerouac, philosophers such as Herbert Marcuse and Norman O. Brown, psychologists such as Erik Erikson, sociologists such as William H. Whyte and C. Wright Mills, and activists such as Saul Alinsky and Paul Goodman all contributed to a climate of thought that delegitimized the old social and cultural order. The effect was akin to the philosophers of the Enlightenment as they undermined monarchy and aristocracy in eighteenth-century Europe, or the Progressives and socialists of the turn of the twentieth century as they shook the moral certainties of American capitalism. Black and feminist writers aroused skepticism of the status quo among their particular constituencies. A new paradigm of thinking was ready when events prodded the impending social movements into life.

Triggers of Revolution: The New Frontier and the Vietnam War

However deep their ultimate causes may run, revolutions are typically set in motion by some kind of dramatic triggering event that makes people realize that things do not have to go on as they have, and that releases held-in hopes and hatreds. In this sense the Fourth Revolution in America can be dated with precision: it began with the election of John F. Kennedy as president in 1960.

JFK's impact was testimony more to the rising hunger in the nation for political change and social justice than to any intrinsic radicalism in his initiatives. Arthur Schlesinger called the New Frontiersmen who came to Washington with Kennedy "a new breed," who "proposed to roll up their sleeves and make American over."[6] A mystique grew up around the new president even before it was magnified by the tragedy of his assassination, a picture of youthful vigor leading the country on new paths of idealism. The Peace Corps, a modest overseas service gesture in the Truman tradition, epitomized this exaggerated spirit of optimism. "Nothing in the Kennedy years," wrote Schlesinger, "was more spectacular than the transformation of American youth."[7] The historian Eric Goldman advanced the theory of the rising type of "Metroamericans," young, educated, suburban, ambitious, "liberal but without ideology," to explain enthusiasm for Kennedy as well as disdain for all his successors.[8] The Kennedy era was the last time that educated American youth showed any faith in their government.

A recent chronicler of the Kennedy years recognized the doomed euphoria of a fresh and still moderate revolution, where "hope will get so far ahead of experience that the gap will bring hope itself crashing to the ground." This implicitly set up the extremist upheaval, "turmoil ... the result of frustration that was derived from that kind of disappointment."[9] Enjoying only a razor-thin mandate and faced with the familiar Republican–southern Democratic conservative coalition in Congress, Kennedy moved gingerly in most areas of domestic policy, including the contentious sphere of black civil rights. He held the Republicans to a minimal gain of three House seats in 1962 in the midterm election that usually goes more heavily against the party in power. Yet his initiatives in equal employment opportunity and housing access, and challenges to southern segregation laws, were enough to energize the civil rights movement as never before. Work done in his administration laid the groundwork for much of the Great Society program that followed, perhaps, as Schlesinger believed, as an agenda that he would have undertaken had he survived to govern in a second term.[10]

Kennedy's assassination in November 1963 turned him into a martyr and made his political impact seem larger than life. For the younger generation, the crime was a stunning blow, disillusioning many minds about the prospects for peaceful change that the youthful president had raised up with such hopefulness. The assassination was equally important as the chance event that put in the White House its most dynamic incumbent since Franklin Roosevelt, and one of the most enigmatic leaders in all of American history.

Noted for his arm-twisting style as Senate majority leader for six years under President Eisenhower, Lyndon Johnson was usually dismissed in his vice-presidential role as a ticket-balancing concession to southern conservatism. What a surprise, then, when he became free to proclaim his own agenda, in fact more radical than the Kennedy program, and more relentlessly pursued. A congressman from Texas since the late Roosevelt years, Johnson proved to be an ardent New Dealer still, committed to reviving the economic banners of fairness and security in his War on Poverty and his ideal of the Great Society. At the same time, he was the first president

to make the condition of the black minority a top priority for his administration, as he attempted to extend the rewards of the Second Revolution in
political rights and the rewards of the Third Revolution in economic benefits to America's most underprivileged citizens. Thus Johnson personally
bridged the Third and Fourth revolutions.

Johnson's dream, like Roosevelt's, fell afoul of war. His entanglement in
Vietnam was ironic, pursued as it was to shield his domestic program from
charges of a foreign policy soft on Communism, yet ultimately a cause of
such national anguish and division that the president was brought down
by it. Unlike American involvement in the two world wars, the Vietnam
War did not dampen the impulse of reform but sharpened and accelerated
it. The war intensified the Fourth Revolution much as wartime emotions
drove the Second Revolution onward in eighteenth-century America
and France and the Third Revolution in early twentieth-century Russia.
Vietnam and the antiwar movement radicalized the student generation
and the youth culture as never before and evoked the kind of uncompromising emotion typical of any revolution in its extremist phase.

The Revolution and Government: The Great Society

Like the Third Revolution in the New Deal era, the Fourth Revolution
proceeded on two distinct planes, inside and outside government. Unlike
the New Deal, which apart from the labor movement was mainly a govern-
ment-driven turnabout in American life, the Fourth Revolution took on a
radical life of its own and surged ahead even when the governmental effort
was faltering. Yet initially the federal government's role was decisive in
leading and encouraging the Fourth Revolution, above all in its racial
component.

There was a remarkable parallel between the trajectories of the New
Deal and the Great Society, if we take Kennedy's thousand days of tentative
exploration as the equivalent of Roosevelt's early experiments. Johnson
assumed the presidency in 1963 with a vision of reform at least as clear as
Roosevelt's in the "Second New Deal" of 1935. Shortly after taking over, he
admonished the nation, "The meek and the humble and the lowly share
this life and this earth with us all. We must never forget them. President
Roosevelt never did."[11] He pursued his aims with a force of leadership and
a feeling of urgency that were even more intense than his model, unaided
by any national crisis equivalent to the Depression.

As president, the old New Dealer Johnson responded with alacrity
when he learned what the Kennedy administration had planned to do to
address chronic poverty. He told Walter Heller, chairman of the Council of
Economic Advisors, "Go ahead. Give it the Highest Priority. Push ahead

full tilt."[12] Poverty, restored to the intellectual agenda, was lent new urgency in a report on manpower troubles by Assistant Labor Secretary and future senator Daniel Patrick Moynihan, and Johnson made the issue his own.[13] In his message to Congress in January of 1964, he declared "an unlimited war on poverty," and he went on to hammer this theme into the national consciousness.

But this was only the beginning. Johnson's banner of the "Great Society" came from the British socialist Graham Wallas by way of Walter Lippmann.[14] In a commencement address written by the Kennedyite Richard Goodwin that he delivered at the University of Michigan in May 1964, Johnson proclaimed the "Great Society" as an ideal to elevate the quality of life for all: "In your time we have the opportunity to move not only toward the rich society and the powerful society, but upward to the Great Society. The Great Society rests on abundance and liberty for all. It demands an end to poverty and racial injustice, to which we are totally committed in our time. But that is just the beginning." The president cited the need to uplift American cities, the American environment, and American education—goals that are scarcely any nearer satisfaction more than a third of a century later. "You can help build a society where the demands of morality, and the needs of the spirit, can be realized in the life of the nation," he exhorted the graduates. "So, will you join in the battle to give every citizen the full equality which God enjoins and the law requires, whatever his belief or race, or the color of his skin? Will you join in the battle to give every citizen an escape from the crushing weight of poverty? … Will you join in the battle to build the Great Society, to prove that our material progress is only the foundation on which we will build a richer life of mind and spirit?"[15]

Johnson's vision entailed a sweeping agenda of governmental action, under a timetable compressed by his fear that political support for his program would not endure. In the words of his biographer Doris Kearns, "Johnson wanted to give his people everything this principle suggested and he wanted them to have it at once …; the Great Society would offer something to almost everyone. Impelled by an intense anxiety that his popular mandate might be swiftly eroded, Johnson felt that it was necessary to act swiftly, since he could not know how long his consensus would last." The inevitable result was "a politics of haste."[16]

Neither Johnson nor Doris Kearns put it in these terms, but the Great Society president had become a revolutionary, a revolutionary in power—albeit a moderate in methods, hewing to the constitutional framework. Like every great revolutionary leader in history, Johnson sensed that a brief window of opportunity for radical change had presented itself, and he was determined to seize that moment. Hence the extraordinary series of initiatives that he brought forth with bewildering rapidity and wrestled through the Congress.

To launch his attack on poverty, Johnson issued an executive order to create the Office of Economic Opportunity and charged it with developing a "Community Action Program." To head it he appointed the Kennedy brother-in-law and Peace Corps director Sargent Shriver. The philosophy, originally formulated by Robert Kennedy's assistant David Hackett, was to encourage and empower the poor to overcome their own conditions, through "maximum feasible participation."[17] Statutory authority for the War on Poverty was conferred by the Economic Opportunity Act of August 1964, with the inclusion of such diverse programs as "VISTA" (Volunteers in Service to America), a "Job Corps" on the model of Roosevelt's Civilian Conservation Corps, and the Head Start Program for underprivileged preschoolers. An important companion piece was the Legal Services Program or Legal Aid.

Results of all this antipoverty action were spotty, owing to the haste of the program and the resistance of local authorities who felt preempted by it. Outright welfare payments to the poor, through the joint federal–state program of Aid to Families with Dependent Children, were not a Great Society innovation but were derived from the Social Security Act, contrary to later perceptions.[18] To be sure, empowerment of the poor—pushed by such groups as George Wiley's National Welfare Rights Organization— significantly upped the call for such help.[19] Actually more distasteful to the powers-that-be in small-town America than the cost of direct support of the poor was the change in the local power structure implied by helping the poor use the system. Conservative animus against Welfare and Legal Aid rivaled hatred of the unions during the New Deal.

Along with his immediate antipoverty measures, Johnson pushed support for the black civil rights struggle, again cashing in on the preparatory work of the Kennedy administration. Breaking a Senate filibuster with the help of Republican leader Everett Dirksen in June 1964, LBJ secured the great Civil Rights Act of that year, with its sweeping antidiscrimination provisions. These terms were extended to include sex discrimination, iron-ically, by the conservative chairman of the House Rules Committee Howard Smith of Virginia, who mistakenly hoped thereby to sink the whole measure.[20]

The momentum Johnson had built up in his first, abbreviated term supercharged his campaign for election in his own right in 1964. A Repub-lican lurch to the right under Senator Barry Goldwater, appealing covertly to racism and overtly to anti-Communism, backfired and delivered to Johnson an electoral triumph rivaling Roosevelt's in 1936. The heavily Democratic congress that came in on Johnson's coattails (68 Senators, a gain of 2, and 295 House seats, a net shift of almost 40 seats) gave him a majority strong enough—for the first time since the height of the New Deal—to act independently of southern conservatives and forge ahead with far-reaching reforms. "Thus," wrote another chronicler of this era, "Johnson had the two years of the 89th Congress to put over his Great Society. The old Republican–southern Democratic coalition that had dominated the Congress since 1938 was temporarily disabled. He could get whatever he wanted, but he would have to hurry."[21] A small cloud on the horizon was the showing of Alabama's segregationist governor George Wallace against Johnson stand-ins in several Democratic presidential primaries, an intimation of the potential white working-class backlash that ultimately turned the political balance against the Fourth Revolution.

Over the next two years the Great Society forged ahead. At Howard University in June 1965, responding to a probing and prophetic report by Moynihan on ghetto social conditions,[22] Johnson declared, "We seek not just freedom but opportunity. … We seek not just equality as a right and a theory but equality as a fact and equality as a result."[23] Congress passed the Voting Rights Act two months later. In September it followed up this epochal step with immigration reform, to erase the racist premises of the national origins quota system dating from the 1920s. (The measure proved to be loaded with weightier demographic consequences for American society than its sponsors ever imagined.)

The Democrats' executive–legislative team then turned its attention to the gaps in the Welfare State left over from the New Deal, above all in the health area. Medicare and Medicaid, huge undertakings to provide health insurance for older people and the poor, respectively, were put in place. Aid to education came in for its share of attention in the Elementary and Secondary Education Act and the Higher Education Act, along with the National Endowments for the Arts and for the Humanities. Along the way, attacks on water and air pollution were initiated, and in 1966 the Model Cities Act and new consumer-protection legislation were adopted.

But resistance to Johnson's reforms was quickly growing. By the end of 1966, wrote the presidential historian Robert Dallek, "The anti-poverty crusade was in trouble," especially because of its challenge to local power structures. "Johnson knew full well … that his public pronouncements trumpeting the end of want in America were unrealizable."[24] Fearing a setback in the off-year elections, Johnson kept his distance to deflect the blame;[25] in the event, the Democrats lost all the congressional seats they had gained in 1964 and more. California, already shaken by the "Free Speech" movement at the University in Berkeley and by the Watts riots in Los Angeles, turned back from its vanguard liberalism and elected the actor-turned-conservative-ideologue Ronald Reagan as its new governor.[26]

In part, these democratic electoral setbacks reflected the usual falloff for the party in power without the president's coattails, but they also demonstrated that the country had been force-fed more reform than it could digest. Dallek cited a memo to LBJ to this effect by his Special Counsel Harry McPherson: "I think we have had about all the social programs we need. ... We may have too many."[27] The Gallup Poll had found just before the election that 52 percent of whites thought the administration was pushing too fast on civil rights, compared with only 32 percent of naysayers in 1962. In any case, the Republican–southern Democratic coalition took charge again in Congress; the only major pieces of Great Society legislation still to pass were the Occupational Health and Safety Act (OSHA), and the Civil Rights Act of 1968 directed at discrimination in housing.

After the Democrats' electoral setback in 1966, Johnson could no longer get Congress to finance both the Great Society and the Vietnam War simultaneously. Bit by bit, he had to sacrifice the former for the latter, while courting inflation in the meantime. "For the moment," Moynihan commented, "the confidence of many persons in the nation's ability to master the congeries of social, economic, regional, and racial problems that were subsumed under the heading poverty in the winter and spring of 1964 has been badly shaken."[28] All in all, the mood in government was turning back from revolution even before the full impact of the Vietnam War was felt in the crisis of 1968. Johnson had had just three years, the same short time that Roosevelt had from 1935 to 1938, to accomplish his agenda.

In the minds of some observers, the Great Society never transcended the limits imposed by business interests on the New Deal legacy after World War II. According to Professor Ira Katznelson, "The Great Society substantially expanded the policy themes of American politics, but it did so in a way that simultaneously ruled out a politics of more vigorous intervention in the market place."[29] The Boston University historian Bruce Schulman concurred: "Johnson could not, would not, see that the interests of rich and poor, business and labor, must sometimes collide; he could not win everyone's cooperation without compromising the effectiveness of his programs."[30] Moynihan closed the governmental revolution as he had opened it: "The great failing of the Johnson Administration was that an immense opportunity to institute more or less permanent social changes—a fixed full-employment program, a measure of income maintenance—was lost while energies were expended in ways that very probably hastened the end of the brief period when such options were open."[31]

The Great Society resembled the New Deal as a government-sponsored revolution, heavily dependent on extraordinary leadership and enjoying only a brief period of popular and legislative favor before it faltered. It differed in its circumstances and in its focus: it enjoyed a time of prosperity (enhanced by the Keynesian stimulus of the January 1964 tax cut), and it concentrated on the social margins—the poor, the black, and the elderly. Much more than the New Deal, it unleashed revolutionary movements in society, with a major shift in objectives from the economic condition of the whole to the social status of particular segments of the population. All these changes left by the wayside the Third Revolution's commitment to the economic interests of the preponderantly white and often ethnic working class. And liberalism acquired a bad name: as Michael Kazin and Maurice Isserman put it, "The imagery of class conflict in America was turned on its head. Liberals ... were viewed by many as an arrogant elite of 'limousine liberals.' And conservatives ... were emerging in the 1960s as the new populists."[32] The Great Society opened up long-term fissures among the forces for reform of any sort.

The Revolution in Society

The revolutionary upheaval in society, independent of direct governmental action, is the heart of the Fourth Revolution's story. It is the subject of the next three chapters of this book, devoted to the three main areas of struggle for social equality—race relations, youth and the counterculture, and the women's rights movement along with the sexual revolution.

These components of the social revolution differed among themselves not only in the constituencies they represented but also in the forms their development took. The black revolution was the first component to take shape, and was the most violence prone, as well as the one most directly linked to the initiatives of the Great Society. The youth revolution was the most antigovernmental and even antisocial, inflamed as it was by the Vietnam War and countercultural defiance. It shared more obvious international counterparts, but in its overt aspects it was also the most transitory of these movements. The revolution of gender equality was the slowest to pick up steam, and it was the revolutionary component that aroused the most stubborn resistance among social conservatives. Each of these currents of protest displayed the variegated spectrum of revolutionary views from moderate to extreme, along with the tendency to fragment and break apart as the radicals overreached and counterrevolutionary resistance mounted. Each component of the Fourth Revolution included offshoots that matured later on—the American Indian movement and the cult of diversity in the wake of the civil rights movement; the overthrow of sexual mores and the emergence of open homosexual politics; and antielitism in education and culture, accompanied by deep debates extending from standards of language to the meaning of Western civilization.

Despite differences among the revolutionary social trends that the Great Society stimulated, the various currents displayed striking political parallels. They all found their main governmental support not in the legislative branch that in centuries past had embodied the revolution for political rights, or in the executive branch that had led the charge for economic revolution, up to and including the Great Society, but in the judiciary, the same institution that had been such a drag on the New Deal. Often going far ahead of legislative intent, the courts of the 1960s and 1970s found meaning in the Constitution in regard to equality, due process, and privacy for individuals that had scarcely been dreamed of by the Founding Fathers, though those words the founders had used in justification of their own revolution of political equality were there for all to see. Thus, the landmark steps in the social revolution were more often than not judicial decisions—*Brown v. Board of Education,* the epochal school desegregation case of 1954; *Roe v. Wade,* the decision on legalizing abortion in 1973; *Miranda v. Arizona* (1966) and other decisions bearing on the rights of criminal defendants; and the democratization of state government effected by the "one man, one vote" decision in *Baker v. Carr* of 1962. All this work of the "Warren Court" and of Chief Justice Earl Warren, who guided the nation's judicial destinies from 1953 to 1971, aimed at the consistent implementation of a society of free and equal citizens, far beyond where legislative bodies would have gone on their own. The achievement earned for Warren a place equal to Roosevelt and Johnson in the pantheon of conservatives' devils.

Enjoying the blessings of the judicial branch, after the Third Revolution had had to struggle against it, the Fourth Revolution was confronted by a different counterrevolutionary force from inside the government, in the form of the secret police; in other words, the FBI under Director J. Edgar Hoover.[33] Exercising virtually a free hand in choosing his priorities, thanks to his skill at bureaucratic maneuver and intimidation, Hoover carried on a persistent, ideologically driven campaign to disrupt the civil rights movement as well as the youth culture in its more militant, antiwar manifestations. What the net effect of these machinations added up to is hard to gauge, but they may actually have exacerbated the radicalism and alienation of the more extreme elements among the revolutionaries.

The pursuit of equal rights for groups that had previously been discriminated against turned out to be the most successful and lasting aspect of the Fourth Revolution in America. At the same time, ironically, public sympathy turned sharply away from the Great Society's focus on the economic woes of the nation's unfortunates. Thus, as in all revolutions, the net result of the Fourth Revolution in class terms was far different from the initial promise. The ironic outcome of the Third Revolution in its various forms around the world was to elevate the bureaucracy and the salariat at the expense of the class of manual workers, which was its ostensible concern. In the Fourth Revolution, the practical economic effect of nondiscrimination and affirmative action in matters of race and gender was not an advance toward equality for the whole class of victims of discrimination but rather what amounted to the redistribution of inequality.

The primary beneficiaries of the Fourth Revolution were successful representatives of heretofore disadvantaged social categories, particularly racial minorities and women. Such individuals gained access to all levels of the political and economic pyramid, often on the basis of implicit or explicit quotas, but without change in the form of the pyramid. Meanwhile, the impoverished and unproductive underclass of the unemployable and welfare dependent, disproportionately black and female, grew worse off both in absolute economic terms and in its social marginalization, at the same time that it drained public resources and fed resentment against aid to the unfortunate. Much later, the Reverend Jesse Jackson faulted the emphasis on "horizontal disparity" among racial categories, to the neglect of "vertical disparity" in economic and social status within all categories.[34]

The Great Society did not settle the class struggle. Instead, it shifted the alignments and provoked a new class struggle, as it were. This new face-off opposed the middle class (broadened in its definition to include everyone who worked) and the newly identified "underclass." The rich were thereby insulated from invidious attention, while the poor were virtually demonized.

The Fourth Revolution Abroad

Like all the previous types of revolution, the Fourth Revolution was an international phenomenon. Protest movements erupted in the 1960s in an unforgettable revolutionary wave throughout the Western world and evoked peculiar echoes in the Far East as well. Such a surge of defiance against the social order immediately recalled the explosion of the Second Revolution for political rights all over Europe in the dramatic year 1848. Other international parallels were the democratic responses of sympathy with the French Revolution in the 1790s, and the socialist responses to the Russian Revolution after World War I that fueled the creation of the Communist International.

At the same time, there were some signal novelties about the Fourth Revolution as an international experience. This time, the United States was not just a peripheral participant, as it had been in the eighteenth century, or a pale reflection, as it was of twentieth-century socialism. America became the epicenter of the social revolution, pursuing it more broadly than any other country. Abroad—even in China—the Fourth Revolution was felt primarily as an uprising of youth, with a mainly antielitist and antibureaucratic direction. In these locales, the movement reached a degree of fervor and violence beyond in America, where the Fourth Revolution was more diffuse. Its most militant component, the black civil rights movement, was unique to the United States; feminism was more advanced; and far more national energy than elsewhere went into the cultural side of the youth movement and pursuit of the sexual revolution.

It is hard to account for the intensity as well as the timing of the youth rebellion abroad. Germany was the initial European center of radical protest, particularly at the Free University of Berlin, an institution that combined American-style social nonconformity with radical European and Maoist political ideology. Breaking out there in February 1968, the movement of student demonstrations and riots quickly spread around Europe, including the Communist East, in a quixotic passion to overturn the old society of hierarchy and alienation. In Czechoslovakia it was the student movement that precipitated the democratic reforms of the "Prague Spring" and the subsequent tragedy of Soviet intervention, though these events did not specifically bring up the issues of the Fourth Revolution. It was in France that the movement of student anarchism against Establishment meritocracy attained its most spectacular height and its widest popular support.

Growing antiauthority defiance among French youth, led by "Danny the Red" Cohn-Bendit, a German exchange student at the University of Nanterre near Paris, erupted early in May 1968 into a series of clashes with the police. The upshot was a mass revolt in Paris' Latin Quarter, complete with barricades, a situation verging on civil war with the forces of order. In turn this confrontation triggered a sympathy strike movement among industrial workers, quite the opposite of the antipathy between labor and the New Left in the United States. Defying the caution urged by their own old-line Communist leadership, the French strikers came to the brink of overturning Charles de Gaulle's government and prompted the general to prepare a military coup. This last resort proved unnecessary, after he succeeded in mobilizing conservative resistance by blaming the Communists for the trouble, and triumphed in the parliamentary elections of late June.

The European student rebellion, like its American counterpart, aimed not so much to redistribute the wealth as to overcome the sense of alienation in big organizations, to correct what the German student leader Rudi Dutschke called "an acute feeling of powerlessness in relation to the established system."[35] The rebels found inspiration in what they perceived to be the most radical versions of Communism, particularly the ideas of the Cuban visionary Che Guevara and the "Cultural Revolution" in China.

Jacques Servan-Schreiber, editor of the liberal *L'Express,* captured the essence of the Fourth Revolution when he wrote, "This was not a 'socialist' movement as the term is applied traditionally and so dogmatically in Eastern Europe. … What it dared to question was not the legitimacy of property, which was treated as a secondary problem, but above all, power and authority. It made no attempt to seize the means of production, but rather the centers of command."[36]

What was happening in China to engage the sympathy of the Ultra-Left in Europe and America was unique in the annals of revolution. The so-called Great Proletarian Cultural Revolution was set in motion by Chairman Mao Tse-tung in 1966 as a deliberate effort to mobilize youthful discontent against a Communist bureaucracy that had allegedly betrayed the true revolutionary spirit and, in Mao's view, taken the Soviet path of postrevolutionary bureaucratic degeneration. Organized in the so-called Red Guards, the Chinese youth movement quickly took on a violent life of its own, first on the French model of protest against bureaucratized education, and then as a massive assault on the educated class and the nationwide power structure of the Communist Party. Mao capitalized on the turmoil to sack most of his top leadership, while radicals independently seized local power in Shanghai and other points.

The heyday of this social extremism in China did not last long. By mid-1967 the army closed ranks against the radicals, and Mao became convinced that the Cultural Revolution had gotten out of hand. Yet the process of restoring the previous bureaucratic order was both protracted and violent, encountering continued resistance by radicals around Mao and his wife Chiang Ch'ing. One final flare-up occurred in Peking in 1968, in the "Hundred Day War" between the most radical faction of students and those who were a shade less extreme, until Mao intervened, sent workers into the universities to restore order, and dispatched millions of people to the villages, both perpetrators and victims of the Fourth Revolution. By 1969 the Cultural Revolution was over, and the Fourth Revolution in China had effectively been suppressed, despite one last gasp in 1976, led by Mao's wife and the so-called Gang of Four. These diehards were easily removed from power by the military the moment the aging leader died, allowing China to return to the path of modernization based on a post–Third Revolution, bureaucratic model of the social system with gradual concessions to the private economy.

The Fourth Revolution in China was unique as a new kind of revolution within the context of an ongoing revolutionary process that had not yet worked its way to the end. The Cultural Revolution was the most impassioned and violent instance yet seen anywhere in the world, of rebellion against the authority of age, expertise, and hierarchical position.

It also had bizarre international ramifications in the encouragement it lent to the most radical student elements in Europe and America. The Chinese demonstratively recognized these hotheads as their ideological confrères, along with the black civil rights movement in the United States. "The revolutionary masses in Europe and North America," trumpeted the *People's Daily* in May 1968, "dared to look down on the law and bayonets of the reactionary ruling cliques, showed no fear of suppression, persisted in their heroic struggle, and demonstrated a lively, revolutionary spirit."[37] The Cultural Revolution was also the direct inspiration for the fanatical Khmer Rouge movement in Cambodia, devoted during their rule from 1975 to 1979 to the deadly extirpation of the entire urban and educated sector of society.[38] Declared Cambodia's revolutionary dictator Pol Pot, "Political consciousness is the decisive factor. If we chose 'culture,' it would lead to a life and death disaster for the Party."[39] If there was an ultimate embodiment of the Fourth Revolution in power, it was the Khmer Rouge.

The Crisis of 1968

The year of international youth rebellion—1968—was also the point when the diverse elements of the Fourth Revolution converged in America to produce a social and political crisis without precedent since the Civil War. With the governmental side of the revolution already under assault, the components of revolution in society at large, above all among blacks and youth, came together in a peak of defiance, dismissing the efforts of the Great Society and articulating demands for the total overthrow of the social order. But it was not long before the forces for change splintered among the extreme, the moderate, and the fainthearted, as they typically do in revolutions. There was no chance for a true seizure of power by the hopelessly minoritarian extremists. To be sure, the Johnson administration foundered, and the Great Society was halted in its tracks, but the outcome of the crisis was not more revolution—it was the onset of the inexorable downturn in the revolutionary process.

The solvent that broke up the alliance of forces sustaining the Great Society was the same circumstance that had brought the Fourth Revolution to a head—namely, the war in Vietnam. The war had always been as much political as strategic, pressed by the Kennedy and Johnson administrations to parry any potential Republican charge of "losing" another country to Communism, such as had plagued the Truman administration after the Communist victory in China in 1949. Johnson continued stubbornly to pursue the war in the fear that his putative nemesis Robert Kennedy would use the issue against him if he backed off.[40] Intended to protect the political right flank of the Great Society, the Vietnam War ironically opened it up to assault from the left.

Johnson's escalation of the war in 1965 immediately galvanized an antiwar student movement, centered on the increasingly radical Students for a Democratic Society (SDS) and driven by fear of the military draft. The experience proved that a country cannot use drafted troops to conduct a limited war of power politics, in distinction to a genuine struggle for national survival, without provoking deep national discord. The antiwar movement sharpened dramatically in the March on Washington in October 1967, with the attempted storming of the Pentagon vividly chronicled by Norman Mailer.[41] Almost simultaneously, egged on by the civil rights veteran and future congressman Allard Lowenstein, the mystical junior senator from Minnesota Eugene McCarthy announced for the forthcoming Democratic presidential nomination as an antiwar alternative to Johnson.

The contest of wills over the war was intensified by the so-called Tet Offensive launched by the Vietnamese Communists on January 31, 1968, the day after the Vietnamese New Year. Militarily the offensive was a disaster, particularly for the South Vietnamese Viet Cong guerrillas, but politically it was just as much a disaster for Johnson's policy. It demonstrated that the American client government in Saigon had no will to fight and that the war was pointless from the standpoint of American interests and unwinnable except at unacceptable cost. On the heels of Tet, McCarthy astounded the nation by nearly beating Johnson in the New Hampshire presidential primary. Robert Kennedy, now a senator from New York, added an aftershock to this political earthquake by deciding to challenge Johnson in his own right with an agenda of Great Society revivalism as well as a renunciation of the war. The president, agonizing over his accumulated political liabilities, astounded the nation in turn by announcing his withdrawal as a candidate for reelection. Johnson was truly a tragic figure, fatally undone by what Eric Goldman called "the fact that he was not a very likeable man, ... ready to double-talk about anything ... in order to protect votes."[42] Halfheartedly, he left the role of Establishment leader to his vice president, Hubert Humphrey.

Kennedy, though he had driven a bitterly felt split into the antiwar forces when he undertook to upstage McCarthy, displayed a charismatic ability to mobilize all kinds of social groups in a new crusade for economic and racial justice riding the antiwar wave. "Alone among national politicians," observed the historian Allen Matusow, "Kennedy could walk through the streets of both white working-class and black neighborhoods and be warmly cheered in each."[43] He might have gone on to win the presidency and reinvigorate the Great Society, had he not, like his brother, fallen victim to an assassin's bullet, at the height of his presidential campaign in June 1968. From that time on—almost simultaneously with the assassination of Martin Luther King Jr.—the Fourth Revolution was left leaderless in any coherent national sense.

Nevertheless, against this backdrop of politics in turmoil, the social forces of revolution were peaking in every quarter of American society. The black civil rights movement, gaining momentum from the late 1950s on under King's charismatic leadership, had entered a phase of escalating violence and widening fissures between moderates and extremists, climaxing in the huge riots in Washington and elsewhere triggered by King's assassination in April 1968. The antiwar movement and radical youth protests reached a peak at almost the same time, in the revolutionary student takeovers at Columbia University and other big campuses, paralleling the student uprisings taking place simultaneously in Europe. Youthful defiance was intensified by the influence of the counterculture, which repudiated the whole gamut of bourgeois values from hard work to cleanliness to monogamy. This contrarian state of mind, intensified by the new fashions in rock music and consumption of psychedelic drugs, was epitomized by the congregation of youth in San Francisco during the "summer of love" of 1967. At the same time, radical feminism, intertwined with the counterculture, made its appearance in such manifestations as picketing of the 1968 Atlantic City Miss America pageant (though "bra burning" proved to be an unfounded legend).

All of the currents of revolution in 1968, combining passions of defiance both in the political realm and in radical social and cultural styles, came to a head at the Democratic National Convention in Chicago in August. Antiwar politics within the normal process, left to depend on the faltering leadership of Senator McCarthy after Robert Kennedy's demise, was steamrollered by the Johnson–Humphrey forces. Only the streets were available to the revolutionaries, who made the most of the Vietnam issue and came ardently to grips with the forces of order represented by the Chicago police and the Illinois National Guard. Humphrey's campaign was almost fatally discredited among both moderates and radicals by the tumultuous events of those days, and belated efforts by the nominee and finally by President Johnson to appease antiwar sentiment failed to turn the tide. George Wallace's third-party campaign, diverting the votes of anti–Fourth Revolution Democrats, proved to be decisive. He carried five states in the South and drew away enough Democrats to account for Nixon's margin of victory in thirteen others, including California and Illinois, more than enough to have swung the Electoral College the other way. Thus did Richard Nixon narrowly prevail in the 1968 election, and the inexorable Thermidorean Reaction set in.

Thermidor and Counterrevolution

All revolutions overreach in their trajectories. One way or another they are then compelled to fall back to a level more compatible with society's habits and traditions, whatever advanced rhetoric may persist. However, the setback is never total; some revolutionary changes are bound to survive.

So it was with the Fourth Revolution, as currents of radicalism within it alienated some of its supporters while carrying its demands beyond the limits of the tolerable for most of society. The characteristic generational cycle of reform in the United States, at this point beginning to turn downward, constricted the popular sources of enthusiasm for change. Yet unforeseeable contingencies in the succession of national political leadership gave the descending postrevolutionary curve a prolonged and peculiar character.

Richard Nixon, demonized by liberal opinion on account of his political exploitation of anti-Communism, as president confounded his critics. Like Truman in the aftermath of the New Deal, he proved to be not a counterrevolutionary but only a Thermidorean, content to implement the scaled-down aims of the revolution he had inherited, without undertaking major new initiatives either to advance or to scuttle the new social arrangements. Nixon left intact the antipoverty and Welfare State innovations of the Great Society and even tried, unsuccessfully, to bridge the welfare–work gap with his ill-fated "family assistance program" (killed by an odd congressional alliance of uncompromising liberals and immovable conservatives). His administration continued to enforce the Kennedy–Johnson civil rights programs, despite his electoral dependence on southern enemies of equality for blacks. His years in office saw the feminist movement gain momentum, though here the judiciary was the key, through its decisions advancing abortion rights and equal opportunity. Nixon may have contemplated a shift to the right once he had been personally validated by reelection, but the Watergate scandal of political burglary and cover-up, and the ensuing constitutional crisis, deflected any such intention. In any case, it is noteworthy that the Reaganites and their successors from the 1980s on, crusading against liberalism and all its works, never distinguished the Nixon era from the Johnson and Carter administrations in their litany of "failed programs."

The one area where Nixon showed no compromise toward the spirit of the sixties was the youth rebellion and the antiwar movement. Like Johnson, Nixon covered his political right flank by continuing the war in Vietnam, until his secretary of state Henry Kissinger managed to negotiate the appearances of a successful withdrawal in 1972–73. He pressed the legally preposterous trial of the "Chicago Seven," radical celebrities charged with inciting the disorders surrounding the 1968 Democratic convention (all either found not guilty or acquitted on appeal). Nixon's antiradical posture stood him in good stead in the 1972 campaign, when he was able to represent his opponent George McGovern as the champion of the hippies and social disorder, and he thereby scored an unprecedented victory (without, however, substantially altering the political balance in Congress).

In a democratic country, the era of retrenchment between a revolutionary peak and avowed counterrevolution can be a long period of pulling and hauling, as the post-Progressive and post–New Deal times showed. Watergate, confounding and then destroying Nixon's presidency shortly into his second term, kept outright counterrevolution against the sixties at bay. These singular events allowed the postrevolutionary standoff to persist during the Nixon–Ford term of 1973–77 and on through the Carter administration of 1977–81. Watergate produced a congress that was almost as Democratic as Johnson's of 1964–66, though it lacked executive leadership under the Republicans. Guided only modestly by Carter, Congress barely held the line on reform. Thus, under the conditions of the 1970s, government moved neither ahead nor back on the principles of the Fourth Revolution. Revolutionary forces outside government were allowed, with judicial encouragement, to consolidate their gains where they could.

The Fourth Revolution and the End of the Third

In contrast to the continuing momentum of most social components of the Fourth Revolution in the seventies, the Great Society's legacy in economic empowerment and equality steadily deteriorated. In part, this loss of ground was the consequence of broad economic conditions, including the chronic inflation of the seventies and the government's abandonment of the macroeconomic goal of full employment. Real wages for the unskilled and the value of welfare support for the needy began a long decline, while social disintegration brought the numbers of clients dependent on public assistance, and the total cost of these programs, to ever-higher levels. Testimony to the new power of Fourth Revolution principles was the tendency to couch lingering Third Revolution issues such as labor and welfare rights in terms of the civil rights struggle, by pointing up the racial aspect of economic disparities. But this connection had already cut the other way: the legal theorist Cass Sunstein noted the role of southern racism in defeating Truman's full employment act in 1946, as well as popular hostility to more recent welfare and redistributive spending on the same grounds.[44]

In addition to the discouraging circumstances of the national economy in the 1970s, the principles of the Third Revolution were caught up in the shift of opinion against the excesses of the Fourth. Formerly radical intellectuals, led by the one-time Trotskyist Irving Kristol and *Commentary* editor Norman Podhoretz, appalled by feminism, legal permissiveness, and the welfare culture, abjured economic liberalism along with the social revolution, and invented "neoconservatism" as their new ideological home.[45] The ever more costly Great Society programs beamed at society's unfortunates came under a heavy cloud, as the new class struggle between the poor and the not quite so poor (often a thinly disguised racial antipathy) intensified.[46] Beckoned by the "Coalition for a Democratic Majority" that was set up in 1972 after George McGovern's disastrous defeat to be followed later by the "Democratic Leadership Council" (1985), most Democratic leaders shied away from the liberal label, verbally confused as they were about the distinction between Third and Fourth Revolution issues. Michael Dukakis and Bill Clinton personified the party's quandary as they danced around any identification with the "L word." John Kerry never came near it. Such maneuvering nevertheless failed to stanch the loss of southern Democrats and northern working-class white men to the national Republican ticket, the political trends that had set up the Reagan counterrevolution of the eighties.

By the 1980s, economic and social conservatism converged in rejecting governmental responsibility for the condition of the underclass; it would be only "throwing money at problems." In the war on poverty, "Poverty won." At the federal level and in most states, the Office of Economic Opportunity and Community Action programs withered and died. The labor movement, disparaged by both Right and Left as merely one more special interest, steadily lost ground in numbers, bargaining power, and sense of public purpose. Among the beneficiaries of the Great Society, only the elderly saw their fortunes improve, to the point where their average income rose higher than that of the population as a whole, though the actuarial storm clouds of an aging population were visible ahead. All in all, revulsion against the principles of the Fourth Revolution worked more to undermine what remained of economic egalitarianism than to reverse the gains of social equality.

Real counterrevolution in the cycle of the Fourth Revolution, at least at the symbolic level, began with Reagan's election in 1980 on a sweepingly antigovernment platform. Though his popular vote victory over Jimmy Carter and independent John Anderson was a narrow one, Reagan took his Electoral College triumph as a mandate for tax cuts intended to cripple the fiscal basis of the Great Society's commitments. His real triumph came in his reelection in 1984, when he overwhelmed Walter Mondale, the last true economic liberal to lead the Democrats. This victory marked the deepest point of the counterrevolution, coming exactly half a generational cycle—sixteen years—after the revolutionary peak of 1968.

The Reagan counterrevolution, however, proved to be attenuated and anticlimactic, leaving in place most of the sixties agenda that had survived Nixon. In 1984 Reagan lost the Republican Senate majority that came in with him in 1980, and he was never able to break the Democrats' hold on the House of Representatives. To be sure, there were signs of the party realignment that marked the 1990s. Southern conservatives began to extend their Republican voting preference from the presidential level down to their congressional and state choices, and they threatened the Democrats with permanent minority status in the region. Meanwhile, a devilish compromise ensued from divided government: tax cuts on one hand, deficit financing on the other to sustain programs both for the military and for the poor and the elderly—a politically palatable stopgap. But major new initiatives of the Great Society sort were henceforth out of the question, as President Clinton discovered in 1994 when he tried to revive the unrequited aim of national health insurance.

Not until the Republican takeover of Congress in 1994, aided by the rapid realignment of southern conservatives into the GOP's ranks, did the counterrevolution hit with full ideological force. Speaker-elect Newt Gingrich of Georgia vowed to extirpate "liberalism" for all time. Such a goal reflected the strange alignment of middle-class disgust with the Great Society, free-market resistance to the Third Revolution, and religious fundamentalism's determination to wage cultural war by undoing even the First Revolution and the separation of church and state.

The Fourth Revolution Revived?

As the counterrevolutionary spirit personified first by Reagan and then by Gingrich blew through the eighties and into the nineties, it began to encounter currents of a diametrically opposite character. Old principles of the Fourth Revolution embodied in the diverse social movements that made it up began to revive and display new militancy, in racial politics, in feminism and the gay and lesbian rights movement, and throughout the educational establishment. Seen in the classical pattern of revolutions, this recrudescence of the Fourth Revolution fits the concept of the moderate revolutionary revival.

Actually, the cause of revolution in its moderate form was never unequivocally put down. A sharper edge appeared in the social thinking of the late eighties and the nineties, in the new militancy and exclusiveness of extremist elements in the various social movements, especially race and gender related. The revolutionary upturn was felt most keenly in universities, under the pressure of "cultural diversity" and "political correctness," along with the ongoing requirement of affirmative action in hiring and admissions.

Thus in the nineties and since, the militant spirit of counterrevolution has found itself face-to-face with a vigorous revival of the aims of social revolution. No wonder that the public and its leadership have had a hard time setting their political bearings. No wonder that political discourse is muddled, that social life is anxious, and that slogans and code words have taken the place of real analysis and choice in public affairs. No wonder that people of all persuasions, left, right, and center, feel alienated and adrift, without their old certainties to turn to.

CHAPTER **5**

The Racial Revolution

The earliest, deepest, most violent, and most uniquely American component of the Fourth Revolution in the United States was the black civil rights movement. Civil rights was, moreover, the prototype for all the new social struggles of the era. The most distinctly revolutionary of all the facets of the Fourth Revolution in America, the black civil rights movement served as a battering ram opening the way for all the other potentially revolutionary forces in American society, and encouraged them to assert the whole gamut of radical demands for social change. At the same time, the black civil rights movement was the most successful component of the new revolution in terms of the ground it gained and the conquests it held, even if its attainments fell short of its adherents' maximum hopes.

Most clearly and consistently of all the currents of the Fourth Revolution in the United States, the black civil rights movement fit the classic mold of the revolutionary process. Its deep causes are discernable in the broad evolution of modern American society toward more complex, urbanized forms. The movement had its own distinct intellectual preparation in the work of writers, white as well as black, who helped delegitimize the old racial values of supremacy and subordination. It began gradually and moderately, both from below and from above, as a series of local protests and favorable judicial decisions. It picked up steam and programmatic focus in an advanced moderate stage with remarkable, principled leadership, together with energetic support from the executive branch of government. Then came a social explosion from below, accompanied by the ideological split of the movement between moderates and extremists. Finally, there was a distinct Thermidorean Reaction, as mass protest exhausted itself, extremist groups dissipated, opposition regrouped, and moderates had to content themselves for the time being with the substantial though incomplete gains they had made.

This process in the classical revolutionary form was played out, to be sure, in a restricted context. Directly, it involved only a particular segment of the country's population, a minority defined by race, although its successes ultimately depended on changing the values and attitudes of the white majority. Its timing and its achievements were heavily dependent on the orientation and actions of the national government, especially as a counterweight to the unabashedly antirevolutionary state governments in the South. By the very nature of its minority racial basis, the black civil rights movement could never move beyond the limits of a semirevolution, however radical and violent some of its constituent elements might become within their own sphere.

Origins of the "Black Revolution"

Any great historical development poses two questions for explanation: Why did it happen, and why did it happen when it did? What, in other words, were the basic causes, and what were the immediate, triggering causes?

Obviously the black revolution was rooted in the unique racial character of American society, where one-tenth of the population was descended from slaves and subjected to varying forms of discrimination and obloquy, open and legal in the southern states, less consistent and more subtle in the North. Blacks were left out of the American Revolution, except for its abortive post–Civil War epilogue, and this history bequeathed a gaping hole in the application of America's basic political and legal principles. Little was done for blacks directly in the economic revolution of Progressivism and the New Deal, except as the lot of the poor generally was improved. Nevertheless, as the achievements of modernization—urbanization, education, and principles of personal rights—reached the black population, movements to remedy their oppressed status were bound sooner or later to sprout up.

In the immediate background of the black civil rights movement, as of the other components of the Fourth Revolution, was the impact of World War II on American society. Much longer and more intense than the nation's involvement in World War I, World War II generated opportunities for both geographic and occupational mobility that made it possible for millions of blacks to escape peonage in the rural South. Sporadic moves toward desegregation in the armed forces pointed the way to basic social change, and the labor movement, despite its overall ambivalence and inner divisions on the race issue, did nurture the black activism of such leaders as A. Philip Randolph of the Brotherhood of Sleeping Car Porters. Perhaps most important, the war and its aftermath saw the extraordinary migration of rural southern blacks into metropolitan areas both northern and southern, focusing them as a potential force for political action as well as intensifying the conditions for agonizing social disintegration.

Like the great classical revolutions, the black upheaval of the 1960s was long foreshadowed by a series of black critics of American society, supported by the contributions of white writers. The protest tradition can be traced all the way back to the abolition of slavery and the failure of Reconstruction, with the militant Christian moralism of Frederick Douglas followed by Booker T. Washington's "politics of accommodation" and W.E.B. Dubois's socialist separatism.[1] Protest gained a sharper edge after World War II, the turning point being the publication of Gunnar Myrdal's *American Dilemma* in 1944.[2] A whole school of black writers, from Richard Wright (*Black Boy* and *Native Son*) to Ralph Ellison (*The Invisible Man*) and James Baldwin (*The Fire Next Time*) articulated black distress and brought it home to open-minded whites as well. Black musicians opened up a wide hole in the armor of White Supremacy. All this helped achieve the change of mood that is essential to the onset of any revolution: the undermining of the will and self-assurance of the masters of the old order. Attracting many people who had previously sympathized with the New Deal agenda, the cause of racial justice opened a new dimension to the American understanding of "liberal" and "liberalism."

Not to be neglected, at the same time, was the role of religion among the black population. The churches had taught forbearance in the name of a heavenly ideal, but they could also take a hand in the cause of justice on earth. The moderate southern leadership of the black civil rights movement in its early phases, above all as it was associated with Martin Luther King Jr. and his immediate followers, was deeply and specifically Christian. One specialist on black thought speaks of the civil rights movement as "primarily a religious event, ... part of the historical tradition of religious revivals."[3] By contrast, secularism, a more typical expression of modernization, was the prevailing standpoint of the northern component of the black civil rights movement and especially of its radical elements. Inconspicuous at first, but more prominent later on, was black interest in Islam as a rationale for extremism and separatism.

As social changes and literary critiques highlighted the question of equity for blacks in the immediate postwar years, political responses were quick to follow. A high-level Civil Rights Commission appointed by President Truman in 1946 under the chairmanship of Charles Wilson, CEO of General Electric, called for an extraordinary reform program, including voting rights, employment rights, and school desegregation—all of the great issues that lay ahead. Pressured from the left by Henry Wallace's Progressive Party and the dying moans of the New Deal, Truman embraced most of his commission's recommendations.[4]

The Democratic Party, already enjoying the bulk of the black vote outside the South since New Deal days, took a historic step at its 1948 convention when, at the urging of senator-to-be Hubert Humphrey, it adopted an explicit civil rights plank. This famous document, in retrospect quite mild and indirect, called only for "equal political participation," an antilynching law, and the revival of the wartime Fair Employment Practices Commission. Nonetheless, the platform was enough to provoke the defection of a large fraction of southerners, who nominated Governor Strom Thurmond of South Carolina as the standard bearer of the "States' Rights" Party and carried five states in November.

Two weeks after the Democratic convention, in the teeth of this defiance, Truman ordered an end to racial discrimination in the armed forces and the civil service. Full desegregation came later, over the protests of generals who objected to making the military a laboratory for social experiments. Since that time, the armed forces have stood in the national vanguard in terms of practical desegregation, personified by the career of General Colin Powell. In the meantime, in 1947 the great American spectator pastime of Major League Baseball took its first step on the road to racial desegregation when the Brooklyn Dodgers brought Jackie Robinson up from the minors to play first base.

The epochal event steering the civil rights issue in the direction of revolutionary confrontation was the 1954 school desegregation decision of the Supreme Court under the new leadership of Earl Warren. In *Brown v. Board of Education* (a Kansas case, not from the Deep South), the Court overturned the "separate but equal" doctrine in public schools on the ground that separate was inherently deprecatory and unequal. The decision was met by a firestorm of defiance throughout the South, as a clash of fundamental principles shaped up between equality and inclusion on one hand and segregationist White Supremacy on the other, embodied in the fascistic White Citizens Councils and the revived Ku Klux Klan. However, the judiciary, transformed by constitutional argument into the spearhead of the Rights Revolution, went steadily against the segregationists, provoking almost insurrectionary resistance. The worst came in Little Rock, Arkansas, in 1957 when President Eisenhower had to dispatch regular troops and federalize the Arkansas National Guard to enforce court-ordered desegregation of the city's high school. Meanwhile, in 1956 the Supreme Court extended the new principle of educational integration to state-supported universities, where desegregation was much less militantly resisted, in part because it was impossible to argue that at the level of higher education, separate could nevertheless be equal. "The decade spanned by the 1954 Supreme Court decision on school desegregation and the Civil Rights Act of 1964," wrote the civil rights organizer Bayard Rustin from the perspective of the mid-1960s, "will undoubtedly be recorded as the period in which the legal foundations of racism in America were destroyed."[5]

The legislative branch of the national government, hobbled by the power of southern senators armed with the filibuster, was much slower and weaker than the judicial branch in its responses to the new civil rights efforts. Lyndon Johnson, becoming majority leader in the Senate when the Democrats regained control in 1954, strove to produce civil rights reform but managed to secure only a modest measure for federal injunctions in voting rights controversies. Further progress by governmental action awaited the mobilization of the black civil rights movement outside of government.

King, Kennedy, and the Moderate Revolution

The saga of the Montgomery, Alabama, bus boycott and the emergence of Martin Luther King Jr. on the national stage is the best-known facet of the civil rights story. When the preconditions are ripe, one small incident—in this case, the refusal of seamstress Rosa Parks to move to the back of the bus in December 1955—can grow into a mighty torrent of angry activism. King, a newly established Baptist minister in Montgomery, found the resulting black boycott of the Montgomery bus system just the point to apply his philosophy of Christian nonviolent resistance. Escaping a bomb attack on his home, he proclaimed, "We must meet hate with love."[6]

By the time the Supreme Court ruled in 1957 that Montgomery had to desegregate its buses, King had become a national figure. He set up a broad organization, the Southern Christian Leadership Conference (SCLC), to advance the cause of desegregation and voting rights, and with this show of strength he helped secure the passage of Johnson's early civil rights bill, the first such legislation since Reconstruction. Beginning slowly, King's movement picked up momentum in 1960 when black college students began the sit-in movement to desegregate restaurants and stores in the southern states. With King's blessing, the students formed the Student Non-violent Coordinating Committee (SNCC), led by a very young Baptist minister, not yet out of college, John Lewis (the future congressman from Georgia). Joining personally in the sit-in campaign in Atlanta, King was briefly jailed, until presidential candidate John Kennedy successfully interceded on his behalf.

Kennedy's election in November 1960 injected new hope and governmental encouragement into the black civil rights movement. Even before the inauguration of the new president, the Supreme Court ruled against segregation in any form of interstate transportation and in the terminals serving it. In turn, this action opened up an opportunity for the New York–based Congress of Racial Equality, an interracial organization founded by the black minister James Farmer in 1942 on Quaker and Gandhian principles of nonviolence.[7] CORE undertook to organize the celebrated "freedom rides," with biracial teams traveling the South by bus and braving vigilante violence to challenge segregation rules. Attorney General Robert Kennedy threw his support to the movement, came to speak at the University of Georgia (the first such institution in the Deep South to capitulate to an integration order), and prevailed upon the Interstate Commerce Commission to enforce the Supreme Court's order on desegregation in travel.

Following the example of previous administrations, President Kennedy issued an executive order to establish an Equal Employment Opportunity Commission, chaired by Vice President Johnson. The order introduced for the first time the phrase "affirmative action."[8] For the time being, however, all this was confined to federal agencies and contractors. Otherwise, to the great dismay of black leaders, the Kennedy administration held back from broad intervention in the civil rights struggle, out of concern for congressional conservatives and the 1964 elections. It was nonetheless forced to send troops when black student James Meredith, armed with a federal court order, attempted to enroll in the University of Mississippi. Both the King people and the Kennedys tried to walk the narrow path between overcaution and rashness, to keep their most ardent supporters satisfied while avoiding violent confrontations with the enemies of reform. Neither the black leaders nor the government seemed fully aware of the depths of emotion, both revolutionary and counterrevolutionary, that they had tapped.

Birmingham

A critical turning point in the civil rights movement came in the spring of 1963, in Birmingham, Alabama.[9] Birmingham could fairly be described as the storming of the Bastille for the black cause. As in France in July 1789, or at Lexington and Concord, it was the event that turned a movement into a revolution. It made Martin Luther King Jr. the nationally recognized leader of the black revolution, swung the sympathies of the nation at large toward the revolutionary aims of its black segment, and, not least, impelled the Kennedy administration in Washington to take the initiative in the civil rights cause.

Birmingham was deliberately targeted by SCLC as the most unyielding bastion of southern segregation, despite King's apprehensions about this tactical boldness. Organized protest demonstrations and a boycott of white businesses commenced in April 1963; King, defying an injunction against these actions, was arrested and put in solitary confinement until President Kennedy protested. This was the occasion of King's "Letter from Birmingham Jail"—the testimonial of a revolutionary who still clung to moderate methods. "Freedom is never voluntarily given by the oppressor; it must be demanded by the oppressed," he wrote. "I have almost reached the regrettable conclusion that the Negro's great stumbling block in his stride toward freedom is not the White Citizens Councilor or the Ku Klux Klanner, but the white moderate, who is more devoted to 'order' than to justice. ... If they refuse to support our nonviolent efforts, millions of Negroes will, out of frustration and despair, seek solace and security in black-nationalist ideologies—a development that would inevitably lead to a frightening racial nightmare."[10]

Though King was soon bailed out of jail, the demonstrations continued. On May 3 Birmingham police commissioner Eugene "Bull" Connor made himself nationally infamous by assaulting the protesters with dogs and fire hoses, an action flashed immediately onto every TV screen in the country. Under pressure of Justice Department mediators, the Birmingham business community agreed to a truce that granted many of the blacks' demands, while Ku Klux Klan holdouts attempted to bomb King and his brother, and young blacks rioted. Once again, President Kennedy had to deploy federal troops, and he threatened to federalize the Alabama National Guard, while Bull Connor lost a court fight to continue in office. Birmingham quieted down, but its national impact was indelible.

Meanwhile, a federal court had ordered the desegregation of the University of Alabama at Tuscaloosa, the last public institution of higher education in the nation to hold out against admitting blacks. Governor George Wallace, already incensed about federal intervention in Birmingham, threatened to "stand in the schoolhouse door," and on June 11 he appeared personally to bar the enrollment of two black students at the university. Kennedy again deployed troops and officially federalized the Alabama Guard to protect the blacks; Wallace, having made his point, backed down, but not without accentuating the national impact of southern intransigence.

The Tuscaloosa crisis finally convinced Kennedy that he had to gamble on unequivocal support of the civil rights movement. Aware that it might be his "political swan song," he went on radio and TV to make "equal rights and equal opportunity" a "moral issue" for the nation, while warning of a "rising tide of discontent that threatens the public safety."[11] On June 19 he sent Congress a civil rights bill that would ban discrimination in public accommodations, put legal teeth in school desegregation, and extend the authority of the Equal Employment Opportunity Commission to the entire private sector.

Taking this progress in stride, the black leadership pressed on with plans to carry their protest to the national level with a massive march on Washington. Conceived by the trade unionist Randolph and the pacifist Rustin, and backed by King after the Birmingham crisis, the idea of a march was intended to put pressure on Congress to advance the civil rights agenda and to push "a broad and fundamental program of economic justice" (according to King's biographer David Garrow), despite fears in the Kennedy administration that the effort would become violent and hence counterproductive. "King had come to appreciate that it was the coercive direct action of Birmingham, and not persuasive moral appeals aimed at winning over the hearts of southern whites, that the movement would have to pursue."[12] John Lewis, at the time one of the hotheads, spoke of "the great social revolution sweeping our nation."[13] In the actual event, on August 28, the march proved to be an altogether peaceable assemblage of a quarter of a million people, the largest ever in the capital up to that time, who heard King's memorable "I Have a Dream" speech with its peroration from the old spiritual, "Free at last! Free at last! Thank God Almighty, we are free at last."[14] Two weeks later a bomb explosion at a black church in Birmingham killed four young girls. Congressional action on the civil rights bill was ensured.

Birmingham was the critical turning point for black rights. It turned a local movement into a national one, it brought the federal executive in unequivocally on the side of civil rights, and it truly opened a new revolutionary chapter in American life. In the eyes of the New Frontier historian Irving Bernstein, "The Birmingham crisis was decisive in making civil rights the central domestic issue of the decade. ... It was Bull Connor and his fire hoses and snarling dogs playing on television."[15] Linking the revolutions of the 1930s and the 1960s, Arthur Schlesinger saw "no such surge of spontaneous mass democracy in the United States since the organization of labor in the heavy industries in the spring and summer of 1937. Characteristically," he added, "each revolution began with direct local action—one with sit-downs, the other with sit-ins. In each case, ordinary people took things into their own hands, generated their own leaders, asserted their own rights and outstripped not only the government but their own organizations."[16] John Morton Blum saw the black civil rights movement's progress as an interaction between courageous initiative from below and sympathetic response from above: "Without the hopes and the boldness, the frustrations and the ideals of anonymous thousands of Blacks who were determined to win their full rights as Americans, the leaders of the civil rights movement would have had no flocks. ... Without those leaders and the pressures they generated, Presidents Kennedy and Johnson would not have acted when they had, nor could they then have won the votes they needed on the Hill." Still, "Kennedy and Johnson had the personal sympathies and essential convictions that their immediate predecessors and successors lacked."[17]

For the moment, the new black revolution remained essentially moderate. To be sure, "moderate" in the revolutionary scheme does not imply unwillingness to struggle for an ideal goal. In the American black civil rights movement, it meant two things, one tactical and the other strategic. Tactically, moderation was expressed in the commitment to nonviolence; strategically, it was embodied in the goal of inclusion in the broader society. It was religiously inspired and based in the South. All of this was soon to be called into question in the extremist phase that was shortly to take over in the black revolution.

The Great Society and Acceleration of the Black Revolution

Kennedy's assassination in November 1963 did not set his civil rights agenda back, despite wide distrust of his southern successor. To the contrary: on civil rights as well as on economic issues, Lyndon Johnson proved to be more consistently liberal and aggressive than his predecessor, and he enjoyed the aura of JFK's martyrdom besides. An immediate monument to Kennedy's efforts was ratification of the anti–poll tax amendment to the Constitution, approved by Congress in 1962 and finalized by thirty-eight states in January 1964. The legislative drive continued, and the Civil Rights Act of 1964 became law in July, with the sweeping aim of suppressing discrimination everywhere in public accommodations, education, and employment. Considering the precarious makeup of Congress, the 1964 act was an epochal achievement; it was the black revolution's equivalent of the Declaration of the Rights of Man in the French Revolution. "Critics belittled the act," Allen Matusow observed, "because it did not attack de facto segregation or ... subtle discrimination or ... the scandal of black poverty. None of these were its purpose. The act's main intent, limited but indispensable, was the accomplishment of legal equality in a region where it did not exist."[18]

The federal role in civil rights was not entirely positive. Early on, King ran afoul of J. Edgar Hoover and the FBI, who conducted a long vendetta against the black civil rights movement, with little distinction at first between the moderates and the radicals. As early as 1962, King aroused Hoover's ire by criticizing the FBI's unenthusiastic record in civil rights, whereupon Hoover made an issue of ex-Communists in King's entourage and got Robert Kennedy's approval to bug the black leader's conversations—an activity that quickly shifted in its focus from politics to sex. Presumably investigating murders in Mississippi, the FBI director made bold to assert at the state capital in July 1964 that his agency "does not and will not give protection to civil rights workers."[19] Hoover was particularly incensed when King was awarded the Nobel Peace Prize for 1964, but he overplayed his hand in public and private attacks on the black leader, and his political clout began to weaken. Nevertheless, for the balance of the decade, Hoover continued his active measures through "COINTELPRO" (Counterintelligence Program), a secret campaign of disruption directed primarily against black radicals.[20]

As is typical when a country has entered into a revolutionary condition, political gains by their movement only sharpened the outrage of the black revolutionaries and elevated their aims. Frederick Douglass had observed, "Under a harsh master, a slave could but think of survival; under a good master, he began to think of freedom."[21] Black voting rights were one area not further addressed in the 1964 Civil Rights Act, and the leading black groups, cooperating as the Council of Federated Organizations, decided to go ahead on their own to crack Mississippi, the most laggard of all the southern states. The resulting "Freedom Summer" of 1964 was the heroic moment in the voting rights struggle, as student volunteers of both races from all over the country flocked to Mississippi to help push voter registration in the face of violent white resistance that extended to bombings, church burnings, and the murder of three student volunteers. "The United States is unique among contemporary Western democracies," wrote Ted Gurr in his study of violence, "in nurturing an enduring tradition of private political murder in resistance to change."[22] Yet the barriers were broken. In the words of one chronicler of the movement, "The fortress of white supremacy, once believed impregnable, had been breached."[23]

To the embarrassment of the Johnson administration, anxious about southern support in the forthcoming election, the momentum of the black voter registration drive encouraged the "Mississippi Freedom Democratic Party," a largely black group that made bold to challenge the all-white official Mississippi delegation to the 1964 Democratic National Convention in Atlantic City. An attempt by the Johnson administration to impose a compromise succeeded only in precipitating a walkout by the regular Mississippi and Alabama delegations, while simultaneously alienating black radicals. By the time of the convention crisis, according to Joseph Rauh, who was counsel to SNCC at the time, the blacks had already found allies among the remnants of the Communist Party, specifically in the National Lawyers Guild.[24] Meanwhile, Alabama's George Wallace had thrown his hat into the presidential ring, and in primaries in Wisconsin, Indiana, and Maryland he demonstrated the potential of white working-class backlash against black rights by winning a third or more of the vote against Johnson stand-ins. All this trouble presaged Republican Barry Goldwater's sweep of the Deep South in the November election, mainly the same states that had gone for Thurmond in 1948. That outcome in turn pointed the way to the historic regional realignment of the parties that was completed in the 1990s. But for the moment, the Democrats were better off without the South than with it; Johnson scored the greatest Democratic victory since 1936, and brought in with him the first unabashedly liberal Congress to take office since the New Deal.

President Johnson's triumphal reelection accelerated the whole gamut of Great Society initiatives, and with them a continuing drive on the civil rights front. Pressured by radical blacks, King escalated his voting rights campaign and focused on the ultrasegregationist city of Selma, Alabama, in the hope of prodding further federal action. Caught between headstrong black militants, local police and Klan violence, and a federal government in search of compromise, King nonetheless scored decisively in the arena of national opinion. Congress responded with the Voting Rights Act of 1965. This step, according to Hugh Davis graham, the leading historian of civil rights legislation, was "both radical in design and extraordinarily effective in enfranchising the southern blacks."[25] It overrode all manner of discriminatory registration tricks in the southern states and permitting direct federal registration wherever the voting rolls remained unnaturally low. Johnson followed up this legislative triumph with an executive order, Number 11246, instituting the doctrine of affirmative action in hiring or admissions in any firm or institution benefiting from federal aid or contracts. With this measure, it seemed that the fundamental political demands of the black civil rights movement had been achieved.

In any event, the Voting Rights Act of 1965 was the last significant piece of civil rights legislation, except for the housing act of 1968. Thermidorean Reaction, signaled by Republican gains in the 1966 congressional elections and recovery of power by the Republican–southern Democratic coalition, began to blunt the cutting edge of the Great Society on all fronts. Further black gains at the governmental level had to depend on the judiciary.

Extremism, Violence, and Black Power

Exhibiting the typical revolutionary pattern of moderate protest followed by violent outburst, the black civil rights movement moved rapidly into its extremist phase between the summer of 1965 and the summer of 1966. There ensued a struggle not just between resisters and reformers but also between reformers and radicals, while potential sympathy for the movement within the larger society and in the federal government was divided and often hamstrung by this new confrontation. The black civil rights movement and the Fourth Revolution as a whole still bear the marks of the extremism that erupted in the mid-1960s and continue to carry its liabilities.

Black extremism, like the movement in general, can be traced back to direct ideological incitement on the part of a number of radical black writers, as well as to changing circumstances in modern American society. James Baldwin had enormous influence in his anticipation of a violent crisis in the American polity. There were foreign influences, notably the equation of racism and imperialism by the Franco-Caribbean writer Franz Fanon in such works as *The Wretched of the Earth*.[26] Some of the inspiration went back decades, to Marcus Garvey and the notion of black nationalism. More recent was Islam, exemplified by Elijah Muhammed and his sometime protégé and eventual victim Malcolm X, preaching the racial tolerance of Moslems and the incompatibility of black society with the American mainstream.[27]

The extremist cause was consciously or reflexively amplified by new conditions of life for millions of American blacks as they migrated from the rural South to northern ghettos. Here new forms of discrimination and deprivation were encountered, not legal but de facto, accompanied from the second generation on by all the familiar social pathologies of the inner city and an even starker sense of alienation from society at large. There was new and more volatile leadership as well, reflecting the sociological findings about the "status discrepancy" that encourages radicalism among people who have progressed economically and educationally but suffer contempt or discrimination socially, as blacks did almost universally.[28] All this was powder that needed but a short ideological fuse to set it off.

As early as the Birmingham crisis and the march on Washington in 1963, there were signs of an undercurrent of radical impatience with the moderate black leadership exemplified by King. Observed Robert Kennedy, "There's obviously a revolution within a revolution in the Negro leadership. ... These younger people [believe] ... that the way to deal with the problem is to start arming the young Negroes and sending them into the streets."[29] Bayard Rustin described this new thinking as the "no-win policy," giving up on the nation's willingness to consider massive reforms. "They conclude that the only viable strategy is shock; above all, the hypocrisy of white liberals must be exposed."[30] The summer of 1964 saw riots in New York and other northeastern cities; typically, the larger the black population, the more likely a riot, and northern cities were more susceptible because the blacks were more thoroughly packed into racial ghettos than in the South.[31] Then, five days after President Johnson signed the Voting Rights Act of 1965, two weeks before he was to launch his affirmative action program, came Watts—two days of intense rioting, looting, and arson in the black ghetto of south-central Los Angeles, touched off by the speeding arrest of a young black and heavy-handed police conduct. It took nearly fifteen thousand National Guardsmen to restore order, and thirty-four blacks were killed.

Watts was another critical turning point, when the revolutionary anger of young urban blacks became uncontainable. President Johnson at first refused to believe that such an outburst could be the answer to his reform efforts: "How is it possible, after all we've accomplished? How could it be? Is the world topsy-turvy?"[32] But this is the irony of revolution. Watts, unfortunately, was to be the prototype of similar explosions of black rage, focused on the police and spearheaded by the young, unmarried, and unskilled—but not usually unemployed—in every large American city over the next four years.[33] It was a decisive moment, when the moderate phase of the black revolution reached its limits, and the radical phase of uncompromising defiance commenced, marked by what the urban historian Robert Fogelson termed "the erosion of restraint" and a "sharp rise in Black expectations."[34] But more often than not, though the behavior was extreme, the objectives really were not; the commission chaired by Illinois governor Otto Kerner found, "Despite extremist rhetoric, there was no attempt to subvert the social order of the United States. Instead, most of those who attacked white authority and property seemed to be demanding fuller participation in the social order and the material benefits enjoyed by the vast majority of American citizens."[35] The riots thus manifested the deep irony of the revolutionary process, as the pursuit of attainable goals surged over into gestures of futile assault on the whole social system.

Following Watts, there were some key leadership changes in the major black organizations. CORE's moderate founder James Farmer (later on an assistant secretary of Health, Education, and Welfare under Nixon) was forced out late in 1965 by the militant lawyer Floyd McKissick, who announced a new mission to free blacks from "economic bondage."[36] Stokely Carmichael, a brilliant native of Trinidad who had invented the slogan "Black Power" and the Black Panther symbol in a local political experiment in Alabama (the "Lowndes County Freedom Party"), seized control of SNCC in May 1966 in a virtual coup d'état. He ousted chairman John Lewis, who was radical enough to worry King, and even ejected the radical but nonviolent executive secretary James Forman, while installing an all-black staff. Commented historian Thomas Brooks, "SNCC became a handful of fanatics."[37]

A few months later, Bobby Seale and Huey Newton, two young blacks of Oakland, California, took their cues from Carmichael and Malcolm X and organized the "Black Panther Party for Self-Defense" to promote armed resistance in the ghettos. As their ideologist they brought in Eldridge Cleaver, noted for his prison memoir *Soul on Ice*,[38] and the nearest of the black leaders to the classical Left. These men exemplified professor Inge Bell's warning, "The nonviolent philosophy was destined to fail as an ideology that could give meaning to the efforts and sacrifices demanded by a prolonged and often bloody struggle."[39]

The split in black ranks between moderates and extremists opened up for all to see when James Meredith, having graduated from the University of Mississippi four years after his government-ordered matriculation, was wounded by a shotgun blast in June 1966 as he set out on a demonstrative voter-registration march from Memphis to Jackson, Mississippi. Carmichael and McKissick turned the affair into a Black Power crusade, shouting, "White blood will flow"; their manifesto denounced American society in general and the Johnson administration in particular.[40] Traditional black organizations like the NAACP and the Urban League disavowed the radicals and distanced themselves from King because of his perceived tolerance of them, just when King was breaking with the newly radicalized SNCC. This left the great black leader virtually isolated. A year later, he was bereft even of the support of the White House, after he ventured to criticize the war in Vietnam.

In the summer of 1966, black rage exploded all around the country. King was inadvertently the catalyst of this extremist surge, as he took his equal rights campaign to the toughest northern bastion of segregation and "slumism," Chicago, in an effort to restart the flagging momentum of his leadership. Unfortunately, he excited the ghetto more than he appeased it, and a bad riot broke out that left three black youths dead. More rioting, mainly involving black teenagers and alienated young men, quickly followed in Cleveland and other large cities, typically touched off by trivial clashes or misunderstandings with the police but fueled by deep antagonism between the black communities and the municipal authorities. The riots were not altogether mindless but implicitly a rational response to felt grievances.[41] Yet, as the Kerner Commission later found, they were "not caused by, nor were they the consequence of, any organized plan or conspiracy."[42]

Trying to keep up with events, King allowed himself to be sharply radicalized, as he plunged into antiwar politics in 1967 and shifted his racial agenda to the economic arena to mobilize the black poor. But events ran still further ahead of him. The summer of 1967 saw terrible race riots in the North, worst of all in Newark and Detroit. In each case the National Guard was called in to restore order, but, untrained in riot control, they turned disorder into carnage—a contrast with the relatively bloodless restoration of order in France and elsewhere in 1968.[43]

Detroit and the Kerner Commission

Detroit was a paradox. Under the leadership of Mayor Jerome Cavanagh, blacks in the city had been enjoying considerable economic opportunity and political benevolence—bearing out the thesis that radicalism erupts where progress points the way.[44] Harry McPherson grasped this truth intuitively, as he recounted a White House staff debate on the riots: "[James] Gaither: 'But why have law and order broken down now, when we've begun to move?' McPherson: 'Because we've begun to move. It's always been this way.'"[45]

The July 1967 riot in Detroit was spontaneous; it was not led by any prominent black figures. Like most other cases of black urban violence, it was sparked by a casual incident, when police raided an illegal after-hours bar in a black entertainment district early Sunday morning, July 23. Rumors of beatings and a few thrown bricks triggered an orgy of violence, looting, and arson, according to the mob dynamics that Michael Barone described as "the widely shared expectation that others would join in, and in numbers sufficient to render all the rioters immune to any arrest or hindrance."[46]

Michigan governor George Romney ordered in the National Guard—98.5 percent white—to suppress the riots. But by the second day the rioting was so bad that the forces of order had to withdraw from whole city blocks. Romney, at the time an aspirant to the Republican presidential nomination, reluctantly turned to Washington for federal troops, but President Johnson temporized for still another day until he figured how he could put the blame on Romney for inability to control the situation. Order was finally restored by Thursday, July 27, after seven thousand people had been arrested and forty-three killed (mostly blacks shot by nervous National Guardsmen), along with thirteen hundred buildings destroyed.

The Detroit riot—if one event may be singled out—was perhaps the crucial turning point in the black revolution. Allen Matusow called it "the worst American riot in a century," a manifestation of "sheerest nihilism,"[47] and the civil rights scholar Stewart Burns saw it as "the most catastrophic urban rebellion in U.S. history."[48] Detroit was the moment when the semi-revolution of the civil rights movement, already boiling over into extremist violence, clearly threatened a disruptive impact on the larger society.

Taken together, the 1967 riots deeply shocked the whole nation, evoking a reaction not so much antiblack as one of panic about disorder. As the Kerner Commission was to report, "There is a willingness among the white population of these northern cities to see government play a strong hand in helping bring about improvement in the condition of the cities."[49] Abhorring the possible violence that Detroit and similar riots were exemplifying, the mainstream of white thinking became convinced that justice had to be done, economically as well as legally, to parry the danger of an underclass permanently in a state of revolt. This was an unspoken premise in all the subsequent history of integration, affirmative action, and the social safety net, at least until overt counterrevolution regained its aggressiveness in the 1990s.[50]

The very day that the violence in Detroit was brought to a halt, President Johnson proclaimed the establishment of a National Advisory Commission on Civil Disorders to investigate the crisis. That was the Kerner Commission, under the chairmanship of the Democratic governor of Illinois, with New York's Republican mayor John Lindsay as vice chair. The president's aim, as his aide Joseph Califano recalled, was "to help whites understand the plight of black ghetto dwellers and help assure blacks that he was working to alleviate their plight."[51]

The Kerner Commission set to work with alacrity, after receiving new assurances from J. Edgar Hoover that the black riots were not the product of a Communist master plan. Its report, delivered ahead of schedule in February 1968, was candid if in retrospect obvious about ghetto misery as the setting for riot, and it concluded with the famous warning, "Our nation is moving toward two societies, one black, one white, separate and unequal."[52] Of course, the nation had always been so divided, and if anything was making progress to bridge the gap—a point perhaps lost on someone who does not understand Tocqueville on the revolutionary implications of reform. But the Kerner report did usefully underscore social conditions as a cause of rioting: "Segregation and poverty have created in the racial ghetto a destructive environment totally unknown to most white Americans."[53]

Unfortunately, the Kerner report landed on the desk of a president deeply enmeshed in the Vietnam quagmire and already retreating from the Great Society's fiscal liberalism. Johnson had just broken with Martin Luther King Jr. over the latter's endorsement of the antiwar movement. Commission member and NAACP president Roy Wilkins recalled, "LBJ seemed to take the conclusions as a personal rebuke and affront. He did not accept and act on it. As a matter of fact, he refused to receive us when the work was done."[54] Left and Right dismissed the report as platitudinous or anodyne, while Robert Kennedy jumped on LBJ: "This means that he's not going to do anything about the war and he's not going to do anything about the cities either."[55] Hubert Humphrey almost alone hailed the commission's call for massive action, until Johnson jerked his chain; the vice president was compelled to plead that he had been misquoted.[56] Shelving the Kerner Commission's work, Johnson waited until June to appoint a brand-new commission on "Violence in America" under Milton Eisenhower, the ex president's brother, to focus on the assassinations of King and Kennedy that had occurred in the meantime. The work of this new body, lamenting that Americans had become "a rather bloody-minded people," did not come out until President Nixon had taken office.[57]

As the tumultuous events of 1967 and 1968 showed, the natural but disconcerting eruption of extremism drove a deep wedge between the black semirevolution and its liberal sources of support in the broader society. Developments in the next few months, both in leadership politics and mass movements, opened this cleavage to the point of a national crisis, as black extremism expended itself in a paroxysm of rage. Black leaders continued to be radicalized or else displaced by more radical personages. Impatient with mere equal rights and nonviolence, the movement turned ideologically to Black Power, in one interpretation or another. A new wave of urban riots demonstrated the force and seriousness of revolutionary disaffection among the black masses. Finally, and inevitably, patience and idealism in the white mainstream began to yield to vexation, fear, or the reflexes of racism, covert or overt.

Martin Luther King Jr. and Black Radicalism

In his last year King was visibly moving beyond the dogged moderation that had marked his earlier civil rights efforts. "The storm is rising against the privileged minority of the earth," he warned."[58] Harboring doubts about the Vietnam War ever since Johnson's escalation of American involvement in 1965, King openly endorsed the antiwar movement in the spring of 1967, thereby incurring the president's outrage.[59] "Johnson was unhinged by disloyalty and betrayal," opined Stuart Burns, while King concluded that Vietnam had "broken and eviscerated" the war on poverty.[60] As he turned to the economic plight of the urban black masses, King expressed ideas of a distinctly socialist nature. He even proclaimed himself a "Marxist," as he called for "restructuring the whole of American society" and asserted, "The Black Revolution … is exposing evils that are rooted deeply in the whole structure of our society.… We are engaged in the class struggle."[61] These were the sentiments prompting the "Poor People's Campaign" that took him fatefully to Memphis in April 1968. King thus placed himself at that distinctive point in the revolutionary spectrum, no longer moderate, not altogether extremist, that might be described as "advanced moderate" or perhaps "liberal radical"—radical in goals but still moderate in methods, like the French Girondists or the Russian Mensheviks.

King was pressed to move in the radical direction by the changing leadership and attitudes of other components of the black civil rights movement that were surging ahead of him and threatening to strip all initiative away from him. These people were the true extremists, rallying under the slogan of Black Power. To be sure, Black Power was not a simple idea; as the historian John McCartney explained in his analysis of the movement, it had three distinct readings.[62] The least extreme was the perspective of the people whom McCartney termed "Black Power pluralists," exemplified by New York congresswoman Shirley Chisholm (a disciple of Marcus Garvey's cultural identity politics). They sought to be one distinct force within the pluralistic American whole. Second, and truly extremist, were the "countercommunalists," such as Huey Newton and Eldridge Cleaver, who anticipated a total revolution in society at large, with the blacks in the vanguard. Finally, and most commonly identified with Black Power, were the "Black Power separatists," often inspired by Islam in the tradition of Elijah Mohammed and Malcolm X, who aimed at some form of territorial and administrative self-rule. Thus, black ideology moved full circle, away from the integrationist inclusiveness of the early civil rights movement to a defiant repudiation of white society—just when white society was opening its doors to equal black participation.

King's grip on the black civil rights movement and on the public mind was tragically restored by his shocking assassination on April 4, 1968. Nothing succeeds like martyrdom, in this case a searing stab at the conscience of white America that did as much to raise the cause of equal rights beyond public dispute as the whole civil rights struggle had up to then. At the same time, in the outpouring of outraged national sympathy, the lately radicalized version of King was expunged from public consciousness, so thoroughly that within a few short years his birthday could be proclaimed as a national holiday on a par with the two greatest presidential birthdays combined.

In the immediate term, King's newfound radicalism was transcended by the renewed wave of urban riots that his death set off. Washington, where Stokely Carmichael helped incite the gathering crowds, was the worst, with three days of mob looting and arson on the model of Detroit the previous year, before the army could impose order. Chicago, Baltimore, and Kansas City followed in quick succession, all trenchantly validating the Kerner Commission's conclusions about the black ghettos. There were limits, however. Few cities had more than one big riot in the course of the black revolution, and none in two successive years. Each metropolitan center experienced its own cycle of revolutionary commotion, not necessarily linked in timing to the overall progress of the movement. By the summer of 1968, the course of spontaneous popular extremism had by and large expended itself; Cleveland saw the last serious riot, in July. In Chicago in August, contrary to the expectations of the radical protesters concentrated there for the Democratic convention, the blacks failed to rise.

Thermidor in the Black Revolution

Just as the escalating phases of the black revolutionary struggle were the most sharply defined of all the components of the Fourth Revolution, so also was the abrupt downturn in black extremist efforts after the climactic events of the spring and summer of 1968. In part, this was the effect of outright repression (more on the local level than federal until the Nixon administration took office), which was virtually invited by the exponents of Black Power as they taunted the forces of law and order. The curbs that the extremists consequently encountered illustrate the limits on any semi-revolution among a minority component within a larger society: moderate protest could win white sympathy, whereas violence or the threat of it caused doors to slam. There were also positive reasons for the waning of extremism, including rising incomes and widening opportunity for political participation, though these improvements did not come fast enough to explain the drop-off in violence.[63] The revolution was becoming emotionally exhausted.

Faced with these constraints, black extremism quickly tore itself apart. Infighting among the diverse black factions in the first half of 1968—often heightened by FBI provocations and disinformation—crippled key organizations such as SNCC, while it alienated white sympathizers at the same time. The Panther leaders were jailed, Seale briefly for an armed incursion into the California State Assembly, and Newton on a charge of murder in the course of a shootout with police (which occasioned large "Free Huey Newton" rallies in California). Cleaver took over the Panther leadership as "minister of information" and launched a bizarre scheme to merge with

SNCC by making Stokely Carmichael his "honorary prime minister" and H. Rap Brown his "minister of justice." Brown, Carmichael's successor as SNCC chief, had achieved notoriety with his exclamation during the 1967 riots, "Violence is as American as cherry pie."[64] However, Carmichael railed against any alliance with the "white ideologies" of the Left that Cleaver espoused, and Brown was jailed on a weapons charge. SNCC moderates seized the chance to oust Brown and Carmichael, but only at the cost of emasculating the organization. "What remained," according to the historian of SNCC, "was a withering institution waiting to be picked clean by the urban black militants seeking to expand their influence, by police agents and informers seeking to undermine black militancy, and by staff members more concerned with institutional control than with the painstaking work of building mass struggles out of black discontent."[65]

Undaunted by this turmoil, the Panthers shook off a challenge by the even more violent "U.S. Organization" of Ron Karenga (later noted for inventing the Kwanzaa holiday celebration). They merged with the white radical Peace and Freedom Party in California, and nominated Cleaver for president. But the tide was going out; Cleaver polled only two hundred thousand votes in the November election, while Panther candidates for legislative offices in black districts in California were swamped by black moderates. Meanwhile, other diehard black nationalists held a "National Black Government" conference in Detroit to plan a "Republic of New Africa," while what was left of CORE opted for "autonomous" black and white societies in America. But sustained mass support for these ideological ventures, as distinct from riotous outbursts, proved to be lacking.

Most of the black extremist leaders gave up in despair. Carmichael went off to Africa; Brown, after a jail term, did likewise, then returned as a Moslem cleric, only to go back to jail in 2002 for killing a deputy sheriff. Cleaver jumped bail and fled via Cuba to Algeria, eventually returning to the United States as a born-again Christian. Seale, though repeatedly put on trial, escaped conviction and abandoned radical politics; by the 1970s, he was working for the Nixon administration. Newton spent the rest of his life in and out of jail until his death in 1989 in a drug fight.

In Washington the conservative recovery in Congress in the 1966 midterm elections, coupled with reactions against the riots and black extremism, changed the mood on racial troubles from remedies to repression. President Johnson's bill to promote equal access to housing passed in April 1968 only with the "Rap Brown amendment," making it a federal crime to cross a state line with intent to provoke a riot. The "Poor People's March" undertaken by King's followers in May 1968, followed by their rainy encampment in Washington—"Resurrection City"—was a dismal failure in its effort to impress white opinion. While equality before the law was no longer overtly questioned, Congress was by now more interested in order than in equity, as illustrated by the tough crime control act of June 1968. A more direct reaction showed itself in George Wallace's 1968 third-party presidential campaign, which polled 13 percent of the nationwide vote.

Yet civil rights as such could no longer be openly called into question. The key to mainstream thinking, as Michael Barone put it, was "a deeply disturbing cultural phenomenon: disorder, prompting a response not primarily racist per se but one of anxiety over the disruption of ordinary life."[66] The premise that still prevailed for the next decade and a half was to make amends and forestall the causes of violence. As Senator Dirksen put it, "I do not want to worsen the restive condition in the U.S."[67] This was the context for the ongoing pace of affirmative action, both legal and voluntary, and for the explosive growth in welfare programs that proceeded even under Republican administrations.

Nixon's win over Humphrey in November 1968 was the sharpest single stroke of Thermidorean Reaction against the Fourth Revolution in the United States. It was as clear a turning point as the fall of Robespierre in the original French revolutionary month of Thermidor. For the black revolution, however, the Republican victory was neither the beginning of the downturn nor the end of any revolutionary advances. For all his reliance on southern, antiblack, and law-and-order sentiment, Nixon did not try to roll back any of the Johnson-era civil rights legislation. Great Society programs of special import to blacks—welfare, economic opportunity, and so on—continued to be funded, while attempts were made to marry civil rights and economic conservatism in the promotion of "black capitalism." In the fall of 1969, Labor Secretary George Shultz launched the so-called Philadelphia Plan to impose integration quotas on the building trades unions, thereby initiating the affirmative action philosophy that was to mark federal policy for the next three decades. On the other hand, the Nixon administration stepped up repression of black extremists. It targeted what was left of the Panthers—"the greatest threat to the internal security of the country," in the eyes of J. Edgar Hoover[68]—and by the time of Nixon's reelection in 1972 the radicals had essentially been stamped out.[69] Subsequent black gains came mainly from the judiciary, in affirmative action regarding employment and education (notably the *Bakke* decision of 1973 on compensatory racial preferences in university admissions), and in efforts to overcome de facto residential segregation (housing rules, busing of school children, etc.). But the extraordinary thing is that despite the momentary exhaustion of the movement and the self-discrediting of black militancy, the revolutionary gains of the civil rights era held firm.

Outcomes of the Black Revolution

The black civil rights movement was a semirevolution, a revolution in one segment of society, within the broad envelope of the Fourth Revolution in America. It was a true revolution in its dynamic process, as it moved from moderate protest to radical defiance. Equally, it was revolutionary in its impact on both governmental policies and the public psyche.

By and large, the lasting accomplishments of the black revolution were prefigured in the agenda of the moderate phase of the movement. First and foremost, the structure of legal segregation and exclusion from the democratic process in the southern states was smashed. The society of racial discrimination and subordination that had been taken for granted, North as well as South, ever since the abolition of slavery became a thing of the past. "Racism as an ideology," wrote Robert Fogelson as early as 1971, "is losing its impact not only because it runs counter to the American creed … but also because it has lost its credibility." And the flip side: "The Blacks refuse to see themselves through white perceptions or judge themselves by white standards."[70] The tradition of black subservience evaporated as completely as the old "society of deference" had in the American Revolution. In sum, the principles of equality and integration became as self-evident as their opposites had been before, though subsequent decades would see new complications in applying these norms. Writing of white attitudes about blacks, one public opinion expert observed, "In no area do ideals and practice come into greater conflict."[71]

In conjunction with the initiatives of the Great Society, the black civil rights movement started its long march toward nondiscrimination in American economic life. With the aid of affirmative action programs and compensatory reverse discrimination, blacks began to win remarkable access to the hierarchy of social, educational, and business success. This progress in the redistribution of inequality, as it were, obviously helped—for the time being—to let the steam out of black revolutionary endeavors. But it was not the kind of progress that would alter the shape of the socioeconomic pyramid in America or improve the circumstances of the black underclass. Ghetto conditions, whether in terms of unemployment, social disintegration, or criminal violence, only grew worse in the decades that followed the revolution.

Did black extremism contribute anything to the gains of the revolution? Obviously it fell short of its announced goals of overturning the whole society or establishing black self-rule. Perhaps it helped open the way for less utopian achievements by delegitimizing white complacency and threatening white society with endemic violence if reforms were not forthcoming. At the same time, black extremism pointed the way for other elements of the Fourth Revolution, especially radical students and the antiwar movement. The blacks made violent resistance and riotous protest the fashion of the moment for others to emulate.

A full accounting of the effects of the black revolution, including its carryover to other racial minorities, must await assessment in later chapters of the events of the decades that followed. In its time, however, the changes that the black revolution brought about were extraordinarily fast and far-reaching. By no means did it solve all the problems of black–white relations or the economic condition of the multitude. Yet for all its shortcomings, the black movement was as successful an example of revolutionary change as one could find anywhere in history, and all without overthrowing the government.

CHAPTER 6

The Revolution of Youth

Unlike the black movement, which was quite specific in its clientele, its aims, and the trajectory of its efforts and evolution, the revolutionary youth component of the Fourth Revolution in the United States was complex, diffuse, confused in its aims, and indistinct as a revolutionary process. This force was nevertheless intense and far-reaching, and as a movement in the broader society its impact was even more profound than the racial revolution, especially in the cultural realm as distinct from the political and legal. "The youthful turbulence of the late sixties was too powerful, too extreme, to be dismissed as a modern version of 'sowing wild oats,'" was the judgment of a CBS News inquiry in 1969. "It was characterized by anger and despair rather than exuberance, by violence rather than prankishness. It represented a depth of feeling unmatched by the superficiality of past generational rebelliousness."[1]

The axis of the youth revolt, as everyone has recognized, was the movement to protest the Vietnam War. Around this galvanizing issue moved a variety of revolutionary challenges to the old social and cultural order—student protests, the counterculture, so-called, and everything falling under the rubric of the "New Left." Accompanying all these forms of protest, and shared with youth revolts abroad, was a novel sort of class struggle, an antielitist and antiexpert outburst directed against the managerial meritocracy of modern society. Some of these elements of the youth revolution, including its terrorist fringes, flared out quickly and passed into history. Other components persisted, in tandem with the racial revolution and the gender revolution, to change the whole face of private as well as public life in America.

Origins of the Youth Revolt

In the background of the youth revolution in America, some of the same circumstances may be cited that underlay the black revolution. Both broke out in a mature urban and suburban society, where educated but restless youth turned with moral fervor against the system that begat them. The British historian Ronald Fraser observed "the uneven development of postwar Western societies in which the actual and ideological authority structures were out of synchronization with the rising expectations seemingly afforded by rapid economic growth."[2]

There was a remarkable parallel between young middle-class rebels in America and the young "nihilists" of the Russian revolutionary movement of the last third of the nineteenth century, except that the Russians for the most part came from a much narrower privileged social pyramid in a much more backward and oppressive country. The youth agitation of the 1960s was also fed by purely demographic factors—the surge in the numbers of young citizens born in the immediate post–World War II baby boom, and a leap in the proportion of youth attending institutions of higher education. In the hyperbole of one student of the phenomenon, "The baby boom ... gave ... the most rebellious years of youth a weight and impact they never had before. ... The baby boom became a huge cannon on the deck of society, rolling and smashing whatever stood in its path."[3] These considerations, to be sure, fall short of explaining why the youth revolt burst forth when it did and in the way it did. The social philosopher Lewis Feuer argued that generational restiveness is endemic in modern society and that it erupts in open revolt whenever the generation in power is delegitimized by events.[4] In America such delegitimization stemmed above all from the Vietnam War, the accelerator and conditioner of all manner of protest, though the moral issue of racial discrimination and the civil rights movement had already begun to radicalize of the more sensitive youth. Underlying these reactions was the crass commercialism of the post–World War II era, alienating many young and thinking elements from society's prevailing values. Early on, C. Wright Mills sensed that something new was afoot: "The Age of Complacency is ending. ... We are beginning to move again."[5]

As to intellectual preparation, the youth revolution was well cultivated, as much or even more than the black movement, and by some of the same writers. During the 1950s and early 1960s, a time of social stasis when many commentators were decrying the lack of political involvement among students, the writers and social critics of the "Beat Generation" articulated an angry sense of personal alienation and cultural defiance of bourgeois norms. Among the avant-garde, religion yielded to the human potential and self-realization school of psychology as the main reference point for addressing life's troubles. Philosophers like Norman O. Brown and Herbert Marcuse tore at the certainties and complacencies of the bourgeois scheme of things; democratic freedom Marcuse dismissed as "repressive tolerance."[6] Sociologists such as Mills and William Whyte took issue with the hierarchy and dehumanization that in their eyes went with the new meritocracy.[7] Educational critics like Paul Goodman attacked traditional authoritarian didacticism.[8] Historians like William A. Williams challenged the legitimacy of American foreign policy, labeling it a form of neoimperialism,[9] while films such as Stanley Kubrik's *Dr. Strangelove* and *Seven Days in May* (both of 1964) evoked the absurdity of the Cold War. All this helped set the stage for the antiwar movement. In sum, by the early 1960s a surge of antiestablishment criticism in all modes of thought had built up, waiting for the requisite social force to translate it into action.

The Moderate Phase

The most obvious trigger of the youth revolution in America was Kennedy's election as president in November 1960, unleashing as it did a surge of idealistic, if diffuse, enthusiasm for change. Kennedy's brief time in office, with the new opportunities for service that it offered at home and abroad, above all the Peace Corps, represented the short-lived moderate phase of the youth movement.

Contributing to the new ferment, though soon with a more radical edge, was Fidel Castro's revolution in Cuba in 1959. Castro appeared to show that there could be an alternative to the corruption and exploitation that repelled idealists when they looked around at America's international sphere of influence. His associate, the Argentine physician turned guerrilla–philosopher Ernesto "Che" Guevara, became an international hero of romantic anti-imperialism, especially as he was echoed in the work of the French political theorist Regis Debray.[10] Cuba's excitement for American radicals fit the pattern of the international impact of intersecting revolutions, and it was an unspoken factor in the hard line that the American government took toward Castro, from the severance of trade and travel contact to ventures in outright counterrevolution.

Disillusion with the Kennedy administration began very early, from the moment of the abortive CIA invasion of Cuba at the Bay of Pigs in April 1961. Signs of radicalization among the student generation appeared soon thereafter, notably in the formation of the Students for a Democratic

Society (SDS) and the organization's adoption of the "Port Huron Statement" of 1962. Simultaneously, the incipient youth movement began to interact with the accelerating black movement, which drew idealistic young whites into civil rights activism beginning with the Freedom Rides of 1961 and climaxing in the Freedom Summer of 1964. For any number of subsequently prominent white rebels, the civil rights struggle was a training ground and a radicalizing experience. SDS president Carl Oglesby said of his organization, "At our best, I think, we are SNCC translated to the North."[11]

The New Left

The political expression of the new generational radicalism was the New Left, so called to distinguish it from the Old Left of Communism and Socialism. Though many of the early leaders of the New Left had family roots in the Old Left, their emotional drive had become quite different: an antiauthoritarian quest for purification and moral honesty rather than attachment to a systematic program of political and economic reconstruction. Wrote Maurice Isserman, "New Leftists repudiated dogmas they never shared and then turned with the passionate intensity of the newly converted to building a movement based on what was left to them: personal morality, ethics, and sincerity."[12] New Left rebels have been diagnosed psychologically as self-righteously arrogant, narcissistic, and power hungry,[13] but these are characteristics that would apply to any revolutionary activists, not to mention plenty of politicians of other stripes. In any case, the psychological hard core was small in numbers, though its influence was multiplied by the sympathetic resonance of its preachments among much broader segments of the youthful generation.

The New Left was not a party but a movement. Apart from a few self-destructive fringe groups, the New Left abhorred formal structures, ultimately to its own undoing. It had no central leadership, organization, or ideology, though plenty of publicity-hungry individuals came forth to trumpet its spirit. The watchword was "participatory democracy" (a slogan coined by University of Michigan philosopher–activist Arnold Kaufman, who subsequently initiated the antiwar "teach-in" movement).[14] "Don't trust anyone over thirty," was the tactical principle. As the critic Diana Trilling defined it, the New Left was "existential," in "its improvisational character, its disdain of ideology and of any fixed political program, and its appeal as a means of personal definition."[15]

Starting in the early 1960s, the New Left gospel was spread by a host of new, irreverent, often "infantile" radical publications—up to five hundred of them—most successful of which was the Berkeley *Ramparts,* professing communal principles and patronizing the Black Panthers.[16] Many of the underground rags were shadowed and harassed by the FBI, which in its counterrevolutionary naïveté "took the fantasy seriously—to the surprise and, one senses, the pride of the guerrilla journalists."[17]

In reaction to the sectarianism of the Old Left, as Isserman observed, there was "a distaste for ideological hairsplitting and rigidly centralized organizations,"[18] qualities, it may be noted, that distinguished the American New Left from its counterparts in Europe. The New Left wanted to go deeper; Paul Potter, briefly president of SDS in the midsixties, said of the enemy, "I refused to call it capitalism because capitalism was for me and my generation an inadequate description of the evils of America—a hollow, dead word tied to the 'thirties.'"[19]

The SDS was the nearest thing to an organizational embodiment of the New Left. It was an offshoot of the former Socialist Party youth arm, revived by a student radical at the University of Michigan by the name of Robert Alan Haber. Committed to deep social change, Haber proposed that students rather than the proletariat could be the force for such an overturn. He drew in the student journalist and civil rights activist Tom Hayden to help him organize SDS chapters on other campuses and to draft a program for the movement. This document was adopted by the SDS as the "Port Huron Statement" in June 1962 at the same time that the group elected Hayden its new president.

In the main a pessimistic sermon about apathy, Port Huron zeroed in on the universities as the political base for the future: "A new left must consist of younger people who matured in the postwar world. ... The university is an obvious beginning point." Bemoaning America's tarnished image and popular apathy about the public problems of the age, the statement endorsed a broad program of civil rights, peace, and social reform, to be spearheaded by students but reaching out to "an awakening community of allies" throughout society.[20]

Hayden soon shifted his interest from students to an "interracial movement of the poor," and with some SDS friends he plunged into a project to build participatory democracy in the inner cities, mainly in Newark and Cleveland. Funded by the United Auto Workers, this "Economic Research and Action Project" (ERAP) met with indifferent success, though Hayden kept it going in Newark until black nationalism and the 1967 riots preempted the attention of the ghetto. Paul Potter wrote in disillusionment later on, "People in SDS had seen a chance to go directly for the jugular vein of the system. We leapt and missed."[21] But the political scientist James Miller thinks the ERAP experience was inspirational: "Long after the experiments had wound down, it was possible to point to an example like Cleveland and say, 'Look, *this* is participatory democracy in practice; *this* is the radical alternative.'"[22]

The New Left broke openly with the social basis of the Old Left in the labor movement. Ironically, the Old begat the New organizationally—the Socialists inspired SDS through their League for Industrial Democracy, and the United Auto Workers gave it logistical support. Nevertheless, the antiwar and countercultural associations of the younger radicals quickly drove them apart from their early patrons.[23] The New Left perceived the union bureaucracy as part of the "corporate liberal" establishment and shifted its sympathies to the most marginalized elements in society: "Sharecroppers were always more likely than steelworkers to engage their sympathies," as Isserman observed.[24] The socialist Irving Howe wrote retrospectively, "Each day the New Left kept moving away from its earlier spirit of fraternity toward a hard-voiced dogmatism, from the ethic of non-violence toward a romantic-nihilist fascination with a 'politics of the deed.'"[25]

Internationally, the New Left encompassed student radicals all over the industrialized world, including Japan. It was antinational and anti-imperialist, and it was implicitly subversive of modern Western civilization, an attitude that was to revive a generation later. The international New Left was deeply opposed to the waging of the Cold War, though it was simultaneously anti-Soviet: Moscow-style Communism was just another variant of the bureaucratic, alienating enemy. Moscow returned the sentiment, calling the New Left "werewolves."[26] By contrast, the Chinese, in the frenzied era of their "Great Leap Forward" and "Cultural Revolution," happily claimed kinship with the New Left, whose most extreme elements in turn identified themselves proudly as Maoists. In the later sixties, the Maoist-inspired Progressive Labor Party (PLP), a splinter from the old-line Communist Party–USA, figured in the explosive breakup of the SDS.

The American New Left stood in awe of black militancy. This was a concrete instance of how the black movement opened the way for other components of the Fourth Revolution. Rooted in the participation of white radicals in the civil rights movement in the early 1960s, New Left deference to the black revolution continued and even intensified with the emergence of violent black nationalism in the mid- and later sixties. Whenever the two currents intersected, white radicals shrank to the back of the bus. A benchmark instance was the "National Conference for a New Politics," convened in Chicago in September 1967 with representatives of hundreds of diverse radical organizations. A small black caucus demanded equal voting power with the majority and the condemnation of Zionism as racism, and, in the words of the historian Charles DeBenedetti, "A majority of whites ... deferred in the belief that Black America really constituted the cutting edge in the domestic drive toward radical change."[27]

The Antimanagerial Revolution

The unfolding of the Fourth Revolution twisted old theories of class structure and class struggle into a sociological pretzel. Race and culture proved more decisive than social standing and economic interests in the formation of political alignments and in the choice of ideological allegiances. The working class and the poor divided on racial lines, and the white majority perceived the black minority to be a fiscal burden and an economic threat on top of more traditional forms of prejudice. The middle class split on generational and educational lines, as its younger, more schooled but less seasoned cohorts embraced a series of righteous reform causes and in the most extreme manifestations of these goals completely rejected the moral validity of existing society. Two new forms of social struggle tore at the body politic: the economic resentment of wage earners against welfare beneficiaries, and the psychological struggle of the alienated against the established.

What was established in American society was and is a highly complex matter, but in any case it has been changing, well beyond the compass of old ideologies either of individualism or of collectivism. One clear trend, recognized by sociologists for at least a century, notably by Max Weber, is the movement toward bureaucratic organization and the domination of all social functions by trained and salaried experts, in a word, toward the managerial society.[28] As James Burnham argued in *The Managerial Revolution*,[29] managerialism is the logical outcome of every form of the Third Revolution, whatever their professed aims and ideologies—Communist, Fascist, or Welfare State. Nor is conservative attachment to Second Revolution classical liberalism an alternative: its contemporary outcome is simply the unregulated corporate version of managerialism.

Managerialism and the rule of the experts were targeted by the youth component of the Fourth Revolution, by the Americans as one of their enemies and by the Europeans as their paramount foe. Sloan Wilson's novel *The Man in the Gray Flannel Suit* highlighted the whole way of life that the youth revolution rejected.[30] C. Wright Mills's *White Collar* and *The Power Elite* became the rebels' basic ideological texts.

Surprisingly, very little youthful anger was vented in the workplace in the sixties against the business hierarchy, not to speak of any significant trade union agitation (except for France, where the unions, in coming out for the students and against their own Communist leadership, nearly brought on a nationwide insurrection). Rebels beyond student age either contented themselves with participating part-time in the counterculture and political protests or dropped out of the gainfully employed world altogether. Only the hierarchy closest to students was targeted, the universities, including their educational aims and standards as well as their institutional authority. Here the enemy was education conceived as training for career competence, to the neglect of psychic self-expression; the radicals would have pulled the plug on everything that made up the so-called postindustrial society.

The Counterculture

The most distinctive face of the youth revolt in America was less political than psychological, in the form of the so-called counterculture. The counterculture was not so much an act of rebellion as it was a revolutionary state of mind. Perhaps it could better be described as a secessionist mood, a movement of withdrawal from conventional life, in the spirit of drug guru Timothy Leary's slogan "Tune in, turn on, drop out." But the counterculture was powerful enough to infuse almost all other elements of the Fourth Revolution in America with its defiance of accepted social norms, an "angry no" and a "transcendent yes," in the phrases of the critic David Pichaske.[31] Jean-François Revel called it "*the* revolution of our time, ... a total affirmation of liberty for all in place of archaic prohibitions."[32]

Although the counterculture overlapped with the New Left, the two movements were not coterminous. The true New Left was political and puritanical, whereas the pure counterculture was a personalistic quest for deviant experience. Only in certain manifestly insane expressions like the "Yippies" ("Youth International Party"), led by Jerry Rubin and Abbie Hoffman, did the extremes fully coincide. However, the countercultural aura of "acid, amnesty, and abortion" was enough to discredit the New Left, in the eyes not only of the American mainstream but of the surviving elements of the Old Left as well. The public's association of George Mcgovern's candidacy with the counterculture was one of the liabilities that dragged his presidential campaign of 1972 down to such a disastrous defeat. Yet, ironically, the counterculture left a far deeper and more lasting imprint on American life than the abstruse political radicalism of the New Left.

The main lines of the counterculture were familiar to all contemporaries, and they have persisted to the present day. There was a revolution in entertainment, not only in its content of violent music and corresponding lyrics but also in the commanding place that entertainment seized in the public psyche at the same time that it embraced themes of political and social protest.[33] Drug use became a focal ritual for counterculture participants, most spectacularly the newly discovered hallucinogen LSD (outlawed only in the mid-1960s).[34] Among its users, according to the researchers Martin Lee and Bruce Shlain, "There was a sense that LSD had changed all the rules, that the scales had been lifted from their eyes and they'd never be the same. The drug was supposed to provide a shortcut to a higher reality."[35] Odds and ends of unbuttoned oriental religion, notably the Zen Buddhism popularized by the philosopher Alan Watts, figured prominently alongside the drug culture.[36] The counterculture incorporated the gender revolution, more particularly its strictly sexual aspect, being more interested in free love than in the overall status of women or homosexuals (more of this in the next chapter).

Extreme devotees of the counterculture—the "beatniks" (from the "Beat Generation," presumably beaten down by bourgeois convention) and then the "hippies" (from "hipsters," those who are hip, in the know, that is, about the alleged falsity of bourgeois values and lifestyles)— became a class apart in their centers such as Haight-Ashbury in San Francisco and Greenwich Village in New York. Hundreds of thousands if not millions of other youth and young adults became part-time, often weekend participants in the counterculture or at least served as the clientele for the entertainment and stimulants that it provided.[37] Like black nationalists, the extremists of the counterculture gave up on reforming the national society and sought salvation in a separate mode of existence. This was the import of the counterculture as embraced by Broadway in productions of *Hair* (1967) and *Oh Calcutta* (1969).

The acme of the countercultural urge of withdrawal and renunciation was the commune movement. Youthful devotees of drugs, rock music, and the sexual revolution, sought collective solace, sometimes in enclaves like the "Diggers" in Haight-Ashbury, who collected free goods and distributed them free, sometimes in out-of-the-way rural locales like New Mexico and Vermont. For all their appearances of rule-smashing self-indulgence, these countercultural extremists were antimaterialistic and even puritanical in their own way. This was a mentality typical of radical revolutionaries throughout history. However, the communards had largely given up on the broader society. "For them," wrote a student of the movement, "the lesson of the sixties is the futility of political reform, and the only viable radical alternative is to begin to create a new society in microcosm."[38] They had something in common with medieval monasticism, happily rejecting what one of their theorists, Theodore Roszak, called "the myth of objective consciousness."[39] Religious inspiration, Buddhist or Hindu, was just another indication of the far-fetched questing going on in the minds of these cultural rebels. Of all the elements of the Fourth Revolution in the United States, the commune movement in its mood of radical withdrawal came nearest to the model of ultrarevolutionary utopianism.

As the least political aspect of the youth revolution, the counterculture had no definite trajectory or turning point. If there was any discernable climax, it may have been the so-called Summer of Love in San Francisco in 1967. A drug-fed orgy of musical and sexual self-expression, the Summer of Love was a more or less deliberate promotion by offbeat entertainers and communards to multiply their following. The project was all too successful, swamping Haight-Ashbury with thousands of excitement seekers and turning the district onto the road of degradation, so abruptly that in the fall of that year, the Haight-Ashbury old-timers conducted a mock funeral to mark "the death of hippie." From that time on, in its main urban centers, the hippie life began to decay in an atmosphere of drug excess, police incursions, common crime, and internal violence, at its worst when the Hell's Angels motorcycle gang intruded into Haight-Ashbury. The much celebrated Woodstock rock music festival of August 1969—actually held in Bethel, New York, in the Catskills—proved to be only the Indian Summer of the counterculture as idealistic protest, just a step toward being taken over as the new fashion in commercialized mass entertainment.

Despite the seaminess into which it had sunk by the end of the sixties, the counterculture proved to be the most enduring and the most broadly influential element of the youth revolution. Precisely because it was nonpolitical in its essence, it was immune to the normal cyclical decline of revolutionary movements. Commented sociologist James Drane, "The older militant youth who believed in the principle of 'sacrifice now for the new society which is coming' have almost disappeared. Much more enduring are the non-political hippies of the sixties who believe that the only way to bring in the new society is to start enjoying it right now."[40]

By the time the decade of the 1970s had passed, the counterculture in all its major aspects—the music, the drugs, the sex, the long hair and unkempt demeanor—was no longer counter but rather the dominant youth culture in most parts of the country. It not only extended throughout the middle-class student population but had percolated down among working-class youth as well and readily fused with the predilections of the antisocial underclass. In the course of the 1970s, the pollster Daniel Yankelovich found a broad popular shift from the "ethic of self-denial" to an "ethic of self-fulfillment."[41] The disreputable lifestyle signaled by beads and beards that brought opprobrium upon the deviant individual in the early sixties had by the end of the seventies become simply a badge of generational membership.

Not only was the counterculture a measure of generational change in life styles; in some of its more extreme manifestations—its rejection of productive commercialism, its embrace of antiscientific and "New Age" thinking—the counterculture prefigured, more than any other aspect of the Fourth Revolution, the advent of a totally new kind of revolutionary protest, a Fifth Revolution, as it were, that we consider in the final chapter. Thus, the excesses of the counterculture in the Fourth Revolution corresponded to those utopian excrescences in each previous revolution pointing the way for future protests against the social order.

The Antiwar Movement

The counterculture was less a movement than a condition. Another condition powerfully feeding the youth revolution in America was the war in Vietnam, intensifying in tandem with the social upheaval at home. Vietnam was the occasion for the most vigorous politically focused effort of the sixties, bringing together all of the elements of the generational upheaval. It was the first military involvement in U.S. history since the Civil War to arouse widespread public opposition, to the point of civil disobedience. Charles DeBenedetti, himself a pacifist, went even further, to call the antiwar movement "the largest domestic opposition to a warring government in the history of modern industrial society."[42]

Vietnam churned up powerful antinationalist and anti-imperialist sentiments in America that gave the Fourth Revolution a tenuous link with the Old Left, as well as marking it sharply off for a time from the patriotic majority of Americans. Antiwar feeling prompted a self-righteous rejection of the whole American tradition of a triumphant and uncontroverted national history, as Frances Fitzgerald showed in *America Revised*: "The society that was once uniform is now a patchwork of rich and poor, old and young, men and women, blacks, whites, Hispanics, and Indians. ... What is remarkable about the American-history texts of the late sixties and early seventies compared with those of the past is the sense of uncertainty they show."[43] The antiwar movement opened the way for history "from the bottom up," featuring the grievances of the downtrodden and marginalized that came to distinguish American historical thinking in the 1980s and 1990s.

Vietnam was not a prominent element in the early phases of the Fourth Revolution, although the origins of American intervention went back as far as the Truman administration and its containment doctrine directed against any advance by Communism. American connivance in the assassination of South Vietnamese president Ngo Din Diem in 1963 took more of the bloom off the idealism of the Kennedy administration, following its troubles in Cuba, but Vietnam did not become a widely divisive issue until President Johnson's escalation of American involvement during the first half of 1965. Opposition to the war then burgeoned on American college campuses, first of all in the teach-in movement of informed protest. The teach-ins served as a mobilizing and consciousness-raising experience for the broader student revolt that was to follow. SDS, announcing against the war, experienced a surge in membership and chapter organization.

In April 1965, overriding objections to its acceptance of Communists and other Old Left radicals, SDS took the lead in the first of many marches on Washington, and twenty thousand protesters gathered on the Mall, mostly peaceful but a few confrontational. Here was the characteristic cleavage between moderate and radical revolutionaries: "Every subsequent antiwar demonstration," wrote two observers of the scene, "would see the same split between those who wanted peaceful, legal demonstrations (thus, they hoped, broadening the movement's appeal) and those who urged more radical tactics (thus 'upping the ante')."[44] The extremists shocked the public by idealizing the North Vietnamese, "as honest a revolution as you can find anywhere in history," in the eyes of SDS president Carl Oglesby, who went on to link the antiwar movement with a "humanist reformation in American society."[45] Late in 1965 SDS leaders Tom Hayden and Staughton Lynd together with the Communist historian Herbert Apteker made the first of a series of well-publicized pilgrimages to Hanoi by New Left leaders to express solidarity with the enemy.

A practical focus of antiwar agitation was military conscription, still in effect though college students were deferred until graduation. In November 1965 a group of New York pacifists first burned their draft cards as a gesture of antiwar protest, and the practice quickly spread. Ironically, it was the middle-class student population, temporarily immune from military service, who protested the war while noncollege youth, disproportionately poor and black, went as called and took their chances. By 1967 antiwar and antidraft resistance had become intense, with the formation of the National Mobilization Committee to End the War in Vietnam, sparked by the long-time radical pacifist A.J. Muste and led after his death by David Dellinger.[46] The "Mobe" promoted a series of marches on Washington and elsewhere. This was when Martin Luther King Jr. threw his lot in with the antiwar movement: in a sensational speech in New York in April 1967, he protested sending black and white Americans to "kill and die together for a nation that has been unable to seat them together in the same schools" and called the war "a symptom of a far deeper malady within the American spirit."[47]

Radical pacifists of the *Catholic Worker* group, particularly the Jesuit brothers Daniel and Philip Berrigan, played a distinctive role. They were joined in their violent antiwar protests by the eminent pediatrician and child care author Benjamin Spock. Put on trial for physical raids on draft board offices, where they poured blood on the records or burned them with napalm, the Berrigans went underground and eluded capture for more than two years. Spock and Yale chaplain William Sloane Coffin were convicted of counseling draft evasion. Heavyweight boxing champion Mohammed Ali was stripped of his title for refusing induction. In the face of all this defiance, the authorities fed the fire by terminating the deferment of graduate students and threatening to draft all protesters.

Antiwar and antidraft protests escalated, along with the war, in the fall of 1967. Pacifists and New Leftists organized a "Stop the Draft Week" in October. Demonstrations and draft-card burnings provoked sporadic violence by police and counterdemonstrators, particularly in the San Francisco Bay area. Most climactic was the march on Washington called by the "Mobe" for October 21, with the participation of the countercultural radicals Rubin and Hoffman but against the misgivings of moderate pacifists like SANE (the National Committee for a Sane Nuclear Policy). "We are now in the business of wholesale and widespread resistance and dislocation of American society," said Rubin.[48] Fifty to a hundred thousand protesters, the largest antiwar manifestation ever, gathered at the Lincoln Memorial to hear Dellinger call for "confrontation" and "active resistance,"[49] before they crossed the Potomac to demonstrate at the Pentagon. The event, as Norman Mailer described it in his self-conscious participant memoir *The Armies of the Night*, was a chaotic and undirected flux of people and emotions, a Tolstoyan battle scene reduced to farcical theatrics.[50] Some of the leaders and a group of SDS radicals with Viet Cong flags tried to invade the building, inviting and achieving arrest and beatings. After this near insurrection and a night of attempting to propagandize the troops on guard despite more arrests, the demonstrators withdrew, their objective of national notoriety accomplished. President Johnson was so incensed that he demanded of the CIA—probably illegally—that it find proof that foreign powers had instigated the protests; Director Richard Helms had to confront him with the truth that there was "no trace" of such involvement.[51]

Into the heated atmosphere of antiwar protest and anti-Johnson politics the Vietnamese Communists' "Tet Offensive" burst out in late January, early February 1968. Tet abruptly made victory seem either senseless or unattainable, in the minds of the government as well as the general public. No sooner had the disillusioned defense secretary Robert McNamara been replaced by long-time presidential confidant Clark Clifford in March 1968 than the latter called for a freeze on any further buildup of American forces in Vietnam. From this point on, the question for the American government was not how to win but how to get out.

With President Johnson's withdrawal from the presidential race at the end of March, it would seem that the antiwar movement had sufficiently prevailed. Actually it gained even more steam from its victory over President Johnson and pumped its energy into disruptive politics as well as campus rebellions. Robert Kennedy's assassination and Johnson's dominance of the Democratic nominating process on behalf of Vice President Humphrey left the antiwar radicals no avenue of effective protest except the streets. This was the mood, capitalized on by the Mobilization to End the War and by the exotic Yippies, that climaxed in the spectacular demonstrations and clashes with police around the Democratic convention in Chicago in August 1968. "Some of them may have hoped actually to stop the war in this way," wrote Nancy Zaroulis and Gerald Sullivan about the resistance movement; "others, more attuned to the reality of American life in the mid-sixties, understood that armed revolution, domestic violence, the mobile tactics of guerrilla street warfare were simply unacceptable to the vast majority of the American people—far more unacceptable than the war in Vietnam. And more, that a great deal of police action would be tolerated by the American public in order to preserve their domestic tranquility, war or no war."[52] The Thermidor of the youth revolution was already on the horizon, though the war had four more years to go.

It is remarkable that in the face of all the political disasters the Democrats experienced during 1968, their ticket did as well as it did in the November presidential election. Bereft of the traditional southern Democratic support that now swung to Richard Nixon or to George Wallace, Humphrey nevertheless turned the corner in his celebrated Salt Lake City speech in September, in effect declaring his independence from Johnson's war policy. A week before election day, the president relinquished his own obsessions by halting the bombing of North Vietnam. A dramatic reversal of Humphrey's prospects was in the offing, had it not been for a back-channel conspiracy between the Republicans and the government of South Vietnam to stall the initiation of peace negotiations.[53]

Nixon's narrow victory, helped by his claim of a "secret plan" for peace (a plan that never existed), meant in actuality four more years of war, while frustrated antiwar outrage turned step-by-step into cynical alienation. Anti-Establishment militancy on the nation's campuses continued to draw fuel from the war for another year and a half, culminating in widespread demonstrations to protest Nixon's "incursion" into Cambodia in April 1970. Meanwhile the administration pursued its prosecutions of the "Chicago Seven" and other alleged perpetrators of antiwar violence, despite an appeals court's reversal of the conviction of Dr. Spock in July 1969. But Cambodia proved to be a final turning point in the aggressiveness of both the protesters and the government. American society is acutely sensitive about serious violence—a reservation that is one of the differences between a semirevolution and a real one. When student protest over Cambodia culminated at Kent State University in Ohio in the killing of four students by frightened National Guardsmen, both the authorities and the rebels recoiled in horror, a sentiment only underscored a couple of months later when a protest bomb explosion at the University of Wisconsin killed an innocent researcher.[54] This was the effective end of the antiwar component of the Fourth Revolution, despite the occasional provocations still being wrought by such radical New Left fringe elements as the Weatherman.

The Student Revolt

Of the various elements of the revolution of youth in the United States, it was the currents of revolt on college campuses that most closely paralleled the upheaval of 1968 abroad. However, the American student movement was less ideological in the traditional sense, the New Left supplying only vague slogans and an antiauthoritarian mood in lieu of a program. The Vietnam War and the race issue loomed larger than socialist and anarchist theories in the thinking of American college youth; the war and civil rights were the challenges that precipitated "a crisis in loss of generational confidence" and "de-authorized" the older generation, as Lewis Feuer described it, thereby legitimizing in young minds the most extreme tactics of violent or obscene protest.[55]

Bringing to a focus all of the elements of the youth revolution—New Left ideology (such as it was), antibureaucratic a lienation, countercultural defiance, and antiwar self-righteousness—the student revolt exploded and burned out in a relatively short span of time. Heralded by the Free Speech Movement at the University of California in 1964, student rebelliousness burst forth into violent confrontation in the prototypical campus uprising at Columbia University in the spring of 1968. Running a little later in its phasing than the black civil rights movement or the antiwar movement per se, the student revolution reached its peak in 1969 in ugly campus takeovers at Harvard and Cornell, among other places. By 1970 the worst student violence was over, though antiwar protest still had its tragic consequences.

Like so many decisive episodes in the history of this and all other revolutions, the Berkeley Free Speech Movement originated in a relatively trivial dispute, over the permissibility and location of student political rallies.[56] Its escalation into violent demonstrations and battles with the police was in great measure the accomplishment of another veteran of the civil rights effort, the graduate student Mario Savio. "The operation of the machine becomes so odious," Savio exhorted his followers as they prepared for a sit-in, "that ... you've got to put your bodies upon the gears and upon the wheels, upon the levers, upon all the apparatus and you've got to make it stop."[57] Berkeley simmered down after Chancellor Clark Kerr was sacrificed, but its reverberations rocked student circles all over the country and prepared thousands of minds for confrontation with the forces of authority. Observed the German historian Klaus Mehnert, "The true enemy was 'society'—whatever that might mean for the individual—the university simply being that segment of society with which the students happened to be confronted."[58]

Student protest was closely intertwined with the antiwar movement and expanded rapidly along with the latter after Johnson's escalation in Vietnam in 1965. Thanks in part to the media spotlight that its antiwar activities attracted, the SDS grew so rapidly that the national organization could not keep in touch with its local chapters, and the locals could not restrain the radicalization of the national.[59] Under the influence of the New Left, and with the example of the Cuban revolution and guerrilla movements around the world, wrote Ronald Fraser, a "culture of insubordination" took hold, flaunting obscenities and antinationalism.[60] J.-F. Revel called the phenomenon "a New American Revolution, ... the only revolution that invokes radical, moral, and practical opposition to the spirit of nationalism."[61]

Rather than support universities as the base for broad societal change, as the Port Huron Statement proposed, rebellious students now turned against the very institutions that nurtured them, as the target of opportunity for generational rage. The observer David Westby commented, "Increasingly, universities and colleges came to be seen no longer as scholarly sanctuaries but rather as closely tied to and implicated in, perhaps even essential to, the maintenance of the interests of American capitalism at home and around the world."[62] Strictly campus issues—parietal rules, curricular requirements, the discipline of *in loco parentis*— played a part, especially in the initial phases of the student movement. But as the campus uproar escalated in the later sixties, hapless college administrators found themselves only the stand-ins for the villainous rulers and war makers of the larger society.

Individual extremist leaders played a more conspicuous part in the campus revolt than in the more diffuse aspects of the youth revolution. In this they paralleled the efforts of the extremists in the black movement, where most of the student radicals won their spurs. SDS most commonly served as the fuse for campus disorders, though its metastatic growth in the climate of antiwar protest vitiated the organization as a coherent national source of direction.

All the gathering emotion of rebel youth, relatively restrained in action until 1968, broke through to mass revolutionary action at Columbia University. Responding to the urgings of the national SDS and its condemnation of universities as part of the social status quo, the "action faction" of the Columbia SDS group, led by the dogmatically visionary undergraduate

Mark Rudd, laid plans to use the war and race issues to revolutionize the campus and set up a "provisional government of the university run by students, employees, and Harlem citizens."[63] Rudd relished the opportunity for generational as well as political defiance, and asserted in an open letter to President Grayson Kirk, "We will destroy your world, your corporation, your university."[64] Said Columbia provost David Truman, "They regard the universities as a soft spot in a society that they're trying to bring down."[65]

Allied with radicalized black students, SDS seized on the issue of Columbia's construction of a new gymnasium on parkland adjacent to Harlem, provoked university disciplinary responses, and in late April led an occupation of a number of university buildings including the president's office. The university administration believed that they could not appease the rebels without, in Provost Truman's words, "betraying not only Columbia but the whole of higher education."[66] Faculty mediation failed, and the university administration summoned massive intervention by the New York police, ushering in a cycle of demonstrations and repressions until the end of the spring semester. At Columbia as everywhere else, student revolution took a vacation for the summer, but a victory of sorts was racked up by the radicals as at Berkeley when President Kirk resigned.

Columbia reverberated on campuses all over the country in the late spring and again in the fall of 1968. Paraphrasing Che Guevara on Vietnam, Tom Hayden called for "two, three, many Columbias."[67] The most spectacular sequel was a student strike at San Francisco State College in November, led by Black Panthers, but the rebels were faced down by President S.I. Hayakawa (who later won a U.S. Senate seat on the strength of his antirevolutionary backbone). In all this, the university was not the primary enemy but only the most easily assaulted symbol of the political authority and perceived social oppressiveness that had incurred the generalized ire of radical students. Fed by antiwar sentiment and disappointment over the failure of peace initiatives in 1968, the campus revolt continued strong for another year after Nixon's election put a damper on most components of the Fourth Revolution. The year 1969 was even more tumultuous than the year before, with massive uprisings stimulated by SDS activists on the Columbia model.

An especially sharp edge was acquired by the student revolt where it intersected with the black civil rights movement. This connection took two different forms, first in the association of white student radicals with the civil rights movement, and then in the campus revolts of 1968 and 1969, notably at Columbia, San Francisco State, and Cornell. Diana Trilling observed that the Columbia University administration was "effectively paralyzed" by fear that any action against black student insurgents would trigger a mob invasion from Harlem.[68] At Cornell, black students took up arms, and the university administration avoided a shootout only by surrendering abjectly.

In the face of the rebellious student upsurge, university administrators behaved like Louis XVI—rigid and provocative in the first instance, but timid in the face of violence or its threat, and over the long pull soft on students' demands. They yielded to calls for abolishing parietal rules and relaxing curricular requirements, or even anticipated them. Complaints about authoritarian teaching methods were often answered by younger, radicalized professors and teaching assistants: Who, they questioned, has the right to tell anyone else what the truth is? After 1968–69, protests within the campus context were pushing against an open door.

Meanwhile, as the student movement peaked and ebbed, the national organization of SDS went into climactic agony, much like the black radicals. The Maoist Progressive Labor Party joined SDS en masse and attempted to take over the organization. The challenge prompted leaders such as Rudd and the budding terrorist Bernadine Dohrn to take equally radical but pro–North Vietnam positions to head off the pro-China people. At the last convention that the SDS held, in Chicago in June 1969, the anti-PLP forces walked out and regrouped as the "Revolutionary Youth Movement," which promptly split in turn between its more and less violent elements. All that survived of these schismatics was the terrorist Weathermen group, led by Dohrn, taking their name from a line by the singer Bob Dylan, "You don't need a Weatherman to tell which way the wind is blowing." They went on with futile bomb-planting tactics until arrest or flight ended their activity. Another small sect of bitter-enders was the biracial "Symbionese Liberation Army" in California, who achieved notoriety by kidnapping and brainwashing the heiress Patricia Hearst and involving her in a fatal bank robbery. But on the broader scene, by the time the Kent State killings triggered massive campus protests and presented a new opportunity for revolutionary student action, there was no nationwide organization left to capitalize on it.

The Youth Revolt in Retreat

The national turn away from revolution, marked by the failure of protest within the Democratic Party and the Republican victory of November 1968, did not immediately dampen youth agitation against the Vietnam War and for social and educational change, though the leadership of the movement had fallen into self-destructive turmoil. After the spring riots of 1969, however, student radicalism rapidly subsided. The Kent State tragedy evoked national outrage and the greatest outpouring of peaceful student demonstrators in the whole history of the Fourth Revolution, but students by and large had no stomach for either killing or getting killed. It did not take much repressive action by the authorities to curb a movement that was already losing its fire.

Many observers have noted how reformism was ground down between the extremist wing of the youth movement and the forces of reaction. Paul Berman wrote, "There was bafflement that a movement so grand and touching in its motives as the student leftism of the 1960s could have degenerated and disappeared so quickly." But he drew the obvious parallel with the revolutionary process and its disappointments throughout modern history.[69] Walter Laqueur commented at the time, "The American youth movement, with its immense idealistic potential, has gone badly, perhaps irrevocably, off the rails," for which he blamed the ideological "gurus" of the intelligentsia.[70] But this pied-piper conception of the youth revolt misses the character of the movement as essentially unled and unorganized, except in a very local and ad hoc way. Both the causes and the effects of the youth revolt ran much deeper.

The Nixon administration was as uncompromising in its attitude toward youthful radicalism as it was circumspect in dealing with racial minorities, perhaps sensing intuitively where the actual weaknesses as well as resiliencies were in the revolutionary front. Prosecutions of disrupters and terrorists proceeded apace, though not always with the political benefit intended; an exceptional failure for the forces of law and order was the trial of the Chicago Seven for fomenting the 1968 riots (Hayden, Rennie Davis, Yippies Rubin and Hoffman, and the militant pacifist David Dellinger, plus two manifestly innocent hangers-on, the black radical Bobby Seale having been consigned to a separate process because of his courtroom disruptiveness). Ultimate acquittal of the Chicago Seven (two immediately, the others on appeal) wrote finis to judicial attempts at nullifying the Fourth Revolution, except for sundry Weathermen and draft dodgers who were lightly handled when they eventually turned up, or even amnestied.

Drug misuse proved to be a stronger antirevolutionary rallying point in the popular mind, a subject of continued and often enhanced prosecution often as it progressed from the hippie subculture to the population at large. The drug issue endured as a sharp dividing line between the heirs of the youth revolution and the nation's anxious postrevolutionary leadership.

The last gasp of the youth revolution, politically, was George McGovern's presidential campaign of 1972, a veritable children's crusade. Capitalizing on the splits and disillusionments of 1968, youthful reformers prevailed in the presidential primaries, snubbed old-guard Democratic organizations like the Daley machine in Chicago, and went down to the most disastrous defeat in the Democratic Party's history. This was the beginning of the much-analyzed breakup of the "New Deal coalition," though the event had been prefigured in George Wallace's overtly counter-revolutionary candidacies and in the passage of Southern voters over to the Republicans in presidential contests ever since the Goldwater campaign in 1964. Thanks to the cultural controversies raised by the youth revolution and the antiwar movement, as well as reaction against the Great Society and the oncoming gender revolution, much of the Northern base of the Democratic Party—Catholics, ethnic groups, trade unionists—now began shifting to the Republican camp, as their economic interests in an epoch of prosperity were overshadowed by lifestyle issues. Represented as the party of "acid, abortion, and amnesty," the Democrats were left in shock and disarray by the McGovern debacle, and only Nixon's stumble in the Watergate scandal saved the two-party balance. But the days of concerted leadership for social change by one avowedly liberal party were gone for a generation to come.

The Legacy of the Youth Revolution

Like all revolutions, including the other components of the Fourth Revolution in the United States, the youth revolution was mixed and contradictory in its impact on the American nation. As a coherent movement it was ephemeral, a flash in the pan, yet it profoundly transformed the national psyche. In attitudes toward tradition, authority, and discipline, in the assertion of personal freedom and the toleration of it in others, American culture after the sixties was almost the antithesis of American culture before the sixties. The extent of these changes was only highlighted by the frantic desperation of the most traditionalist elements of society—the "Religious Right"—who earlier could assume that their censorious values would go without question in public discourse, except by insignificant, marginal elements.

In the broad, cultural sense, it was the amorphous counterculture, of all the elements of the youth revolution, that had the most pervasive and lasting effect on postrevolutionary American society. In a 1971 poll Daniel Yankelovich observed an "unlinking of cultural and political values," as cultural radicalism spread among the student-age generation while political radicalism lapsed.[71] The New Left and overtly political student action collapsed quickly: "ideological diffusion" led to "organizational demise," in the words of David Westby.[72] The war issue that had pumped up the radicals' strength was finally disposed of by the Paris accords of January 1973 and the ensuing withdrawal of American forces from Vietnam. North

Vietnam's forcible takeover of the South two years later, passing as it did with scarcely a murmur from an American public deadened by internal political controversy, showed how far the assertion of national power had dropped below the horizon of concern for revolutionaries and counterrevolutionaries alike.

There were nonetheless a number of specific institutional changes attributable to the impact of the youth revolution. As with the blacks, both national and state governments were quick to offer concessions in the realm of legal equality, in this instance the Twenty-sixth Amendment to the U.S. Constitution lowering the voting age to eighteen, and state laws generally reducing the age of majority and of legal drinking also to eighteen. (This did not prevent all but Louisiana from later restoring the twenty-one-year drinking age, a seeming denial of equal protection of the laws coerced by the federal threat to withhold highway money.)

Of all areas of public policy, education at every level manifested the greatest response to the new value system, with the shift to a doctrine of equal outcomes and the standard of student "self-esteem" (by no means always observed in practice). In 1971 the Supreme Court intervened to restrict the practice of IQ testing both in schools and in employment, as an infringement of equal rights.[73] Education remained the realm where the American ideology of equality, filled out and extended by the Fourth Revolution, could stand as a beacon light of principle in the moral darkness of a competitive class society.

CHAPTER 7

The Gender Revolution

If the struggle for racial equality was the most sharply fought component of the Fourth Revolution in America, and the youth revolt was the most immediate in its effect on everyday life, the gender revolution was the most profound, even epochal element of this upheaval, in its implications for millennia of tradition in cultures of interpersonal hierarchy. These distinctions among the various components of the Fourth Revolution help explain why the gender revolution was the most protracted, the most openly resisted, and to date the most incomplete aspect of the twentieth-century transformation in social relationships.

Overtly, the gender revolution was the least revolutionary of the components of the Fourth Revolution. It generated no great riots or other violent manifestations, no wild calls for overthrowing the government or seceding into separate societies. Compared with the black civil rights movement, it lacked the overarching purpose of civil rights or the compelling national leadership of a Martin Luther King Jr. Yet in a deeper sense it was the most revolutionary side of the social upheaval, in its challenge to axioms deeply embedded in human culture. It prompted a "gut reaction" over "changing a fundamental biological condition," as the radical feminist Shulamith Firestone acknowledged it.[1]

The women's movement was as much a revolt within as between the sexes, resisted by many women as well as men. "Although equality is the objective of Women's Liberation," the pollster Robert Chandler found in the early 1970s, "it is the female more often than the male who seems to resist the objective, ... who seems uneasy about liberation and fears she may forfeit more than she gains."[2] It was logical for the historian Winifred Wandersee to find, "One of the major tasks of feminists was to convince women *themselves* that they had a right to freedom."[3]

The gender revolution did not follow the typical pattern of the revolutionary process as clearly as other components of the Fourth Revolution. It was less politically focused, more sporadic as various episodes burst upon the public consciousness, less concentrated into any major crisis like the black civil rights and youth movements, but in the long run more pervasive. To be sure, it had clear roots in the social changes of an urbanized society, including female employment and the sixties revolution in birth control techniques. It drew on a powerful intellectual impetus from a series of feminist writers. It was charged up by the general climate of protest in the later sixties. But its actual unfolding revolved around a series of specific controversies with different chronologies—legal equality and the Equal Rights Amendment (ERA); abortion rights; equal employment opportunity and workplace issues, including sexual harassment; and the broad question of changes in family relationships and roles. Victories and setbacks came at different times in different areas, with a series of particular climaxes, often of a legal nature, rather than one big extremist surge. Overall, the gender revolution is still going on.

Backgrounds of the Women's Movement

Of the various components of the Fourth Revolution, the gender revolution had the longest continuous roots in the past. Like the black revolution, it took as its point of departure the eighteenth-century principles of political equality—the Second Revolution—as they had been enunciated by the American founding fathers. It then unfolded with a logic that hardly anyone at the time of the American Revolution had thought out to its fullest implications. (Tom Paine was an exception, and a little later John Stuart Mill.)[4] It took almost a century and a half for these principles to bear fruit in women's equality before the law and at the ballot box, and another half century, nearly, before the de facto conditions of gender inequality in American society were widely addressed.

These changes did not come about of themselves. They were the result of unending effort and agitation by a growing corps of feminist leaders, riding the tide of social transformation wrought by the industrial revolution and the multifaceted experience of modernization. The struggles undertaken by these activists have now been made familiar by the literature of women's history, itself a product of the Fourth Revolution and the expanded awareness it has brought to this facet of the American past.

The pre–Civil War generation in America saw the earliest attempts at political action by women, closely associated with the abolitionist movement. Both protofeminism and abolitionism were parallel efforts to extend the legal equality of the Second Revolution to the politically forgotten elements of society. In 1848 the aspiring lawyer Elizabeth Cady Stanton and the abolitionist Lucretia Mott organized a Women's Rights Convention, the now-famous Seneca Falls conclave, the first-ever gathering of its sort. Enumerating their grievances in the format of the Declaration of Independence, these pioneering feminists boldly blamed Man for oppressing Woman: "He has endeavored in every way that he could to destroy her confidence in her own powers, to lessen her self-respect, and to make her willing to lead a dependent and abject life."[5] Subsequent efforts in the cause of women's rights are part of the mainstream of American history—Susan B. Anthony and the crusade for women's suffrage, Margaret Sanger's lifelong struggle to achieve the legalization and dissemination of birth control. The term *feminism* entered the national vocabulary early in the twentieth century, during the Progressive era, when the women's movement became an integral part of the effort to clean up government and society alike, "a fight of the home against the saloon, ... a long strong battle between the selfish citizens and the patriotic ones."[6]

But it was mainly external events in the form of World War I that opened the way to women's participation in most walks of life in America, above all in the political process with the adoption of the Nineteenth Amendment to the Constitution. Indeed, President Woodrow Wilson backed the goal of woman suffrage because it was "vital to the winning of the war."[7] Though major wars in American history have usually been followed by political reaction, the post–World War I era, with the suffrage victory and the flapper age, was a notable exception for women. Nevertheless, the efforts in the 1920s by the National Women's Party (a militant offshoot of the suffrage movement) to promote an ERA came to naught.[8]

The political rights achieved by women as a result of the suffrage movement still belonged to the Second Revolution, rounding out the meaning of equality before the law. As the historian Nancy Cott defined it, "Feminism can be seen as a demand to extend to women the individualistic premise of the political theory of liberalism."[9] The Progressive movement, that is, the incipient Third Revolution in America, impinged on women's issues mainly as a concern to protect the weak, as it tried to do in the case of child labor, treatment of the mentally ill, prison reform, and so on.

Efforts at protection of women in the workplace collided with the feminist determination to achieve equal treatment of women in all respects, a division that persists to the present. University of Chicago philosopher Jean Bethke Elshtain wrote, "Contemporary feminism confronts a whole range of vexed issues: Should feminists pursue a liberal-equalitarian strategy aimed at gender-blind reform—the course advocated by the National Organization for Women—or should they endorse protectionist measures that acknowledge that only a minority of American women meet the ideal of a full-time, salaried employee?"[10] Furthermore, did the feminist cause entail the restructuring of society as a whole, as European socialists maintained, or should it be pursued as an independent goal within the existing social framework? And what of the United States is the connection between feminism and racial justice?

World War II did not boost the feminist cause in the United States as the nation's belligerency of 1917–18 did; its impact was rather the opposite, despite the new employment opportunities and the shake-up of traditional habits of life that the war brought along. The historian William Chafe observed that wartime integration of women into the world of work was socially acceptable only to the extent that it was not seen as "a feminist threat" or "part of an overt revolt against traditional values." Nevertheless, "The fact remained that women's economic status had shifted more rapidly than at any other time in the twentieth century."[11]

In the opinion of many feminists who experienced it firsthand, the postwar era from the late 1940s to the early 1960s was a time of reaction in the status of women, just as it was in American political life in general. Betty Friedan in her feminist manifesto referred to "the recent sexual counterrevolution" based on the "mystique of feminine fulfillment" that "succeeded in burying millions of American women alive." Altogether, she asserted, "The American spirit fell into a strange sleep. ... The whole nation stopped growing up."[12] According to the radical theorist Kate Millett, the sexual revolution that developed from the early nineteenth century to the 1930s (in our terms, the gender revolution more broadly understood) was followed by an international counterrevolution led by everyone from the Nazis to the Stalinists to the Freudians.[13] The British-born economist Sylvia Hewlett was shocked by the postwar retrogression in the status of American women while Europe forged ahead: "The most educated and most independent women in the world became ultradomestic creatures."[14] The sociologist Leila Rupp and the historian Verta Taylor described a state of "deliberate antifeminism" in postwar America, when the media felt no compunctions in disparaging and ridiculing the women's rights effort. Feminism survived, consequently, only as an "elite-sustained movement."[15]

All this oppressive conservatism broke apart as abruptly as the onset of the youth revolution and black militancy, and at just about the same time, as signaled by John Kennedy's election. As Friedan wrote in an oft-quoted line, "In 1960, the problem that has no name burst like a boil through the image of the happy American housewife."[16] Alessandra Stanley of the *New York*

Times, looking back at her college days, discerned a "fault line" in the year 1962, "between the convention-bound 1950s and the era of feminism."[17] Then, in 1963, appeared Friedan's own book, the work of a forty-two-year-old self-described housewife and disillusioned Old Left journalist. By all accounts, *The Feminine Mystique* revolutionized American women's thinking about their status in society as much as Tom Paine's "Common Sense" did for the consciousness of the American Revolution two centuries before. It truly launched the "Second Women's Movement."[18]

The Awakening of the Sixties

Like the youth rebellion in all its ramifications, the gender revolution was energized by the two most compelling circumstances of the sixties, the civil rights movement and the Vietnam War. Shulamith Firestone saw history repeating itself: "Just as the issue of slavery spurred on the radical feminists of the nineteenth century, so the issue of racism stimulated the new feminism; the analogy with racism and sexism had to be made eventually."[19] It was in pursuit of the black and antiwar causes that most women activists of the epoch got their start as crusaders for change, not least because of the put-downs they often suffered at the hands of male black and New Left leaders.[20] Only toward the end of the decade did this momentum shift toward explicitly feminist goals, including equal economic opportunity and legalized abortion.

Thus, the women's movement surged up in the 1960s under ironic circumstances. It was an integral element in the revolt against hierarchical relationships in society, yet it was met with a signal lack of sympathy from other elements of the Fourth Revolution. It was resisted by the black movement, disparaged by the New Left, and exploited by the counterculture, not to mention the indifference, antagonism, or ridicule it encountered among the general public. "The movement never enjoyed the kind of broad moral support and sympathy that the civil rights movement had experienced," wrote Winifred Wandersee.[21] It was more a social and cultural process than a political action, according to William Chafe, "almost without any overarching structure" despite the efforts of the National Organization for Women (NOW) and various radical sects.[22] The revolution in sexual mores, such as it was, threatened to render women's status worse, not better, by abetting what the essayist Barbara Ehrenreich called "the flight from commitment" on the part of men.[23] There was a forlorn quality to sixties feminism; as one participant wrote, "Perhaps the reason membership in the women's movement is so often a painful experience is that the more we know, the more powerless and overwhelmed we feel."[24]

As it was for the youth revolt, the short-lived Kennedy administration was a catalyst for the gender revolution, even though its position, in the eyes of the feminist legal scholar Joan Hoff, was really "benign neglect masquerading as pseudo-concern."[25] Kennedy was signally reluctant to appoint women to high office; he was the first president since Hoover to have no woman in his cabinet. But he was willing to look at the agenda of women's economic needs posed by the Women's Bureau of the Labor Department.[26]

The Estates General of the gender revolution, as it were, was the president's Commission on the Status of Women, set up by Kennedy in December 1961 at the suggestion of Esther Peterson, a former labor lobbyist who, as director of the Women's Bureau, was the highest-ranking woman in the new administration. As urged by then-vice president Johnson, Kennedy designated Eleanor Roosevelt (shortly before her death) as chair of the new body, which, under the prodding of the National Federation of Business and Professional Women's Clubs, was quickly replicated at the state level. These commissions, bringing diverse activists into touch with each other, heightened a shared awareness of women's problems and led, like so many prerevolutionary concessions of reform, to "a climate of expectations."[27] "There is no doubt," wrote the historians Judith Hole and Ellen Levine, "that the Commission created the atmosphere, fashioned many of the tools, and engendered the momentum that has enabled many of today's feminists to challenge head-on ... basic assumptions and popular images of women."[28]

Kennedy followed up his creation of the commission with an executive order removing old legal bars to women in high civil service positions. In the spring of 1963, with the commission's support, Peterson got an equal pay bill through Congress, mandating equal wages for jobs in interstate business that required "equal skill, effort, and responsibility."[29] The commission reported formally in October 1963, just before Kennedy's assassination, with a set of moderate but concrete recommendations, primarily in Peterson's field of labor policy, trying to reconcile the tradition of the female homemaker with equal participation in the world of work.[30]

Much of this agenda was soon realized, at least in the abstract, in a quite backhanded way—the inclusion of sex discrimination as one of the targets of the Civil Rights Act of 1964. This step was the handiwork of Congressman Howard Smith of Virginia and his southern allies, who aimed to sink the entire bill by burdening it with the women's issue, only to find women's leaders and their liberal male allies seizing the idea and winning recognition of a decisive new principle. However, meaningful enforcement of this provision, Title VII of the new law, was another matter.

NOW and Women's Liberation

Radicalization of the women's movement was a direct response to the disappointments it experienced at the hands of the Johnson administration, even while LBJ was trying to do so much for blacks and the poor. The women's movement was the Cinderella of the Great Society. Johnson left women out of his 1965 executive order on equal employment by federal contractors, and the director of the new Equal Employment Opportunity Commission set up to enforce the Civil Rights Act would not take sex discrimination seriously.[31] Women who worked with the national and state commissions on the status of women "experienced and then stimulated a mood of rising expectations among American women," wrote the sociologist Alice Rossi, but "their hopes were dashed" at the Labor Department's conference of the state commissions in June 1966.[32] This governmental foot-dragging in the face of women's newly aroused hopes led directly to the creation of NOW.

NOW, to pursue the French revolutionary analogy, might be thought of as the Jacobin Party of the women's revolution; or perhaps the better parallel is the Girondist Party, revolutionary but not so fanatic. From the radical perspective, NOW was only "the NAACP of the women's movement."[33] Led by Betty Friedan and Kathryn Clarenbach, a university administrator and chair of the Wisconsin commission on the status of women, NOW was formed by members of the state commissions frustrated with the ineffectiveness of federal and state gestures toward job equality.[34] The organization elected Friedan president at its first convention in October 1966 and rapidly built a stalwart corps of enrolled members, ultimately as many as one hundred fifty thousand. Its agenda was ambitious and unflinching: "to take action to bring women into full participation in the mainstream of American society *now,* exercising all the privileges and responsibilities thereof in truly equal partnership with men." NOW broke boldly with the presidential commission on the fundamental question of biologically distinct gender roles: "We reject the current assumption that a man must carry the sole burden of supporting himself, his wife and family, ... or that marriage, home and family are primarily woman's world and responsibility."[35] On NOW's twentieth anniversary, the *New York Times* described the organization as "a towering presence in the struggle for women's rights and the spearhead for a significant social revolution."[36]

NOW was quickly caught up in the dynamics of revolutionary escalation, swinging toward social radicalism and the sexual revolution as envisaged by radical feminist theory. The organization became a microcosm of the revolutionary process, much like the SDS, as it moved ideologically and tactically from the moderate toward the extreme, along the way suffering splits and defections both on the left and on the right. Unlike SDS, NOW survived the turmoil of the revolutionary climax and eventually settled into a more Thermidorean, mainstream role, with lasting influence.

From the beginning, NOW was buffeted by the growing debate between the old Progressive-style programs aiming to protect women as a category and the newer demand for equal rights as individuals embodied in the proposed ERA, the "liberal individualism" that Friedan exemplified. In this spirit, at its second national convention in November 1967, NOW adopted a "Bill of Rights for Women," stressing the ERA and reproductive rights along with equal employment and maternal protection principles.[37] Simultaneously, NOW prevailed on President Johnson to include sex in federal antidiscrimination rules, though as with title VII, enforcement could not be taken for granted.[38]

Unlike blacks, women had to fight their own battles unaided. To the end of the sixties, even in the most radical movements of male-led protest, among the black nationalists, in the SDS, and even in the counterculture, equality for women was not taken seriously, and women in the respective movements were usually relegated to foot-soldier roles.[39] "We know that 'hip culture' and 'radical life style,' " wrote Robin Morgan, a former child TV star turned ardent feminist, "have been hip and radical for the men, but filled with the same old chores, harassment, and bottling-up of inner rage for the women, as usual."[40] A student of the counterculture in Philadelphia noted the persistence of traditional attitudes of male domination, passivity of the "chicks," and monogamous jealousy in the communes.[41]

Women in the Student Non-violent Coordinating Committee (SNCC), including Tom Hayden's then wife (before whites were excluded from the organization), were victims of a "common-law caste system" that "uses and exploits women"; she only incurred obscene derision from Stokely Carmichael and others.[42] Women were howled down or, worse, ignored when they tried to bring up feminist issues at SDS meetings in 1965 and 1966.[43] By the late sixties, the most radical and activist women were convinced that they had to fight their battles independently, to tack the gender issue onto the other components of the Fourth Revolution. The breakthrough for them came in the revolutionary year 1968.

A foretaste was offered at the National Conference for a New Politics in Chicago in September 1967, the New Left conclave where the whites had caved in to black demands for a 50 percent voice. To present their agenda to the conference, a group of women at the University of Chicago formed what Hole and Levine called "the first known independent radical women's group."[44] To little avail: the male leadership at the conference buried the women's "trivial demands."[45] But within a scant two or three years, all this had changed; among the radical splinters of the disintegrating New Left, notably the Weathermen, violent young women played an equal if not preponderant role.[46]

The Spirit of '68 set off a vigorous series of protests specifically on behalf of the women's cause. In December 1967 NOW picketed offices of the Equal Employment Opportunity Commission all over the country, and in February 1968 the organization went to court to make the commission enforce the sex provision of the Civil Rights Act. A "Jeannette Rankin Brigade," led in person by the former Montana representative who had voted against U.S. entry into both world wars, responded to the rising antiwar fever by carrying a feminist–pacifist protest to Congress in January 1968. At the same time, a "Women Doers" luncheon hosted by Lady Bird Johnson was scandalized by the entertainer Eartha Kitt when she tried to turn it into an anti-Vietnam protest.[47]

In-the-streets feminist activism was concentrated in New York City. One of the feminist protesters at the Conference for a New Politics, Shulamith Firestone, moved to New York and helped organize the "New York Radical Women." This new group went to Washington with the Jeannette Rankin Brigade but split off to stage a "Burial of Traditional Womanhood" at Arlington National Cemetery.[48] In June they started the first of many small radical feminist journals, *Notes from the First Year,* brandishing the new slogan of "women's liberation." An even more defiant group, calling themselves "Witches International Conspiracy from Hell" (WITCH), aped the antics of the Yippies, even to disruption of the New York Stock Exchange.[49]

During much of 1968, activist women were absorbed in the presidential campaign and the antiwar movement. Young women as well as young men rang doorbells for Robert Kennedy and Eugene McCarthy; women as well as men got their heads cracked and their faces gassed in Chicago in August. After Chicago, as the political process turned anticlimactic, radical feminists bent the street theater of the New Left to their own cause.

In September 1968 the New York radicals, led by Robin Morgan, sprang a protest demonstration at the Miss America beauty pageant in Atlantic City. Their stunts included crowning a sheep as Miss America and tossing their underwear and "other instruments of torture" into a "freedom trashcan" (from which the myth of bra burning spread through the mass media).[50] The impact of Atlantic City was electrifying: it was "a moment that changed the world's view of this rebellion—and therefore perhaps the rebellion itself—forever," wrote the chronicler Marcia Cohen.[51] "Women's Lib" polarized the nation, and radical feminism became a national fact even as it was inviting ridicule among the male population. Atlantic City proved that under modern American conditions the way to make a revolution—which means above all a revolution in people's minds—is to create spectacles that seize the attention of the sensation-seeking mass media.

Along with its sudden new national visibility, the women's movement experienced the usual splits and fissures of revolutionary times—Mensheviks, Bolsheviks, and all the other sectarians. A wide spectrum of positions from the moderate to the extreme rapidly emerged in the late sixties and early seventies, marked off by divisions over both tactics and goals. One argument had been simmering since the early sixties, over the basic aims of the movement: group protection, as in labor law, favored by the old-style reformers, versus equality of individual legal rights, expressed in the off-again, on-again agitation for the ERA. NOW was caught besides in the divergence between the political–legal approach of "women's rights" and the champions of "women's liberation," who thought the organization too "integrationist and legalistic," too much interested in women's success within the existing system rather than repudiating the social pillars of marriage and capitalism.[52] In turn, the radicals divided between the "politicos"—New Left and often Marxist adherents of an economic overturn to solve the women's question—and the "cultural feminists" rebelling against the male oppression they saw in all extant social systems, even to the point of a "lesbian/separatist solution" paralleling the separatism of the black nationalists.[53]

In this spirit, a radical faction broke with NOW as early as October 1968 to form the "Feminists," repudiating marriage and all differentiation of sex roles as well as NOW's middle-class basis.[54] Shulamith Firestone sparked a new group, the "Redstockings," devoted to "consciousness raising" against "male chauvinism": "We are an oppressed class. ... We identify the agents of our oppression as men."[55] Firestone's previous followers, now the "New York Radical Feminists," took a slightly different tack, attributing women's oppression not to the economic and social system but to male psychology and "the politics of ego."[56]

Events in the streets and agitation by the extremists rapidly pulled NOW toward social radicalism and the sexual revolution. Friedan was distressed by the rising lesbian question, which she attributed to an FBI–CIA provocation to discredit the movement. Advocates of "lesbianism and hatred of men" were "disrupters of the women's movement" who risked provoking "sexual McCarthyism."[57] She went so far as to denounce the "pseudo-radicalism" of "infantile deviants" and their "sexual shock tactics and man-hating down-with-motherhood stance."[58]

Forced to surrender the presidency of NOW in 1970 by a four-year term limit in the bylaws, Friedan undertook to perpetuate her leadership by calling a nationwide "women's strike for equality" on the fiftieth anniversary of the adoption of the Women's Suffrage Amendment. The strike was a success in New York, to the point of drawing endorsements from Mayor John Lindsay and Governor Nelson Rockefeller; even President Nixon issued a proclamation on women's "wider role." Nationally the strike effort multiplied NOW's membership, brought in younger members, and broadened its social and ideological diversity. To Marcia Cohen, the strike was the point when the nation had to start taking women's liberation seriously.[59]

Two key Friedan supporters in the strike were on their way to becoming national figures in mainstream, that is, moderate, feminism, Bella Abzug and Gloria Steinem. Abzug, a lawyer who had plunged into civil rights issues and the antiwar movement, won election to Congress in 1970 from a Manhattan district. A flamboyant gadfly under the Nixon administration, she fought for the ERA and abortion rights along with a broad agenda of liberal causes. Steinem, half a generation younger, was a conventional liberal journalist until she was radicalized by the abortion issue in the late sixties; she went on to found *Ms.* magazine and became a feminist icon.

Despite the success of the 1970 strike, leadership of the women's movement was slipping away from the tempestuous but programmatically moderate Friedan. Revolutionary turmoil continued to build up in NOW under a series of more radical though less charismatic leaders. Rapid growth in membership (to forty thousand by 1974) had the same effect as in SDS, the breakdown of communication between the national organization and the local chapters, amid wrangling over bureaucratic centralism versus participatory democracy.[60] Ideological splintering at the top also paralleled the travails of SDS. The organization yielded to lesbian demands for an equal place on its agenda and turned away from its hitherto dominant middle-class white constituency. In 1974 a minority faction calling themselves the "Majority Caucus" (shades of Bolsheviks and Mensheviks!) seized control and drove the moderate wing out of NOW's leadership, only to lose to the middle-of-the-roaders under Eleanor Smeal three years later.[61] That comeback finally signaled the Thermidorean Reaction within NOW and the women's movement, and a sharp turn toward conventional political participation.

Well before this, in 1971, Friedan had turned back to the mainstream political process, where women were making steady if unspectacular progress. Between the election of John Kennedy in 1960 and the reelection of Richard Nixon in 1972, women's presence in the U.S. House of Representatives more than doubled, from seven to fifteen. In 1971, giving a push to the trend, Friedan along with Abzug, Steinem, Kathryn Clarenbach, and Shirley Chisholm (the first black congresswoman, elected in 1968 from a Brooklyn district) formed the National Women's Political Caucus. Their principles were distinctly moderate, based on devotion to the advancement of women's concerns through the electoral process. Clarenbach became the group's first chairperson.

The impact of the National Women's Political Caucus was immediate. When the Democratic National Committee adopted the reforms in organization and rules proposed by the McGovern Commission that had been formed after the 1968 electoral loss, it included "demographic balance" in party bodies and in the delegate selection process. The result was to bring the Democratic National Convention from 13 percent women in 1968 to 40 percent in 1972, while the 1972 party platform included practically all the concrete demands on discrimination and economic equity that the women's movement had been pressing for the decade past. With less fanfare, the Republicans followed suit and adopted almost the same set of principles.

Theory in the Gender Revolution

Much more than the black movement, even more than the New Left, the women's movement generated a storm of theoretical pronunciamentos. Black writers were more literary, appealing to pathos, and the youth movement was polemical or satirical. But the gender revolution in its various currents shouted out the most impassioned philosophical justifications for its challenge to the traditional order.

The core of all revolutionary ideology is very simple: some malevolent force has been conspiring to take away our traditional liberties and privileges, and the time has come to fight back. In feminist theory, a series of sensational writers located the antifemale conspiracy in one area of life after another: cultural, then economic, then political, then biological. Their charges added up to a cumulative repudiation of the entire social order.

Betty Friedan initiated this genre of revolutionary rejectionism with her *Feminine Mystique* of 1963. As the first major theorist of the new feminism, she viewed the conspiracy against women more in cultural terms than in the political: somehow, a "mystique" had been conjured up that trapped women in their unfulfilling roles of housewife and helpmeet. The solution lay with individual women—throw off the internalized fetters of an imprisoning ideology, and be yourself. No ingenue, but a veteran of militant trade unionism, Friedan was a personal link between the Old Left and the New, the Third Revolution and the Fourth.[62] However, turning to equally militant feminism, she experienced a deep change in her philosophical emphasis, to try to rescue not just a class but indeed half the human race.

A more materialist critique of the status of women, focusing on the world of work, was Caroline Bird's *Born Female* of 1968. Likening the economic condition of American women to that of the blacks, Bird argued for the equity of equal pay and equal opportunity, backed up by equal sharing of household tasks with men. Moreover, she stressed the loss to national life when women of talent could not realize their abilities to the fullest: "We are destroying talent, ... we are wasting talent, ... we are hiding talent."[63] In retrospect, Bird's plea for equal access to the top in business seems entirely uncontroversial, which only shows how quickly the economic aspect of the feminist case was absorbed into mainstream American thinking. This was a big step toward the concentration of contemporary social criticism on the goal of equal access to an essentially hierarchical social structure, to the neglect of everyone lower down.

Going deeper into the roots of gender inequality was the 1970 work of the young sculptor and literary scholar Kate Millett, *Sexual Politics,* "probably the first feminist study to have a major impact on mainstream culture and social criticism," in the view of Winifred Wandersee.[64] An avowed lesbian, challenging Friedan's heterosexual orthodoxy,[65] Millett excoriated the patriarchal bias and exploitive sexism expressed in modern Western literature, in particular such putatively radical targets as D.H. Lawrence, Henry Miller, and Jean Genet. She did not spare Sigmund Freud either, "beyond question the strongest individual counterrevolutionary force in the ideology of sexual politics during [his] period," his sin being "to rationalize the invidious relationship between the sexes."[66] Instead, Millett called for "a truly radical social transformation—the alteration of marriage and the family as they had been known throughout history," meaning "the end of the patriarchal order through the abolition of its ideology."[67]

Earlier, in 1968, Millett had written the manifesto for the newly organized Columbia University women's liberation group. There she charged, "When one group ... the master class ... rules another, the relationship between the two is political. ... All historical civilizations are patriarchies: Their ideology is male supremacy."[68] Yet in her later and larger work new hope had arisen, that "a second wave of the sexual revolution might at last accomplish its aim of freeing half the race from its immemorial subordination."[69]

The reaction to *Sexual Politics* was one of shock across the spectrum. Irving Howe called it "arrogant ultimatism,"[70] while *Time* magazine branded Millett "the Mao Tse-tung of Women's Liberation."[71] Millett's open lesbianism was the axial issue splitting moderate and radical feminism; predictably, she was disavowed by Friedan.[72]

A very different, radically heterosexual statement was *The Female Eunuch* by the Australian-born British essayist Germaine Greer. This was a biologically based demand for women's sexual equality, to remedy the "castration of women" through liberation of the female libido. "Sex," Greer insisted, "must be rescued from the traffic between powerful and powerless."[73] Her aim, she explained when preparing this polemic, was to "have woman release her last clutch at man, not to have her retreat into some absurd Amazonian society, but to improve female congress with the male, to ally female with male in a way which is not mutually limiting. ... 'I have a dream.'"[74]

Greer wanted not "rebellion" or "war" but "revolution," a revolution against marriage and every other convention about gender roles. "The chief means of liberating women," she asserted, "is replacing of compulsiveness and compulsion by the pleasure principle." This meant, ultimately, a total overturn in all social relationships: "Women's liberation, if it abolishes the patriarchal family, will abolish a necessary substructure of the authoritarian state, and once that withers away Marx will have come willy-nilly."[75]

Greer was the theorist *par excellence* of the sexual revolution as a specific component of the movement for gender equality. There was no more extreme and compelling denunciation of the old patriarchal culture than hers. But the reality proved to be more complex.

The sequence of more and more intense theorizing on behalf of the gender revolution corresponded closely to the rising curve of the classic revolution, proceeding from the moderate phase toward the extreme. Thus, the moderates such as Friedan and Bird addressed issues of women's legal equality and economic opportunity in existing society, while the radicals exemplified by Millett and Greer broke with the fundamentals of that society by pointing toward women's separation from the mainstream or by kicking over traditional taboos that hitherto had applied to both sexes. This is not to suggest that the moderates were not revolutionaries: as in every classic revolution of yore, they clearly were, in temperament and in their defiant stance. But their objectives were essentially those of practical adjustment. The radicals, like their precursors in past revolutions, were irreconcilable utopians in their urge to supplant the whole social and cultural order.

The Sexual Revolution

In line with radical feminist theory, a new dimension of controversy entered the picture of the gender revolution with the emergence of an alternative code of sexual mores in personal life. This was the sexual revolution per se, a movement both broader and more diffuse than the political history of feminism, though closely linked to it in the minds of both the radical feminists and the conservative public. The sexual revolution was a cultural, attitudinal, and behavioral phenomenon, impinging one way or another on every member of society, whatever they thought of it.

A word is in order about the meaning of the sexual revolution. All aspects of the Fourth Revolution have affected the language, with new meanings and new distinctions. The gender revolution was originally called the "sexual revolution," but in the course of the transformation wrought by the movement in public discourse, "sex" and "sexual" came more and more to denote strictly physical relationships between the sexes, or more exactly, interpersonal activity involving the sexual organs. To fill the linguistic gap, "gender" was extended from its original grammatical meaning, to designate a sex in the sense of the female sex and the male sex; so it is the "gender revolution" that refers to changes in the overall status of women. "Sexual revolution" is reserved here for that aspect of the gender revolution involving changes in the specifically sexual relationships between men and women.

As a cultural change, not a political movement, the sexual revolution naturally cannot be mapped on a clear line with any definite beginning, peak, or completion. The sexual revolution was more a transformation in overt attitudes than in individual conduct, more a change in social expectations and standards of acceptability than in personal beliefs, which typically shift much more slowly than the public climate. This is not to mention actual behavior, which statistics and literature since time immemorial show to have diverged widely from socially and religiously correct standards in almost every society. The point is that traditionally, before the revolution in public attitudes, the norm everywhere was to condemn open sexual transgressions and the objective exploration of sexuality. "Properly speaking," wrote William O'Neill, "there was no sexual revolution. ... What had changed was the attitude of many people toward it."[76] As Helen Perry, a chronicler of the counterculture put it, "There is rather a surfacing and exposure of fears, doubts, and behavior that have been around for a very long time; the exposure itself constitutes reform."[77] Indeed, at the beginning of any kind of revolution, the climate of expectations may lag behind the development of private belief and desires and then quite suddenly surge ahead to catch up and sweep well beyond what the average person will normally tolerate.

Some of the groundwork for the sexual revolution as an attitude reversal was laid by the scientific pioneers of a century ago—Havelock Ellis, Freud, and others—as well as by the leaders of the birth control movement, all of whom initially scandalized Western societies. Freud's position is curious, because prior to the sixties he was considered a beacon of sexual enlightenment, only to be damned by radical feminists as an ideologist of female oppression. In any case, by the time of Alfred Kinsey's researches and publications from the late 1940s on,[78] American culture was getting prepared to absorb the revolutionary blow.

Apart from the breakthrough into the public consciousness by behavioral research, signs of the coming sexual revolution, if it was a revolution, were apparent by the early 1960s in the realm of popular culture. It became acceptable to discuss sexual functions and issues more or less explicitly, first in print and then in the electronic media. Publishing was liberated in the sexual respect when, in the name of free speech, obscenity laws gave way to the elastic judicial formulas, "prevailing community standards" and "redeeming social value," according to which D.H. Lawrence's *Lady Chatterly's Lover* was finally ruled not obscene in the United States.[79] Helen Gurley Brown, taking over *Cosmopolitan* magazine, touted in 1962 the excitements of personal freedom in *Sex and the Single Girl.*[80] Fashion pushed ahead provocatively with miniskirts and bikinis. Under the heading "Do Your Own Thing," the *World Book Encyclopedia* reported, "In 1968 a woman was finally allowed to wear her skirt as long as she pleased."[81] At the same time the advent of the pill made it easier for women to yield: "Women had begun to feel," wrote Helen Perry, "that indeed they could enjoy sex and admit to it without feeling unladylike. The concept of a woman being 'used' by a man as a slave either at the table or in bed had begun to seem ridiculous, at least theoretically."[82]

Colleges were caught in the middle, between the traditional rules and sanctions presumably expected by parents and benefactors and increasingly assertive student behavior claiming rights of personal freedom and privacy in the sexual realm. "Standards of sexual conduct and sexual morality are rapidly changing," reported one policy study in 1966. "The double standard increasingly is being discarded," while "the adult world lacks consensus, ... the underlying values of human relations are murky as well."[83]

Under such circumstances of prerevolutionary tension between belief and reality, a very small incident—like the Boston Tea Party—can tear aside the curtains of the old orthodoxy, to show that the Emperor has no clothes. In the sexual realm, the scene of this breakout was Columbia University, just when it was becoming the epicenter of the broad youth revolt. In March 1968 a Barnard College undergraduate was threatened with expulsion for the sin of cohabiting with her boyfriend (technically, for lying about the relationship). Rousing heated student protests simultaneous with the uprising at Barnard's parent institution, the incident captured widespread press and public attention.[84] By highlighting its extent, the publicity suddenly made nonmarital sex seem normal. Abruptly, marital status ceased to be a matter of expectation or censure in living arrangements and public accommodations. The Census Bureau adapted, with the new category "Persons of opposite sex sharing living quarters," from which the acronym POSSLQ, immortalized by Charles Kuralt of CBS News in his series, "On the Road."[85]

Responding quickly to the new sense of what was demanded by their students and tolerated by the parents, colleges and universities dropped parietal rules and instituted coed dormitories. Permissiveness on sex, as college and university administrators conveniently discovered, helped defuse the campus revolt that was sweeping the country. "With contraception, and now abortion, eradicating the old puritan bludgeon of fear," proclaimed the abortion activist Lawrence Lader in 1973, "the barriers against cohabitation on most college campuses have been wiped out."[86] Europeans were experiencing the same readjustment between appearances and reality; university parietal rules were one of the main issues when the French student revolt first broke out at Nanterre in May 1968. At Barnard the original offender was amnestied by the college authorities. Ironically, she dropped out anyway, after being arrested in the main Columbia student melee across Broadway.[87]

The sexual revolution paralleled the nation's change in public values about race, as expectations and standards of acceptability that had long since been running behind personal sentiments and behavior jumped ahead of them instead. Conventions of verbal restraint in public were trampled by the extremists and left undefended by intimidated moderates, thus illustrating the kind of attitudinal leap that marks a real revolution. As a result, though, both the racial and the sexual shifts in American culture left a reservoir of resentment among the "silent majority" who found public standards sweeping far ahead of their personal values, resentment that was often expressed in indirect ways. In race it came out in hostility to such originally race-neutral programs as welfare and affirmative action. In sex, charged up by religious conservatism, it eventually found its focus in the antiabortion movement and in resistance to homosexual rights.

Some radical feminists also had their reservations about the sexual revolution. "The so-called sexual revolution was only another form of oppression for women," said Robin Morgan as the movement was accelerating in 1970.[88] Be careful what you wish for.

In time, the sexual revolution went much deeper than its more articulate champions expected, deeper than purely material factors such as the pill can account for. The results were clear in the demographics of the 1970s and beyond. The divorce rate climbed rapidly, though to be sure this was not a new trend, while illegitimate births rose sharply. The economists George Akerlof and Janet Yellin cited figures showing a truly catastrophic increase in out-of-wedlock births to black mothers, from 24 percent in 1965 to 64 percent—almost two-thirds of all babies—in 1990; but whites followed the same path, from a mere 3 percent rate of recorded illegitimacy in 1965 to 18 percent in 1990.[89] To explain the paradoxical surge in illegitimacy in the era of improved contraception and available abortion, Akerlof and Yellin adduced a theory of "technology shock": "Women who were willing to get an abortion or who reliably used contraception no longer found it necessary to condition sexual relations on a promise of marriage in the event of pregnancy," while the sexual revolution eased the social stigma on either the behavior or its consequences. "With premarital sex the rule, rather than the exception, an out-of-wedlock childbirth gradually ceased to be a sign that society's sexual taboos had been violated."[90] In addition, Akerlof and Yellin conceded, the greater availability of welfare benefits from the 1960s onward contributed to the virtual disappearance of "shotgun marriage" and adoption among black mothers.

Male irresponsibility, freed up by the sexual revolution, was the common denominator in all this social pathology. It was sadly accompanied by violence and, one suspects, by depression and drug dependency, among both isolated men and overburdened women. The outcome of burgeoning calls on welfare entitlements that these developments generated threatened to sink the promises of the Great Society, as its benefits, in the minds of the majority, became associated overtly with loose living and the undeserving, and covertly with the deviance imputed to racial minorities. The social fabric was badly stretched, though not in the way that radical feminists intended.

Campaigns in the Legal Trenches: Abortion

Once the gender revolution had attained full force in both the political and the cultural respects, it spread into a multitude of diverse—and divisive—issue areas. Here it was no longer a matter of basic principles that could be advanced by taking to the streets but a series of long drawn-out contests mainly in the forum of the courtroom. This was further testimony to the leading rule taken by—or forced upon—the judicial branch of government in pursuing the social goals of the Fourth Revolution. The areas of legal struggle were manifold, but three in particular stand out as key components both of the gender revolution and of the rising counter-revolutionary resistance to it: legalized abortion, the Equal Rights Amendment to the U.S. Constitution, and gender equality in the workplace.

Just as for the black civil rights movement, the landmark breakthrough for women in the governmental realm occurred in the judicial branch. The 1973 Supreme Court decision on abortion rights was the school desegregation case of the women's rights movement—a revolutionary victory won through litigation that could not be easily or universally achieved legislatively. Like black civil rights, it was a success won by appealing to the broad revolutionary principles that the Founding Fathers had enunciated to justify an originally far more modest agenda of individualism.

Unlike the black civil rights movement, the signal judicial victory for women in abortion rights came after rather than before their upsurge of direct action. *Roe v. Wade* would have been unthinkable until the outburst of women's liberation and the sexual revolution had shifted the ground in public attitudes. The Court's decision, wrote the political scientist Rosalind Petchesky, was "the product, not of judicial innovation or fiat, but of a groundswell of popular feeling and practice, ... the product of a social and political movement."[91] Indeed, capping as it did an extraordinarily quick and deep reversal in public opinion—in publicly acknowledged opinion, that is—*Roe v. Wade* consummated a veritable minirevolution within the broader revolutionary transformation in women's rights and in the Fourth Revolution as a whole.

The abortion question had long made the women's movement uneasy, in its challenge to the public sexual mores that prevailed until the mid-1960s. "Abortion," wrote Lawrence Lader, "stood at the apex of all our nightmares and inhibitions about sex, and to tamper with it meant that the whole system could come tumbling down."[92] In the matter of reproductive rights, birth control had been the salient issue for half a century, until medical advances and the demise of the last restrictive state statutes removed it from the realm of serious controversy. The last state law barring the supply of contraceptives even to married persons (in Connecticut) was voided by the Supreme Court in 1965,[93] and Congress finally came down on the side of birth control with the Family Planning Services and Population Research Act of 1970.

The legal establishment stepped gingerly into the question of abortion in the 1950s. A benchmark in this adventure was the proposal adopted in 1959 by the law-drafting American Law Institute (ALI) to legalize abortion in the event of rape, incest, or grave threat to a woman's health.[94] By the mid-sixties, supported by opinion polls, the medical profession caught up with this principle; by 1967 the reform was being considered in half the states and had been passed in several.[95]

Direct attacks on state abortion laws emerged simultaneously with the rise of the organized women's liberation movement. An Association to Repeal Abortion Laws was formed in California in 1966, and Colorado led a succession of states from 1967 on to relax their abortion statutes. California's law on the ALI model was signed by the state's new governor, Ronald

Reagan, in June 1967. Betty Friedan added to the momentum for repeal in her first-year report to NOW in November 1967, where she asserted "the right of every woman to control her own reproductive life, ... by removing contraceptive information and abortion from the penal code," all in the name of "sexual equality."[96]

The feminists found an important ally in John D. Rockefeller III and his Population Council. Rockefeller opined in 1968 that because abortion could not be stopped, it might as well be legalized, for reasons both of health and of respect for the law.[97] The American Public Health Association concurred immediately, and the American Medical Association and the American Bar Association followed suit, in 1970 and 1971.[98] Another boost came in 1968 from the Citizens' Advisory Council on the Status of Women (successor to President Kennedy's commission, chaired by former Senator Maurine Neuberger and congresswoman-to-be Shirley Chisholm), when it endorsed general repeal. Planned Parenthood joined in a few months later.[99]

The broad social changes that were being expressed in the gender revolution made the argument for repeal hard to resist. The simultaneous trends of rising participation by women in the workforce, better education, deferral of marriage, and a rising divorce rate set the stage so decisively that a Harris poll of 1969 showed nearly two-thirds of respondents opposing the prevailing state bans on abortion.[100] All in all, as Professor Amy Kesselman put it, "A sea change in attitudes toward abortion occurred during the five years before *Roe v. Wade.*"[101]

In 1969 a National Conference on Abortion Laws, held in Chicago, set up an organization to carry the fight forward. This was the National Association for the Repeal of Abortion Laws (NARAL), also under the leadership of Neuberger and Chisholm. NARAL staged nationwide demonstrations for repeal on Mother's Day, May 8, 1969, while radicals like the Redstockings picketed court proceedings and the Bar Association.[102] One by one, NARAL appealed to state courts, invoking the federal constitution and the concept of the right of privacy against all prohibitions on abortion.[103] Decisions won in California and the District of Columbia in the fall of 1969 eviscerated the local abortion laws, and in the spring of 1970 state legislatures began to join the repeal movement—first Hawaii and Alaska (the latter over the governor's veto), and then, signally, New York.

One of the many local abortion appeals pressed by NARAL, this one in Texas in the name of a young woman who went down in history as Jane Roe, was destined to set the national norm. The case was *Roe v. Wade,* where a Federal District Court ruled in May 1970 against the Texas anti-abortion law as "unconstitutionally overbroad" and "unconstitutionally vague," and sustained "the right of choice."[104] The case made its way to the U.S. Supreme Court late in 1971, and it was finally decided for the plaintiff, by a seven to two margin, in January 1973. Summing up for the majority, Justice Harry Blackmun wrote, "A state criminal abortion statute of the current Texas type that excepts from criminality only a *life saving* procedure on behalf of the mother, without regard to pregnancy state and without recognition of the other interests involved, is violative of the Due Process Clause of the Fourteenth Amendment." While he recognized the legitimacy of "increasing restrictions on abortion as the period of pregnancy lengthens," Blackmun concluded, "Up to these points the abortion decision in all its aspects is inherently, and primarily, a medical decision."[105] Lawrence Lader commented, "What the abortion movement accomplished in six years was to shake up the country as it has only been shaken by the abolitionists and Alabama bus boycotts and early peace marchers."[106]

The Equal Rights Amendment

The abortion rights movement had a very specific objective that lent itself to a clear decision in the courts, once the groundwork had been established in public and professional opinion. Much more complex and diffuse was the concept of an equal rights amendment to the U.S. Constitution, despite the apparent simplicity of its proposed language against discrimination on account of sex. The ERA had to go through the legislative process, first in Congress, and then in the state legislatures for ratification. Its ultimate failure testified to the limits and fears about gender equality among a substantial minority of the American population, female as well as male, and highlighted the persisting regional differences in the United States in response to the Fourth Revolution.

The idea of an equal rights amendment to write gender equality into the Constitution arose almost simultaneously with the adoption of the Nineteenth Amendment on woman suffrage. Backed by the National Women's Party, it was first introduced in Congress in 1923 by two Kansas Republicans, Senator Charles Curtis and Representative Daniel Anthony (who happened to be Susan B. Anthony's nephew).[107] The Senate actually approved the amendment twice in the 1950s, though House action was blocked in committee. It recurred in party platforms, but real progress had to wait until the force of the Fourth Revolution in all its aspects was felt in the 1960s.

At Betty Friedan's urging, NOW came out for the ERA in the "Bill of Rights for Women" that it put forth at its second national convention in 1967 and pressed it before the Congress.[108] President Johnson and candidate Nixon both endorsed it, as did their advisory councils on the status of women. By 1970 public opinion polls recorded more than 50 percent for the ERA.[109] Congressional hearings commenced that year, though passage was delayed by the issue of subjecting women to the draft. Nevertheless, "The feminist drive in Congress was superbly organized and unstoppable," as legal historian Hugh Davis Graham observed.[110] Congress adopted the ERA overwhelmingly, in the House by a vote of 354 to 23 in October 1971 and in the Senate by 84 to 8 in March 1972, thereby sending it to the states for ratification. Shorn of qualifying amendments, the text was a model of simplicity: "Equality of rights under the law shall not be denied or abridged by the United States or any State on account of sex."

Opposition to the ERA during and after the congressional process came from two very different quarters. One element was grounded in the women's movement: the old sentiment that legislative protection of women, especially in the workplace, should take precedence over the assertion of an abstract equality that could compromise the unequal character of gender-protective statutes. This was the position taken by most of Organized Labor until the late 1960s, driven in part by the fear of losing protections for both sexes. Labor helped keep the ERA out of Democratic Party platforms despite the turbulence of the decade. Besides, many defenders of women's status agreed with the position taken by Kennedy's Commission on the Status of Women in 1963, that an equal rights amendment was unneeded in the light of legal protections afforded by the Fifth and Fourteenth amendments (however unrealistic this argument may have been in practice).[111] Esther Peterson was dismissive of "troublesome and futile agitation" for the ERA.[112] This split over the ERA, as much as any other issue, highlighted the difference between the Third and Fourth revolutions, in this instance between the struggle to improve the condition of the economically downtrodden and the crusade for pure principles of social equality and sameness of treatment under the law.

The other base of resistance to the ERA was the regional one, in the southern states, still smarting from their defeat in the black revolution and determined to resist further erosion of the traditional patriarchal culture to which the region was attached. To be sure, cultural opponents of equal rights regularly appealed to the protection issue, as well as to the tradition of male responsibility for supporting the family, to try to kill or at least delay the ERA. In addition to these generalized conservative sentiments, opposition to the ERA was galvanized by the abortion issue and *Roe v. Wade*, coming as it did in the midst of the ratification process. "Conservative activists," wrote the political scientist Jane Mansbridge, "saw abortion and the ERA as two prongs of the 'libbers' general strategy for undermining traditional American values," and "sought to turn the ERA into a referendum on ... *Roe*."[113]

Ratification of the ERA at first seemed easy, Hawaii's legislature acting literally within minutes after word arrived of final passage of the measure by the U.S. Senate. Twenty-one more states ratified before the end of their 1972 legislative sessions, and eight ratified in 1973. Three followed in 1974, one in 1975, and Indiana, the last, in 1977. Supporters of the ERA could not advance beyond this total of thirty-five states, three short of the thirty-eight required to implement the amendment, even though Congress extended the deadline for ratification from 1979 to 1982.

Boundless explanations have been offered for the failure of ratification, above all the power of conservative lobbying and advertising campaigns. Joan Hoff attributed the trouble to "the cultural and political backlash that had set in across the country after the end of the Vietnam War."[114] But the main reason for the demise of the ERA is much simpler: it was the regional resistance of the South. Nine of the eleven states of the old Confederacy failed to ratify, excepting only Tennessee and Texas. The border states of Missouri and Oklahoma also held out along with Utah's Mormons and their neighbors in Arizona and Nevada. This was enough to deny the three-fourths of the fifty states necessary for adoption of the amendment. (Five Western and border states subsequently rescinded their ratification.) Much has been made of the role of conservative activists such as Phyllis Schafly and her Eagle Forum, but the only northern state that Schafly swung against the ERA was her home state of Illinois. Actually, the ERA failed in Illinois only because of the state's unusual rule requiring a three-fifths majority in the legislature to ratify federal constitutional amendments. Besides, as the count shows, Illinois was not even needed to block ratification. Thus, the ERA failed primarily because of the regional veto that the amending process of the Constitution allowed the South, nationwide public opinion notwithstanding.

In any event, defeat of the ERA was a setback for the women's movement more in symbol than in substance. Judicial and legislative action driven by the gender revolution and evolving public opinion was recasting the scene in terms of equal rights in one area after another. "The ERA would have had much less substantive effect than either proponents or opponents claimed," opined Professor Mansbridge.[115] For Joan Hoff, formerly Joan Hoff-Wilson, "The ERA may be more important in defeat than in victory, as a symbol of how far women still have to go ... to seek creative legislative and judicial solutions in their continuing struggle for full and equal legal status with men."[116] In spite of this uphill perspective, the due process and equal protection doctrines usually sufficed in court tests of gender discrimination.

Gender in the Workplace

The earliest of the legal struggles for equal treatment of women was also the longest lasting. This was the campaign for equality on the job, in all its ramifications throughout the diverse levels and areas of the national economy. Here the advance of women in the 1970s and beyond was extraordinary even if not totally satisfying.

Equal economic rights and opportunities became a contentious issue with the rise in women's participation in the workforce during and after World War II, and particularly with the spread of female employment beyond the areas traditionally reserved for women—elementary teaching, nursing, retailing, secretarial tasks, and domestic service. Changes in the family in the 1960s associated with the sexual revolution, above all rising rates of divorce and single motherhood, put an increasing premium on employment opportunity and equity. At the same time, gains in these respects encouraged the further progress of the sexual revolution by lessening women's dependence on men as well as men's responsibility for women.

Added to these mass trends was a cultural change in the upper and middle reaches of society, as educated and affluent women rejected the role of homemaker and helpmeet to successful men and struck out for careers of their own. Ironically, the percentage of women among persons achieving advanced university degrees actually declined between the 1920s and 1950s,[117] but this was only a relative rather than absolute drop as the total number of degree-seekers exploded after World War II. A factor keeping the number of professional women relatively low was the presumption until the 1960s that marriage and a career were incompatible and that women in responsible jobs should remain unmarried or even (for schoolteachers) unattached. The overthrow of this social taboo in the course of the sexual revolution cleared the way for a massive advance of women into the upper, not just the lower, levels of the workforce. "In the professional middle class," wrote Barbara Ehrenreich, "women were working not only because they had to ... they were pursuing demanding, fast-track professional careers. ... Perhaps the greatest single achievement of the feminist movement has been the opening up of formerly all-male professions, such as law, medicine, and management."[118]

These advances in women's aspirations collided with the old Progressive agenda of special protection for women in employment, designed for an era when women worked mainly in menial and exploited capacities. That tradition, ensconced in federal legislation and in the Women's Bureau of the Labor Department, did not suffice for the new era when women sought opportunity in the most prestigious professions with equality of access all the way to the top. The backhanded inclusion of sex discrimination in the 1964 Civil Rights Act broke new legal ground for this urge and ushered in a period of dogged controversy, spearheaded by NOW, over federal action through the Equal Employment Opportunity Commission (EEOC).

The focal question in this wrangle was whether to treat gender discrimination under the new law with the same seriousness as racial discrimination. Much energy was spent by the contending forces of old and new feminism over the seemingly marginal issue of gender segregation in help-wanted advertising. But with rising feminist pressure and President Johnson's appointment of a majority from the "affected classes," the EEOC came around in 1967 and 1968 to "a path that would tightly link race and sex in EEO enforcement," in the words of Hugh Davis Graham. This goal had to be pursued, however, against the conservative shift in Congress resulting from the 1966 midterm elections.[119]

Meanwhile, through its Task Force on Family Law and Policy, President Johnson's Advisory Council on the Status of Women developed a broad program for reform in property and marital rights.[120] In 1967 Executive Order No. 11375 banned sex discrimination on the part of federal contractors. Following up this initiative, under pressure of litigation by the women's rights movement, President Nixon ordered "an affirmative action program of equal employment opportunity" in federal agencies themselves (Executive Order No. 11478), thereby opening up an area of controversy that would run through the remainder of the century. George Shultz as Nixon's secretary of labor issued requirements for "action plans" in the hiring and promotion of women by federal contractors. At the same time, the federal government began to scrutinize sex discrimination in academic institutions receiving federal grants, a move supplemented by the Educational Amendments Act of 1972.[121] Discrimination lingered in the classification of certain positions as inherently male or female, until the Supreme Court in 1971 overturned an Idaho rule allowing only men to be appointed estate administrators.[122]

Joan Hoff credited the "establishment or mainstream wing of the Second Women's Movement," based among professional women in the Northeast and only tenuously linked with the new radical feminists, with most of these successes at the governmental level.[123] In any case, by the time of the 1974 amendments to the Civil Rights Act, gender equality was well established as a fundamental principle of public policy.

Executive action was often decisive for women's employment opportunities, as it had been for blacks when President Truman decreed the desegregation of the armed forces. Once the draft had ended in 1973, the military rapidly broadened women's options beyond their traditional role of nursing, and by the 1990s every military occupational specialty save literal hand-to-hand combat was open to women. The same shift could be noted in local police forces. More broadly, federal power exerted through contracts and research grants applied leverage to private business and the academic world, drawing the issue of women in with that of race in the pursuit of employment equity.

As the employment of women progressed in higher-status and nontraditional jobs—even in construction, for example—the conditions experienced by females in formerly all-male or male-dominated work environments became a central question in public policy. Specifically, the phenomenon of sexual harassment, up to and including the extraction of sexual favors as a condition for job retention or advancement, made women's gains in employment opportunity less than fully gratifying. Congress and the courts tried to respond, though these difficulties testified to the depth of cultural change and resistance that the gender revolution entailed.

The Legacy of the Gender Revolution

The gender revolution had no dramatic climax such as the black revolution or the youth revolution had in the late 1960s. It was not marked off by a clear beginning or end or by any point where its protagonists could say with unanimity, "We have won!" It was a process of social transformation, deep in its impact, though still inconclusive. Yet within the span of just a few years it had set the forces in motion for the most profound social change that America had ever experienced, certainly since the abolition of slavery, perhaps in all its history.

With the gender revolution, America took the lead in the international social revolution. The black revolution was specific to the United States, and the youth revolution, though spectacularly international, was felt mainly in a limited span of time, the late 1960s and early 1970s. But the gender revolution applied open-endedly to the whole world and to decades of the future.

The gender revolution cut more deeply into the universals of human culture than any other element of the Fourth Revolution, perhaps more deeply than any revolution in history. It challenged the most deeply entrenched habits and traditions of family, sex, and reproduction, of the fundamental relations between the two biologically established halves of humankind. Little wonder, then, that the gender revolution was the most tenaciously resisted component of the Fourth Revolution, particularly when it came to issues that were exclusively sexual: abortion and, later on, homosexuality.

The impact of the gender revolution on the status of women in the United States was extraordinary both in its extent and in its rapidity, considering that it involved deep changes in society at large as well as in the governmental sphere. As Joan Hoff observed from the perspective of the 1990s, "The legal status of women in the United States changed more rapidly in the last twenty-five years than in the previous two hundred."[124] Naturally, both the conservative and the radical extremes remained unsatisfied. As in any revolution, overt policy changes outran the more slowly evolving instincts of the general public. And this disconnect left an enduring challenge of catch-up work to be accomplished.

Like the other components of the Fourth Revolution, the gender revolution went beyond the premises of the Third Revolution that addressed only economic justice. In practice, those goals of the Third Revolution were eclipsed by the principle of equal opportunity, pressed within the increasingly inegalitarian structure of American society at large. In the realm of educated expertise, women made extraordinary gains in the course of the gender revolution; at the bottom of the meritocratic ladder, for women and men alike, progress was problematic at best. This was the basic issue dividing the adherents of pure legal equality from the old Progressive and New Deal campaigners for women's material betterment within a movement to improve the economic condition of everyone who worked for a living.

The new feminist inegalitarianism, to coin a phrase, meshed more with the actual outcome of the Third Revolution than with the hopes of those who had waged it. The deepest social consequence of the Third Revolution was the shift from proprietorship and entrepreneurship to managerialism and meritocracy as the primary basis for individual status and success. What the women's movement accomplished was to secure for its following more or less equal access to higher status within this new social structure, while liberating them from dependence on fathers and husbands as the guarantors of their station in life. In this embrace of the meritocratic society, the gender revolution parted company with the youth revolution and its antimeritocratic bias. Meanwhile, for women at the bottom of the heap, often on their own economically even under the old order, the new kind of equality represented only a remote benefit, made all the more exasperating by the chimerical ideology of meritocracy that urged everyone to "get ahead" through education.

In the intimate relations of women and men, the gender revolution perhaps achieved more than it bargained for. Sexual liberation—traditionally an unspoken male prerogative under the old double standard—may have been won at a price in psychological security, the downside of the doctrine of sameness in this respect. While the shedding of old constraints on social roles and self-expression may have meant opportunity for upper-class women, it meant irresponsibility for lower-class men. The consequence was evinced on one hand in the drop in the U.S. birthrate from the 1960s on, and on the other hand in the surging percentage of illegitimacy among the children actually born, despite the availability of legal abortion. Radical feminists who denounced marriage and the nuclear family found their wish untowardly fulfilled in the proliferation of impoverished single-motherhood.

Who won in the gender revolution? The answer eludes us, because the gender revolution remains the least complete of all the elements of the Fourth Revolution. The struggle for liberty and equality on behalf of women continues, more successful in some areas and in pragmatic minds than in other respects and in more purist views. New generations of women may expect new opportunities, and perhaps new burdens, but the propagation of the species, regardless of how it is arranged, will never be easy.

CHAPTER 8

Revolution and Reaction

After the volcanic events in America between the mid-1960s and the early 1970s, it was inevitable that a reaction would follow, even if its exact form and extent could not have been anticipated. As matters turned out, the reaction was neither quick nor complete. Indeed, no postrevolutionary retreat ever turns the clock completely back: the Old Regime is never fully restored. All the more so with the three great revolutions in American history, Independence (combining the First and Second revolutions), the New Deal (the Third), and the Fourth Revolution. Reaction, however fervent, could not altogether eradicate the revolutionary changes that had taken place in each turbulent era in public life and in the nation's governing assumptions.

It is hard, of course, to find simple meaning in the most immediate past. The trees overshadow the forest. But the generation's span that elapsed between the upheavals of the 1960s and the millennium was a particularly complex time for the American nation. The aftermath of a revolution worked itself out against the backdrop of deep changes in the social and economic fabric of the country as well as dizzying transformations in its international environment. All this played out within a political context of bitter division over principles and a practical immobilism frustrating to all sides.

The sixties were etched into the American national consciousness as the era when everything was overturned. Of course, the revolution was not actually that total, and the country's basic political and economic institutions were affected hardly at all. Where profound change did in fact take place was in the realm of life that was central to the Fourth Revolution, namely, social relationships and cultural standards in everyday experience. There was a reaction, to be sure, but the extraordinary thing about the Fourth Revolution in America was how successfully it not only resisted reaction but also went on to develop and spread, and to implant itself irretrievably in the fabric of American life.

The Postrevolutionary Pendulum

As a violent and disruptive experience, the Fourth Revolution came to an end in the early 1970s. But revolutions do not conclude with one dramatic overturn in the social order; their influence continues to work deep changes, through the gradual osmosis of revolutionary innovation into the body social. Moreover, revolutions are usually followed by a series of aftershocks, so to speak, when new though diminished efforts may be made to rescue and advance the revolutionary agenda.

The familiar political metaphor of the pendulum is altogether apposite here. The initial revolutionary shock gives the political pendulum a big push toward change—to the Left, one used to be able to say—followed by a natural swing back toward the status quo ante, and then one or more lesser swings back and forth. These oscillations usually run about a generation apart. The history of France after the Great Revolution illustrates the point most clearly: 1789 was followed by new revolutionary beats in 1830, 1848, and 1871. In America the generational pendulum has never stopped swinging; the force of new revolutionary impulses has kept the motion going from the eighteenth century right down to the present. This is the source of the generational cycles of reform and reaction in American history that Arthur Schlesinger and others have noted.

The initial force of the Fourth Revolution in the United States caused a period of public commotion running from the early 1960s to the early 1970s. After such an experience, it is normal for a revolution to be followed by a Thermidorean Reaction. This was the meaning of Harry Truman's promise, "no more experiments," after the tumultuous struggles of the New Deal era. Next, it is likely for the principles of a revolution to be attacked head-on by counterrevolutionaries, who are not content with the retrenchments of the Thermidorean era. But in the Fourth Revolution, with its complex strands of the struggle for social equality, there was no such clear-cut aftermath. The backswing was not severe, in part for political reasons, and the revolution was able to extend and consolidate itself in much of the institutional and policy-making structure of society.

A secondary leftward swing of the pendulum in the late 1980s and the 1990s also can be discerned. This again is typical in the later trajectory of a revolution—a modest upturn after a long postrevolutionary trough, in other words the "moderate revolutionary revival." To be sure, this second wave of the Fourth Revolution was not as sharply defined politically as were most of the previous cyclical peaks in the American past. The Fourth Revolution kept running through the 1970s and 1980s in one social arena or another, and the 1990s did not represent a distinctly new break. Moreover, random events and personality quirks in presidential politics disturbed the clean revolutionary curve. The Watergate crisis with Richard Nixon's resignation in 1974, and Jimmy Carter's election in 1976, delayed and dampened the counterrevolution that finally came with Ronald Reagan.

Then the revolutionary revival misfired. The election of 1988 that Michael Dukakis should have won when the political cycle had turned favorable to liberalism was reversed by his incompetence as a candidate and his apprehension about the "L-word." Bill Clinton's election in 1992 and his initial affirmation of the positive role of government were seemingly a belated fulfillment of the revolutionary renewal. This last gasp of Great Society liberalism peaked in 1993–94 with the Clintons' ambitious but complex scheme for universal health insurance, and the pendulum started back again when, in the face of rumblings in the media and the business community, they withdrew the plan from consideration without even subjecting it to a congressional vote. President Clinton's tepid liberalism was being undercut by the political realignment of the South, and upon the Republican congressional triumph of 1994 it died. That opened the way for the first major governmental retreat from the New Deal–Great Society Welfare State, the 1996 reform "to end Welfare as we know it." Meanwhile, the "culture wars" simmered down, with both revolutionaries and counterrevolutionaries dug in for the long haul. The standoff resembled France of the Third Republic, where the representatives of the revolutionary and antirevolutionary traditions faced each other in a long-term but inconclusive contest for the nation's soul.

Thermidor and Counterrevolution

November 5, 1968, was the Ninth of Thermidor for the Fourth Revolution in America. Like the overthrow of Robespierre in revolutionary France, the election of Richard Nixon as president signaled an end to the revolutionary push and a national revulsion against extremist violence. In neither case, however, did the Thermidorean Reaction mean an immediate counterrevolutionary effort to undo everything the revolution had accomplished—whatever Nixon's enemies may have feared, and despite his own secret proclivities.

Nixon's narrow victory ushered in a long and complicated era of postrevolutionary adjustment. On the governmental plane there was, to be sure, vigorous repression of the revolutionary extremism associated with the black and youth revolutions, but basic policy accomplishments of the revolution were sustained and even advanced. The deepest reaction against the Fourth Revolution was societal rather than governmental, and it was muted because the revolution had shifted in public standards of acceptable advocacy. Societal reaction did not stop the deepening of revolutionary change in the main channels of the Fourth Revolution, the black civil rights movement, the women's movement, and popular culture. Indeed the revolutionary spirit went on to rouse newer social groups—other ethnic minorities, homosexuals, the handicapped and their advocates. Cumulatively, the changes in American life during the last third of the twentieth century added up to a profound overturn both in human relations and in thinking about them, even though the nation's political institutions were barely touched.

The Ideology of Reaction

Ideologically, reaction against the Fourth Revolution was seamlessly linked with lingering reaction against the Third. Doctrinaire, so-called Movement conservatism, had its roots in the frustration of right-wing Republicans on account of the ascendancy of the moderate, Eastern wing of the party in the 1940s and 1950s. The conservatives were particularly aggrieved by the failure of the Eisenhower administration to move aggressively against the legacy of the New Deal, the Welfare State, and "creeping socialism." In the 1960s and 1970s, these frustrations fused with new ideological elements—the opposition of conservative southern Democrats to the nascent Fourth Revolution, especially in its black expression; the political mobilization of religious conservatives against the cultural and sexual expressions of the Fourth Revolution; and the so-called neoconservatives who demanded a more nationalistic foreign policy.

Amalgamation of the Republican right, heir to the old isolationist tradition, and southern conservatism, traditionally the most interventionist and anti-Communist element in American politics, was the accomplishment of Senator Barry Goldwater. Goldwater, in the words of William O'Neill, was "an ideologue who hoped to replace the limited welfare state with an unlimited warfare state."[1] Theodore White called the senator "a Trotsky of the far right."[2] In a venomous struggle for the 1964 Republican nomination, Goldwater prevailed over the internationalist champions of moderate Republicanism, Governor Nelson Rockefeller of New York and Pennsylvania senator William Scranton. Then he went on to the most disastrous Republican defeat since Alf Landon's in 1936. Nevertheless, in a sign of the political realignment still to come, Goldwater carried most of the Deep South (plus his home state of Arizona, but nothing more.)

Goldwater's conservatism, if it can be called that, became an ideological benchmark for the self-conscious conservative movement for the rest of the century and beyond. It was never couched in very specific terms, however, apart from its anti-Communism and its antigovernment animus. In social terms this counterrevolutionary conservatism was for the most part expressed in a set of vaguely defined code words whose meaning was more felt by the faithful than intellectually grasped. "Traditional values" meant almost anything one sensed in the slogan, including, one suspects, covert racism and patriarchalism along with hostility to the Welfare State and the income tax. "Family values" seems to have come into play primarily as code for opposition to abortion, sexual freedom, and homosexual rights. "Virtue" was invoked in the 1980s,[3] but it boiled down in practice to a code word for sexual restraint and economic self-reliance; that is, the qualities that were hoped to reduce illegitimate births, mass influx onto the welfare rolls, and attendant taxpayer expense.

A more sophisticated injection of ideology into the reaction against the Fourth Revolution was the contribution of the neoconservatives, typically Third Revolution radicals who were repelled by the excesses of the Fourth Revolution in the racial and cultural realms, and who turned against their Third Revolution roots besides. As intellectuals—academics and publicists—they provided a veneer of sophistication to an inherently Know-Nothing movement. Among the most prominent leaders of this turn were two articulate man-and-wife teams: Irving Kristol and his historian spouse Gertrude Himmelfarb, and *Commentary* editor Norman Podhoretz with his wife, the essayist Midge Decter. To them one might add a man who defied all classification, in career as in ideology, Daniel Patrick Moynihan, the flamboyant social scientist turned government official. These leading lights were seconded by a variety of old and new journals of a militantly counterrevolutionary character, ranging from William Buckley's *National Review* to Hilton Kramer's *New Criterion*. Joining these elements in the 1970s were many so-called Jackson Democrats, followers of Washington senator Henry Jackson, who rebelled at what they perceived to be the party leadership's foreign-policy softness in the later stages of the Cold War. Neo conservatives rejected most of the premises of the Fourth Revolution, except for black legal rights, and accommodated themselves to the anti–Third Revolution elements of the "Reagan Revolution."[4] In the view of its chronicler Peter Steinfels, neoconservatism was the ideology of "policy professionals" in retreat from the problems raised by social reform; it verged on "the legitimating and lubricating ideology of an oligarchic America."[5] That point was underscored by generous business contributions to conservative think tanks such as the Heritage Foundation and the American Enterprise Institute that incubated the anti-intellectual intellectuals of neoconservatism.

Relatively late in the movement of reaction against the Fourth Revolution came a third infusion of antirevolutionary ideology, most explicitly in reaction to the gender revolution. This was the so-called Religious Right, more or less quiescent until the abortion issue galvanized them into political action. Initially, as the historian of religion William Martin pointed out, the reaction was primarily Catholic. The conservative Protestant mobilization came on in the late 1970s, with theologians such as Harold O.J. Brown and Francis Schaeffer and, above all, with the televangelist Jerry Falwell and his Moral Majority (founded in 1979).[6] Their ultimate bugbear was "secular humanism," embracing a litany of the evils of the Fourth Revolution. "To understand humanism," wrote one religious publicist, "is to understand women's liberation, the ERA, gay rights, children's rights, abortion, secular education, the 'new' morality, evolution, values clarification [a fashionable school program of that day], situational ethics, the separation of church and state, the loss of patriotism, and many of the other problems that are tearing America apart today."[7]

The religious conservatives found waiting for them an improbable champion, the one-time Hollywood actor Ronald Reagan. They swung into action to fight for his nomination and election, and they contributed measurably to his victories. At the same time, through their grassroots organizing efforts, they won a decisive role in Republican Party councils.

By the 1990s, the various elements of counterrevolutionary ideology were well positioned to contend with the now-reviving enthusiasm for Fourth Revolution causes. This confrontation set the stage for the culture wars, in the media, in the law, and, above all, in academia, where the two sides have since been fighting bitterly, if inconclusively, to command the nation's consciousness.

Reaction in Government

It is typical in revolutions for political reaction in defense of the status quo to arise almost simultaneously with the revolution itself, even its moderate phase. So it was with the Fourth Revolution, barely underway when the forces of reaction began to mobilize against it. Conservative Republicans, still targeting the vestiges of the Third Revolution in the Welfare State, made common cause with southern Democrats restive over the civil rights movement. Not only Goldwater but also Ronald Reagan in his political pronouncements of the mid-1960s openly courted the racist South. That appeal accounted for Goldwater's main success.

At the national level the political tide began to turn against the Fourth Revolution as early as the congressional elections of 1966, when President Johnson lost the super-majority he needed to make him independent of conservative southern support. In the same year Reagan won the governorship of California, in large part as a popular reaction against the excesses of the youth revolution already raging in that bellwether state. Richard Nixon got the message and turned it into his "Southern strategy" of 1968, to win both the Republican presidential nomination and the general election.

As befits a Thermidorean era, Nixon's antirevolutionary moves were limited and selective, despite his enemies' fears that he would try to roll back all the social gains of the 1960s. Official animus was directed more at extremist manifestations of all sorts than at the moderate mainstream of reform, and more at the youth revolution than anyone else. In January 1969 incoming attorney general John Mitchell bracketed antiwar activists and campus disrupters with common criminals in his law and order promises.[8] He put the ill-founded case of the Chicago Seven at the top of his agenda, pursuing it to the bitter and futile end of dismissals and acquittals.

Nixon was not, in the view of his biographer Richard Reeves, "a small-minded conservative" but only an opportunist,[9] who lacked, as Hugh Graham put it, "any inherent and internally consistent ideology."[10] His ill-fated "Family Security System" of 1969 with its guaranteed minimum income together with work requirements (actually Moynihan's baby) was the most ambitious extension of the Great Society that has yet been attempted.[11] His 1973 imposition of price and wage controls to fight inflation was arguably the most radical economic measure an American president has ever proposed in peacetime. Though Nixon was privately an unabashed bigot, his approach to the black civil rights movement was mixed, reflecting the narrow political path he was trying to tread. He was vengeful in prosecuting black extremists, above all the remnants of the Panthers. Toward the mainstream of the movement he was uncomfortable. He was skeptical of his own government's desegregation efforts, and he toyed with the idea of a constitutional amendment to ban school busing for integration.[12] Women gave him the least problem; he was actually supportive of the Equal Rights Amendment, and he did not interfere with the abortion rights effort.

All this time, the American political landscape was being transformed by the step-by-step realignment of the South from the Democratic to the Republican column. The shift proceeded from the top of the ticket downward, as conservative southern whites gradually embraced their traditional Republican enemies, the culprits a century before in pressing the final stage of the Second Revolution to emancipate the blacks. Republicanism would be the South's new vehicle to resist the social and cultural changes of the Fourth Revolution. Strom Thurmond's Dixiecrat revolt of 1948 started the process, taking votes away from the Democrats without having to give them to a Republican (though in the event, not enough to deny Truman his victory over Thomas Dewey). Below the presidential level, for the time being, the Solid South remained true to its regional Democratic allegiance, while its representatives in Congress maintained the coalition with the Republicans that had dominated the national legislative branch ever since the waning days of the New Deal. The high-sounding but nonthreatening Adlai Stevenson scored his only wins against Dwight Eisenhower in 1952 and 1956 in southern or border states, and John Kennedy, with the Texan Lyndon Johnson on his ticket, claimed most of the region in his narrow victory over Nixon in 1960. Then, under the impact of the civil rights movement, the Solid South began to dissolve. In 1964 five Deep South states gave their electoral votes to the counterrevolutionary Goldwater. In 1968 the South moved more aggressively to the right; George Wallace carried four of the five southern states that had gone for Goldwater in 1964, and all the rest of the South except Texas went for Nixon, to clinch his slim victory over Hubert Humphrey. The election of 1972, when almost the entire nation voted for Nixon and against "acid, amnesty, and abortion," finalized the southern shift to the Republicans in national politics.

From that point on, the southern realignment worked its way down through the congressional delegations and governorships and finally into state legislatures and local elections. Not even the Democrats' nomination of the all-southern Clinton–Gore ticket in 1992 and 1996 could stem this tide; indeed, the surge of 1994 led by Georgia's Newt Gingrich gave the Republicans for the first time a majority of the South's seats in the House of Representatives. In many parts of the South, Democrats survived only as a heavily black party in majority-black districts. But the national legislative balance between liberals and conservatives did not change substantially, as older conservative southern Democrats were replaced by younger (and, to be sure, more aggressive) southern Republicans. If anything, the liberal character of the Democratic Party emerged less diluted.

With the realignment of southern conservatives into the Republican ranks and the drift of moderate Republicans in the opposite direction, the two major parties became more sharply polarized than at any time since the Civil War. Moreover, this polarization took a starkly ideological form along the lines of the Fourth Revolution, either for it or, implicitly or explicitly, against it. Beneficiaries of the Fourth Revolution lined up strongly with the Democrats, blacks overwhelmingly so, other racial minorities substantially. Women, to the degree that they were politically energized by the gender revolution, disproportionately supported the Democrats, thereby creating the so-called gender gap in the electorate. Gays voted almost exclusively Democratic. A majority of straight white men, on the other hand, was left to the Republicans—in some parts of the country, the South and the mountain West, in a ratio of two or three to one. Considering the proportion of each of these groups in the population, the Democratic Party came to depend for at least 50 percent of its support on voters aligned with the Fourth Revolution.

Meanwhile, with the South's conversion and the political mobilization of the Religious Right, hard-line conservatives easily captured the Republican Party machinery. The signal shift, of course, was Reagan's nomination in 1980 over the putatively moderate George H.W. Bush, following his close run for the Republican nomination against President Gerald Ford in 1976. Reagan's victory over Carter in the 1980 general election was not a popular landslide, as the press has always represented it since then—he scored a bare majority of 51.6 percent against the 41.7 percent for Jimmy Carter and the 6.7 percent for the moderate Republican protest candidate, Illinois representative John Anderson. But the lopsided Electoral College majority for Reagan—489 from forty-four states to 49 from six states plus the District of Columbia for Carter (including only his home state of Georgia from the South)—is what stuck in the public mind. The counterrevolution had finally won both the White House and an apparent mandate to undo everything its partisans hated about the sixties.

Reagan's election marked the end of the long retrenchment phase in the Fourth Revolution, drawn out by the Watergate crisis and the ensuing Carter interlude. Now came avowed reaction. It is interesting that most subsequent expressions of the conservative movement date its origins to 1964 and its triumph to 1980, while they implicitly disown both the Eisenhower and Nixon–Ford administrations. To be sure, Reagan was always an elusive character, even to the aides and biographers who knew him best. In contrast to the hard-driving Goldwater, it remains unclear what Reagan's personal commitments really were and how much of himself he really put into his political posturing.[13] He seems to have trod the path of the Henry Jackson neoconservatives before their time, moving from the role of an anti-Communist trade unionist in the film industry to become a media propagandist for the corporate interest. Then he won the governorship of California in 1966 on the earliest crest of the backlash against the youth revolution. By 1968 Reagan's abortive challenge to Nixon for the Republican presidential nomination made him the national standard bearer of the counterrevolution, a role he accepted with relish and convincingness whatever the depth and consistency of his personal beliefs. On this basis he ran against the incumbent Gerald Ford in 1976 and split the Republicans between the bland conservatives and the more doctrinaire sort. Four years later he led the hard-line faction to victory, overwhelming George Bush at a convention that would not allow a tribute to the late Republican vice president Nelson Rockefeller even in death.

The shifting tides of political sentiment toward the Fourth Revolution had a critical effect on the federal judiciary. In contrast to their vanguard role during the heroic period from 1954 to 1973, the position of the courts in the years that followed was ambivalent at best. The changeover depended, of course, on judicial vacancies and new Republican presidential appointments, but cumulatively the courts came to reflect closely the nation's turn to the right after 1968. From a locomotive of revolution, the judiciary was turned into a brake on it.

At the level of the Supreme Court there was a close symbolic connection of successive chief justices and the phases of the revolutionary process. The "Warren Court" represented the revolution, even sparked it. The "Burger Court," under Nixon's appointee Warren Burger from 1969 to 1986, stood for the temporizing Thermidorean Reaction, no longer revolutionary, not yet counterrevolutionary. The final role was reserved for the "Rehnquist Court," led from 1986 on by Reagan's choice William Rehnquist and often bitterly divided in its decisions.

Chief Justice Earl Warren personified the Supreme Court of the civil rights era, at the price of impeachment initiatives against him all over the country. He retired in 1969 after Lyndon Johnson's abortive effort to nominate Justice Abe Fortas to succeed him. Burger, the Minnesota appeals court judge Nixon selected to replace Warren, was a choice that turned out to be almost as surprisingly liberal as Eisenhower's pick of his predecessor. The same held of the other of the "Minnesota Twins," Harry Blackmun, appointed by Nixon in 1970 after the Senate's acrimonious rejection of two conservative southerners, Clement Hainsworth and G. Harrold Carswell. Among Nixon's four appointees only Rehnquist proved to be an unyielding conservative and the only one of them to vote in the negative on *Roe v. Wade* (along with JFK's disappointing selection, Byron White). Jimmy Carter had no bite at the Supreme Court apple. Reagan's choices—Sandra Day O'Connor, Antonin Scalia, and Anthony Kennedy, along with his elevation of Rehnquist to be chief justice—were another matter. Along with the first Bush's appointee Clarence Thomas, they made up the counterrevolutionary majority that persisted past the millennium and settled the disputed presidential election of 2000 by installing Bush the son.

Reaction in Society—The New Class Struggle

After the retrenchment of 1968, purely political reaction against the Fourth Revolution did not go much further. Mainly, it reflected the realignment of southern conservatives from their anomalous Democratic allegiance to their true ideological home in the right—and now dominant—wing of the Republican Party. Deeper reactions took place in the broader society, beyond the institutions of government. Even here, however, the black revolution had so thoroughly justified itself in moral terms that hardly anyone was willing publicly to challenge it head-on, though sublimated and surrogate expressions of such resistance fed other expressions of counterrevolution.

An early and sharp form of reaction against the sixties centered on the practical side of the Great Society and its war on poverty. These initiatives of the Johnson administration were hated by broad elements of the wage-earning and taxpaying public, who viewed them as handouts to undeserving freeloaders. Legal Aid particularly galled bourgeois America, even though it was the Nixon administration that institutionalized the program, as the Legal Services Corporation.[14] By empowering the poor, Legal Aid was sensed as a threat to the natural social order.

In effect, the Great Society set up an unprecedented kind of class struggle. Now it was not the capitalists versus the working class but the workers themselves versus the dependent and putatively antisocial underclass. (That term, introduced into the English language by Gunnar Myrdal and popularized by Ken Auletta, served as a convenient rallying cry for anti–Great Society resentments.)[15] Postrevolutionary reaction turned the war on poverty into a much more popular kind of campaign, a war against the poor—exactly the title of a trenchant book by the sociologist Herbert Gans.[16] In this new, unequal form of class struggle, victory was easily won simply by states' letting their welfare-matching appropriations fall behind the Great Inflation of the 1970s. The living standards of the dependent poor fell precipitously.

This development did not assuage the growing popular animus toward the poor, nor did the slide in real incomes of working-class Americans between the mid-1970s and the mid-1990s. A common reaction among pundits and public alike was to blame government and resist taxes, as in the tax revolt that began with California's Proposition 13 in 1978—all of which contributed to the victory of Reagan's brand of conservatism in 1980. Rancor toward the underclass played a big part in disrupting the old New Deal political coalition and splitting off much of the white male working-class electorate from their traditional Democratic allegiance.[17] And underlying this reaction was the fact that the poor and in general beneficiaries of the Great Society were disproportionately black: the New Class Struggle inescapably became a conduit for sublimated racism. Challenged in their sense both of status and of fairness, "Reagan Democrats" took the same path of realignment as the southern conservatives, though for different reasons and with less consistency. Resentment of the poor, encouraged even by President Clinton, bore ultimate fruition in the 1996 welfare law. That measure set absolute cutoffs of aid to the able-bodied, mothers included, without assuming any public responsibility for the provision either of work opportunity or of child care.[18] The New Class Struggle, where conservatism was identified with the working majority and liberalism with the spongers, was the looming danger that made Michael Dukakis shy away from the "L-word" in 1988 in his flailing effort to define himself ideologically.

A measure of academic respectability was conferred on the New Class Struggle by the sociologist Charles Murray in his 1984 book *Losing Ground*.[19] Murray argued that antipoverty programs had only multiplied the poor and worsened their dependency, and ought to be abandoned completely. The *New Republic* called his work an "intellectual mugging of the Great Society."[20] The book's import for Reaganism has been likened to the effect of Michael Harrington's *The Other America* on John Kennedy and the architects of the Great Society.

Average citizens meanwhile lost interest in contesting the power of the corporate economic hierarchy, if they could beat back the perceived encroachments on their own pocketbooks by the undeserving poor, who in the main were the black poor. Thus, sublimated hostility to the Fourth Revolution carried over into defection from the Third Revolution and left the corporate heirs of the Second Revolution virtually unchallenged.

Reaction in Society—The Religious Right

Just as striking as the alienation of the middle and working classes from the Welfare State in the aftermath of the sixties was the political mobilization of religious conservatives. They were enemies not only of the Fourth Revolution but also even of the First, the revolution for freedom of conscience embodied in the American separation of church and state. Leaders of the Religious Right constantly asserted that America was a "Christian nation," and they railed against "humanism" and "secularism" as notions subversive of the social order. The Supreme Court heard them. In a five-to-four decision of 1984 in a Rhode Island case about a Christmas nativity display, Chief Justice Burger found, "Nor does the Constitution require complete separation of church and state. It affirmatively mandates accommodation, not merely tolerance, of all religions."[21]

In the form of evangelical and fundamentalist Protestantism, the Religious Right had deep roots in American culture, going back to Colonial times. Its new political involvement in the latter part of the twentieth century, however, was a direct response to the revolutionary movements of the 1960s and 1970s. Toward the black revolution the Religious Right displayed little overt animosity, thanks in part to the religious associations of the civil rights movement in its earlier stages; Martin Luther King Jr., after all, was a Baptist minister. Toward the youth movement and the counterculture, not surprisingly, there was sweeping condemnation, reflected in the name that the Reverend Jerry Falwell gave his "Moral Majority." But it was the women's movement and the issues associated with it—abortion, the ERA, and homosexual rights, all coming to the forefront of national debate in the 1970s—that most exercised religious conservatives.

The political alignment of the Religious Right with the conservative wing of the Republican Party was slow to be cemented. During the 1970s the movement was uncertain where to turn politically. Some of its adherents disliked Nixon for his gestures of social liberalism and had little taste for Gerald Ford, not to mention his vice presidential designee Nelson Rockefeller. Jimmy Carter with his Southern Baptist credentials looked attractive, and the televangelist Pat Robertson actually backed him for president in 1976.[22] But Carter's support for the ERA and gay and lesbian rights, lukewarm as it was, turned his religious following off. Said the Reverend Tim La Haye, a leader in the Moral Majority, "We had a man in the White House who professed to be a Christian, but didn't understand how un-Christian his administration was."[23] La Haye went on to coauthor the immensely popular "Left Behind" series of Judgment Day novels.[24]

Eventually Falwell's Moral Majority was upstaged as the main vehicle of religious political mobilization by Robertson's "Christian Coalition." Like Falwell a Virginia Baptist minister, Robertson rose to prominence as head of the Christian Broadcasting Network, exploiting the medium of TV to draw in millions of followers. He was more sophisticated and more political than Falwell, and at the same time he was harder edged, inclined to satanic conspiracy theories.[25] In 1988 Robertson made bold to put himself forward as an aspirant to the Republican presidential nomination, challenging Vice President Bush. Failing in that venture, in 1989 he set up the Christian Coalition, with the young historian Ralph Reed as executive director, and through that organization he continued to pursue his antirevolutionary agenda.

In the course of the Reagan Revolution, aroused by the cultural excesses of the youth revolt, inflamed by the gender revolution, and fed by sublimated racism, the Religious Right made common cause with the rising Republican right wing. This alliance, strong in the South as well as the intermountain West, coincided with the southern political realignment in the same direction. Actively or tacitly fighting the Fourth Revolution and all its works, the combined and overlapping forces of southern and religious conservatism secured a stranglehold on the Republican Party machinery. This proved decisive in keeping an avowedly counterrevolutionary Republican leadership in power in Washington for years and restoring it after the Clinton interlude.

New Coalitions

For all their fervor about social and cultural principles, neither the Fourth Revolution nor its enemies have represented a serious threat to the established political and economic power structure in the United States. From the standpoint of the powers that be, the Fourth Revolution has been a tolerable diversion, while anti–Fourth Revolution reaction has led millions of Americans to the uncritical defense of the status quo. In their joint support of Reagan, business and the Religious Right entered into an unholy alliance, overcoming the logical antithesis between the values of God and those of Mammon. Cultural conservatives went out of their way to embrace the causes of tax cutting and deregulation. At the same time, the corporate power structure willingly absorbed much of the force of the Fourth Revolution by accommodating itself to affirmative action and promotion for women and members of racial minorities. Its ire was more often reserved for environmental protesters (of all this, more later).

Even the youth revolution and the counterculture proved to be no long-term threat to the Establishment, as former hippies and antiwar protesters matured psychologically and succeeded economically. The absorption of these elements into the national mainstream and their impact on cultural convention was described by David Brooks in his book *Bobos in Paradise*. "Bobos"—"bourgeois bohemians"—are aging devotees of the Fourth Revolution, especially on the cultural side, whom prosperity has weaned away from any spirit of economic radicalism. "If you investigated people's attitudes toward sex, morality, leisure time, and work, it was getting harder and harder to separate the anti-establishment renegade from the pro-establishment, company man. Most people, at least among the college-educated set, seemed to have rebel attitudes and social-climbing attitudes all scrambled together. ... People seemed to have combined the counter-cultural sixties and the achieving eighties into one social ethic."[26] Thus, the bobos embody a new libertarian synthesis of the Fourth Revolution and its cultural freedom with the Second Revolution and its premium on the pursuit of individual affluence. The corporate power structure has had no difficulty accepting this new mentality, even while the culture wars have been raging in academia and the law. And the Third Revolution with its principles of economic equity and social responsibility has again been the loser.

CHAPTER 9

Deepening of the Revolution

Neither the on-again–off-again mood of reaction in government nor the conservative climate in most of American society during the 1970s and 1980s could put a total stop to the unfolding of the Fourth Revolution during those years. In a variety of areas, efforts to advance the cause of social equality continued to score successes by appealing to the courts and to the principles of equal treatment that had been written, by this time, into the playbook of any organization, be it commercial employment or an educational institution receiving federal funds. This applied not only to the black civil rights effort and to feminism but also to a wide range of new movements for equal treatment that are detailed in the following chapter.

Overcoming Reaction

While reaction in government and in society held center stage in American public awareness throughout the seventies and eighties, the main revolutionary forces generated by the sixties—blacks, politicized women, and the counterculture—continued to press ahead undeterred. As is often the case with revolutions, including eighteenth-century America, the principles of the Fourth Revolution were really implemented and consolidated only after the revolution in its more active sense had passed. In the broad reaches of American life, the greatest changes initiated by the sixties upheaval took hold only gradually, but they did take hold, leaving a nation transformed beyond any possibility for counterrevolutionaries to turn all the way back to the old regime. Testifying most visibly to the grip of the revolution was a literal transformation in the faces of the mass media and of higher education, with the appearance of blacks and women where up to the 1970s they had been conspicuous by their absence.

Resistance to the progress of the revolution was selective. There was less of it, overtly, to the black civil rights movement; more, to aspects of the gender revolution, specifically abortion and homosexual rights. But running beneath these controversies was the pervasive extension of the youth revolution's cultural defiance into all levels of society and all aspects of everyday life, from entertainment and dress to educational standards and work habits. Illustrating this point, Professor Ralph Whitehead spoke of a revolt against "industrial discipline" on the part of the "new collar class" of culturally radicalized young workers.[1] Observes the British social historian Arthur Marwick, "The various counter-cultural movements and subcultures ... did not *confront* mainstream society but *permeated* and *transformed* it."[2] Since the 1970s the Fourth Revolution has defined every sort of national issue, whether governmental, legal, or purely private. Ultimately, the quantitative deepening of the revolution added up to a fundamental qualitative change in national life.

The cumulative postrevolutionary success of the Fourth Revolution's constituent elements accords with the historical model of the revolutionary process, calling as it does for a moderate revolutionary revival after a period of conservative reaction. It is hard to pinpoint such a phase in the course of the Fourth Revolution, but it had certainly set in by the 1990s in some sectors of society. If Michael Dukakis had won the presidency in 1988, that event would have clearly marked the next turning point in American political life.

Outside of government, starting in the later 1980s and early 1990s, there was a gradual but perceptible invigoration of the revolutionary spirit, expressed in new militancy among blacks, feminists, and cultural radicals, as well as the newer beneficiaries of the Fourth Revolution. A milestone in this revival was a "Mid-West Radical Scholars and Activists Conference" in Chicago in October 1990 that burgeoned into a conclave of more than one thousand nostalgic revolutionaries.[3] But there was no violence or disorder in this new movement—it was, after all, a *moderate* revolutionary revival. Direct action in this era was rather the province of counterrevolutionary diehards who felt their position eroding.

Three areas of contention stand out where the forces of the Fourth Revolution tightened their hold. These controversies correspond roughly with the movements of women, blacks, and the counterculture, though there were overlaps. Sharpest was the ongoing struggle over abortion rights, obviously specific to women. Broadest in terms of the groups it affected was the issue of affirmative action, emphasizing the status of blacks but extending to other minorities as well as to women. Third was the spread of Fourth Revolution–style thinking in education and cultural life, generating the so-called culture wars between liberal and conservative ideologists. In every case, the outcome was one-sided. However much conservatives may have resisted, in none of these areas was the advance of the revolution seriously checked.

The Women's Movement and Abortion

Unlike the black civil rights movement, which hit a plateau after the turmoil of 1968 and Nixon's electoral victory, or the youth protest movement, which lost its drive as the Vietnam War wound down, the women's movement continued to battle for its basic goals. And battle it had to, against rising resistance and newly mobilized conservative—that is, counterrevolutionary—forces. Its successes were checkered: an epochal breakthrough in reproductive rights, a discouraging failure to secure the Equal Rights Amendment (ERA), and an uneven record in advancing equality in employment and in family relations.

While the Nixon administration leaned toward counterrevolution in its attitude toward black and youth extremism, it was relatively congenial toward the women, despite stiffening resistance to the gender revolution outside of government. One of the new administration's first acts was to form a President's Task Force on Women's Rights and Responsibilities, chaired by Virginia Allan of the National Federation of Business and Professional Women's Clubs. The task force reported in December 1969 to recommend the creation of a permanent office of Women's Rights and Responsibilities and to endorse the ERA, which the administration helped to get through Congress in 1971–72 with an overwhelming margin.[4] Gerald Ford sustained the sunny mood. He responded to the United Nations' proclamation of 1975 as International Women's Year, by establishing a National Commission on the Observance of the International Women's Year, under Jill Ruckleshaus, wife of Environmental Protection Agency (EPA) head (and former assistant attorney general for civil rights) William Ruckleshaus.

Jimmy Carter initially kept up the momentum, appointing Bella Abzug to chair the International Women's Year commission. The commission in turn endorsed the ERA, though by this time the measure was dead in the water, and it organized (with federal funding) what was supposed to be a landmark National Women's Conference in Houston in November 1977. At the conference, the popular black congresswoman Barbara Jordan gave the keynote address, and the body adopted a "national plan of action" embracing the whole range of feminist issues, from the ERA and abortion rights to equal treatment of lesbians.[5] There was a futile protest by the small minority of conservative delegates, while outside the conference locale a much more vociferous "national profamily rally" denounced all the evil works of the feminist movement.[6] Faced with such signs of popular reaction, President Carter reversed course. He broke with Abzug, ousted her as cochair of the National Advisory Commission on Women, and allowed that group to fall away from her economic agenda to the purely legal arena.[7] The gender revolution, like other components of the Fourth Revolution, was thrown into retreat. Feminist success had provoked greater conservative resistance, as Winnifred Wandersee explained: "If there was an awakening feminist consciousness in the 1970s, it was countered by an awakening conservative consciousness, and the feminist reformers were providing the focus for a conservative mobilization."[8]

The Supreme Court's abortion decision of 1973 stirred religious and social conservatives into a degree of political activism that they had never before manifested. "The *Roe* decision set off some of the most strident and sustained criticism that the American judiciary has ever experienced,"[9] said Deborah Rohde. The National Right-to-Life Committee, already formed in 1970 on the initiative of the Catholic Church to fight liberalization of state abortion laws, became the legal focus of antiabortion efforts.[10] Meanwhile, once legality had been achieved, the controversy was exacerbated by pressure from the most ardent reformers to include abortion under Medicaid's pregnancy coverage for free public funding for low-income women. Congress reacted in 1976 with the so-called Hyde Amendment, banning such federal support except in cases of rape, incest, or danger to the woman's life—exceptions that confirm the essentially punitive character of antiabortion thinking. Nevertheless, such monetary restrictions on access to abortion were upheld by the Supreme Court in decisions of 1977, on which President Jimmy Carter commented only, "There are many things in life that are not fair."[11] So in practice, efforts to curb legal abortion became another part of the American nation's class war against the poor and, by sublimation, against emancipated but impoverished black women.

By the 1980s the conservatives' capture of the presidency with Ronald Reagan, coupled with the mood in Congress and most state legislatures and the cumulative effect of Republican Supreme Court appointments, turned all levels of government against abortion rights. Even so, it was not easy to move the clock back. Besides, as the political scientists Karen O'Connor and Lee Epstein noted, Reagan's opposition to abortion was "largely symbolic."[12] Later on, in 1989, the Supreme Court, now headed by Rehnquist, took a big step back in the case of *Webster v. Health Reproductive*

Services, where it voted 5 to 4 to uphold a Missouri statute barring public employees and even public buildings (i.e., hospitals) from any role in abortions.[13] The National Right-to-Life Committee exulted, "*Roe* is dead. ... *Roe* and its progeny are de facto overruled."[14] Joan Hoff lamented that the decision "eviscerated *Roe v. Wade*" and "set a new precedent in the history of second-class citizenship for one-half of the American population."[15] While the rhetoric on both sides may have been a bit overblown, it seems fair to say that by the end of the 1980s, at least with respect to women's rights, the federal judiciary had been turned from the spearhead of social revolution into its opposite.

In its outrage over abortion rights the counterrevolution turned to a variety of responses. These ranged in tactical extremism from demands for a constitutional amendment to overturn *Roe v. Wade,* to bans on abortion counseling by agencies receiving federal funds, and even to outright terrorism against abortion clinics and providers. The Reagan administration threw its weight—though unsuccessfully—behind the constitutional amendment approach. In 1984 it went so far as to institute a ban (still in effect) on American aid to any organizations abroad, including population-control programs, if they countenanced abortion.

Abortion, the great breakthrough issue for women in the early 1970s, has remained thenceforth more than any other domestic question the focal point of controversy between liberals and conservatives. It intensified the sharpening polarization of American politics that followed the realignment of southern conservatives to the Republicans and northeastern liberals to the Democrats. Politicians, judges, and executive appointees all had to subject themselves to the abortion test. Ever since, the prolife–prochoice division has been the defining fault line in American politics.

Affirmative Action

In the realm of public policy, postrevolution, the issue with the widest import for all the social movements aligned with the Fourth Revolution was affirmative action. Primarily linked with the hitherto most oppressed minority, the blacks, affirmative action by its logic quickly extended to all other groups—the protected classes, so-called—who had experienced discrimination and the indignities of traditional social inequality. It applied especially to the largest disadvantaged category of all, namely, women. With little resistance, affirmative action rolled ahead during the 1970s and the decades that followed, gathering strength both in the extent of its application and in the meaning that was ascribed to it. President Nixon got behind it, in the view of Professor John Skrentny, "as a preemptive strike at the liberal agenda."[16] Its primary focus has always been the terms of participation in the economy, but its principles have readily been extended to everything from club membership to college athletics. In many respects affirmative action was the signature achievement of the Fourth Revolution.

In the course of its extension over the last third of the twentieth century, the concept of affirmative action saw its meaning change substantially. Originating as an effort to give practical effect to the ideal of equal opportunity, affirmative action turned progressively into a campaign for equal outcomes in a competitive, achievement-oriented society. At the extreme, it became a euphemism for a thinly disguised quota system to benefit racial categories, women, and any other group who could claim special privilege on the basis of a prior history of discrimination.

Affirmative action in its initial, narrower sense was an integral part of Johnson's Great Society program. Before that, affirmative action can be traced all the way back to the New Deal and World War II, notably to Roosevelt's Fair Employment Practices Commission and to the wartime opening of opportunities for blacks and women in industry and the armed services. Firmer roots were implanted during the Kennedy and Johnson administrations, with their early steps to overcome racial and gender discrimination in employment. Affirmative action was basic to the logic of the Equal Employment Act of 1965, envisaging a good-faith effort by employers to seek out and encourage minority and female applicants for their job openings. The term originated in Kennedy's executive order of March 1961 creating the President's Commission on Equal Employment Opportunity, into which a legal aide, the black Texan Hobart Taylor Jr., had inserted those memorable words.[17] Vice President Johnson, taking the chair of this new body, endorsed the "affirmative duty" of government contractors to hire members of minorities and to treat them equally.[18] The implications of these gestures, however, were not clearly spelled out for another decade, until some far-reaching executive and judicial steps were taken under the "putatively conservative" Nixon administration (as Hugh Graham characterized it).[19]

Critics of affirmative action were quick to spring into action even before the program was fairly underway. As early as 1971 Nathan Glazer published his thesis of "affirmative discrimination," holding that civil rights enforcement had shifted "from *equal opportunity* ... to an attempt to ensure a full equality of achievement for minority groups."[20] Even earlier, Moynihan warned openly against "ethnic quotas" and their threat to Jewish achievement in education and other public institutions.[21]

These caveats notwithstanding, both the Nixon administration and the courts pushed ahead with affirmative action in its broader sense. In 1970–71 the administration endorsed the so-called Philadelphia Plan to set proportionality targets for minority hiring in the construction trades, with minorities enumerated as "Negro, Oriental, American Indian, and Spanish Surnamed Americans."[22] This step was quickly followed by the Supreme Court's decision in the case of *Griggs v. Duke Power,* where it held that the use of tests for prospective employees was illegal if it resulted in a "disparate impact" on the status of minorities, even if there was no demonstrated intent to discriminate. Chief Justice Burger further injected the doctrine of "compensation" to undo "the status quo of prior discriminatory employment practices," all of which implied "a model of proportional representation in the workplace."[23] To the conservatives Paul Craig Roberts and Lawrence Stratton, the *Griggs* decision amounted to "a new law defining discrimination as unintended status disparities between racial groups."[24] To the usually restrained Hugh Graham, "The historical logic of the Warren Court had achieved a snowballing momentum that swept the reluctant Chief Justice Burger before it."[25]

Thanks to these decisions of the 1970s, affirmative action became the guiding principle in American policy toward disadvantaged groups. "Resistance to Affirmative Action," wrote Skrentny, "was almost nonexistent. ... Anyone who questioned the Civil Rights tradition risked their own legitimacy."[26] Neither political reaction nor the conservative revamping of the judiciary in the era of Reagan and Bush Sr. sufficed to reverse the national commitment to affirmative action even in its broad, quota-setting sense. In the Civil Rights Act of 1991, Skrentny continued "The premise of Affirmative Action as appropriate in cases of minority group underrepresentation was accepted."[27] Affirmative action stood firm despite a groundswell of criticism, not just from conservatives, that it was running contrary to the American tradition of equal individual rights before the law, while spokespeople for its intended beneficiaries continued to complain that its application did not go far enough.

Affirmative Integration

Parallel with affirmative action in employment opportunity, the classic civil rights aim of racial integration underwent a transformation in the 1970s in a broader framework. Going beyond the original goal of removing barriers of legal segregation, integration was broadened to almost ensure the proportionate inclusion of racial minorities in all aspects of American social life. At the same time, in the face of this advance, a countercurrent of self-segregation set in among some of the beneficiaries of mainstream inclusion, notably in academic life.

Most contentious of all areas in positive integration, like the earliest efforts at desegregation, was the national public school system. Paradoxically, actual school desegregation was initially achieved most fully in the rural South, while a "return to passivity" on the part of the judiciary left desegregation incomplete in the North and in southern cities.[28] There, the greater size of urban school districts allowed residential segregation by neighborhoods to express itself in widely different racial proportions among individual schools. Cries went up among minority advocates for steps to promote "racial balance" among the schools in a given district, on the theory, first expressed in the 1954 Supreme Court desegregation decision, that pupils from minority groups would learn better if they were mixed in with white pupils. The answer, imposed by court rulings, was to bus pupils to schools outside their neighborhoods.

In practice, busing mostly meant transporting black children to predominantly white schools. It was met with vociferous opposition, both legal and spontaneous. Violent protests were common, especially in white working-class neighborhoods like Irish South Boston. Everywhere, busing prompted "white flight," as families who could afford it relocated to the suburbs (which were usually immune to busing from the central-city jurisdiction) or transferred their children to private (mainly parochial) schools and agitated for state vouchers to help pay the tuition. As a result, the proportion of white children in inner-city public schools dropped precipitously.[29] Moreover, practices of "second-generation discrimination," as the Georgia political scientist Charles Bullock termed it, reduced white–black contact even within nominally desegregated schools.[30] Experience suggests that when the proportion of minority or otherwise culturally deprived pupils much exceeds their proportion in the general population (12 percent in the case of blacks), the uplifting effect of the white environment will be nullified. Thus, white flight and the resulting demographic revolution in inner-city schools undercut the whole rationale for busing to put minority pupils in a better white environment.

Housing was another area where the federal authorities tried to attack de facto segregation after the civil rights legislation of the sixties had ruled out legal discrimination. In its public housing measures of the early 1970s, Congress tried to require racial balance in filling new housing projects, as well as to fight discrimination by private landlords, mortgage lenders, and insurance companies (including the so-called practice of red-lining dubious districts on a city map). The result, as often as not, resembled the public school situation—whites avoided or left the projects and areas subject to affirmative integration, and the proportion of minorities in such places often rose far above the balance that might yield positive social results. All too often the policies of affirmative integration ended by intensifying residential segregation of the races rather than easing it.

In higher education and in the mass media, affirmative integration was ultimately much more successful. During the 1970s, under pressure both from the federal government, through its criteria for research grants and student support, and from minority advocates, universities instituted preferential admission policies for members of protected minorities to promote racial balance among their student bodies and graduates. A limit to this practice was reached, however, in the Supreme Court's celebrated *Bakke* decision of 1978.[31] In this case, the court ruled against an absolute quota for minority group admissions to the University of California Medical School, though it still allowed universities to take race into account in the interest of social diversity in their student bodies. Even the most liberal members of the Burger Court, as Professor Lawrence Fuchs understood them, "never wavered in maintaining that group-conscious measures based on race, ethnicity, or gender should be considered temporary remedies to protect the individual rights of individuals who were members of the designated beneficiary groups."[32] There remained a longer-term way around this stricture: affirmative action in admitting students from poverty backgrounds—which disproportionately meant racial minorities.[33]

The mass media and the advertising industry followed education in the promotion of racial representation. By the 1990s this sector of society was leaning over backward to accentuate minority participation, often well beyond what any proportional quota system might require. Yet such gains only whetted the appetite, notably stimulating demands for "reparations"—in other words, payments to today's blacks to make amends for white exploitation of black slaves in times past.[34]

Multiculturalism and the Culture Wars

Where the Fourth Revolution went deepest, arguably, was in the cultural realm. Here, peaking in the late 1980s and early 1990s, were the most vocal mainfestations of the return of revolutionary thinking, exemplifyung the moderate revolutionary revival seen at the end of any revolutionary cycle. Ultimately the cultural revolution energized by the youth revolt of the sixties, seemingly the least successful component of the Fourth Revolution, came back triumphantly.

Multiculturalism was the signature ideal of the end-of-century revolutionary revival.[35] It may be defined as the proposition that American society is made up of a number of distinct cultural entities, each of which is entitled to equal recognition and respect in all sectors of life. "Multiculturalism," according to three students of the phenomenon, "tends to focus on the welfare of peoples or cultural groupings, which are seen as the source of the socially constructed identities of individuals."[36] In practice, multiculturalism corresponds exactly to the diverse racial identities in America—one culture equals one color.

The activist reading of multiculturalism is encapsulated in the slogan "cultural diversity," or "cultural pluralism" as it is sometimes rendered. This is really a value statement, implying that the uniqueness of various cultures—that is, the distinctive virtues of each racial group—should not only be recognized but actually be promoted by all the institutions of social life, from government on down. By contrast, cultural differences among populations of a similar racial character are largely excluded from multicultural consideration. Given the racial understanding of culture, *cultural diversity* becomes a euphemism for racial quotas everywhere in society, even though the actual word *quota,* with its disturbing echoes of an era of anti-Semitism, has been assiduously avoided in favor of *preferences* or *targets* or whatever.

Initially, the philosophy of multiculturalism was driven by the ongoing momentum of the black revolution—a case of unintended consequences, so to speak. Nathan Glazer called the blacks "the storm troops in the battles over multiculturalism."[37] Bit by bit, the understanding of multiculturalism was extended to embrace all the racially defined minorities in American society, as they were specified in various official enactments, extending to American Indians, Hispanics (in their case, construed as a cultural group transcending race), Asians, Alaskan Natives, and Pacific Islanders. With this expansion in its meaning, multiculturalism moved beyond deepening the original components of the Fourth Revolution and toward extending them to new classes of people—a topic for the next chapter.[38]

Multiculturalism first gathered momentum in the public school system, in the course of the 1970s. It caught on quickly in teacher-training institutions. As early as 1972 the American Association of Colleges for Teacher Education set up a commission on multicultural education and adopted its recommendations to push the concept.[39] Congress chimed in at the same time with earmarked funds for "ethnic heritage studies" programs.[40]

By the early 1980s the multicultural movement hit higher education, where it has been pursued by various means, sometimes reminiscent of the totalitarian heirs of the more radical instances of the Third Revolution. Students of whatever color are often required to take courses on ethnic (i.e., racial) diversity intended to inculcate the ideology of the new revolution, including collective hereditary guilt on the part of the heretofore dominant group, white males. (The courses, incidentally, appear to be disliked as much by American students as their Marxist–Leninist counterparts were in the old Soviet Union.) College political commissars may be appointed under such titles as "coordinator of multicultural affairs" to see to the observance of Fourth Revolution rectitude in the general curriculum and especially in the humanities. Woe betide the professor himself (it is naturally "him") who incurs charges of racism or sexism in the conduct of his courses. Student behavior may be monitored to investigate and root out manifestations of alleged racism or sexism, even in casual conversation, and formal debate of the propositions of the Fourth Revolution is practically excluded. Black studies and women's studies have proliferated. (These curricula were originally conceived on the multidisciplinary model of foreign area studies, but in time they have usually been elevated to the status of separate university departments, where study is hard to distinguish from advocacy.) Special centers for minority students have become commonplace. Thus, the sixties ideal of racial integration has given way to an ideal of racial distinctiveness and a new, voluntary *apartheid* (however little students may observe it in practice).

Multicultural needs in the educational system and in the media have encouraged a profound rewriting of American history.[41] The same de facto standards of group recognition and respect demanded by the Fourth Revolution in contemporary policy have been extended back to the recasting of the nation's past, to bring out the "contributions" of each racial group and to highlight the achievements of individual blacks and members of other minorities as well as of women. However, because the political and cultural life of the past was largely the realm of white males, the diversity movement requires a diminution of the traditional historical emphasis on these realms in favor of the social life of ordinary people. History in the old sense has been supplanted more and more by a form of sociology turned toward the past.

In this new orientation, the American melting-pot ideal has been denigrated as empirically inaccurate when applied to racial categories in distinction to European-derived ethnic groups. It is even rejected as a desirable objective, because it implies the superiority of the white European pot in which other elements were supposed to submerge their identities. And other elements have been quick to assert their separateness.

CHAPTER 10

Extensions of the Revolution

As the main contingents of the Fourth Revolution consolidated their impact on American society during the final decades of the twentieth century, other movements followed in the paths that they had opened up. Violence and resistance varied from case to case, but the widening of the revolution usually went more easily than the initial struggles of the 1960s. After the black revolution came a series of ethnic efforts, most of them facilitated readily by the Establishment, in the name of cultural diversity, so that they hardly had time to crystallize as movements. The sequel to the gender revolution was a different story, as conservatives closed ranks to resist the movement for homosexual rights as stiffly as they did to fight abortion and other perceived cultural threats to the nuclear family. Finally, a variety of other challenges to invidious group distinctions prevailed with ease, from rights for the handicapped to deinstitutionalization of the mentally ill. By century's end, so thoroughgoing was the revolution that no claim for equal rights and equitable treatment could be denied.

The American Indian Movement

Even more than the blacks, though in very different ways, the native peoples of the United States had historically been victimized, suffering incessant violence to the point of partial extermination. By the beginning of the twentieth century, Indian resistance to white settlement had been stamped out, and the Indian population remained relatively quiescent until the black revolution shook up their fatalism along with the self-assurance of the white majority. A minimum of Indian protest then sufficed to wring one concession after another from the powers that were.

Compared with the black movement, potential Indian militancy was limited, obviously, by the much smaller numbers involved (perhaps one and a half million), the lack of a clear Indian racial identity in the case of some mixed-blood and assimilated people, and the divisiveness of traditional tribal loyalties. Like the black movement, the new Indian restiveness was stimulated by the national pot stirring of World War II and of migration to urban centers. The old tribal consciousness was challenged by a new racial consciousness, while another cleavage cut across this one, as the philosophy of assimilation and "termination"—meaning the termination of special government recognition and services to Indian tribes—was challenged by a new nationwide Indian activism. A modern-style lobbying organization, the National Congress of American Indians (NCAI), founded during World War II, opposed both the paternalism of the federal government's Bureau of Indian Affairs and the goal of termination. A more militant organization, the National Indian Youth Congress (NIYC), took shape in 1961 to represent the more educated and urban-based element. This division paralleled and even anticipated the moderate–extremist cleavage among blacks. As early as 1964, talk of "Red Power" emanated from NIYC.[1] They took part in the Poor People's march on Washington in 1964, though worrying about losing their identity. "We do not want to be pushed into the mainstream of American life," said NIYC president Mel Thom.[2] Vine DeLoria, director of the NCAI from 1964 to 1967, tried to be less threatening by defining Red Power as "the power, the political and economic power, to run our own lives in our own way"—in other words, some form of local racial autonomy.[3]

The Great Society did not overlook the Indians and their gross economic and cultural grievances, but its reception among Indians was ambivalent. Help offered by the War on Poverty through the Office of Economic Opportuning (OEO) and the Community Action programs was badly needed, but in the same measure governmental paternalism was resented. In 1966 President Johnson actually appointed an Indian to head the Bureau of Indian Affairs and promised "a new goal for our Indian programs, a goal that ends the old debate about termination of Indian programs and stresses self-determination, a goal that erases old attitudes of paternalism and promotes partnership and self-help."[4] However, such assurances, not matched by equivalent action, did little to curb growing unrest among Indians. The historian Paula Marks noted, "All of this governmental activity to address Indian problems and concerns actually fed activism rather than defused it."[5] Here was another demonstration of Tocqueville's thesis about reform encouraging revolution.

What corresponded to the Storming of the Bastille in the American Indian movement came shortly after Johnson's Great Society gave way to the Nixon administration. This was the occupation in November 1969 of Alcatraz Island, site of the former federal prison in San Francisco Bay, by a couple of hundred young Indian activists excited by black student militancy in California. The impact on Indians all over the country was electrifying. "I experienced ... the excitement of seeing and watching our people put their heads up," said the Chippewa leader Leonard Peltier, on his own path to more violent action.[6] Ultimately liquidated by federal marshals in 1971, the occupation failed in its immediate aim of recognition for an independent Indian center on the island. Nevertheless, as Troy Johnson observed in his history of the occupation, its hope "to awaken the American public to the reality of the plight of the first Americans and to assert the need for Indian self-determination" was attained immediately.[7] President Nixon promised "to break decisively with the past and to create conditions for a new era in which the Indian future is determined by Indian acts and Indian decisions."[8]

Alcatraz, like the original Bastille, was the signal for a rising tide of direct action by Indian militants, a "decade of Red Power activism," in the words of journalist–historian Alvin Josephy.[9] A march on Washington known as "the trail of broken treaties" turned into a forcible takeover of the headquarters of the Bureau of Indian Affairs, with the formulation of "Twenty Points" to reaffirm old treaty relationships with the U.S. government and to fight any move to put Indians under the jurisdiction of the states.[10] The occupiers had to be bought off with immunity from prosecution, while the price they paid in return, in the opinion of Paula Marks, was "a schism between more moderate Indians and the militants" as well as a "tempered non-Indian sympathy for Native American demands."[11]

Meanwhile, an organization among Indians living in Minneapolis for self-defense against the police had blossomed into the American Indian Movement (AIM), "the most radical of all the new Native American organizations," according to the historians James Olson and Raymond Wilson.[12] Led by two city Indians, the Chippewa Dennis Banks and the Sioux Russell Means, AIM was a culprit in the violence that erupted in the march on Washington. Then, early in 1973, they tried to take advantage of a political dispute at the Pine Ridge Sioux Reservation in South Dakota and staged a takeover of the Wounded Knee trading post (bearing the name of the infamous massacre of Sioux in 1890). An armed standoff with federal agents ensued, climaxing in a declaration of Sioux independence by the radicals and the deaths of two Indians by gunfire. Federal negotiators finally defused the confrontation by acknowledging Congress's responsibility to review the long history of treaty violations. To be sure, this episode was a pale reflection of the massive protests and riots brought on by the black civil rights movement and black nationalist agitation, but it became a historic beacon in the cause of Indian self-determination. Boasted Means long afterward, "We lit a fire across Indian country."[13] Banks was a bit more modest: his goal, he said, was "to survive as a cultural species."[14]

Indian militancy continued throughout the 1970s, while activists complained of harassment by the FBI like the tactics the black civil rights movement had experienced.[15] In another fracas at Pine Ridge in 1975, two FBI agents were killed, and Leonard Peltier was imprisoned for the crime. But Congress responded to the tension with further concessions, notably the Indian Self-Determination and Educational Assistance Act of 1975, which enhanced tribal powers, curbed the Bureau of Indian Affairs, and at the same time put an end to any notion of termination. Simultaneously, an American Indian Policy Review Committee was established, as an admission of the failure of past policies and the need of further reform in the direction of tribal sovereignty.

Nonetheless, in 1978 AIM went on to organize another march on Washington. This was the "Longest Walk," all the way from San Francisco, to protest potential congressional backsliding from tribal sovereignty. But the Longest Walk marked the end of direct-action militancy and a shift to litigation and lobbying to pursue Indian aims (everything from land claims and fishing rights to exemption from state gambling laws). Thus did the Indian movement adjust to the lowering climate of retrenchment and counterrevolution that had descended on the country at large.

In the Reagan years assimilation again became the federal government's preference, powerfully supported by the pull of the urbanized and materialistic mainstream of American society. By 1990 the rate of intermarriage for American Indians passed 50 percent.[16] At the same time, with the aid of newly trained Indian lawyers or sympathizers in the bar, Indians continued to pursue land claims and extraterritorial exemption from state laws, with signal success. And Indian cultural purists locked horns with anthropologists and museums over control of presumptive tribal bones and artifacts.[17] The outcome of all this was a form of cultural diversity unanticipated by any party when the Indian movement began.

Hispanics and Other Minorities

The beneficiaries of the Fourth Revolution were not limited to those who made it. Through the hole blasted by the black civil rights movement in the old wall of prejudice and discrimination came all the diverse racial and ethnic groups desiring to claim the rights of equal treatment won by the revolutionaries of the 1960s.

These claims took advantage of the deep change that the revolution had wrought in the way the American nation conceived the relation of individuals to society at large, to define the individual in terms of membership in groups and above all in racial groups. Nathan Glazer traced the origins of this form of "color consciousness" all the way back to the 1964 Civil Rights Act and the Equal Employment Opportunity Commission, which defined the protected classes—not only blacks but Hispanics, Asians, and American Indians as well.[18] The census bureau implemented this concept in 1980, when it introduced questions about membership in these particular groups and added the categories of Alaskan Natives and Pacific Islanders. On the basis of these classifications, racial minorities were accorded not just equal rights but compensatory rights as well, both to assert racial group identity and to participate on a proportionate basis in society at large; thus the doctrines both of cultural diversity and of affirmative action. To its critics, this new paradigm represented the Balkanization of America and the subordination of individual equality to racial quotas and privileges.[19]

Ironically, the group who had borne the brunt of the struggle for equal rights—the blacks—found themselves being overshadowed by passive beneficiaries of their effort, by the Asians in achievement and by the Hispanics demographically. Hispanics, of all the protected groups, presented the most complex and often contradictory picture. To begin with, they were the one group not defined precisely by racial origin but were distinguished only by a common linguistic identity or heritage. Unlike blacks, Asians, and European ethnics, who immigrated (voluntarily or involuntarily) into an established white Anglo-Saxon Protestant society, Hispanics were originally brought under the American roof by U.S. conquest of their homelands, in the Mexican War of 1845–48, and, Puerto Ricans, for the in the Spanish-American War of 1898. The analogy is more with the subjugation of American Indians and with the continental expansion of Tsarist Russia in Asia in the nineteenth century. There were usually identifiable racial characteristics to the two main Hispanic groups—part black in the Puerto Rican case, part Indian among Mexicans—but neither saw its identity primarily in racial terms, so linguistic culture was recognized as the common denominator. That opened the door for membership in the protected Hispanic category to any immigrants claiming a Spanish-language background, however disparate their national and cultural antecedents. They included Cubans, Iberians, or any Latin Americans (other than Portuguese-heritage Brazilians, among whom, ironically, there was a greater black element in the population than anywhere else in South America). Thus the Hispanic category actually came to resemble the Soviet concept of a language-based national minority. Richard Rodriguez, an ardently assimilationist journalist, wrote sardonically, " 'Hispanic' is not a racial or a cultural or a geographic or a linguistic or an economic description. 'Hispanic' is a bureaucratic integer—a complete political fiction."[20]

Because of the group's linguistic basis of identity, language use and language discrimination have been a running issue for Hispanics. With Puerto Ricans primarily in mind, a clause in the Voting Rights Act of 1965 barred denying the vote to persons educated in a language other than English. But with the surge in Latino numbers since the 1970s, the issue of education in Spanish, or bilingual education, became a subject of heated contention, especially in the Southwest. On this front the counterrevolution continued to fight the Hispanic cause right up to century's end.

Unlike the blacks and the American Indians, Hispanics developed no broad protest movement in the 1960s, whether violent or nonviolent. They were by and large passive beneficiaries of the Fourth Revolution's philosophy of groupism, while they profited through entry into the mainstream political system. Federal court decisions as early as the 1950s recognized Mexican Americans in Texas as a "distinct class" meriting protection from discrimination in such matters as jury service and school segregation.[21] As might be expected, small radical Latino organizations sprang up in the late sixties and early seventies, "inspired," says the journalist–historian Juan Gonzalez, "by the black power and anti-Vietnam War movement at home and by the anticolonial revolutions in the Third World, especially the Cuban revolution."[22] Cesar Chavez and his United Farm Workers have been compared with Martin Luther King Jr. and the nonviolent civil rights movement, but they were only regional and focused only on a small sector of economic life.[23] At the radical end of the spectrum, the Young Lords gang of Hispanic youth in Los Angeles, turning political, briefly linked up with the Black Panthers.[24]

What the late sixties and early seventies did bequeath to the Hispanic population in America was, in the words of Geoffrey Fox, a writer on Latin-American affairs, a "paradigm shift" toward a sense of national identity expressed as "La Raza," embracing all the diverse ethnic elements of Spanish-language heritage.[25] By the 1980s, Fox observed, there was a further shift "from outlaw to routine politics." At last, "Latinos had found their way into the system."[26] In the 1990s, thanks simply to their burgeoning numbers, Hispanics won a major role in the mainstream political process: Democratic for most Mexican Americans and Puerto Ricans, Republican for Cuban Americans. Hispanic intellectuals debated the propriety of claiming the preferences of a protected group, including affirmative action, but the group as a whole continued to enjoy them. One outside critic bemoaned the demand "to grant every Latino, whether disadvantaged or affluent, special educational, economic, and political privileges that are denied to disadvantaged whites solely on the basis of their race."[27]

Other racial groups exhibited even less activism than the Hispanics, but fell heir equally to the preferences created by the federal government in the spirit of the Fourth Revolution. Here lay more irony, for certain Asian immigrants and their descendants, specifically Japanese and Chinese, having overcome nineteenth and early-twentieth-century discrimination, proved so successful in political, economic, and educational integration that their statistical indicators of achievement in all these realms have actually outshone the averages of the white population. The Fourth Revolution was most successful where it least needed to be fought for.

Immigration

As both the Hispanic and Asian cases show the greatest impact of the Fourth Revolution on the U.S. population, in terms of its numbers and ethnic mix, came from immigration, and specifically from changes in the law on immigration introduced under the revolution's influence. This was a direct outcome of the new philosophy of groupism and racial equality as applied to immigration policy. Immigration reform was one of President Kennedy's initiatives after taking office in 1961, as he called on Congress to scrap the national origin preferences embodied in the statutes of the 1920s. In the spirit of the sixties, Congress overcame southern and nativist opposition and passed the Hart–Celler Act of 1965 to eliminate national quotas and the virtual bar against Asians, though broad limits were retained—100,000 yearly for the Western Hemisphere and 170,000 for the Eastern, and a top of 20,000 for any one country (regardless of its population, illogically). "It is not coincidental," wrote one authority, "that the 1965 Immigration Act was enacted in the wake of the country's civil rights movement."[28]

Ironically, the Immigration Act and its 1976 modifications set limits on Mexican immigration for the first time, just as the pressure to enter the United States was rising and creating the huge problem of illegal residents. The 1965 act also introduced preferences for certain skilled workers and for relatives of U.S. residents, whose numbers could override the overall numerical limits. "In 1965," reported the National Research Council, "few policy makers foresaw that this provision would increase immigration, particularly from developing countries," thanks to what the environmentalist Mark Nowak called "chain migration."[29] The surge in arrivals from Asia and Latin America that followed was truly a "Second Great Migration."

Nevertheless, in the late seventies Congress eased numerical limits on immigration, and the annual influx doubled, from three hundred thousand a year in 1965 to more than six hundred thousand in 1990. The law of 1990 further expanded the eligibility of relatives of residents, instituted a special category for college-trained workers, and introduced a lottery system for others, all in all allowing legal immigration to approach one million a year by the late 1990s. A Commission on Immigration Reform chaired by former congresswoman Barbara Jordan proposed rolling the limit back to half a million a year, but implementation of the commission's report failed in Congress. In fact, talk of immigration curbs galvanized the broadest Latino political protest movement to date, in the form of a march on Washington in the fall of 1996. Whatever their reservations about the social and economic impact of immigration, it seemed that few political leaders were willing to incur the charge of racism for opposing looser rules. "Legislators' fears of being labeled 'nativist,' 'anti-immigrant,' 'anti-family,' or worse, have made honest debate impossible," said Mark Nowak. "Any proposal to reduce immigration is considered taboo."[30]

The cumulative effect of the broadened post-1965 immigration policy was dramatic.[31] According to the 2000 census, foreign-born residents of the United States (not counting illegals) had reached nearly 10 percent of the total population, the highest proportion since the 1920s. During the nineties, Hispanics, mainly of Mexican origin, increased by 58 percent to become 12.5 percent of the total population and by a whisker to exceed the number of blacks. Asians increased by 46 percent, reaching 3.5 percent of the total, while Native Americans, though they increased by a quarter (mainly by reidentifying themselves), remained less than 1 percent of the whole. Economically, most studies indicate that the new wave of immigration, preponderantly unskilled and poorly educated, had a depressing effect on the low end of the wage scale, which means blacks above all.[32] Demographic momentum now guaranteed the future of racial diversity in America, but with growing black–Hispanic competition, this was not the same kind of diversity that the early proponents of this ideal had envisaged.

Homosexual Rights

Just as the black civil rights movement prepared the ground for efforts at equality on the part of all racial minorities in America, so the gender revolution and the sexual revolution in particular opened the way for homosexuals. Historian Jeffrey Escoffier summed it up: "The gay liberation movement emerged in the wake of the women's movement."[33]

The task in the case of gay rights was particularly difficult, given on one hand the traditional animus in American and most other cultures toward overt homosexual behavior and on the other hand the ease for the homosexual minority to take refuge in invisibility, "in the closet." Campaigns by McCarthyite superpatriots of the 1950s were notorious for equating homosexuals and security risks, despite the closet homosexual inclinations that have recently been inferred among some of Senator McCarthy's own entourage.[34] Only after the revolts of blacks and females against their subordinate status, the challenge to public taboos posed by the sexual revolution, and the discovery of the judicial route to claiming equality was it even conceivable for homosexuals to brave the obloquy and discrimination attendant on "coming out" and to campaign for their place in the new revolutionary social order.

The homosexual rights movement paralleled the women's movement both in its challenge to deep-rooted cultural standards and in the difficulty of mobilizing its potential constituents for action to advance its aims. Even more than the women's movement, it met with dogged and prolonged resistance based on the counterrevolutionary force of religious fundamentalism. As bitter controversy over legalizing the unions of gay and lesbian couples testified, the homosexual revolution was far from secure even at the turn of the century.

Several recent histories have brought out the early stirrings of homosexual-rights organizing in the 1950s and early 1960s, as well as the influence of such diverse literary figures as James Baldwin and Michel Foucault.[35] While the New Left was generally as icy toward the homosexual movement as it was toward feminism, numerous future exponents of gay rights got their training in activism while still in the closet, so to speak, as participants in the civil rights movement and the antiwar movement. This background illustrates how the main stem of the Fourth Revolution spawned various offshoots. In addition, the counterculture in San Francisco and a few other spots served as a friendly incubating milieu. In a diatribe against straight culture that he called "A Gay Manifesto," the advocate Carl Wittman wrote, "San Francisco is a refugee camp for homosexuals. ... We are refugees from Amerika."[36]

By all accounts, homosexual rights became a real political movement only from the moment in June 1969 when the New York City police raided a gay bar, the Stonewall Inn, in Greenwich Village. "Stonewall," wrote the historian Martin Duberman, "is *the* emblematic event in modern lesbian and gay history."[37] While the counterculture and the black and student movements had provided a vehicle for activist participation, this was the first occasion when gay victims fought back directly, in a classic riot. "For the first time," asserted two other chroniclers of the movement, "the usual acquiescence turned into violent resistance. ... From that night the lives of gay men and lesbians, and the attitude toward them of the larger culture ... began to change rapidly."[38] The journalist Charles Kaiser compared the effect of Stonewall to the impact of the Six Day War of 1967 for Jews everywhere: "For the first time, thousands of members of each tribe finally thought of themselves as warriors."[39] In a word, Stonewall was the Bastille of the homosexual revolution in America.

Once inhibitions against openly resisting persecution had been broken, homosexual politics both intensified and fragmented in the manner of all revolutions. The moderates, in Jeffrey Escoffier's formulation, were "assimilationist," while the extremists rallied around the "cultural minority thesis."[40] Lumping the latter with radical women, another author wrote, "Feminists and gay liberationists often thought of themselves as revolutionaries rejecting a fundamentally unequal and corrupt power establishment in favor of participatory democracy."[41] For the radicals, in the name of "liberation for gay people," Carl Wittman demanded not only lifestyle freedom but also political autonomy in the manner of black nationalism: "To be a free territory, we must govern ourselves, set up our own institutions, defend ourselves."[42] For any homosexual, the very act of publicly identifying with the movement was a personally revolutionary step.

Stonewall immediately led to the formation of a Gay Liberation Front, espousing a radical doctrine of anarchistic pan-sexuality and expressing solidarity with the most extreme elements of the Fourth Revolution, notably the Black Panthers. Huey Newton wrote in 1970, "The Women's Liberation Front and Gay Liberation Front are our friends, they are potential allies"—which did not prevent gays from being barred by the Black Panthers' Philadelphia convention shortly afterward.[43] Not surprisingly, the Gay Liberation Front soon split, as a more moderate Gay Activists Alliance broke away to concentrate on the homosexual agenda alone and to sponsor the first Gay Pride Week in New York on the anniversary of Stonewall.

The cleavage between the two gay organizations paralleled the division among feminists over whether justice for the group could be pursued without revolutionizing society as a whole. Gay Liberation adherents, rooted in the fading counterculture, soon splintered politically and disappeared as a movement.[44] In 1973, finding themselves still harassed by the radicals, the leadership of the Gay Activists Alliance dissolved the organization and formed the National Gay Task Force, with an assimilationist agenda aiming to uphold the rights of homosexuals to participate as equals in the social mainstream.[45]

The feminist movement, of course, split sharply over the issue of homosexuality. Betty Friedan exemplified the fear that animosities stirred up by the lesbian question could endanger the progress of women overall.

Meanwhile, like every other facet of the Fourth Revolution, homosexual rights activity attracted the indiscriminate though ineffective attention of the FBI.

By the mid-1970s, militant homosexual extremism had largely yielded to tactics of political pressure in the spirit of the civil rights movement, aiming to achieve equal treatment before the law. Successes in the legal area, if not in the minds of the public at large, came quickly: as early as 1971, individual states began to repeal their sodomy statutes, and the federal courts held against the firing of government employees solely on grounds of homosexuality. From that time on, the movement pursued a long, slow effort to get sexual orientation into nondiscrimination laws generally. The Democrats first advanced the principle of equal rights for gays in their 1980 platform. It was a tempting target for the Reagan campaign, though Reagan himself hewed to his Hollywood origins by accepting closet gays in his entourage.[46] By the 1990s, state referenda against homosexuals were running afoul of the courts. Here and there, openly gay candidates won election to local and state office and ultimately to the U.S. Congress.

A landmark of sorts was reached in 1973, when the medical and psychiatric establishments responded to gay pressure and dropped homosexuality as a category of mental illness.[47] Physical illness was another matter, in the form of the AIDS tragedy, which in the United States, apart from intravenous drug users, was largely specific to gay men. The epidemic had its politically positive side, however, providing both a rallying point for the movement and a source of public sympathy.

Even more than the women's movement and the sexual revolution in all its senses, the homosexual rights movement was targeted by the counter-revolution, whereas the black civil rights movement and other racial minorities remained relatively immune from direct public attack. Religious fundamentalism and the South as a region led the reaction, and the FBI, carried along by the momentum of the Hoover years, tracked gay activists on into the 1970s as a menace to national security. Tensions peaked in the military, especially when the Clinton administration supplanted the old dishonorable discharge policy with its fence-straddling "Don't Ask, Don't Tell" doctrine of 1993. On the other side, homosexual rights were fully absorbed into the liberal agenda in its Fourth Revolution sense, and sexual orientation became one of the criteria for cultural diversity in academic circles. By the 1990s, gay pride demonstrations and marches became routine. In no other sector of society was legal change as dramatic, from the 1970s when criminal penalties and police harassment were still common, to the 1990s when, with local exceptions, sexual orientation became a matter of right and of official protection. "There is reason to think that the battles over gay liberation will go on wavering, now forward, now back," wrote Paul Berman, "but there is reason also to think that … the final vector will point toward more liberation, not less."[48]

The ultimate goal of public acceptance seemed to be at hand in the year 2000 when the state of Vermont legalized "civil unions," falling only verbally short of gay marriage.[49] The Massachusetts Supreme Court took that last step in November 2003, to the intense disgust of conservatives around the country. For the most dedicated activists, on the other hand, the time seemed to be near when victory and assimilation could actually drain the life out of the gay rights movement. This is the ultimate fate of successful revolutions.

Disability Rights

The ideologically purest extension of the Fourth Revolution in America reached into a sector of society distinct from all the vigorous movements of protest—racial, gender, cultural—that made up the main thrust of the national upheaval. This realm consisted of people who were often helpless to represent themselves and who therefore depended on the idealism of their advocates. They included both the physically disabled and the mentally ill or handicapped, brought within the terms of the Fourth Revolution by the belief that they were entitled to the same provisions of group equality and protection from discrimination as all the other beneficiaries of the new social philosophy. "The historical record indicates that people with disabilities, with few exceptions, have not been a part of the American mainstream," wrote the advocates Don Fersh and Peter Thomas,[50] and acceptance into the mainstream became the overriding objective of supporters of the disabled. The movement reached out in particular to handicapped children, especially the mentally retarded, and posed the complex issue of how to treat these unfortunates within the public education system. At its farthest reach, the new egalitarianism and libertarianism extended to the criminal justice system and what had long been known euphemistically as "correctional institutions," taking them to task, like treatment of the mentally ill and the retarded, in accordance with the new doctrine of deinstitutionalization.

All of these campaigns to protect the disabled had their ideological roots in the civil rights movement and their legal roots in the Civil Rights Act of 1964. As two influential advocates for the handicapped wrote, "The experiences of women and racial and ethnic minorities in battling for civil rights in our society have provided an invaluable model for handicapped people's civil rights efforts."[51] Just as the civil rights movement had fought for equal treatment of blacks and subsequently of other racial minorities, the new movements for the disabled targeted the prejudice of "handicap-ism" and undertook to remove the stigma that had traditionally been attached to these groups.[52] Such attitudes, it was believed, underlay the discrimination that the various categories of the disabled had always experienced. Any objective limitations to their participation in the main-stream would be overcome by legal action, just as the effects of racial prejudice had been.

As early as 1947, President Truman set up a President's Committee on Employment of People with Disabilities. This body has continued through the years to push the cause of the physically handicapped, especially in employment, with emphasis on educating and persuading employers. An early concrete step came in the waning months of the Great Society, when Congress passed the Architectural Barriers Act of 1968 to require wheelchair access to any federally funded buildings. But, as the National Council on Disability later contended, "The political climate of the late 1960s and early 1970s worked against the advancement of civil rights for persons with disabilities."[53] In 1972 Senator Hubert Humphrey unsuccess-fully proposed to include the disabled under the Civil Rights Act. Separate legislation was twice vetoed by President Nixon. Finally a compromise measure passed, the Rehabilitation Act of 1973, with a key provision, Section 504, that had quietly been slipped in: "No otherwise qualified handicapped individual in the United States ... shall, solely by reason of his handicap, be excluded from the participation in, be denied the benefits of, or be subjected to discrimination under any program or activity receiving Federal financial assistance." For enforcement, the act added protection of the handicapped to the responsibilities of the Equal Employment Oppor-tunity Commission along with racial minorities and women, pursuant to Title VII of the Civil Rights Act.

The 1973 law was the first high-level signal to the handicapped that they might claim status as a distinct class, an oppressed minority like the blacks, with the right both to desegregation and to the assertion of their own distinctiveness as a culture.[54] Nevertheless, the issuance of regulations to implement the Rehabilitation Act was hamstrung by fiscal anxieties for nearly four years, under Nixon, Ford, and even the incoming Carter admin-istration. Legal closure only followed direct action by disabled demonstra-tors, mobilized by the short-lived American Coalition of Citizens with Disabilities, who invaded the office of Health, Education and Welfare (HEW) secretary Joseph Califano in April 1977. They staged a prolonged sit-in— a "mini-Woodstock"—at the HEW regional office in the protest-friendly climate of San Francisco. "We will not accept more segregation," was the cry, and they won.[55] The Carter administration got the message, forthwith holding a White House Conference on Handicapped Individuals, creating the National Council for the Handicapped (originally an advisory body in the Department of Education, later made an independent agency, renamed the National Council on Disability in 1988) and pushing the independent living movement.

The early 1980s, the years of the Reagan counterrevolution, was a time of rearguard holding action for the handicapped, fighting both the courts and the executive branch, as their advocates pursued their case in Congress. These efforts culminated in the Fair Housing amendments of 1988, which gave disabled individuals civil rights protection in that area. Meanwhile the National Council on the Handicapped pushed for broader economic protection of their constituents. Calling for a "national policy for persons with disabilities," the council stressed the goals of "independent living," "self-determination," and "participation in the day-to-day life of the community." In its 1986 report "Toward Independence," the council invoked the spirit of the civil rights movement in affirming, "Discrimination against persons with disabilities will no longer be tolerated by our society."[56] Then in March 1988 came what the journalist Joseph Shapiro called "a defining moment for the disability rights movement": students at Gallaudet University for the deaf in Washington, calling for the appointment of a deaf president of their institution, closed the school down until their demand was met. "It was the closest the movement has come to having a touchstone event, a Selma or a Stonewall," wrote Shapiro, and it added to the momentum for legislative action.[57]

The upshot of all this pressure was the Americans with Disabilities Act of 1990, sponsored by Senator Tom Harkin and Representative Tony Coelho on the basis of groundwork by the National Council on Disabilities. The new act was a sweeping expansion of the 1973 law, extending its protections to all employment, private as well as public, and strengthening the 1968 rules on access to public facilities and accommodations. Finalizing the legislative process, President George H.W. Bush held the largest signing ceremony in history.[58] Ferth and Thomas described the new statute as "a mandate to mainstream people with disabilities into millions of America's workplaces." In the framework of the Civil Rights Act, "Disability is placed on the same level as race, color, religion, national origin, and sex."[59] Declared Bernard Posner, a longtime director of the President's Committee on Employment of People with Disabilities, "The Americans with Disabilities Act creates an entirely new focus by making the employment of people with disabilities, not just 'good business,' or the 'nice thing to do,' but the law of the land."[60] Thus, subject to the dictates of "reasonable accommodation," the social equality of the Fourth Revolution became a national principle for including the physically disabled into the mainstream of society.

Like all revolutionary advances, this great gain failed to silence the voices of extremism in the disability rights movement. There were protests, even violent, that the Americans with Disabilities Act did not go far enough in aiding the handicapped to be integrated into society. Other spokespeople took the opposite tack, holding that the disabled constituted a new culture that should be respected like the homosexuals, and like the homosexuals they found attempts at cures actually offensive.[61] This was what Joseph Shapiro described as "the new thinking by disabled people that there is no pity or tragedy in disability, and that it is society's myths, fears, and stereotypes that most make being disabled difficult."[62] Perhaps the ultimate public dilemma was how to memorialize President Franklin Roosevelt—with or without emphasis on his wheelchair (which, contrary to the belief of some present-day activists, was not concealed in his lifetime).

If equality of treatment for the physically disabled was a signal success for the Fourth Revolution, the same cannot be said of programs and policies regarding the mentally ill. In the early sixties, the psychiatrist Thomas Szasz and others, encouraged by Michel Foucault, popularized the belief that mental illness is just a flaw in the general culture.[63] This "myth that mental illness is a myth," as the psychiatric social worker Ann Braden Johnson termed it,[64] led to a revolutionary overturn in the treatment of mental patients. Targeting the decrepit institution of public mental hospitals as oppressive instruments of social control, the reformers launched a national program of deinstitutionalization. Despite the best of intentions, unfortunately, the consequences were little short of disastrous.

The movement for a revolution in the mental health area began to take shape as early as the 1950s. In 1955 Congress established a Joint Commission on Mental Illness and Health, whose report of 1961 recommended the establishment of a national system of community mental health centers in place of the big state hospitals, though the commission recognized that it would be hard to persuade the public to cooperate in this move. At the height of the civil rights movement, with the backing of the Kennedy administration, the report bore fruit in the Community Mental Health Center Construction Act of 1963, launching the policy of deinstitutionalization though failing to make realistic provision for the chronically psychotic. Said Ann Braden Johnson, "What we now call deinstitutionalization was brokered, not planned."[65]

By the late sixties, the states were scrambling to save money by emptying their mental hospitals. Beds nationwide were cut by more than two-thirds, from 475,000 in 1965 to 138,000 in 1980.[66] At the same time, the old legal order in mental health was challenged by an "intellectual assault on psychiatry" among mental health professionals and by young lawyers who have been described as "a mental health liberation bar."[67] Targeting the law on involuntary commitment as yet another form of discrimination, the advocates invoked the same legal principles of equal protection and due process that had served the civil rights movement so effectively. These were "potent tools for dismantling state-sponsored segregation," asserted the psychiatrist Paul Appelbaum. "The changes that ensued were of astonishing scope and intensity."[68] Involuntary commitment became a rarity, as the courts swung behind the doctrine of the "least restrictive alternative."[69] In 1982 citizens of Berkeley, California, actually voted by referendum to ban electric shock therapy within the city limits. Although deinstitutionalization depended heavily on the new tranquilizing drugs, the legal push for equal rights for the mentally ill extended to "the right to refuse treatment with medication."[70]

Unfortunately, as the psychiatrist E. Fuller Torrey described it, the "synergistic combination" of state budget cutting and legal curbs aimed at "liberating" patients "caused deinstitutionalization to career out of control."[71] The director of the National Institutes of Mental Health confessed, "We psychiatrists saw too much of the old snake pit, saw too many people who shouldn't have been there and we overreacted. The result is not what we intended."[72] Chronic patients, said Paul Appelbaum, "were essentially abandoned,"[73] dumped onto the streets to swell the army of the helpless homeless.

Yet momentum for the civil equality of the mentally ill carried on through the eighties. The Protection and Advocacy for Individuals with Mental Illness Act of 1986, Torrey contended, made matters worse by providing federal funding to these ends. Public policy, he said, attempted to "deny the existence of mental illness."[74] And it sidelined personal responsibility as well, as Professor G.E. Zuriff said of the regulations written to include under the Americans with Disabilities Act a long list of "personality disorders."[75] Ann Braden Johnson's words succinctly express what happened to the Fourth Revolution in the mental health sector: "Sincerely held beliefs ... based on false belief and wishfulness ... had been indiscriminately, though zealously, misapplied."[76]

Compared with the substantial success of the Fourth Revolution in bringing the physically handicapped into the mainstream of American society, and the failure of utopianism as regards the mentally ill, the achievements of the social equality movement in addressing the problems of disabled and retarded children were a mixed story. The aim of this effort, a "natural segue from Brown v. the Board of Education of Topeka,"[77] was to extend the principles of equal protection and integration exemplified by the civil rights movement to the large class of children traditionally excluded from normal schooling and life by reason of their handicaps, particularly mental retardation.

As with the physically handicapped and the mentally ill, a powerful movement of advocates, in this case organized around the American Association on Mental Retardation and the Council for Exceptional Children, was inspired to promote fairness in education and treatment as yet another civil rights issue. A leading advocate, Stanley Herr, invoked the "civil rights imperative": "Among all minorities suffering discrimination the retarded are the least able to assert their rights."[78] Defenders of the retarded found legal basis for action both in the 1954 desegregation decision of the Supreme Court and in the major Great Society legislative initiatives of the 1964 Civil Rights Act and the 1965 Elementary and Secondary Education Act. Grants specifically for education of the handicapped followed quickly. Then in 1971 came a breakthrough in the judicial branch when the Supreme Court found, in the case of *Pennsylvania Association for Retarded Children v. Commonwealth of Pennsylvania* (in the paraphrase by the plaintiffs' attorney Thomas Gilhool), that "all retarded children should be granted access to a program of free public education and training appropriate to the capacities of each of them," with "a presumption that placement in a regular class is preferable."[79] Four years later, Congress took a great leap forward with the Education of All Handicapped Children Act of 1975, universally recalled as "PL 94-142," which mandated and funded (though never adequately) a "free appropriate public education" in the "least restrictive environment."[80]

In practice these principles conveyed an element of revolutionary utopianism, suggesting that mental disabilities were "merely social constructions" and "cultural sequelae." The extremists demanded the deinstitutionalization of all retarded children and their inclusion in regular school classrooms pursuant to the philosophy of "mainstreaming."[81] These goals won the imprimatur of the National Council on Disability: "Students of all ages and ability levels who are placed in non-restrictive environments can learn the skills and behaviors needed to fully participate in society as contributing adults."[82] In 1989 a federal appeals court sustained this reasoning, holding that the act of 1975 "mandates an appropriate public education for all handicapped children regardless of the level of achievement that such children might attain." This despite the plea of the National School Boards Association, "School districts are getting to the point they are asked to do everything and spend more on education services than education."[83]

Simultaneously with the movement to support special education in the public schools came legal attacks on state institutions for the retarded. Here again the courts were the key, in a series of decisions from the early 1970s to the celebrated case that led to the closing of the Willowbrook Developmental Center on Staten Island in 1987. In the words of Stanley

Herr, the lead attorney in that matter, "The regimes of segregation and exclusion for children with disabilities rivaled the worst abuses and humiliations of Jim Crow schooling that once beset African-Americans."[84]

As with the mentally ill, the practical problems entailed by PL 94-142 and its application did not derail the movement for deinstitutionalizing and mainstreaming the mentally retarded, even though, according to one commentator, "Logic, careful total planning, and thoughtful leadership have often been conspicuous by their absence."[85] Such was the difficulty in challenging a revolutionary ideology once it had gained the advantage in public discourse. Interestingly, the term *exceptional,* as a euphemism for retarded children, underwent a reversal of meaning from its old sense of exceptionally bright. One critic of the trend tried vainly to turn the revolution against itself by urging the educational establishment to "celebrate a diversity of restrictive environments."[86]

But the tension between revolutionary theory and the constraints of reality, fiscal as well as substantive, continued to afflict the public education system. Standardized testing, a mainstay of the principle of meritocracy and a modern panacea for conservatives, was repeatedly assailed for discriminating against students who were handicapped in any respect, despite repeated concessions by the formulators of the tests. Problems of classroom management escalated, as a leader of the National School Boards Association explained when mainstreaming had taken full command in the 1990s: "Nobody envisioned back then the kinds of discipline problems that are on the table now. And no one anticipated how much the culture would change and how big an issue discipline would become in the schools."[87]

Prisoner Rights

The Fourth Revolution and its movement for social equality and liberation extended to some unlikely places in American society. One was the prison system, caught up in the fever of deinstitutionalization and mainstream inclusion. Riding on the momentum of the Great Society and the civil rights movement, a vociferous prisoners' rights movement developed by the early 1970s, with a strong base, like the physical and mental disabilities movements, among young lawyers. It was all part of "the extension of rights to previously marginal and relatively powerless groups," wrote the criminologist C. Ronald Huff.[88]

There was a logical link between prisoners' rights and the civil rights movement, in that the percentage of blacks in the American prison population was, rightly or wrongly, out of all proportion to their numbers in the country at large. As the civil rights lawyer Alvin Bronstein asserted,

"Prison is central to the Black experience because it is the culmination of so many other repressive and discriminatory forces in society."[89]

The precipitating event in prison reform and prisoners' rights was the 1971 uprising at the Attica State Prison in New York. Attica, according to an editorialist in *The Nation,* was a new kind of "politicized" prison riot, inspired by "black nationalism," and at the same time "a class action—the class of the disinherited."[90] The Columbia University historian David Rothman likened the event to the 1968 student uprising at his institution[91]—even though the bloody suppression of the Attica revolt took more than forty lives, including a dozen hostages.

Attica was outrageous enough to set in motion the broader movement for prison reform and prisoners' rights, appealing, like the civil rights movement, to the U.S. Constitution. Due process, cruel and unusual punishment, free speech, and the doctrine of privacy were among the principles invoked. The results, however, were problematic. To be sure, programs of probation, parole, and prison furloughs were liberalized across the country. Some advocates at the extreme called for a radical reduction in the use of imprisonment as a punishment, in the name of "a new calculus" of "decarceration."[92] Writing in 1980, Alvin Bronstein observed, "The judicial attitude has changed drastically from the de facto rightlessness that was almost universally accepted for prisoners little more than a decade ago."[93] There were even attempts to organize labor unions for prisoners, with some success in California, until the U.S. Supreme Court rejected the concept in a 1977 decision that Ronald Huff considered "an anachronism, ... refusing to continue the evolutionary trend in prisoners' rights."[94]

Prison reform became an easy target for the counterrevolution. Republican exploitation of the case of a murder by a furloughed prisoner in Massachusetts, one Willie Horton, helped trip up the presidential campaign of Michael Dukakis in 1988. At the same time, the prison population was exploding, thanks especially to tough drug-law enforcement, itself a reflection of the prevailing counterrevolutionary reaction against the youth culture. What the country achieved with respect to prisons, Bronstein sadly complained, was "many years of reform without change."[95]

The Triumph of Antidiscrimination

The rapid progress of most disability rights movements in the 1970s and 1980s exemplified the power of a revolutionary ideology once it has seized the moral high ground. As long as the ideology holds sway, hardly anyone, whatever the merit of their reservations, wants to challenge it directly in public discourse, for fear of seeming a hard-hearted opponent of human betterment. This was the secret of the Fourth Revolution in all its aspects, as it has been of every revolution in history at the height of its influence.

Testifying to the pervasiveness of the Fourth Revolution as an ideology, every sort of antidiscrimination appeal emerged in America during the last quarter of the twentieth century. Most serious, perhaps, was the matter of "ageism," specifically, age discrimination in employment, addressed in the Age Discrimination in Employment Act of 1967 and then revisited by state legislators in the 1990s when the courts appeared to be curtailing this right. Other pejorative "isms" sprang up on the political margins—"weightism" as prejudice against the obese, and "lookism," as discrimination against the ugly. That such factors were no joke in employment was demonstrated in research conducted in the 1990s.[96] In San Francisco, in response to the problem, the Board of Supervisors enacted a "fat ordinance," adding height and weight to the usual categories in the city's antidiscrimination code.[97] Sometimes individuals allegedly disadvantaged by these conditions even obtained legal relief by invoking the Americans with Disabilities Act.

Odd consequences ensued from more firmly established categories of group protection and rights as well. Indian tribes, gaining partial immunity from state laws, discovered an economic bonanza in the establishment of gambling casinos, located on their reservations but open to the entire odds-defying public. New immigrants, especially Hispanics and Asians, found themselves set against blacks in competition at the lower rungs of the American economy. Racial stereotyping, all but brushed under the rug at century's end, erupted again in the new millennium in the wake of Middle Eastern terrorism.

Nevertheless, such excesses and exceptions did not diminish the ramifying impact of the core principles of the Fourth Revolution, in its face-to-face social egalitarianism and its taboo on public expression of group-based prejudice. By the close of the nineties, following the path opened up by the black civil rights movement, the revolution had temporarily returned, to overcome most forms of postrevolutionary reaction or drive them underground.

Addendum: The Fourth Revolution and Language

All revolutions change the language. Language encodes the structure and assumptions of the old social order and challenges the revolution to find new ways of expressing its aspirations for justice. Toward this aim, language becomes an instrument for revolution to establish its new hegemony of values.

The Fourth Revolution was no exception to this rule. Indeed, linguistic standards, especially the politically correct vocabulary, appeared at the cutting edge of revolutionary protest and became the mark of the new social orthodoxy. Each component of the Fourth Revolution conveyed a series of demands to change propriety in language usage, above all when it came to designations of the particular group waging a struggle for new rights or standing to benefit from them.

The black revolution was the most audible in its demands for changes in nomenclature and in its success in establishing them. This intensity of feeling about words is understandable, considering the arsenal of pejorative terms with which the white majority in America habitually demeaned those whom they judged their inferiors by reason of color. But over time, even the more polite designations of race came to be regarded by their subjects as badges of inferiority or submission. Until World War II, *colored* was the term least intended to offend, though it was the mark of official segregation throughout the South on everything from buses to toilets; *colored* notably survives in the name of the NAACP. From the war until the civil rights movement hit full stride, the term of preference was *negro*, among both the racial minority and benevolent whites; *negro* was, for example, Martin Luther King's usage. But *negro* was too tame for the revolutionary militants; *black* was their banner—Black Power, black nationalism. Later, by the 1980s, even *black* fell into disfavor, yielding to *African American*. The linguist Steven Pinker called this phenomenon the "euphemism treadmill," as "the euphemism becomes tainted by association and the new one that must be found acquires its own negative connotations."[98]

For the American Indian minority, the corresponding shift was from *Indian* to *Native American*, naturally with a strict taboo on earlier appellations for the group even when adopted by popular athletic teams. Place names, heavily derived in the United States from Indian motifs, also came in for protest or sanitizing—any name with *squaw* in it, for instance. Crayola crayons had to alter the color term "Indian Red," lest it suggest a derogatory reference to ethnic skin color.[99] Even the American Sign Language for the deaf had to revise references to physical features of minorities.[100]

Sequences of terminological change like these, loaded with political and emotional depth charges, add a special challenge to the work of the historian. Using too old a term seems condescending; using one that is too new is anachronistic. The best solution is to keep to the usage in play at the time of the events being described, like Russian cities or French revolutionary months; hence, here, the black revolution, not the African American revolution, and the American Indian movement, not the Native American movement.

The gender revolution actually entailed deeper linguistic complications, because maleness and femaleness are embedded in the basic lexical structure of the language, especially, in English, the pronoun system and the vocabulary of agency ending in "-man." Grammarians used to require the use of the masculine of the third-person singular pronoun when the referent could be either male or female, even though the vernacular preferred *they* as a unisex pronoun in the singular as well as in the plural. Now one is supposed to say "he or she," and so forth, however repeatedly. The "-man" terms, implying male exclusivity in the specified capacities or occupations, have yielded to the gender-neutral *chairperson, police officer,* and so on. To end the invidious categorization of married and unmarried women represented by the titles "Mrs." and "Miss"—a distinction not imposed on men—the title "Ms." (pronounced approximately "mizz") was invented in the early 1970s and promoted by the magazine of that name.[101] Finally, as has been noted in connection with the gender revolution, the very term *gender* was extended from its original grammatical meaning, to denote "sex" in the sense of the male or female sex, the word *sex* having come to refer to specifically sexual functions or activity, be they intergender or intragender.

The homosexual offshoot of the gender revolution saw its own terminological evolution. By the 1970s, *homosexual* yielded to the slang *gay* as the self-designation of preference, much as *negro* gave way to *black. Lesbian,* however, held on as the term for homosexual women. In some academic circles, the pejorative *queer* was embraced as a badge of the new self-assertion, in "queer studies" and the like.

A particularly complicated series of terminological changes was generated by the movement on behalf of the mentally retarded. From the traditional *feeble-minded* (excluding the crueler labels), usage moved on to *retarded,* and then to *developmentally disabled. Learning disabilities* recently began to give way to *learning differences.* In the area of physical problems, the traditional *cripple* yielded to *handicapped* and then to *physically challenged,* and so forth. (President Reagan's interior secretary James Watt destroyed himself politically by one intemperate dismissal of affirmative action in the old terms.)[102] It became taboo to call a dwarf a *midget.* Similar unease—taxing the ingenuity of the newly formed National Stigma Clearing House in New York—was evoked by terminology for mental illness, itself a euphemism that came under attack in turn as the imposition of a stereotyped medical model. Throughout, language change was being driven by the urge to mask the reality of actual differences and inequalities among individuals.

Specific language changes associated with the youth revolt did not amount to much—mainly lowering the age, from college graduation to high school graduation, at which boys were supposed to be called men and girls called women. Far more pervasive than any change in group terminology was the impact of the counterculture on the entire universe of public language usage in America. With the demise of censorship laws and conventions, the whole array of four-letter Anglo-Saxon expletives entered everyday discourse in the media (most egregiously, in popular music lyrics). A distinct impoverishment of verbal nuance was one result, not to mention the unrelenting shock administered to traditionalists and the fastidious. This of course was but one aspect of the general assault on received canons of taste and public behavior inflicted by the counterculture. Resistance in a market-driven society was feeble.

By and large, the counterrevolutionary movements of the 1970s and 1980s felt constrained to develop their own code words and phrases to convey sentiments that the Fourth Revolution had tabooed in open form. *School choice,* for example, means de facto racial segregation. *Big government* means the Great Society and the practice of taxing the working majority to support welfare dependency. *Traditional values* or *family values* are code for resistance to the gender revolution and especially for opposition to abortion, women's entry into the workforce, and homosexual rights.

The Fourth Revolution even had echoes in the professional field of linguistics. New linguistic doctrine rejected the "prescriptive" approach to language, in favor of the purely "descriptive," with precedence accorded to oral and vernacular forms over the written standard.[103] In consonance with the revolution at large, linguists turned against the "elitism" implied by notions of correctness and exactitude in language use. A new linguistic relativity extended to arguments for the recognition in public education of negro dialect, "black English" or "Ebonics," as an equally acceptable form of expression.[104] Ironically, the imposition of politically correct vocabulary amounted to a new form of revolutionary prescriptiveness that condemned old group references and demanded new ones. People in sensitive positions such as politics and education would misuse the terminology at their peril.

One social element in the Fourth Revolution carried the linguistic question entirely outside the framework of the English language. This was the Hispanic offshoot of the racial revolution, where the group's overarching characteristic was not physical features but Spanish-language heritage (and often actual language use, in the case of Puerto Rico or recent immigrants from Latin America). The Hispanic factor raised the question of minority language rights in an English-dominated country that was accustomed to the linguistic assimilation of immigrants. The matter came to a head in the issue of bilingual education, whether and how to phase

Spanish-speaking children into an English-language society.[105] In practice, bilingual education often became a shelter for a predominantly Spanish-speaking subsociety, resisted correspondingly by English-speaking conservatives to the point of a 1988 California referendum banning it altogether. This step dovetailed with the English-only movement, a linguistic manifestation of the counterrevolution that prevailed in much of the American Southwest. Ironically, Hispanics largely favored English-language assimilation, even to the point of defying attempts to shunt children into bilingual classes solely because of their surnames.

All through the linguistic echoes of the Fourth Revolution one detects the quasi-religious, liturgical sensitivity to language that characterizes any revolution and its aftermath. One is reminded a bit of the obligatory incantations of Marxism–Leninism that used to prevail in the Soviet Union. Revolutions are notoriously self-righteous, in their linguistic emanations above all. With revolutionaries, just as with religious counterrevolutionaries, there is an implicit faith that universal public use of the proper terminology will make everything turn out right.

CHAPTER 11

The Fourth Revolution
at the Millennium

From the perspective of the year 2000 and after, the recent history of the Western world is a scene of paradox. In terms of material success, it has been a time of almost unblemished progress. Internationally, the West's major challenger in the form of Communism has essentially disappeared, and the economic and cultural ways of the West surge around the world almost without resistance except by radical Islam. Internal politics in the West have become stable to the point of inviting apathy, while the mass media keep the multitude duly distracted. Yet in the intangibles of human values and relationships, a revolution has been going on as deep as any known to history. This revolution, the fourth in a sequence of great transformations in the modern history of the West, has been centered in the most powerful and materially successful country of all, the United States of America.

Hegemonies of the Fourth Revolution

The Fourth Revolution in the United States has scored striking victories. However, its success has been uneven among different sectors of society. That is one of the reasons why the culture wars go on so intractably, without clear resolution.

In certain realms the Fourth Revolution took a commanding position in the course of its second surge in the later 1980s and 1990s. Areas where the revolution of social equality became most firmly ensconced include the law, the federal bureaucracy, the educational establishment at all levels, the mainstream Protestant churches, and, most influential of all, the mass media and the entertainment industry. In society at large, different components of the Fourth Revolution have progressed unevenly in winning general acceptance of their goals. Their enemies are unevenly abashed, while their most avant-garde ideologists remain unsatisfied.

The black civil rights movement was preeminently the most successful element of the Fourth Revolution, measured by the extent of the progress it achieved and the depth of the changes in outlook and relationships that it impressed on society as a whole, whatever the shortfall in its ambitions as viewed from the perspective of the millennium. The movement's most extreme and violent manifestations in the Black Power ideology faded for the time being, and economic integration into the mainstream went on apace, boosted by a commitment to affirmative action on the part of both the executive and the judicial branches of government. A substantive force for progress was the black vote, emancipated in the South by the Johnson-era legislation and mobilized everywhere else by the confrontations of the late sixties. Black gains in access to integrated education, notably court-ordered school busing plans, have remained a focus of controversy and antagonism and may have done the cause of integration more harm than good by prompting white flight from central cities to the suburbs. But overall, a virtual taboo has descended on public endorsement of racial segregation and White Supremacy, even in the South, however much such attitudes may persist covertly. At the same time, racial categories and preferences of a compensatory sort have been built into law and public policy, now extending to all racially defined "protected classes": Hispanics, Asians, Native Americans, and Pacific Islanders as well as African Americans. Beyond the scope of law, blacks have achieved signal representation in the mass media, sports, and entertainment. Thus, whatever its disappointments, the black civil rights movement accomplished an enduring revolutionary change in American society and ideology. Its victory was symbolically consummated in 1985, when Congress proclaimed Martin Luther King's birthday a national holiday, at the very nadir of the Reagan counterrevolution.

Among the various components of the social revolution in America, the women's movement went back furthest in its origins, to the suffrage campaign of the Progressive era and the adoption of the Nineteenth Amendment in 1920. In the sixties, however, women were the last of the various revolutionary elements to express themselves in militant protest. Their subsequent struggles were the longest drawn-out and most resisted, especially over the abortion rights issue after the *Roe v. Wade* decision in

1973. Like the black revolution, and before it the New Deal victories of trade unionism, the women's movement was most resisted in the South, where the old patriarchal culture sufficed in the mid-1970s to deny the three-fourths majority of the states necessary for ratification of the Equal Rights Amendment.

Women's rights were complicated by the movement's association with the sexual revolution in its more literal sense, the overturn of traditional mores governing nonmarital sex, and the sexual content of public discourse and entertainment. These changes, of course, were promoted by the youth rebellion and the counterculture, and were sustained, like other elements of the Fourth Revolution, by purist libertarian and egalitarian readings of the Constitution, often upheld by the judiciary. The practical consequences, unfortunately, were more often a green light for irresponsible males and the victimization of young women, as the rates of divorce and illegitimacy climbed relentlessly and burdened both the public exchequer and the patience of working taxpayers. Meanwhile, sexual liberation reached its most controversial stage as the movement for gay and lesbian rights took shape in the course of the seventies and eighties and became, along with abortion, the focus of militant counterrevolution waged by the Religious Right. The status of women and sexual preference never achieved the kind of public consensus, even at the verbal level, as that won by nondiscrimination in racial matters. "Women's Lib" would be openly disparaged long after the open expression of racial prejudice had become taboo.

Of all the elements of the Fourth Revolution, the youth revolution with its lifestyle accompaniment was the most complex in its impact. Institutionally and legally, it collapsed almost completely, leaving very little imprint compared with women and racial minorities. What was given with one hand—the eighteen-year vote, for example—was often taken away with the other—the restoration of the twenty-one-year drinking age.

By definition, the youth revolution was the most susceptible to generational change. The radicals of the sixties grew up, and they were not replaced. The most hated targets of youthful protest, the Vietnam War and the draft, came to an end, while much of the energy was let out of the student movement by university reforms and by the changes in both rules and mores associated with the sexual revolution. The most radical urges of the youth revolt flared up briefly in the outright terrorism of the Weathermen, a futilitarian gesture of frustration at the failure of the revolution as a mass movement. Overseas terrorist counterparts—notably the Red Brigades in Italy, the "Red Army Faction" in Japan, the Baader-Meinhof Gang in Germany—also continued their struggle into the seventies, perpetrating a series of pointless killings but never succeeding as they hoped in destabilizing society.

At a deeper level, the youth revolution had the most pervasive effect of all the components of the Fourth Revolution, as the counterculture percolated throughout American society. Magnified by the escapism of substance abuse and mass entertainment, it rapidly filtered down to working-class and minority youth and contributed pervasively to the decay both in self-discipline and in social discipline that has marked subsequent decades of American life. Traditional acceptance of authority, whether governmental, educational, or familial, was overturned, just as the original American Revolution dealt a blow to class deference. In educational philosophy, antielitist and antiexpert premises took hold in curricular changes at all levels, playing down the inculcation of factual knowledge and extolling new norms of self-expression and self-esteem, however much these ideals were contradicted by the realities of the workaday world. Standards of conduct and entertainment, even of language, collapsed. Any public act or viewpoint that smacked of elitism came under a cloud.

The spirit of the Fourth Revolution carried over to many other areas of American life. With crucial judicial support, the philosophy of equal rights and minimal constraint was extended to such areas as deinstitutionalization of the mentally ill; equal treatment, access, and employment for the physically and mentally handicapped; and rights and procedures in the criminal justice system. Throughout these reforms, the liberal philosophy prevailed that held social conditions responsible for individual deviance and failure while the conservative faith in individual will and responsibility was left to stew in anger and await its opportunity.

Now diffused throughout society, the Fourth Revolution has stimulated the consolidation of its own base. It has achieved this first of all through the integration and mobilization of its constituencies, above all women and blacks, into the political process. Rare is the politician who will now openly defy the principles of the revolution, except in the contentious area of sexual behavior. Demographics have enhanced the revolution's impact. The baby boom generation growing up in the shadow of the sixties now dominates the middle-aged cohort of power-wielders and opinion-shapers, while the effects of immigration are being felt in a population increasingly diverse in its racial makeup.

Areas of resistance to the Fourth Revolution remain, though expressions of discomfort are often muted by the ideological taboos that the revolution has imposed on public discourse. The South, always the most conservative part of the country, has resisted most, where it was permissible to resist, above all on gender issues, though rarely on race. To be sure, old racial prejudice survives in much of American society in a transmuted form, for instance in resistance to affirmative action on ostensibly constitutional grounds. The gender revolution continues to be fought more openly. Religion has become a focal point of the counterrevolution, dividing the churches between their more liberal elements and denominations on one hand and the Religious Right on the other.

All in all, it is extraordinary how firmly the premises of the Fourth Revolution have been established where it counts and how little effective resistance remains. The culture war is being won by the revolutionaries, despite periodic rumblings of a backlash.

An Accommodation of Revolutions

One reason why all this radical change is acceptable is because it does not seriously challenge either the nation's main political traditions or its basic economic structure. After all, the Fourth Revolution is not an extension of the Third Revolution of the first half of the twentieth century but a fundamentally new phenomenon. The old movement of economic equalization, of people versus property, has almost entirely lapsed, apart from residual entitlement programs. By contrast, the traditions of the Second Revolution of political equality and economic freedom ride higher than ever. At the same time, the First Revolution of liberation from religious authority and dogma has returned to contention as a major subject of the culture wars. And the Fourth Revolution, originally challenging everything that went before it, has in its triumph accommodated itself comfortably to all the revolutionary successes and failures that preceded it.

Central to an understanding of the place that the Fourth Revolution has won for itself in American society is its dissociation from the economic revolution. In shifting from class and property issues to struggles for social equalization, the Fourth Revolution made itself tolerable to the existing hierarchy of economic interests. It was even functionally beneficial to the economic order, insofar as it distracted public attention from issues of the Third Revolution and focused debate in directions that were much less threatening to the business elite. How often has one heard politicians say they are "socially liberal but fiscally conservative"? The Second and Fourth revolutions thus can embrace one another on the ground of their shared libertarianism.

Unlike the Third Revolution, the Second Revolution has proved immune to counterrevolutionary reactions against the Fourth Revolution. These retrograde impulses, mostly encompassed in the Religious Right, have remained attached to the political and economic libertarianism of the American tradition, even though reactions against the new social changes invite rejection of the First Revolution as it has been embedded in doctrines of free thought and separation of church and state. The Religious Right would implicitly override the separation principle and invoke public authority to sustain their version of faith and morals, an urge most salient in the southern states. That region fought the full implementation of the Second Revolution of political equality, dragged its feet on the Third Revolution of economic equalization, resisted the Fourth Revolution as long as and in whatever aspect it remained licit to do so, and always remained in doubt about the original First Revolution of freedom of conscience.

The Fourth Revolution has largely been absorbed into American political culture, despite pockets of resistance, regional or issue specific (abortion and homosexual rights). It has been absorbed without prejudice to the dominant tradition of the Second Revolution and has even capitalized on and abetted that tradition. Meanwhile the First Revolution is played down, or in the case of the Religious Right, implicitly called into question. Finally, the Third Revolution has been abandoned, except for some unintended outcomes.

The Fourth Revolution and Meritocracy

The unintended consequences of a revolution are usually the most enduring ones. The First Revolution burst forth in Europe in the sixteenth and seventeenth centuries as a series of revolts against hierarchical authority in religion, not as a movement for free thought or toleration; if anything, initially, it intensified the pressure for conformity within each religious community. Toleration, intellectual freedom, and the separation of church and state were the unintended consequences of divided religious authority, and only later, in the eighteenth century, did they become ends in themselves. The eighteenth-century revolution, that is, the Second Revolution against hereditary political authority and status, was the most thoroughly successful kind of revolution, first in America and then in Europe, but it never came to grips with the realities of unequal property ownership and economic power to which its libertarian principles gave free play.

The Third Revolution of economic equalization failed signally in its ostensible goal of redressing the imbalance of economic power, whether one considers the violent and totalist version of that urge under Communism or the gradual and partial versions that were attempted under Social Democratic governments and the New Deal. The actual outcome, clearest in Russia, was a shift not in the system of economic inequality but in its basis. In all these cases, society moved away from individual entrepreneurship as the route to success and toward status in hierarchical organizations whether public or corporate. In other words, the outcome of the Third Revolution was the rise of the meritocracy of managers and experts. This was the emerging social reality in the United States when the Fourth Revolution burst forth.

The Fourth Revolution aimed at eradicating social inequality between biologically defined groups. In the pure form, extreme social egalitarianism would entail a head-on clash with meritocracy and its principles of hierarchy and credentialing. This was one aspect of the cause taken up by the youth revolt, especially in Europe, but little came of it apart from an antielitist loosening of educational and cultural standards. Antielitism was even more striking in its rise and fall during the "Cultural Revolution" in China. But in practice, by and large, the Fourth Revolution accepted the reality of meritocracy and settled for working within its terms.

What the Fourth Revolution was reduced to, in its confrontation with meritocratic society, was winning equal access to social hierarchies rather than dismantling them. This was demonstrated by the shift of focus in the black civil rights movement and the women's movement, especially, to affirmative action and de facto quotas for previously disadvantaged groups on the ladder of career success. The effective outcome of these efforts was not the advancement of equality across the board but rather the redistribution of inequality and the removal of racial and gender barriers to the achievement of top status. Rebelling groups, racial and gender, had to be content with seeing proportionately equal numbers of their successful representatives included into the various social hierarchies, whether corporate, educational, or governmental. This was more a symbolic achievement of social equality than the real thing. For the bottom strata of whatever group affiliation, nothing much changed. Perhaps they were left even worse off, in the backlash against the war on poverty and as their natural leadership was siphoned upward by the opportunity for personal advancement.[1]

In the United States, the symbolic approach to social equalization, though mostly applying to the meritocratic hierarchy, was also extended to the vestiges of the Second Revolution economy in the form of small private enterprise. Here the push since the 1970s has been to guarantee quotas, in everything from defense contracts to broadcast licenses, to minority and female-owned businesses. The significance of this practice is more in illustrating the logic of the redistribution of inequality than in really contributing to the economic condition of the clientele of the Fourth Revolution.

Meanwhile, antielitism in education and the movement for symbolic status for women and racial minorities had a certain negative effect on the meritocracy and its standards of operation. Equal access to the system for representatives of these categories meant that for entry and advancement in the hierarchy of success, group status took precedence over strict observance of the standards of merit. This tendency has been underscored in the legal realm by more than twenty years of controversy over affirmative action and cultural diversity, ever since the *Bakke* case. It has become expecially pronounced in higher education and in the general infiltration of casual language, dress, and lifestyle into areas of endeavor that had heretofore rested on discipline and expertise.

The impact of the Fourth Revolution on meritocratic institutions may have much deeper long-term effects than its devotees have anticipated, or that the power structure itself has taken account of in its concessions to social change. Meritocratic industrial–technological society rests on certain assumptions of cultural competence, revolving around the work ethic and the drive to succeed. These cultural foundations of the modern life took a long time to establish, but they may be easily eroded. Seduced by the Fourth Revolution and its tolerance of lower standards together with easier routes to comply with them, the potential population base for recruitment into a demanding meritocracy is more and more depleted. Signs of this escapist effect are already evident in training and hiring for certain difficult occupations ranging from engineering to general-practice medicine, where American institutions are being compelled to rely more and more on foreign applicants. American candidates for the hierarchy see too many less demanding alternatives.

The New Groupism

The Fourth Revolution's adjustment to meritocracy has not only entailed practical and legal complications but also has brought to the surface some profound questions about the nature of modern society. Is society to be understood as a set of individuals, all endowed with equal rights and responsibilities, and ideally with equal opportunities? Or, as the American doctrine of diversity implies, is it more fundamentally an amalgam of distinct groups, based, as Hugh Graham thought, on "an implicit theory of group rather than individual rights,"[2] where equality is approached and judged on a group basis? Is the Constitution color-blind? Or does it require recognition of group rights and the equality of outcomes, at least on a group-by-group basis if not within groups? If equal rights are valid only within a group context, the fundamental principle of individual equality before the law is called into question. An example is the hate-crime issue, where the seriousness of an offense depends on the group status both of the perpetrator and of the victim as well as on the nature and circumstances of the act itself. In this respect, the Fourth Revolution collides with a basic ideal of the Second, namely, equality before the law regardless of the hereditary status of the individual.

The implications of groupism extend even further. In its commitment to rectify intergroup discrimination and to compensate groups even for oppression that their ancestral representatives may have suffered in the past, groupism posits inherent virtues or hereditary guilt that apply to all members of a group whether or not they have personally partaken of the suffering or offense in question. Moral worth or ignominy resides in the group. The measure at one end of the scale is how much a group has allegedly suffered historically and at the other end, how much another group has been responsible in the past for inflicting such suffering. These judgments set up a hierarchical relationship of groups, among the more virtuous and the more reprehensible. This is an ironic outcome: instead of overcoming social inequalities arising from group status, it merely reverses the inequality, at least in the realm of legal and moral claims, if not so far in most of everyday life.

In the end, how are guilt and virtue to be defined, and by whom? There is no answer other than political power and cultural hegemony. Following the millennium, in America, activists of the Fourth Revolution hold the cultural high ground and command effective political conformity, so that naysayers are marginalized. However, considering the instability of most revolutionary achievements, and the ebb and flow of the political tides in U.S. history, this triumphant position of the Fourth Revolution may not hold. A more lasting legacy may be groupism per se, which could become an instrument in the hands of counterrevolutionaries as much as revolutionaries.

Dovetailing with the relativist philosophy of postmodernism, groupism extends to fundamental questions of defining the true and the good. These qualities, by implication, reside in the group and not in any universal standards. There is only group truth and group falsehood, group right and group wrong. The truth of a position is based on the imputed merit of the group that advances it, and the merit of the group derives from its position on the historical scale of victim–oppressor.

The Culture Wars

One of the noisiest consequences of groupism is the culture wars, so called, that have raged mainly in American academic and intellectual circles since the 1990s. In this arena, the second wave of the Fourth Revolution has collided head-on, not only with the counterrevolution represented by the Religious Right but also with moderate-to-liberal elements who have discovered in the light of the issues raised by the Fourth Revolution that they are traditionalists at heart. At issue is the source of public values and moral imperatives. Are they absolutes, derived from some past authority—holy scripture, academic canon—or are they relative to the constellation of power at any particular moment? Each side in this stand off is dug in within the institutions and social sectors where it prevails, with little prospect of resolving the issue. Spectacular resolution to their standoff, but only the prospect of long-term tension. One recalls the division in France—political, intellectual, almost cultural—between the revolutionary and antirevolutionary traditions that endured for almost two centuries and finally passed into the shades only after the civil eruption of 1968.

In the United States, the culture wars have been fought mainly on university campuses, primarily all in departments of the humanities. Professors wrangle over the merits of the Western tradition vis-à-vis other cultural sources and the question of pure cultural values against the social conditioning of cultural creation. These debates parallel the last-gasp battles over the First Revolution occasioned in the nineteenth century by developments in the natural sciences, above all the theory of evolution, and controversies over the socialist ideas of the Third Revolution that roiled the social sciences in the first half of the twentieth century. Federal law and regulations have abetted the Fourth Revolution's ascendancy in the contemporary campus struggles, by requirements ranging from affirmative action in admissions to multicultural criteria in the award of research grants (whether or not related to the subject matter of the grant).

The culture wars have been an asymmetrical contest, between conservatives who have the loudest voices in the opinion journals and liberal professionals who have the numbers. This imbalance is partly demographic, a phenomenon of the baby boom, now employed and aging but still in the main imbued with the ideology of the sixties. "Tenured radicals," the critic Roger Kimball called them.[3] "Conservative" and "liberal" in this context, of course, do not necessarily coincide with political allegiances, where many figures identified as political liberals have taken the conservative side in the culture wars. Some former liberals—and radicals—were driven to political conservatism by their antipathy to the consequences of the Fourth Revolution. Norman Podhoretz and David Horowitz are good examples.[4] Meanwhile, many members of the baby boom generation adhere to liberal cultural values even as their economic interests point them toward political conservatism. This is the phenomenon of "bourgeois bohemians," or "bobos," depicted by David Brooks.[5] On campuses, controversy has swirled around a host of issues—everything from choices of outside speakers to student speech codes to alleged cultural bias in testing, engendering the pejorative "PC" commonly applied to the demands of the new order. Nevertheless, by the millennium the cultural debate seemed to be simmering down.

Like the more radical instances of the Third Revolution, the Fourth Revolution in its most advanced manifestations has not hesitated to resort to the revision of history to advance its cultural agenda. This is not to say that older versions of certain histories might not have expressed the biases of groups dominant in their time, but only to point out that representatives of the Fourth Revolution indulge in the same practice. The furor occasioned by the five-hundredth anniversary of Columbus's "discovery" of America in 1992 is a good case in point, when the American public was rather suddenly presented with a version of this event, emphasizing European imperialism and native victimization, which was practically the opposite of the heroics they had learned in school a generation or two before. Next, the American Founding Fathers—disproportionately Virginians—were taken to task for countenancing slavery and sexual abuse, among other evils. The controversy over Thomas Jefferson and his alleged slave descendants has dramatized the issue. Thus, standards of a more recent revolution are applied in judgment on figures of the past, while in many minds the revolution they were striving to carry through in their day slips into the shadows.

The revision of history and of standards of historical judgment has been abetted in intellectual circles by the new philosophical fashion of postmodernism. Of this, more in the final chapter of this work, which looks at this theory's significance for a new and different form of revolution. Suffice it to say at this point that in questioning the firm meaning and objectivity of any proposition, postmodernism has opened the door to a caustic relativism that eats away at any efforts to uphold traditions or values rooted in the past. Taken to an extreme, it could undermine even the contentions of the revolutionaries who have invoked its principles.

Counterrevolution Again

In the millennium year 2000, the postrevolutionary pendulum appeared to begin another backswing, confirmed in 2004, as the Republican electoral ticket of George W. Bush and Dick Cheney won back-to-back successes. (Incidentally, amid the deterioration of cultural standards in America, no postrevolutionary politician uses his legal first name anymore if he has a familiar nickname.) Though 2000 and 2004 were narrow victories, numerically, for the conservative camp, they had a big enough symbolic effect to recharge all the social elements of counterrevolution, particularly the Religious Right and culture-war retrogressives, with the feeling of a new national mandate.

In practical governmental terms, the main effort of the Bush "revolution," like the Reagan revolution before it, was directed not so much against the Fourth Revolution as against residues of the Third, left over from the New Deal and the Great Society. This was the import of drastic tax-cutting initiatives undertaken under the aegis of both these conservative presidents, along with attacks on Welfare State entitlement programs. In the case of the younger Bush, this campaign went beyond the popular curtailment of welfare programs for the poor to call into question government-sponsored security programs—retirement and medical—for the elderly in general, a much riskier proposition politically.

The renewed counterrevolution had already made itself felt by the mid-1990s, specifically in the Republican takeover of Congress in 1994, the so-called Gingrich revolution. Presidential politics in the nineties lagged behind the general mood, as they had in the opposite direction in 1988. But another element in the shift to conservatism, more a matter of clarifying appearances than of altering substance, was the ongoing realignment of southern conservatives into the Republican ranks, finally reaching down to the level of the House of Representatives and state legislatures.

With respect to specifically Fourth Revolution issues, the efforts of Bush II up through the time of his reelection were, as under Reagan, more rhetorical than substantive. The black revolution remained untouchable except on the outer reaches of affirmative action, and the same held true of the gender revolution except in the contested areas of abortion and gay rights. A telling indicator appeared in the American rationale for war against the governments of Afghanistan in 2001 and of Iraq in 2003, that the enemy needed to be taught to respect the rights of women (though in Iraq, ironically, the status of women actually deteriorated after the overthrow of the secular modernizing dictatorship of Saddam Hussein).

A latent time bomb remained in the makeup of the federal judiciary, already set against any expansion in Fourth Revolution rights and principles. In the Supreme Court, presumptive retirements and conservative appointments could well create a majority prepared not only to curb the revolution, as the Court had since the eighties, but also to actively roll it back. The key test here would be the issue of abortion and the undoing of *Roe v. Wade*. Alternatively, abortion rights could be undone by constitutional amendment, though the requirement of three-fourths of the states for ratification probably confines such an effort to the realm of sound and fury. Gay marriage might more likely succumb to a move overriding the constitutional obligation on each state to recognize the acts of another. But the most pervasive and entrenched elements of the Fourth Revolution, in the realm of culture and personal mores, are likely to remain impervious to judicial interpretation or any other form of governmental action. The Fourth Revolution is here to stay.

The Fourth Revolution and Contemporary Debate

Prompting this book at the outset was the murky confusion in American political argument in recent years as it has addressed basic terms and issues, above the diverse meanings of "liberal" and "conservative." The trouble arises directly from the history of revolutionary change in modern times, and especially its working out in the United States. Nevertheless, it is possible to resolve these problems of political definition by applying the concept of successive revolutionary movements in American history, and above all the Fourth Revolution.

Looking at the history of the United States in terms of the sequence of revolutions readily clarifies the different political positions that have claimed the labels "liberal" and "conservative." The classical liberalism that became the hegemonic American ideology was a compound of the First and Second revolutions, based on individualism, representative government, freedom of conscience and expression, separation of church and state, and laissez-faire economics. Economic liberalism and conservatism were the positions that emerged in the Third Revolution, with the classical liberals taking the conservative, antirevolutionary position this time around. The Fourth Revolution generated yet another kind of liberalism, the social and cultural liberalism advocating the forms of equality and liberty embodied in the revolution's constituent movements. Opposition to the Fourth Revolution or to its extremes—the conservatism of the sixties and after— drew on elements from all across the old political spectrum. Some were economic liberals alienated by the doctrinal extremes and tactical excesses of the Fourth Revolution. Others were religious conservatives who took up arms against the Third Revolution as well as the Fourth and even called into question the legacy of the First Revolution.

Sentiment against the Fourth Revolution rests in part on conservatism in the ultimate sense, that individuals must be made morally and practically responsible for their own condition and that society in the abstract cannot be held accountable. This conviction, eloquently defended by the conservative guru Marvin Olasky,[6] is repeatedly expressed as "self-reliance." It ties in closely with the Protestant work ethic, however unrealistic it may be about the broader economic forces that impinge on an individual's fate. Only the hegemonic tradition of the Second Revolution has been left unscathed in the new climate of reaction. Daniel Bell summed up all this mix of attitudes in a pithy remark: "I am an economic radical, a political liberal, and a cultural conservative."[7]

Considering liberalism and conservatism in the light of the sequence of revolutionary movements, it is finally possible to untangle the confusion that has knotted up American political discourse in the past third of a century. The public understands "liberalism" primarily as advocacy of the Fourth Revolution, especially those elements of it that remain a battleground—the gender revolution where it extends to abortion and homosexual rights, antiauthoritarianism in areas ranging from education to penology, easy welfare policy (which stirs up tacit residual racism), and the whole question of personal liberty in social and cultural matters versus the demand for exercise of personal responsibility. This animus is mixed up with residual Third Revolution issues such as entitlement programs and governmental intervention in the economy. Wary politicians to the left of center have tried to steer around this minefield by calling themselves "progressive" to avoid the emotions that "liberal" in any sense arouses.

The concept of the Fourth Revolution proves to be a sharp tool of analysis to explain a vast range of contemporary controversies. It highlights the links among attitudes one way or the other on educational reform, public morality, sexual conduct, racial preferences, immigration, even on marijuana use. It distinguishes issues—economic versus social and cultural—that have divided the electorate in very different ways. It allows a new and more meaningful depiction of public ideology, as the Fourth Revolution engages the tradition of the Second over the prostrate body of the rejected Third. It underscores how, with minimal change in its political and economic structure, America has become a new land.

Conclusion: What Did the Fourth Revolution Do?

Revolutions never accomplish what they intend. Friedrich Engels observed, "People who boasted that they had *made* a revolution have always seen the next day that they had no idea what they were doing, that the revolution *made* did not in the least resemble the one they would have liked to make."[8] The First Revolution, aiming to free up and rehabilitate religiosity, ended with toleration and freedom of thought. The Second Revolution, aiming to overthrow hierarchies of blood, resulted in concentrations of wealth. The Third Revolution, aiming to abolish inequality of wealth, boosted hierarchies of organizational power. The Fourth Revolution, aiming to eliminate discrimination among social categories, has eventuated in practices of group privilege. The work of revolutions seems never to be done but only to be passed on to a new revolutionary urge among subsequent generations.

Undeniably, the Fourth Revolution wrought vast transformations in American society and in the American consciousness, as well as changes in other lands that were far from negligible. But the depth and permanency of these changes varies from one segment of the Fourth Revolution to another, as does the correspondence between aspiration and result. All in all, the outcome of the Fourth Revolution left many of its original radical hopes marginalized, while other revolutionary strivings were fused seamlessly into the existing social structure.

It is easy to catalog the established successes of the Fourth Revolution. The black civil rights movement scored an extraordinary victory, whatever residual abuses and disappointments may linger. The youth movement won while losing, as the counterculture infiltrated the whole of society. The gender revolution made huge gains, though divisive struggles over abortion and gay rights persist. Education and social services have been revolutionized by doctrines of equality and liberation. In all these respects Americans live in a different country. But the fundamental social structure in America has not been overturned; if anything, it has shown enough resilience to absorb the force of the Fourth Revolution and to gain strength thereby.

Through this synthesis, the Fourth Revolution has become durably embedded in existing society, dovetailing with both the traditional principles of the Second Revolution and the meritocratic outcome of the Third. By pursuing its goals mainly through the legal and judicial system, the Fourth Revolution has meshed with the constitutional tradition of individual rights and equality. At the same time, it has been folded into the meritocracy that moved in alongside the hierarchy of wealth in modern society. To be sure, in its second wave, with the implicit philosophy of group rights and virtues, the Fourth Revolution has clashed with some of the strictures of the Second Revolution. This represents an ironic shift from the original push for equality and integration. At the same time, the Third Revolution base from which the Fourth Revolution was launched in the days of the Great Society has been gravely eroded, with attacks on economic entitlements that particularly threaten the weaker beneficiaries of the Fourth Revolution.

Has the Fourth Revolution run its course? May its deficiencies be remedied, or are its excesses likely to be exacerbated, in a future wave of the movement? Prediction is not easy. Though change is inevitable, the particular form of a new revolutionary surge, perhaps a generation later, is very hard to anticipate. There are lingering controversies—the gender revolution and the culture wars—that may point to new efforts to consummate the principles of the Fourth Revolution. The political realm evidences a renewed backswing against the Fourth Revolution in resistance to affirmative action, deinstitutionalization, and compassionate criminology, to mention just a few points at issue. Still, the most heated disputes in postmillennial politics turn not so much on issues of the Fourth Revolution as on efforts to turn back the legacy of the Third and even of the First.

The Fourth Revolution, like all those before it, remains in contention. Like its predecessors, it may leave some of its agenda forever incomplete. Or it may be superseded, like the others, by an entirely new kind of revolution. There are signs of this already.

CHAPTER 12

A Fifth Revolution?

The historic sequence of great revolutionary causes may not necessarily end with the Fourth Revolution. Certainly, historical change is not suddenly going to stop with the resolution of a certain set of issues, even if the complex challenges of the Fourth Revolution can somehow be brought to closure. While it is impossible to foresee the shape of events very far into the future, a long future there is bound to be, barring the now unlikely eventuality of nuclear annihilation. And enough indications have appeared, since the climax of the Fourth Revolution in the 1960s, of new kinds of revolutionary protest movements taking shape.

It is of course difficult to define the makings of a new revolution within the body of the last one, when the newer movement has not taken a clear and independent form and when the perspective of time is still short. The issues belonging to successive epochs overlap, and at the outset of a new revolution it may be hard to recognize where the old one leaves off and the new one begins. Nevertheless, by applying the past experience of transitions from one set of revolutionary principles to another, and culling recent evidence of a new revolutionary departure, it is possible at least to speculate about the nature of a potential new challenge to the status quo. There are indeed signs of a Fifth Revolution, though its exact character and the timing of its onset are far from predictable.

The Fifth Revolution and the First Four

If the pattern of the past is any guide, a Fifth Revolution will be yet another form of the struggle against authority and inequality in human relations. But what area of protest is left, after the historic struggles against dominance by certain people over others in religion, government, economic life, and social relationships? As the sequence of revolutionary battles has moved down from heaven toward earth, from the more abstract issues of religion and government to the more mundane matters of economics and interpersonal relationships, it points to an as yet inchoate locus of conflict, namely, a contest over the relationship between humanity and nature. Sensing this, the Franco-Russian chemist Ilya Prigogine asserted, "We are heading toward a new synthesis, a new naturalism. ... There is a need for new relations between man and nature and between man and man."[1]

The Fifth Revolution as thus conceived embraces a variety of issues that do not fit clearly into the framework of the earlier revolutionary transformations underlying contemporary society. The nature issue is expressed most literally in militant environmentalism and its resistance to the material progress that is seen to be despoiling the earth. In other words, "Stop the World!" There are signs from time to time of a radical rejection of the division of labor and the whole fabric of mercantile relationships, already expressed in the commune movement of the sixties and seventies. There is a current that rejects technology and demonizes the science that produced it, on the grounds that these accomplishments are dehumanizing transgressions against the humanity–nature balance. At times, the whole of Western civilization is brought under attack, not only for its alleged racism, sexism, and imperialism—targets of the Fourth Revolution—but also for its philosophical sins. Some years ago, anticipating these challenges, I wrote of the prospect of "a revolt against the whole modern tradition of rational and scientific thinking."[2] This kind of protest is now being expressed in everything from herbal medicine to New Age religion. In this respect, the Fifth Revolution parallels the religious fundamentalism that never accepted the scientific worldview begotten by the First Revolution.

In personal terms the Fifth Revolution rejects the whole ethic of individual success. The First and Second revolutions opened the way to self-assertion beyond the bounds of the traditional and hereditary. The Third and Fourth revolutions strove to equalize success for all, utopian as this might seem for a relative goal where the success of one is necessarily the failure of another. Now the portents of the Fifth Revolution point to a general repudiation of the conventional standard of personal competition and achievement.

In some respects the Fourth Revolution shades directly into the Fifth, as, for example, in the commune movement, the attack on expertise, and the critique of Western civilization. This overlap in the sequence of revolutionary principles is not unusual: it is typical for the main features of a new kind of revolution to be prefigured in the ultraradical elements of the previous one. The stirrings of democracy appeared in the religious revolution in England, notions of socialism emerged in the political revolution in France, and the antimanagerial spirit shone briefly in Russia's economic revolution. Movements anticipating a Fifth Revolution cropped up simultaneously with the revival of Fourth Revolution enthusiasm in the late 1980s and 1990s. Again, without more perspective it is hard to be definite about what is fundamentally new in the coming era; impressions must suffice. Nevertheless, a case can be made that a new kind of challenge will be thrust on modern society before another generation is out.

In form, the Fifth Revolution, like the Fourth, will probably not exceed the limits of the semirevolution, at least as far as the United States is concerned. It is not likely in the West to involve a forcible assault on the social system as a whole, though sporadic acts of violence have already occurred in the environmental area and in antiglobalization riots. Presumably the characteristic revolutionary process will get under way, moving from moderate protest to extremist defiance and then to exhaustion and consolidation. Such fissiparous tendencies are already visible among different factions of the movements potentially making up the Fifth Revolution. But nothing approaching the dramatic upsurge of the Fourth Revolution in the 1960s has so far appeared. Apart from isolated harbingers, the Fifth Revolution has not really begun except in the theoretical, intellectual realm.

Like the great revolutions of the past, including the Fourth, the Fifth Revolution will be an international phenomenon, though like its predecessors it is likely to have an epicenter in one or a few particular countries where the pressure for change is greatest and the power to spread the message is present. This is the role that the United States has played in the Fourth Revolution. Now the question arises, where around the world is the strongest inspiration for the Fifth Revolution likely to be centered? One possibility is an emerging non-Western country or group of countries that would raise the banner of anti-Western, antirational, and antimodern revolt, attracting to its standard elements all over the world including people in the West who are restive over the excesses of the Western way of life. Moslem fundamentalism is an example, though one wonders whether by itself it could muster either the geopolitical weight or the ideological appeal to have a worldwide impact. In any case, a Fifth Revolution, like the

Fourth, will not be primarily governmental in the way that the political and economic revolutions were. It will exert its influence by preachment and example rather than by force of arms. Still, wherever the seat of the challenge and its political force may appear, Western modernity could well be rocked again by a new attack on its basic premises, if not by the logic of the critics, then by the economic crunch of energy and resource shortages, including fresh water and even breathable air.

Between the sentiments of the budding Fifth Revolution and the millennial triumphalism of global capitalism there is an extraordinary disconnect. In the United States, particularly, this gap contrasts with the smug absorption of most elements of the Fourth Revolution into the Establishment mainstream. Along with their refusal to take the challenge of worldwide climate change seriously, American political and business leaders are oblivious to the depth of disbelief in the fundamentals of the system and the potential spread of radical rejectionism. Global capitalism, pushing ordinary people too hard in the industrialized countries as well as in the third world, is sowing the seeds of its own undoing. A real global proletarian revolution may be brewing, though it will emerge under the banner of ideologies that would baffle the theorists of Marxism.

Sources of the Fifth Revolution

From the perspective of earlier revolutions, the forces and frustrations feeding the Fifth Revolution can readily be suggested. Many of the elements of a new social explosion are clearly present—intellectual critiques, a mood of nihilistic questing, a new generational revolt against the status quo, an obtuse and unresponsive public sphere. Rebels looking for a cause are fed up with the demanding routines of an overtechnologized economy and the frenetic, wheel-spinning style of life that managerial society entails. They are disillusioned with the outcome of the Fourth Revolution that only reshuffled access to the hierarchical system while leaving the system itself intact. All that is lacking is an overt outbreak somewhere around the world of defiance against the reigning social and cultural order. It would need to be an event with the capacity to excite and rally the international potential of disaffection as the United States more than anyone else did for the Fourth Revolution.

Underlying the new kinds of rebelliousness are the peculiar trends of social and economic development in the Western world since the mid-1970s. The long era of economic expansion and rising living standards for all, dating with only minor interruptions from the early nineteenth century, came to an end, at least for the time being, on a contentious plateau of inflation, unemployment, and third world competition. In the

United States, inequalities sharpened while corporate economics dictated new pressure on the salaried middle class. This, combined with the success of the Fourth Revolution in opening access for women and racial minorities into the upper employment levels, made achievement opportunities in the success hierarchy even tighter for white men. The industrialized world approached a no-growth or "zero-sum" society (to cite the economist Lester Thurow).[3] While this sense of constraint might have abated somewhat with the global stock market surge of the later nineties, in the long run the relief will likely prove to be only temporary. It may be possible to enhance the satisfaction of material desires but not of everyone's clamor for status and success. A mood of sour grapes sets in: these achievements are felt to be illusory, corrupting, and in any case not worth the human and natural cost.

In the third world, a different, almost opposite, dynamic has gone on: hyperdevelopment, driven by Western investment and consumption, that has produced the characteristic signs of a prerevolutionary situation. Urbanization and industrialization have proceeded apace, along with penetration by Western mass culture. Rising expectations are outpaced by widening income gaps and the disruption of traditional communities, complicated in most places by explosive population growth. Governments, whether constitutional or dictatorial, are unresponsive. The consequence is a rising potential of anti-Western protest and ultimately of revolution, awaiting only whatever ideology and organization can translate the unrest into action.

Intellectual repudiation of the technocratic order is already widespread, though it may still overlap with issues of the Fourth Revolution. Some of these critics may not yet be aware that they are preparing a new kind of revolution, but thinkers such as Murray Bookchin on the environment, Amitai Etzioni on the community, and Nancy Rule Goldberger et al. on the rejection of "masculine" science strike at the heart of the modern way of thinking and its assumptions about relationships among the individual, society, and the natural world.[4] Margaret Atwood's recent novel dramatizes the self-destructive rampage of "men at work" and "monkey curiosity," leading into "endless crumbling."[5] Anyone in a rejectionist mood can readily find philosophical support and justification for a new revolutionary nihilism.

Generational anger is always available to be mobilized against the old order, wherever and whenever the perception of a moral lapse among the ruling cohort triggers a new protest movement. Civil rights and the Vietnam War did this for the Fourth Revolution in America in the 1960s. Evidence of governmental dithering in the face of a global environmental crisis could ignite the forces of the Fifth Revolution, or the same could result from some altercation in the third world that smacked of a new form of Western imperialism. More specific to the present time is the reform–reaction cycle in American politics, which has brought in a new upsurge of anti-Establishment idealism and anger, however much these responses might be confined within age groups (youth) or institutional boundaries (academe). The radical sentiments of the Fourth Revolution have been reinvigorated, but at the same time the new kinds of radicalism comprised in the Fifth Revolution share center stage.

Like the resurgent protagonists of Fourth Revolution extremism, theorists pointing the way to the Fifth Revolution have been emboldened by the premises of the now fashionable postmodern philosophy. "Postmodernism stresses the relativity, instability, and indeterminacy of meaning," in the words of one of its leading exponents.[6] In the postmodern view, there are no objective truths or absolute values; truth and values are "constructed" within cultural frameworks and conditioned by social circumstances, be they race, gender, the imperialist domination of one civilization over others, or any other special influence. From this position it is argued that truth is only the truth that is comfortable for the group that speaks it. Furthermore, groups that have been demeaned by the dominant white-male-oriented Western culture are presumed to have a greater legitimacy in rectifying past skewing of knowledge or even to have greater merit in their thought because the experience of oppression has sensitized them to the shortcomings of the modern mind.

This kind of thinking is a direct carryover from the experience of the Fourth Revolution to the theory of the Fifth. It is particularly striking in the radical feminist critique of science, and among the devotees of non-Western philosophy and religion. There is a disturbing parallel here with the philosophical contentions of Soviet-style Marxism, according to which all truth was class truth, conditioned by social circumstances. The Fifth Revolution, with its own favored constituencies, will not be immune to such totalitarian excesses of political self-righteousness.

Like past revolutions, the Fifth Revolution is emerging from the bosom of its predecessor. Extremist views among the various elements of the Fourth Revolution have been shading into the stands of the Fifth in the same way that radical advocacy of Third Revolution principles of economic equalization shaded into Fourth Revolution issues of social equality. In the counterculture, especially, one can see the new shoots of the Fifth Revolution's militant environmentalism and the antisuccess ethic. The extremes of the black civil rights movement and the feminist movement have fed the repudiation of logical and scientific thinking and the rejection of Western civilization in general—never mind that women, at least, have done better in the modern West than at any other time or place since the dawn of recorded history. In societies where economic progress has also meant greater bureaucratic constraint of the individual in business organizations, the antimanagerial component of the Fourth Revolution has encouraged rejection of the hierarchy of expertise and the hegemony of technology, however impractical this sentiment might be. Finally, the deep new anti-Westernism brewing and spreading in the Moslem Middle East may be only the prototype for like movements in other cultures reacting against their experience of involuntary Westernization. The murderous campaign of Pol Pot's Cambodia in the 1970s against its educated urban population might be an extreme example of the direction these emotions could take.

Militant Environmentalism

Militant environmentalism is the earliest and most distinct element of the Fifth Revolution. It is also the most international, taking political form as it has throughout Europe in the movement of the Green parties. Of all the components of the Fifth Revolution, militant environmentalism has generated the most clashes between single-minded idealists and the established interests of governments and economic systems. It has lent a driving force to the other elements of the Fifth Revolution in much the same way that the black civil rights movement energized the Fourth Revolution in its time.

Militant environmentalism or ecopolitics has old roots in the United States. The environmental chronicler Philip Shabecoff spoke of three "waves" of environmentalism, starting with the conservation movement of the Progressive era before World War I. The second wave was the political effort of the 1970s and the legislative breakthroughs it achieved; this would be the moderate stage of the ecopolitical revolution. The third wave, welling up from the late 1980s on to attack abuse of the environment as a sickness of the whole social system, represents the extremist form of this component of the Fifth Revolution. Writing from the moderate standpoint, the geographer Martin Lewis defined "eco-radicals" by their belief that "human society, as it is now constituted, is utterly unsustainable and most be reconstructed according to an entirely different socioeconomic logic."[7] Militant environmentalism sacralizes the pristine earth, to the point of nature worship. It is prepared to invoke any means, even sabotage and terrorism, to assert its creed. It is the revolutionary defense of nature against technological society.

The intellectual preparation of militant environmentalism has a long history, embedded in the protest campaigns and countercultural attitudes of the Fourth Revolution and elaborated by some of the same figures of that era. A variety of books—Rachel Carson's *Silent Spring* on the abuse of insecticides, Charles Reich's *Greening of America,* and Barry Commoner's *The Closing Circle* on the excesses of technology—helped set the stage.[8] By the early 1970s, serious long-range environmental concerns were being articulated by writers such as Lester R. Brown of the Earth Watch organization and by the Club of Rome with its controversial report on "Limits to Growth."[9] The movement was fed by real dangers to the human habitat posed by the nuclear threat, runaway pollution, and the pressure of population on the earth's carrying capacity, all of which fed a mood of radical rejectionism. But this was still the moderate revolution in ecology, tactically speaking, epitomized by the career of David Brower, executive director of the Sierra Club and founder (in 1969) of Friends of the Earth.[10]

Organized ecopolitics in the United States dates from the first Earth Day in April 1970, the brainchild of Wisconsin senator Gaylord Nelson. The chosen date (April 22) happened to be Lenin's birthday, occasioning allegations that the movement was a Communist plot. Nonetheless it crystallized broad public concern. A Nixon staffer admitted, "We were totally unprepared for the tidal wave of public opinion in favor of cleaning up the environment that was about to engulf us."[11] Environmentalism inherited some of the momentum of youthful activism of the sixties while the goals of the Fourth Revolution were being clouded over by extremism and backlash. It also drew the favor of the Nixon administration, happy to back a cause that would divert some of the protest energy of that era. Congress passed the National Environmental Policy Act (creating the Council on Environmental Quality), followed by the Clean Air Act of 1970 and the formation of the Environmental Protection Agency. The Endangered Species Act came in 1973. These reforms of the early 1970s largely satisfied ecopolitics in America until the Reagan counterrevolution of the 1980s, personified by Interior Secretary James Watt with his free market absolutism and tagged with the president's remark that most air pollution was caused by trees. Movements then proliferated, to protect everything from the destruction of species habitat and biodiversity to the introduction of genetically engineered crops and milk-production hormones.[12] Preservation of wilderness areas, in the spirit of Henry David Thoreau, became an end in itself.

American developments in ecopolitics were paralleled and exceeded in Europe, with the formation of Green parties in the seventies and their electoral breakthrough into parliamentary status in the eighties, notably in Germany. Unfortunately, the effectiveness of the German Greens was hampered by the characteristic revolutionary cleavage between moderates and extremists, in this case between the "Realos" or realists who aimed to promote the ecological agenda through the parliamentary process, as an "antiparty party," and the "Fundis" or fundamentalists who rejected compromise and questioned the political path altogether.[13]

A second Earth Day was organized internationally in April 1990 by a coalition of environmental bodies ranging from Greenpeace and the Sierra Club to broader interest groups such as the National Education Association and Planned Parenthood. In the United States it brought out hundreds of thousands of participants and put environmentalism of one stripe or another on almost everyone's political agenda, much as the marches on Washington had done for the civil rights and antiwar movements in the 1960s. A New York Times/CBS poll found that public support for the strictest environmental controls rose from 45 percent in 1981 to 74 percent at the time of the second Earth Day, and membership in the mainstream environmental organizations rose correspondingly.[14] In contrast to his predecessor, President George H.W. Bush went so far as to claim that he was the "environmental president." Thus the moderate form of ecopolitics was absorbed into the national consensus like civil rights had been earlier. Kirkpatrick Sale, the historian of Students for a Democratic Society who became an apostle of the Green movement, wrote in 1993, "Rarely has a movement in so short a time gained such popular support, had such legislative and regulatory impact, produced so many active organizations, or become so embedded in a culture: a green revolution, indeed."[15]

At the same time, the extremist wing of ecopolitics took a new swing toward radical action. Earliest of the direct-action groups was Greenpeace, founded by Canadian Quakers and environmentalists in 1970 with a mission to fight the battles of the environment at sea, first to protest nuclear testing (especially the French explosions in the atmosphere) and then to combat the slaughter of sea mammals and pollution of the oceans. In the course of the 1970s, nuclear power plants were the focus of a series of ad hoc protest actions drawing their inspiration from the civil rights movement and illustrating what the activist–writer Barbara Epstein called "the idea that culture is a substitute for strategy," with "no conscious direction" and "a celebration of fragmentation."[16]

More aggressive was the group known as "Earth First!" founded in 1980 by David Foreman, a West Coast outdoorsman and one-time Goldwater Republican. Foreman and his friends proposed to implement the fictional program of the novelist Edward Abbey (The Monkey Wrench Gang) by throwing "a monkey wrench into the gears of the machine destroying natural diversity."[17] "A huge gap has developed," warned a writer for the New York Times, "between diagnosing the problem and prescribing the cure."[18] Though it professed the nonviolent methods of Gandhi and Martin Luther King Jr., Earth First! was nothing less than a campaign of sabotage, getting into high gear in the so-called Redwood Summer of

1990. The group attempted to disrupt logging in Northern California by such tactics as driving spikes into trees to destroy saw blades and pouring sugar into the gas tanks of the machinery. Another target of choice for sabotage was the electric lines transmitting nuclear power. In justification of such tactics Foreman went so far as to call humanity "a cancer on nature."[19]

Reactions against militant environmentalism underscore the difference between the public orthodoxy that the Fourth Revolution achieved and the raw edges of the Fifth. Whereas it has become taboo, in public anyway, to disparage blacks or women or other protected demographic groups, frightened conservatives and irritated business interests feel no compunctions about denouncing environmental extremists as maniacal "eco-Nazis." "They are a violent, terrorist group," said one California rancher.[20] The writer Michael Crichton published a diatribe, really a parody in novel form, against a putative environmentalist plot to sabotage civilization.[21] The FBI adjudged Earth First! and its kindred souls to be a new menace to national security and trotted out the same methods of surveillance and harassment that it had developed to obstruct the black civil rights movement.[22] Contended Philip Shabecoff, "The extreme right in America, which had fed for decades on the fear and hatred of Communism, was seeking a new devil.... The environmental movement was being tried as a likely candidate—a green menace replacing the red."[23] But there is some substance to these perceptions: militant environmentalism became a focal point for then distinctive emotions of revolutionary extremism, including self-righteous passion against an evil system and the conviction that the end justifies any means.[24]

In the familiar manner of left-wing radical groups, the environmental extremists splintered over issues both of theory and of tactics. Foreman abandoned Earth First! as the captive of "hippies and yippies," only to be denounced by a coleader as "an unrepentant right-wing thug."[25] Another offshoot of Earth First!, on the radical side, was the "Earth Liberation Front (ELF)" proclaimed in England in 1992 to sustain tactics of violence. They took credit for numerous acts of sabotage in the later 1990s and past the turn of the century, notably against lumber interests in the Pacific Northwest. Anarchist in spirit and leaderless in structure, ELF nonetheless became, in the words of a *New York Times* writer, "One of the nation's most active and destructive domestic terrorist organizations."[26]

More serious, and more widely noted, was the bizarre case of the so-called Unabomber, one Theodore Kaczynski, Harvard graduate and sometime professor who retired at an early age to rural Montana and embarked on a one-man campaign of terrorism to disrupt technological civilization. After years of anonymously planting bombs that randomly maimed and murdered students and university employees, Kaczynski laid out his philosophy of radical environmental action in a manifesto that he coerced the *New York Times* and *Washington Post* into publishing.[27] Arguing that industrialism and technology were destroying freedom and the quality of life, Kaczynski opted for revolution in the most literal terms ever heard among devotees of the Fifth Revolution. "When the system becomes sufficiently stressed and unstable," he correctly observed, "a revolution against technology may be possible. The pattern would be similar to the French and Russian revolutions." Moreover, "The revolution must be international and worldwide." Kaczynski was soon thereafter identified (by his brother, actually) he began; apprehended and convicted serving multiple life sentences.

The Unabomber's ramblings were only one variant of the ideology developed by militant environmentalism. This philosophy goes back to the "Gaia hypothesis" first proposed by the British biologist James Lovelock in the late 1960s, to the effect that the earth (or "Gaia," from the Greek goddess of the earth) is a self-sustaining system with lifelike qualities: "The earth is a living organism."[28] The Czech Republic's first post-Communist president Vaclav Havel, who dabbled in the Fifth Revolution, proclaimed "the awareness of our being anchored in the Earth and the universe, the awareness that we are not here alone nor for ourselves alone but that we are an integral part of higher, mysterious entities against whom it is not advisable to blaspheme."[29]

Under the banner of "biocentrism," proposing to displace "anthropocentrism," some of the followers of the Gaia hypothesis turned it into a quasi religion of the earth, supporting New Age antirationalism and touting cooperation in place of Darwinian competition. Lovelock went along with all this: "Gaia may turn out to be the first religion to have a testable scientific theory embedded within it."[30] Bridging the commune movement of the sixties and the nature worship of the eighties, a "Rainbow Family of Living Light" took to meeting annually on the Fourth of July in different national forests, drawing crowds of up to thirty thousand of the socially alienated to pray and meditate for "healing the earth."[31]

Another line of environmentalist argument is directly rooted in the turmoil of the Fourth Revolution. This is "ecofeminism." Going back to Susan Griffin's *Women and Nature* (1978) and Carolyn Merchant's *Death of Nature* (1980), ecofeminism brackets male domination over females and the domination over nature by an exploitive male-oriented society; "androcentrism" is denounced as the root of both evils.[32] The geographer Joni Seager saw the cause of environmental devastation in "social arrangements, and especially social *derangements*" (particularly corporate) rooted in "a masculinist culture."[33] Here again the Fourth Revolution feeds the

Fifth: "The relationships of power and institutional control that shape our environmental affairs are extensions of the ordinary and everyday relationships between men and women."[34] The feminists Maria Mies and Vandana Shiva claimed a special women's sensitivity to "diversity," biological as well as cultural.[35] The Canadian feminist Judith Plant wrote even more confrontationally, "Ecology speaks for the earth, for the 'other' in human/environmental relationships; and feminism speaks for the 'other' in female/male relations. And ecofeminism, by speaking for the original others, seeks to understand the interconnected roots of all domination, and ways to resist and change."[36] Other than participating in the Green movement, however, ecofeminism remains a current of thought that is more academic than pragmatic. There are complaints of continuing male dominance and sexism in mainstream environmental movements, as well as "professionalization," to the detriment of "human-based needs and quality of life issues."[37]

Some writers have gone further in their critiques. Theodore Roszak questioned the whole science-based civilization that threatens earth and humanity alike: "The urban industrial reality principle represses much that is essential to the health both of person and planet: the primitive, the organic, the feminine, the child-like, the world." He touted an "ecopsychology" based on "the ecological unconscious" and hailed its religious implications in an "animist sensibility" and a "rebirth of paganism."[38]

Shocked at this sort of heterodoxy, the *Wall Street Journal* denounced "a pagan fanaticism that now worships such gods as Nature and Gender with a reverence formerly accorded real religion."[39] Pope John Paul II was equally alarmed: "Sometimes forms of nature worship and the celebration of myths and symbols take the place of the worship of the God revealed in Jesus Christ."[40]

Roszak's ideas reflect the most radical current of all in environmentalist thought, the so-called deep ecology first formulated by Ilya Prigogine and the Norwegian Arne Naess. Deep ecology goes beyond environmental protection for human benefit to assert, "The non-human natural world has a right to exist irrespective of how useful it might be for us" or, in Naess's own words, to proclaim "biospherical egalitarianism."[41] Deep ecology can be traced in America back to the "pastoral tradition" of Thoreau and John Muir, according to which, in the words of a historian of these ideas, "The primary purpose of nature is not so much to service the practical needs of American civilization as it is to offer an alternative, essentially religious source of values and experiences."[42]

This principle of deep ecology was injected into the contemporary environmental debate by the philosopher George Sessions and the sociologist Bill Devall, who attacked the anthropocentrism and selfishness of

"Western views of nature" along with the "imperialism of modernity and urbanism." They proposed a new "biocentric" path to self-realization through "a literal intermingling of person and other, of mind-in-nature."[43] The British philosopher Rupert Sheldrake, idealizing primitive animism, urged his readers to "think of the world as alive" and "participate in the spirits of sacred places and times."[44] Other writers have tried to link deep ecology and conventional religion. Tom Hayden of Fourth Revolution fame, now embracing the Fifth, aimed to "overcome the divide of soul from nature" through an environmentalist interpretation of Genesis. Science, he asserted, "cannot answer every mystery of nature.... We are deficient today not so much in our scientific capacity but [in] our spiritual and ethical resources for approaching the environmental crisis."[45]

All these quasi-religious quests were too much for other radical environmentalists. Murray Bookchin proposed the alternative of "social ecology," to bring humanity into harmony with nature through political action and social change. He wrote, "Ecology raises the issue that the very notion of man's domination over nature stems from man's domination of man, ... hierarchies, ... domination in every form."[46]

Militant environmentalism, to sum up, has established a pattern both theoretical and practical for ongoing activism of the Fifth Revolution sort. Philosophically, it has articulated the moral rejection of modern civilization and its scientific and technological basis. Tactically, it has developed a repertory of confrontational protests taking advantage of the antiauthority qualms that the Fourth Revolution introduced into Western culture. With these steps, ecopolitics has paved the way for a host of other protests, all based one way or another on contraposing nature to "civilized" man.

Animal Rights

Promotion of rights for animals is a particularly intense current of Fifth Revolution thought and action, paralleling militant environmentalism. This cause traces its roots back to Thoreau and even to the Utilitarian philosopher Jeremy Bentham, as well as to such more recent writers as Peter Singer, Bernard Rollins, and Tom Regan.[47] Carrying the issue of man versus nature to a logical extreme, the animal rights movement upholds a natural and ethical equality between humans and the animal world. Singer employed the term *speciesism* to compare human domination over animals with the racism that used to justify domination over blacks by whites.[48] In 2002 the San Francisco Board of Supervisors actually voted to transform pet "owners" legally into "guardians."[49] Regan called for a "bill of rights for animals," while the television entertainer Bob

Barker, a vegetarian, has endowed the study of animal rights law at leading law schools.[50]

Like every other radical movement, animal rights defenders have divided over tactics—moderate pressure politics versus extremist violence. The moderates, in such forms as the Animal Legal Defense Fund begun in the mid-1980s, followed the path of the black civil rights movement in invoking the political and judicial processes to curb hunting, medical research, and other activities deemed egregiously cruel to animals. They enjoyed notable success in the waters charted by Greenpeace for international protection of whales and smaller sea mammals.

In its more radical manifestation, both in confrontational tactics to disrupt the utilization of animal products and in the apotheosis of animal species as the moral equal of humankind, the animal rights effort has put itself at the cutting edge of ecological extremism. One embodiment of this urge is the "Animal Liberation Front (ALF)" an amorphous movement like its kindred Earth Liberation Front, that was launched in Britain in 1976 as a splinter from the "Hunt Saboteurs Association" and was introduced to the United States in the early eighties. The ALF people have often been involved in such publicity-attracting protests as paint-spraying fur wearers, picketing zoos, and sabotaging medical research on animals. Less extreme tactically but equally purist philosophically is "People for the Ethical Treatment of Animals" (PETA), noted for exposing cruelty in laboratory research and meat packing; it even tangled with the Ringling Brothers and Barnum & Bailey Circus.[51] PETA affirmed "the simple principle that animals are not ours to eat, wear, experiment on, or use for entertainment."[52] In this vein, the Green theorist Jeremy Rifkin berated the patenting of genetic engineering: "The United States becomes the first nation in the world to eliminate formally any last teleological distinction that might exist between life and inanimate objects."[53] "Animal Liberation is the perfect revolutionary doctrine," wrote Professor Robert Grant of Glasgow, dating this new line of protest from "the end of the Vietnam War, when ten years' worth of accumulated radical sentiment suddenly found itself homeless."[54]

Giving Up on Success

Militant environmentalism, together with animal rights, is one component of the Fifth Revolution that has already taken form as a vigorous movement. Another, contrasting element of the emerging Fifth Revolution is so far not really a movement but only a mood, though no less radical in its implications. This is the multifaceted rejection of the success-oriented society, including the hierarchy of individual achievement, large organizations that alienate both their staffs and their clientele, and at the extreme the whole concept of material progress and the division of labor. It is a potential revolution against the kind of society that all previous revolutions took for granted as the basis of their efforts.

The antisuccess mood picks up from certain elements of the Fourth Revolution that remained marginal or incomplete in the 1960s and 1970s. It presses the antimanagerial stance of the sixties youth revolution, demanding a genuine "civic equality" instead of "pseudodemocracy."[55] It advances some of the ideals of the counterculture and the commune movement, with reference back to the alleged "pastoral" movement in American political thought.[56] It rejects the values of economic growth and material affluence, as President Jimmy Carter intimated in his unforgettable "malaise" speech of 1979: "Too many of us now tend to worship self-indulgence and consumption.... Owning things and consuming things does not satisfy our longing for meaning."[57]

A profound contrast has emerged between the antisuccess mood of the Fifth Revolution and the actual outcome of the Fourth Revolution. The practical result of the latter, in its emphasis on group equality and nondiscrimination, has been not the advancement of individual equality but only the redistribution of inequality, as certain blacks, women, and members of other previously disparaged categories of the population are allowed to rise within the existing structures of hierarchy and power. This result, though opening paths of "success" to representatives of all these categories, has inevitably denied success to the great majority in every category. There is simply not enough room or economic sustenance for universal enjoyment of the upper levels in pyramids of achievement that by their nature progressively narrow the opportunities they offer, the higher the level one aspires to. The antisuccess philosophy resolves this dilemma by condemning the whole social system of hierarchies.

Rejection of hierarchy implies a radical rethinking of the individual's place in the social system. It calls into question the division of labor, the role of expertise and specialization, and the whole concept of work that has prevailed since the advent of the industrial revolution. Illustrating this doubt, the economics writer Hazel Henderson questioned the monetary definition of value and touted the informal, nonmonetary kinds of production and exchange within the home and the community.[58] Jeremy Rifkin welcomed technological unemployment and predicted a growing role for the "third sector" of nonprofit organizations and voluntary activities in the "post-market era."[59] Ivan Illich, who made a name for himself as a critic of disciplinarian education, attacked "commodity values" as contrasted with "vernacular values" and plumped for the principle of self-sufficiency and individual subsistence.[60] This brings us all the way back to

Karl Marx and the protest against "alienation." Work for another for money is treated by antisuccess writers as an unnatural distortion of human life that sacrifices every other value. Going even deeper, Rifkin attacked the modern attitude toward time as a commodity and the obsession with speed and efficiency: time is money. Instead, humanity should surrender to the rhythms of nature.

Advancing propositions like these about work and achievement, the antisuccess ethic dovetails with the most radical environmentalism. Both currents of thought consider the success society as an affront to human nature, literally sickening in its effect. In 1992 the self-styled "Natural Law Party" ran candidates for president and local offices in the United States, campaigning against "stress" and for a "higher consciousness" based on Transcendental Meditation. With growing frequency people who have in fact achieved success are opting out in favor of low-pressure, self-employed, often rural situations.[61] A "Buy Nothing" movement has appeared in some U.S. cities to protest the hegemony of materialist consumerism, especially at holiday time.[62] Some writers, notably Christopher Lasch just before his death, have taken issue with the whole notion of progress as an inevitable boon to humanity. "Progressive optimism," Lasch wrote, "rests, at bottom, on a denial of the natural limits on human power and freedom."[63]

In a more positive vein, the antisuccess mood is expressed in the communitarian philosophy and the "small is beautiful" ideal. Decades ago E.F. Schumacher made "small is beautiful" a household rallying cry in his critique of the failings of large systems and impersonal organizations. He deplored the hegemony of money and the cult of bigness in modern life: "People can be themselves only in small comprehensible groups" where "we can, each of us, work to put our own inner house in order."[64] Amitai Etzioni developed the theme of "responsible communitarianism" in a series of works, seeking a utopian resolution of the individual–authority polarity through the moral order of the voluntary community.[65] He is seconded by the historian John L. Thomas, who placed communitarianism in the Jeffersonian tradition of proprietary democracy.[66] Community —preferably the face-to-face community—is thus intended to solve once and for all the inequalities and stresses that modern acquisitive, materialistic life has imposed on humanity.

Repudiation of Science and Technology

Implicit both in militant environmentalism and in the abandonment of the success ethic is a deep suspicion of modern society and its claimed achievements in both the material and the ethical dimensions. Technology in most of its manifestations is blamed for subverting the natural life. Science as the foundation of technology is held accountable for all the evils real or potential that mechanization poses for the human condition. And behind science the whole tradition of the rational mind is called into question as a dehumanizing delusion, even a social disease.

Though the atomic monster had bothered thinkers ever since Hiroshima, the first serious revulsion against the boon promised by technology was probably the controversy over nuclear power beginning in the 1970s. Fears about safety and waste disposal compelled expensive countermeasures and invited reflection on the inherent limitations to material progress. Here was an early spillover of environmental concern into the generalized suspicion of technology. The near-disaster at Three Mile Island nuclear power plant in Pennsylvania in 1979 and the real disaster at Chernobyl in the Soviet Union in 1986, dramatized by such fictionalized productions as *The China Syndrome*, made theoretical fears real and charged up antinuclear demonstrations in the United States and the Green movement in Europe. As early as 1980, by popular referendum, Sweden rejected a future based on the nuclear power industry and required a phaseout of all nuclear plants by 2010. No new nuclear plants have been undertaken in the United States since 1975.

Another area where the costs and side effects of high tech began to be challenged was medicine, specifically pharmaceuticals and life-support systems. An early turning point was the thalidomide birth-defect tragedy of 1962. Here again technological innovation seemed to have reached a point of diminishing returns, opening the way to patently antiscientific and mythic thinking in a field where everyone has to balance personal worries and social costs. Since the late 1980s, alternative medicine, including herbal medicine, homeopathy, magnetic therapy, naturopathy, even fire walking and outright shamanism, has spread widely both in use and in public acceptance.[67] Faith healing and mind-over-matter medicine were given new respectability by President Johnson's one-time press secretary Bill Moyers, who jumped from the Third Revolution to the Fifth.[68] In 1991, to the consternation of the scientific Establishment, Congress created the Office of Alternative Medicine at the National Institutes of Health, and in 1994 it exempted alternative medications and food supplements from FDA regulation. Justifying the trend, one of its proponents argued, "It resonates with the spirit of the times."[69]

Nature and the worship of the natural world unite alternative medicine and radical environmentalism. To both, science-driven technology is the enemy. A writer for *Time* magazine noted, "The prestige of the irrational flourishes as traditional authority declines to the point of vanishing."[70] "Objective science," protested another critic of alternative medicine, is being represented as "simply coercion in optimist clothing."[71]

Beyond considerations of cost, safety, and practicality, numerous writers have begun to question the impact of high-tech society on the human psyche, as a sort of "technological addiction." Technology, it is felt, controls people, not the other way around, inducing in them a state that the political scientist Langdon Winner called "technological somnambulism" brought on by a "technolopolitan culture."[72] Computer software technology puts the whole world at the mercy of one corporation with its "secret and proprietary code," as if one company controlled the air we breathe.[73] Christopher Lasch complained of the reduction of the individual to the "minimal self," aiming only to survive amid the stresses of industrialism.[74] The environmental writer Bill McKibben worried about biological fixes getting out of control—gene splicing, artificial intelligence, even the quest for immortality.[75]

In the critique of science and technology, as in ecopolitics, a distinction can be drawn between the moderates and the extremists. This does not mean that the moderates are not revolutionary; in program they are—it is their methods and philosophical assumptions that are more reasonable. They worry about the tangible cost and harm that can come from misapplied science and runaway technology. In this vein the British writer Brian Appleyard blamed science for "appalling spiritual damage" that could undermine civilization itself.[76]

Fifth Revolution extremists find science and technology to be not only dangerous but also inherently wrong. According to the biologist Paul Gross and the mathematician Norman Levitt, "the academic left" displays "open hostility toward the *actual content* of scientific knowledge and toward the assumption ... that scientific knowledge is reasonably reliable and rests on a sound methodology."[77] Vaclav Havel captured the spirit of the new antiscience skepticism among humanists when he declared, "The relationship to the world that modern science fostered and shaped appears to have exhausted its potential.... It produces a state of schizophrenia: Man as an observed [being] is becoming completely alienated from himself as a human being."[78] On the defensive, scientists like the astronomer Carl Sagan have railed against scientific ignorance and pseudoscientific beliefs among the American public.[79] In 1995 a special conference at the New York Academy of Sciences deplored "the flight from science and reason" and the twisting of scientific theories of relativity and quantum mechanics into allegations "that nothing in science is certain and that mystery and magic have an equal claim to belief."[80]

Several issues are involved here. One is the softening of educational rigor since the 1960s, and the rebellion against hard study and the discipline of facts that the youth of the sixties carried into the educational establishment of the eighties and nineties. Another is the convenient rationalizations offered by postmodern philosophy that put science on a par with magic and myth making and, in the words of one well-known cosmologist, "reduce the whole corpus of physics to the status of a mass hallucination."[81] "We now confront," wrote Gross and Levitt, "the emergence of a new body of criticism of science, … that Western science is in fundamental ways blind or blinkered, that it is corrupted by its subtle bigotry and by its servile accommodation of power. That it is the artifact of a world view liable, any day now, to be overthrown."[82]

The sharpest assault on science comes from radical feminism, in parallel with ecofeminism. A growing body of feminist literature holds that science has been a patriarchal, male-oriented activity, not only ignoring the contributions of women and imposing a gender dominance on both its methods and its conclusions. In this spirit, the feminist philosopher Sandra Harding aimed to "show that the specific problematics, concepts, theories, language, and methods of modern physics are gender-laden. … The science we have is suffused with the consequences of gender symbolism, gender structure, and gender identity."[83] Science, in this view, will achieve "strong objectivity" only with the proportionate participation of women and members of racial minorities.[84] Meanwhile, at the other end of the political spectrum, science is under attack by religious fundamentalism with such faith-based doctrines as creationism. In sum, the hegemony of science in Western culture is potentially in grave trouble.

Inevitably the critics of blind technological advance have been denounced by the devotees of material progress as "Luddites," comparable to the original machine smashers of the early English industrial revolution. Undeterred, the skeptics have taken up the challenge and embraced the Luddite label heartily. Roszak, for example, responded to the explosion in computer use with a "neo-Luddite" polemic against this alleged threat to real thought.[85] Kirkpatrick Sale went back to do a history of the original Luddites and added some reflections on the antitechnology views of their modern descendants; he cited the estimate of a Russian scholar that there are "approximately fifty to one hundred million people in the United States, Russia, Europe, and worldwide, who have rejected the scientific, technocratic Cartesian approach."[86] Sale's conclusion is stark: "Resistance to the industrial system, based on some grasp of moral principles and rooted in some sense of moral revulsion, is not only possible but necessary. … If the edifice of industrial civilization does not eventually crumble as a result of a determined resistance within its very walls, it seems certain to crumble of its own accumulated excesses and instabilities within not more than a few decades."[87] In this spirit, some antitechnological Americans have unabashedly formed a new Luddite movement. They would "unplug from technology" through "a revolution of hearts" that would "slow things down, touch the earth again" and thus work for "a counter-culture that provides an alternative to virtual reality."[88]

Apart from militant environmentalist forays, the antitechnology spirit has so far remained more theoretical than activist. A notable exception is the celebrated case of the Unabomber, who killed even while he was composing his anti-industrial manifesto. Typical of the eclectic thinking of the revolutionary quasi intellectual, the document drew from anarchism, radical environmentalism, "small is beautiful," and technological skepticism to denounce the modern regimentation of the individual in a quintessentially Luddite spirit: "The factories should be destroyed, technical books burned." In their place, "The positive ideal that we propose is Nature, ... *wild* nature." To achieve which, "Reform is insufficient. Revolution is required."[89] Kaczynski was put down, even by his legal defense, as a paranoid schizophrenic; perhaps people who think him crazy do not grasp the nature of ideologically justified fanaticism.

The New Age

The Fifth Revolution's critique of science and technology is only the most specific expression of a broader rejectionist mood extending to the entire range of modern thought. Writers in this vein speak euphorically of a "new dawn" and a "spiritual awakening." Civilization may be breaking down, but a "fresh tide," as the British New Age advocate Sir George Trevelyan wrote in the seventies, is "rising in our consciousness, an inner flooding from some secret fountainhead, bring[ing] with it a surge of new optimism."[90] In the spirit of the New Age, radical critics are turning their backs on the whole tradition of rationalist thinking—"Cartesian," they call it[91]—and attaching themselves to a bizarre new assortment of cults and myths, in which traditional religion is one source of inspiration but no longer a containing vessel. In its implications for the fundaments of modern culture, this trend is far more subversive than any of the excesses of Communism or feminism or even radical environmentalism.

Many elements of New Age thinking have roots in the 1960s, particularly in the counterculture and in radical feminism. They include the antirationalist psychology of the Human Potential movement, influenced by Carl Jung; the attraction to oriental mysticism; feminist rejection of patriarchal monotheism in favor of polytheistic goddess worship; and all the alleged spirituality of "the Age of Aquarius" (popularized in the late sixties by the song of that name in the musical *Hair*). In 1980 the psychology writer Marilyn Ferguson published a New Age manifesto of revolutionary change, a "paradigm shift ... integrating magic and science." Behind this movement she perceived "a leaderless but powerful network

… working to bring about radical change in the United States. Its members have broken with certain key elements of Western thought."[92]

Some of the themes prominent in New Age thinking have been present in Western culture for many decades and even centuries. Astrology, parapsychology, faith healing, witchcraft, and Satanism have long histories. But in recent years, with the loosening of society's anchors both in traditional religion and in respect for the scientific explanation of phenomena, cults of all sorts have run wild. The calendrical artifice of the millennium has been a further stimulus to this behavior. Belief in astrology is matched by ignorance of astronomy. UFOs and alien visitations have become part of the folklore, endorsed in high places, by the Harvard psychiatrist John Mack , for example, with tales of alien abduction elicited from his patients under hypnosis.[93] Colleges add to their catalogs courses in everything from "environmental ethics" to "perspectives in ecstasy" and "Who is the Devil?" A cofounder of the Esalen Institute promotes New Age golf as a mystical path to God.[94]

Beliefs such as the shamanism of Native Americans have been brought into the mainstream, to the consternation of some Indians who complain that their heritage is being stolen by a movement "centered on the self, a sort of Western individualism run amok."[95] One Native American historian defended creationism and the supernatural origin of his people, against the "scientific folklore" of archeology and evolution,[96] while some mainstream anthropologists retreated to postmodern relativism: "Science is one of many ways of knowing the world." Indians' mythology is "just as valid."[97]

For all its spirituality, the New Age does not fit well with traditional religion. Belief and practice are down in all the mainline American denominations; only fundamentalist groups and televangelists, emotional and antirational, prosper. "Our churches," said sociologist Robert Wuthnow, "are more modeled on a consumer market where people shop for a spiritual life."[98]

The Vatican has weighed in with a warning in pamphlet form, "A Christian Reflection on the 'New Age,' " to dispute the deification of nature and to date the true New Age two thousand years ago.[99] In the meantime, cults such as Jonestown in Guiana, the Branch Davidians of Waco, Texas, Scientology with its curious doctrine of one hundred million years of reincarnation, and the Unification Church of Sun Myung Moon emanating from Korea have reflected and capitalized on the widespread anomie in modern American life. More entertainment oriented is the "Burning Man" festival held annually on the West Coast, a sort of religious revival of the counterculture.[100] In one form or another, in consonance with the antisuccess ethic, vulnerable individuals rebel against the isolating pressures of a competitive society and seek solace in the cult group as a sort of new family. Rejection of the mainstream is so intense that in some cases cult members are ready to commit mass suicide, as in the Jonestown saga. This is violence directed against the self when the system seems immovable, but it might portend greater trouble for the established order if, for example, it took the form of terrorism or urban guerrilla warfare.

The New Age has directly absorbed the heirs of radical feminism, in the form of goddess worship. "American feminism has combined with American spiritualism," said Wellesley professor Mary Lefkowitz.[101] These developments are a direct challenge to traditional Christianity and Judaism, as well as to Islam: it is logically impossible to entertain female equality within a framework of anthropomorphic monotheism. Goddess worship is the alternative, with its bold system of antinomies: "spirit vs. nature, order vs. chaos, transcendence vs. immanence, mind vs. matter, soul vs. body, thinking vs. feeling, and reason vs. instinct," where the first term in each pair implies the suspect patriarchalism and the second expresses the higher female principle, that is, the goddess.[102] The theologian Rosemary Ruether rejected the Christian scriptures as a "canonization to sacralize patriarchy."[103] A "women's spirituality movement," even extending to witchcraft, embraces a wide range of rebels against male-dominated religion.[104]

Like most elements of the Fifth Revolution, the New Age is so far more a mood than a movement. There have been only a few fanciful efforts to bring the diverse facets of this restlessness into some sort of coherent alliance; one was the attempt in 1987 to establish an annual "Harmonic Convergence Day," with sunrise ceremonies based on the Aztec and Mayan calendars.[105] Yet the observed breadth among sentiments of cultural disaffection should give pause to anyone who thinks that society can rely politically and economically on a rational citizenry. Furthermore, if and when the potentiality of the Fifth Revolution is activated by the requisite triggering events into a self-conscious revolutionary movement, there is no telling what madness may come forth among people who feel used and betrayed by a system of impersonal accounting and efficiency.

Rejection of Western Civilization

All of the evils that the Fifth Revolution protests—the abuse of nature, consumerism and the rat race, the excesses of science and technology, the constraints of rationalism on the human psyche—are directly tied in the minds of the new revolutionaries to the global hegemony of the modern West. This revulsion against the Western way is both internal and external. Internally, within Western society, it is expressed in all of the various components of the Fifth Revolution. Externally, in the non-Western world, it is expressed in the forms, often violent, of nativism and fundamentalism that have arisen in response to the perceived hegemony of a foreign and pernicious way of life.

The internal critics of Western civilization demonize their own society by treating all the developments they dislike, be they environmental degradation, the impersonality of science and technology, the pressures of a competitive economy, or the legacy of patriarchy, as inherent evils of Western culture. At the same time, they project upon the Orient, third world, or primitive society their idealized hopes for a virtuous alternative in the man–nature (or woman–nature) relationship. They draw on postmodernist relativism and the premises of twentieth-century anthropology to contend that all cultures are ethically equivalent and then go on to suggest that non-Western or premodern societies are morally superior. Such cultural self-abasement by some Western thinkers is another sign of profound disaffiliation from contemporary society.

It is easy and fashionable to denounce the West for its history of imperialistic conquest and exploitation, above all in the Americas. The five-hundredth anniversary of Columbus's "discovery" of America in 1992 was turned into an antianniversary by righteous denunciation of his incursion into the supposedly pristine and ecologically balanced world of Native Americans.[106] Some social anthropologists have claimed that primitives waged war less ferociously than moderns, a view that "pacified the human past," according to one anthropologist who dissents from the "neo-Rousseauian concept of prehistoric peace."[107] The archaeologist Mariya Gimbutas maintained that the Stone Age cultures of Europe were matriarchal and pacifistic: "The Indo-European conquest transformed all of society. ... We are still living under the sway of that aggressive male invasion," leading to Hitler, Stalin, and their like. "We dominate nature; we don't feel we belong to her."[108] The West is blamed—again with plausibility—for the global environmental crisis, as it imposes its exploitive ways on the rest of the world. Primitives and non-Westerners, above all Native Americans, are idealized because they have presumably lived closer to the earth, as part of nature rather than as its adversaries. The common Western sense of superiority based on science and technology is repudiated with disgust.[109] Because, in the postmodern mind, scientific conceptions of the world are held to be nothing more than social constructs, non-Western mythologies and folk wisdom are accorded an equal claim to validity and, because of the West's contamination by its own material success, an aura of moral superiority.

However powerful the underlying anti-Establishment resentments may be in America and in the West in general, the greater potential for the Fifth

Revolution lies in the non-Western world. Samuel Huntington's thesis about the coming conflict of civilizations may hold more truth than the author realized.[110] The anti-Western revolt in the non-West is not likely to confine itself to the quieter form of a semirevolution, but it could break out in one or more countries into a true revolutionary process, extending to the violent overthrow of existing governments.

Engagement of the Fifth Revolution with the non-Western world means that, like the classic revolutions, it will be internationalized into a wave of uprisings against the dominance of the familiar Western way of life. Where the anti-Western movement will be centered—whether within Western society or in a particular non-Western region—remains unclear; probably some form of reciprocal incitement will take place. But the non-Western component is likely to be much more destabilizing, both in that part of the world and in its impact on dissidents within the West, than it was in the experience of the Fourth Revolution. In that case, in the sixties, there was only the Cultural Revolution in China to resonate in a marginal way with the more radical currents of protest pouring forth in the United States and Europe. Perhaps the ultimate impact of the Fifth Revolution outside the West, given its ideological idiosyncrasies and its challenge to Western interests, could be to embarrass and inhibit the revolution's most radical exponents within the West.

In one instance the anti-Western revolution has already occurred. This, of course, is Iran, which has become a prototype for any such movements. The elements that went into the Iranian Revolution can be seen all over the world. There is overrapid modernization and urbanization under the pressure of Western economic stimuli and cultural examples. There are all the radical urges for change that the West has experienced, combining and telescoping into a single potential crisis all the issues of every previous kind of revolution. There are moves to rally around an angry anti-Western ideology, especially religious fundamentalism. Fundamentalism with a populist, anti-Western edge takes the place of the Marxism of the first half of the twentieth century.

Whatever the ideological form they may attach themselves to, potential revolutions on the Iranian model can be identified all over the third world. Obvious candidates include Brazil, as the Latin American country most severely stretched by modernization while still enjoying the power to sustain and export its possible revolution; India, where British-sponsored secularism is wearing thin against a background of uneven development and resurgent Hindu nationalism; Southeast Asia, where the financial crises of the late nineties have revealed the fragility of semimodernized societies; and above all the Arab world, with its center of instability in the overpopulated misery and cultural discontinuities of the region's key country, Egypt. Al Qaeda's anti-Western terrorism may be only a harbinger of things to come.

In all of these situations there is a characteristic combination of cultural abasement and mass economic grievance more than sufficient to fuel a revolution. What is less certain is the ideology and organization that may channel the revolutionary potential in each instance. Religion is the most obvious vehicle: Islam; militant Hinduism in India; even a revived Theology of Liberation in Catholic countries, though it has been resisted by the Papacy. There remains plenty of anti-Western nativist tinder in Russia. Conceivably Japan could become another locus of anti-Western fundamentalism, as it was in the run-up to World War II, if its economic setbacks at the millennium prove sufficient to detonate its reserves of traditionalistic national reassertion.

Some forms of interaction between the forces of the Fifth Revolution within the West and outside it can already be observed. Western critiques of the industrial system and the scientific culture do not go unnoticed in the non-West.[111] Non-Western complaints about Western (i.e., American) mass culture and consumerism, also heard loudly in Russia, echo the Western devotees of the Fifth Revolution. A global ideology of cultural rejectionism is in the making, with a common emotional core uniting its varied forms of expression.

The complacency that Western political and economic establishments have exhibited in the face of these challenges both internal and external can readily be compared with the Ancien Regime and late tsarist Russia. If anything, the moderns are blinder—no one on the side of the old order is even saying, "Après nous la déluge." Not that a total and abrupt overthrow of the world order is in the offing: it faces instead the semirevolution of gradual disaffiliation among its own most creative human resources and a progressive nibbling at its cultural and economic hegemony on the third world margins. If the industrial–consumerist order is to go, it will be with a whimper, not a bang.

The Nth Revolution?

Will the Fifth Revolution be the last one? Or will human society go on indefinitely being reshaped by successive kinds of revolution, like waves pounding on a beach? Naturally, the future cannot be foreseen well enough to permit a firm answer, but certain potentialities and limits can be suggested from the experience of the past.

The era of revolutions is the era of society transformed by modernization. We can place its beginning in Europe with the First Revolution in the sixteenth and seventeenth centuries, but we lack the perspective to know whether the long sequence of transformations that have taken place since that time is coming to a close or is still in midcourse. There is no reason so far to expect that the eternal issues of domination and equality in human relationships will be resolved once and for all by the Fourth Revolution or even by the Fifth. History shows too much backsliding from the principles of each revolution and too much yearning for new forms of society as human existence goes on changing. People never know what they are going to want as the generations roll by.

Certain forms of future change can nonetheless be suggested on the basis of the trend line in the history of revolution. In the era of the Fourth and Fifth revolutions, revolutionary change has become on the whole less political and less violent, compared with the bloody struggles of earlier epochs. Revolution is becoming more a matter of culture and of the changes in the hearts of men that the theologians have always preferred to look to. Maybe future kinds of social change will be so attenuated that it will be stretching the concept of revolution too much to apply it to them.

Another prospective limitation on the play of revolution lies in the sequence of revolutionary types. In many ways the direction of the Fifth Revolution suggests a return to premodern culture, to an idealized version of traditional society before it became complicated and corrupted by the excesses of technology and rationalism. This is the implication of nature worship, of the ideology of small communities and self-sufficiency, of New Age faiths that reject the scientific mind. Such nostalgia fixes particularly on the present-day survivals of traditionalism in the third world, but it could just as well refer back to the medieval West, before the epoch of revolutions ever began. Thus the sequence of revolutions, completed by the Fifth, proceeds full circle, to end by rejecting the principles that it started with.

Perhaps these considerations prove that the long era of revolution in the form we have known it is coming to an end. We have learned the lessons of St. Bartholomew's Day, the Bastille, the Winter Palace, Newark and Detroit, the Unabomber, the futility of it all. Or have we?

Notes

Chapter 1

1. E. J. Dionne Jr., *Why American Hate Politics* (New York: Simon and Schuster, 1991), 11–12.
2. James Davison Hunter, *Cultural Wars: The Struggle to Define America* (New York: Basic Books, 1991), 42, 34.
3. Arthur M. Schlesinger Jr., *The Cycles of American History* (Boston: Houghton Mifflin, 1986).
4. Charles A. Beard, *An Economic Interpretation of the Constitution* (New York: Macmillan, 1935).
5. Mickey Kaus, *The End of Equality* (New York: Basic Books, 1992), 5.
6. Dionne, *Why Americans Hate Politics*, 11.
7. Christopher Lasch, *The True and Only Heaven: Progress and Its Critics* (New York: Norton, 1991), 21.
8. Robert Heineman, *Authority and the Liberal Tradition: From Hobbes to Rorty*, rev. ed. (New Brunswick: Transaction, 1994), 16.
9. J. G. Merquior, *Liberalism Old and New* (Boston: Twayne, 1991), 66–67, 99–100.
10. Louis Hartz, *The Liberal Tradition in America: An Interpretation of American Political Thought since the Revolution* (New York: Harcourt Brace, 1955).
11. Alexis de Tocqueville, *Democracy in America* (London and New York: Colonial, 1900), 13.
12. Alonzo L. Hamby, *Liberalism and Its Challengers: From F.D.R. to Bush*, 2nd ed. (New York: Oxford University Press, 1992), 4–5.
13. See Elizabeth Drew in *The New Yorker*, December 12, 1988.
14. Robert Kuttner, "Who Owns Populism?" *The New Republic*, June 9, 1986, 12.
15. Paul Fussell, "A Dirge for Social Climbers," *The New Republic*, July 19, 1980.
16. J. K. Galbraith, "Two Pleas at Berkeley," *The New York Review of Books*, July 17, 1980.
17. Heineman, *Authority*, 10–11.
18. For example, Merquoir, *Liberalism*, 70.
19. See, for example, Irving Kristol, *Reflections of a Neo-Conservative: Looking Back, Looking Ahead* (New York: Basic Books, 1983); and Nathan Glazer, *The Limits of Social Policy* (Cambridge, MA: Harvard University Press, 1988).
20. Frances Fitzgerald, *America Revised* (New York: Atlantic Monthly Press, 1979).
21. See John Sperling et al., *The Great Divide: Retro vs. Metro America* (n.p.: PoliPoint Press, 2004).
22. Thomas Frank, *What's the Matter with Kansas? How Conservatives Won the Heart of America* (New York: Metropolitan Books, 2004).

Chapter 2

1. Crane Brinton, *The Anatomy of Revolution* (New York: Prentice Hall, 1938, 1952).
2. See Robert V. Daniels, ed., "Stalinism as Postrevolutionary Dictatorship" and "Soviet Thought in the 1930s: The Cultural Counterrevolution," in *Trotsky, Stalin, and Socialism* (Boulder, CO: Westview, 1991); and Nicholas Timasheff, *The Great Retreat* (New York: Dutton, 1946).
3. See Robert V. Daniels, "The Revolutionary Process, the Moderate Revolutionary Revival, and Post-Communist Russia," in *De Russia et d'ailleurs: Feux croisés sur l'histoire,* ed. Martine Godet (Paris: Institute d'Études Slaves, 1995).
4. J. Christopher Herold, ed., *The Mind of Napoleon: A Selection from His Written and Spoken Words* (New York: Columbia University Press, 1956), 64.
5. David Apter, *The Politics of Modernization* (Chicago: University of Chicago Press, 1965), 1, 3.
6. Samuel P. Huntington, *Political Order in Changing Societies* (New Haven, CT: Yale University Press, 1968), 53–55.
7. Ibid., 265.
8. Theda Skocpol, *States and Social Revolutions: A Comparative Analysis of France, Russia, and China* (Cambridge: Cambridge University Press, 1979), 19.

Chapter 3

1. William Bradford, *Of Plymouth Plantation, 1620–1647,* ed. Samuel Eliot Morrison (New York: Knopf, 1952), 352. See also James M. O'Toole, "New England Reactions to the English Civil Wars," *New England Historical and Genealogical Register* 129, no. 1 (January 1975).
2. Virginia Dejohn Anderson, *New England's Generation: The Great Migration and the Formation of Society and Culture in the Seventeenth Century* (Cambridge: Cambridge University Press, 1991), 18.
3. William Martin, *With God on Our Side: The Rise of the Religious Right in America* (New York: Broadway Books, 1996), 3.
4. Daniel Boorstin, *The Genius of American Politics* (Chicago: University of Chicago Press, 1953), 68.
5. Denis Brogan, *The Price of Revolution* (New York: Harper, 1951), 4.
6. Carl Becker, *The History of Political Parties in the Province of New York, 1760–1776* (Madison: University of Wisconsin Press, 1909), 22.
7. Gordon S. Wood, *The Radicalism of the American Revolution* (New York: Knopf, 1992), 5. See also Michael G. Kammen, ed., *Politics and Society in Colonial America: Democracy or Deference?* (New York: Holt, Rinehart and Winston, 1967).
8. See Perry Miller, "From the Covenant to the Revival," in *The Shaping of American Religion,* ed. J. W. Smith and A. L. Jamison (Princeton, NJ: Princeton University Press, 1961); and Edmund S. Morgan, "The Puritan Ethic and the Coming of the American Revolution," *William and Mary Quarterly,* 3rd series, 24 (January 1967): 3–18.
9. Bernard Bailyn, "Political Experience and Enlightenment Ideas in Eighteenth-Century America," *The American Historical Review* 67 (January 1962): 344.
10. See Neil R. Stout, *The Perfect Crisis: The Beginning of the Revolutionary War* (New York: New York University Press, 1976), 17–19.
11. Quoted in Pauline Maier, "John Wilkes and American Disillusionment with Britain," *William and Mary Quarterly,* 3rd series, 20 (1963): 394.
12. Lawrence H. Gipson, *The Coming of the Revolution, 1763–1775* (New York: Harper, 1954), 230. See also Merrill Jenson, *The Founding of a Nation: A History of the American Revolution, 1763–1776* (New York: Oxford University Press, 1968), 493–505.
13. Gouveneur Morris to Governor John Penn of Pennsylvania, May 1774, in David C. Douglas, ed., *English Historical Documents* (New York: Oxford University Press, 1953), 9:861.
14. William H. Nelson, *The American Tory* (Oxford: Oxford University Press, 1961), 85–96.
15. J. Franklin Jameson, *The American Revolution Considered as a Social Movement* (Princeton, NJ: Princeton University Press, 1926), 34–35; and R. R. Palmer, *The Age of the Democratic Revolution: A Political History of Europe and America, 1760–1800* (Princeton, NJ: Princeton University Press, 1959), 1: 188.

16. See Gary B. Nash, *The Urban Crucible: The Northern Seaports and the Origins of the American Revolution* (Cambridge, MA: Harvard University Press, 1986), 237–38.
17. Becker, *History of Political Parties,* 193.
18. See Staughton Lynd, "The Mechanics in New York Politics, 1774–1788," *Labor History* (March 1964): 232; and Jackson Turner Main, *The Sovereign States, 1775–1783* (New York: New Viewpoints, 1973), 173–76.
19. Gordon S. Wood, *The Creation of the American Republic, 1776–1787* (Chapel Hill: University of North Carolina Press, 1969), 84.
20. J. Paul Selsam, *The Pennsylvania Constitution of 1776: A Study in Revolutionary Democracy* (Philadelphia: University of Pennsylvania Press, 1936), 71.
21. David Hawke, *In the Midst of a Revolution* (Philadelphia: University of Pennsylvania Press, 1961), 148–49.
22. Thomas Paine, *Complete Writings* (New York: Citadel Press, 1945), 1: 16.
23. John Adams, "Thoughts on Government," in *Works* (Boston: Little, Brown, 1850), 4: 194.
24. Selsam, *Pennsylvania Constitution,* 136–40.
25. Rosalind L. Branning, *Pennsylvania Constitutional Development* (Pittsburgh: University of Pittsburgh Press, 1960), 13–15.
26. See Charles A. Beard, *An Economic Interpretation of the Constitution* (New York: Macmillan, 1935).
27. Bernard Bailyn, *To Begin the World Anew: The Genius and Ambiguities of the American Founders* (New York: Knopf, 2003), 132.
28. Palmer, *Age of the Democratic Revolution,* 1: 240.
29. Edmund S. Morgan, "Conflict and Consensus in the American Revolution," in *Essays on the American Revolution,* ed. Steven G. Kurtz and James H. Hutson (Chapel Hill: University of North Carolina Press, 1973), 299–300.
30. Joseph J. Ellis, "A New Topic for an Old Argument," *The New York Times,* February 29, 2004; cf. Ellis, *Founding Brothers: The Revolutionary Generation* (New York: Knopf, 2000).
31. Samuel I. Rosenman, ed., *The Public Papers and Addresses of Franklin D. Roosevelt* (New York: Random House, 1938), 1: 649, 652.
32. J. M. Keynes, Open Letter to President Roosevelt, *The New York Times,* December 31, 1933, quoted in William E. Leuchtenburg, *Franklin D. Roosevelt and the New Deal, 1932–1940* (New York: Harper and Row, 1963), 337.
33. Leuchtenburg, *Roosevelt,* 116–17.
34. William E. Leuchtenberg, *The Supreme Court Reborn: The Constitutional Revolution in the Age of Roosevelt* (New York: Oxford University Press, 1995), 99.
35. Max Lerner, *Ideas Are Weapons* (New York: Viking Press, 1939), 471, 473.
36. Kenneth S. Davis, *FDR, The New Deal Years, 1933–1937: A History* (New York: Random House, 1979), 493–563.
37. See Edward D. Berkowitz, *America's Welfare State: From Roosevelt to Reagan* (Baltimore: Johns Hopkins University Press, 1991), 153–76.
38. John L. Lewis, address to the 1936 Democratic convention, Chicago, quoted in Melvyn Dubofsky and Warren Van Zine, *John L. Lewis: A Biography* (Urbana: University of Illinois Press, 1986), 183.
39. See Steve Fraser, "The 'Labor Question,' " in *The Rise and Fall of the New Deal Order, 1930–1980,* ed. Steve Fraser and Gary Gerstle (Princeton, NJ: Princeton University Press, 1989), 74–75.
40. Robert H. Zeiger, *The CIO, 1935–1955* (Chapel Hill: University of North Carolina Press, 1995), 372.
41. J.K. Galbraith, *American Capitalism, the Concept of Countervailing Power* (Boston: Houghton Mifflin, 1952).
42. Fraser, "The 'Labor Question,' " 71.
43. See Alan Brinkley, *Voices of Protest: Huey Long, Father Coughlin, and the Great Depression* (New York: Knopf, 1982).
44. See Harvey Klehr, *The Heyday of American Communism: The Depression Decade* (New York: Basic Books, 1984).
45. Robert H. Zeiger, *John L. Lewis: Labor Leader* (Boston: Twayne, 1988), 100–101.
46. See Morris Ernst, *Report on the American Communist* (New York: Holt, 1952).
47. Davis, *FDR,* 676.

48. *Public Papers of Roosevelt,* 5: 232–33.
49. David M. Kennedy, *Freedom from Fear: The American People in Depression and War, 1929–1945* (New York: Oxford University Press, 1999), 783.
50. Adolf Berle and Gardiner Means, *The Modern Corporation and Private Property* (New York: Macmillan, 1933); James Burnham, *The Managerial Revolution* (New York: John Day, 1941); Milovan Djilas, *The New Class: An Analysis of the Communist System* (New York: Praeger, 1957).
51. Alan Dawley, *Struggles for Justice: Social Responsibility and the Liberal State* (Cambridge, MA: Belknap Press of Harvard University Press, 1991), 67 ff.
52. Leuchtenburg, *Roosevelt,* 345–36.
53. See, for example, Theodore Rosenof, *Dogma, Depression, and the New Deal: The Debate of Political Leaders over Economic Recovery* (Port Washington, NY: Kennikat Press, 1975).
54. Davis, *FDR,* 675.
55. Ibid.
56. Joseph Alsop, "The Roosevelt We Knew," *The New Republic,* January 27, 1982.
57. Alan Brinkley, *The End of Reform: New Deal Liberalism in Recession and War* (New York: Knopf, 1995), 6.
58. Linda Gordon, "Welfare Reform: A History Lesson," *Dissent,* Summer 1994, 325.
59. Clark Clifford papers, quoted in Daniel Yergin, *Shattered Peace* (Boston: Houghton Mifflin, 1977), 241.
60. See Michael S. Sherry, *In the Shadow of War: The United States since the 1930s* (New Haven, CT: Yale University Press, 1995).

Chapter 4

1. Jean-François Revel, *Without Marx or Jesus: The New American Revolution Has Begun* (Garden City, NY: Doubleday, 1971), 242.
2. Michael Harrington, *The Other America* (New York: Macmillan, 1962); and Maurice Isserman, "Michael Harrington and the Debs-Thomas Tradition," *Dissent,* Fall 1996, 105.
3. As explained at greater length in the addendum to chapter 10 below, the term *black* is used here as the expression most contemporary with events, in preference to the earlier *Negro* and later *African American.*
4. Nicholas Lemann, *Promised Land: The Great Black Migration and How It Changed America* (New York: Knopf, 1991).
5. Lawrence Lipton, *The Holy Barbarians* (New York: Julian Messner, 1959), 7.
6. Arthur M. Schlesinger Jr., *A Thousand Days: John F. Kennedy in the White House* (Boston: Houghton Mifflin, 1965), 210.
7. Ibid., 739.
8. Eric F. Goldman, *The Tragedy of Lyndon Johnson* (New York: Knopf, 1969), 14.
9. W.J. Rorabaugh, *Kennedy and the Promise of the Sixties* (Cambridge: Cambridge University Press, 2002), xi.
10. Ibid., 1009–12.
11. *Public Papers of the Presidents of the United States: Lyndon B. Johnson, 1963–1969,* 11 vols. (Washington: GPO, 1964–69), 1:250. See Bruce J. Schulman, *Lyndon B. Johnson and American Liberalism: A Brief Biography with Documents* (Boston and New York: Bedford Books of St. Martin's Press, 1995), 82–84.
12. Lyndon B. Johnson, *The Vantage Point: Perspectives of the Presidency, 1963–1969* (New York: Holt, Rinehart and Winston, 1971), 71.
13. See Daniel Patrick Moynihan, ed., *On Understanding Poverty: Perspectives from the Social Sciences* (New York: Basic Books, 1968), editor's introduction, 8–11.
14. John Morton Blum, *Years of Discord: American Politics and Society, 1961–1974* (New York: Norton, 1991), 163.
15. Text in Marvin E. Gettleman and David Mermelstein, eds., *The Great Society Reader: The Failure of American Liberalism* (New York: Random House, 1967), 13–19.
16. Doris Kearns, *Lyndon Johnson and the American Dream* (New York: Harper and Row, 1976), 216.

17. Allen J. Matusow, *The Unravelling of America: A History of Liberalism in the 1960s* (New York: Harper and Row, 1984), 107–25. See Scott Stoessel, *Sarge: The Life and Times of Sargent Shriver* (Washington: Smithsonian Books, 2004).

18. Edward D. Berkowitz, *America's Welfare State: From Roosevelt to Reagan* (Baltimore: Johns Hopkins University Press, 1991), 92–97.

19. Frances Fox Piven and Richard A. Cloward, *Regulating the Poor: The Functions of Public Welfare* (New York: Pantheon Books, 1971), 320–23.

20. Hugh Davis Graham, *The Civil Rights Era: Origins and Development of National Policy, 1960–1972* (New York: Oxford University Press, 1990), 134–39.

21. Irving Bernstein, *Guns or Butter: The Presidency of Lyndon Johnson* (New York: Oxford University Press, 1996), 155.

22. Daniel P. Moynihan, "The Negro Family: The Case for National Action," March 1965, in *The Moynihan Report and the Politics of Controversy,* ed. Lee Rainwater and William L. Young (Cambridge, MA: MIT Press, 1967), 41–124. Originally a confidential memo to the president, the Moynihan report surfaced in the media in August 1965 (ibid., 3–6, 139).

23. James MacGregor Burns, ed., *To Heal and to Build: The Programs of President Lyndon B. Johnson* (New York: McGraw-Hill, 1968), 219.

24. Robert Dallek, *Flawed Grant: Lyndon Johnson and His Times, 1961–1973* (New York: Oxford University Press, 1998), 329.

25. Ibid., 336–39.

26. See Lou Cannon, *Governor Reagan: His Rise to Power* (New York: Public Affairs Press, 2003), 144–57.

27. Dallek, *Flawed Giant,* 329.

28. Moynihan, *On Understanding Poverty,* 5.

29. Ira Katznelson, "Was the Great Society a Lost Opportunity?" in *The Rise and Fall of the New Deal Order, 1930–1980,* ed. Steven Fraser and Gary Gerstle (Princeton, NJ: Princeton University Press, 1989), 187.

30. Schulman, *Lyndon B. Johnson,* 100.

31. Daniel P. Moynihan, *Maximum Feasible Misunderstanding: Community Action in the War on Poverty* (New York: Free Press, 1969), 193.

32. Michael Kazin and Maurice Isserman, *America Divided: The Civil War of the 1960s* (New York: Oxford University Press, 2000), 203.

33. See, for example, Natalie Robins, *Alien Ink: The FBI's War on Freedom of Expression* (New York: Morrow, 1992); and Curt Gentry, *J. Edgar Hoover: The Man and the Secrets* (New York: Norton, 1992). Richard Gid Powers, *Secrecy and Power: The Life of J. Edgar Hoover* (New York: Free Press, 1987), took a more modulated view of Hoover's power.

34. Quoted by William Raspberry, *The Washington Post,* March 7, 1997.

35. Quoted in Gianni Stasera, *Death of a Utopia: The Development and Decline of Student Movements in Europe* (New York: Oxford University Press, 1975), 85.

36. J.-J. Servan-Schreiber, *The Spirit of May* (New York: McGraw-Hill, 1969), 30.

37. *People's Daily,* May 27, 1968; text in Harold C. Hinton, ed., *The People's Republic of China, 1949–1979: A Documentary Survey* (Wilmington, DE: Scholarly Resources, 1980), 4:2092–93.

38. See Ben Kiernan, *The Pol Pot Regime: Race, Power, and Genocide under the Khmer Rouge* (New Haven, CT: Yale University Press, 1995).

39. Pol Pot, "Preliminary Explanation before Reading the Plan," August 1976; in David P. Chandler, Ben Kiernan, and Chantou Boua, eds. and trans., *Pol Pot Plans the Future: Confidential Documents from Democratic Kampuchea, 1976–1977* (New Haven, CT: Yale University Southeast Asia Studies, 1988), 160.

40. Kearns, *Lyndon Johnson,* 251–53.

41. Norman Mailer, *The Armies of the Night* (New York: New American Library, 1968).

42. Goldman, *Tragedy of Lyndon Johnson,* 521, 524.

43. Matusow, *Unravelling of America,* 406.

44. Cass R. Sunstein, *The Second Bill of Rights: FDR's Unfinished Revolution and Why We Need It More Than Ever* (New York: Basic Books, 2004), 134–35.

45. See Peter Steinfels, *The Neoconservatives: The Men Who Are Changing America's Politics* (New York: Simon and Schuster, 1979).

46. See Francis Fox Piven and Richard A. Cloward, *The New Class War: Reagan's Attack on the Welfare State and Its Consequences* (New York: Pantheon Books, 1982); and Herbert J. Gans, *The War against the Poor: The Underclass and Antipoverty Policy* (New York: Basic Books, 1995).

Chapter 5

1. John T. McCartney, *Black Power: An Essay in African-American Political Thought* (Philadelphia: Temple University Press, 1992), 42–45, 54, 69–72.
2. Gunnar Mydral, *American Dilemma: The Negro Problem and Modern Democracy* (New York: Harper, 1944).
3. David L. Chappell, *A Stone of Hope: Prophetic Religion and the Death of Jim Crow* (Chapel Hill: University of North Carolina Press, 2004), 87.
4. The report, "To Secure These Rights," was released in October 1947. See William C. Berman, *The Politics of Civil Rights in the Truman Administration* (Columbus: Ohio State University Press, 1970), 55–56, 67–78.
5. Bayard Rustin, "Black Power and Coalition Politics," *Commentary,* February 1965, reprinted in Marvin E. Gettleman and David Mermelstein, eds., *The Great Society Reader: The Failure of American Liberalism* (New York: Random House, 1967), 261.
6. Quoted in Thomas R. Brooks, *Walls Come Tumbling Down: A History of the Civil Rights Movement, 1940–1970* (Englewood Cliffs, NJ: Prentice Hall, 1974), 113.
7. Inge Powell Bell, *CORE and the Strategy of Nonviolence* (New York: Random House, 1968), 9.
8. Irving Bernstein, *Promises Kept: John F. Kennedy's New Frontier* (New York: Oxford University Press, 1991), 55–56; and Hugh Davis Graham, *The Civil Rights Era: Origins and Development of National Policy, 1960–1972* (New York: Oxford University Press, 1990), 27–28, 33–35.
9. Diane McWhorter, *Carry Me Home: Birmingham, Alabama, the Climactic Battle of the Civil Rights Revolution* (New York: Simon and Schuster, 2001).
10. Text in Martin Luther King Jr., *Why We Can't Wait* (New York: New American Library, 1964), 82, 87, 91.
11. Bernstein, *Promises Kept,* 96, 102.
12. David J. Garrow, "Betraying the March," *Christian Science Monitor,* August 28, 2003, and *Bearing the Cross: Martin Luther King Jr., and the Southern Christian Leadership Conference* (New York: Morrow, 1986), 273.
13. Quoted in John Morton Blum, *Years of Discord: American Politics and Society, 1961–1974* (New York: Norton, 1991), 165.
14. Quoted in Garrow, *Bearing the Cross,* 238–84.
15. Bernstein, *Promises Kept,* 95.
16. Arthur M. Schlesinger Jr., *A Thousand Days: John F. Kennedy in the White House* (Boston: Houghton Mifflin, 1965), 966.
17. Blum, *Years of Discord,* 169.
18. Allen J. Matusow, *The Unravelling of America: A History of Liberalism in the 1960s* (New York: Harper and Row, 1984), 95.
19. Quoted in Jon Margolis, *The Last Innocent Year: America in 1964, the Beginning of the "Sixties"* (New York: Morrow, 1999), 260.
20. See David J. Garrow, *The FBI and Martin Luther King Jr.: From "Solo" to Memphis* (New York: Norton, 1981).
21. Quoted in Brooks, *Walls Come Tumbling Down,* 75.
22. Ted Robert Gurr, "Political Protest and Rebellion in the 1960s: The United States in World Perspective," in *Violence in America: Historical and Comparative Perspectives,* ed. Hugh Davis Graham and Ted Robert Gurr, rev. ed. (Beverly Hills, CA: Sage, 1979), 73.
23. Ibid., 246.
24. Ronald Radosh, *Divided They Fell: The Demise of the Democratic Party, 1964–1996* (New York: Free Press, 1996), 15–21.
25. Graham, *Civil Rights Era,* 171.
26. Franz Fanon, *The Wretched of the Earth* (1963; New York: Grove Press, 1968). See also David Macey, *Franz Fanon: A Biography* (New York: Picador, 2001).

27. See Robert Dannin, *Black Pilgrimmage to Islam* (New York: Oxford University Press, 2002).
28. Bell, *CORE,* 128–30.
29. Quoted in Bernstein, *Promises Kept,* 103.
30. Bayard Rustin in Gettleman and Mermelstein, *The Great Society Reader,* 269–70.
31. Joe R. Feagan and Harlan Hahn, *Ghetto Revolts: The Politics of Violence in American_Cities* (New York: Macmillan, 1973), 120–21.
32. Quoted in Doris Kearns, *Lyndon Johnson and the American Dream* (New York: Harper and Row, 1976), 305.
33. Robert M. Fogelson, *Violence as Protest: A Study of Riots and Ghettos* (Garden City, NY: Doubleday, 1971), 46, 59, 76–77.
34. Ibid., 105, 118.
35. *Report of the National Advisory Commission on Civil Disorders* (Washington: Government Printing Office, 1968), 110–11.
36. Brooks, *Walls Come Tumbling Down,* 267.
37. Ibid., 265–67.
38. Eldridge Cleaver, *Soul on Ice: With an Introduction by Maxwell Geismar* (New York: McGraw-Hill, 1967).
39. Bell, *CORE,* 171.
40. Brooks, *Walls Come Tumbling Down,* 273–74.
41. Feagin and Hahn, *Ghetto Revolts,* 197.
42. *Report of the National Advisory Commission,* 89.
43. Gurr, "Political Protest," in Davis and Gurr, *Violence,* 73.
44. See Sidney Fine, *Violence in the Model City: The Cavanagh Administration, Race Relations, and the Detroit Riot of 1967* (Ann Arbor: University of Michigan Press, 1989), 17–37.
45. Harry McPherson, *A Political Education* (Boston: Little, Brown, 1972), 368.
46. Michael Barone, *Our County: The Shaping of America from Roosevelt to Reagan* (New York: Free Press, 1990), 418.
47. Matusow, *Unraveling of America,* 363.
48. Stewart Burns, *To the Mountaintop: Martin Luther King Jr.'s Sacred Mission to Save America, 1955–1968* (San Francisco: Harper San Francisco, 2004), 335.
49. Angus Campbell and Howard Schurman, "Racial Attitudes in Fifteen American Cities," *Supplemental Studies for the National Advisory Commission on Civil Disorders* (Washington: Government Printing Office, 1968), 38.
50. See James W. Button, *Black Violence: Political Impact of the 1960s Riots* (Princeton, NJ: Princeton University Press, 1978), 158–79.
51. Joseph A. Califano Jr., *The Triumph and Tragedy of Lyndon Johnson: The White House Years* (New York: Simon and Schuster, 1991), 219.
52. *Report of the National Advisory Commission,* preface, 1.
53. Ibid.
54. Roy Wilkins, with Tom Matthews, *Standing Fast: The Autobiography of Roy Wilkins* (New York: Viking, 1982), 328.
55. Carl Solberg, *Hubert Humphrey: A Biography* (New York: Norton, 1984), 320–21.
56. Quoted in Jules Witcover, *85 Days: The Last Campaign of Robert Kennedy* (New York: Putnam's, 1969), 53.
57. *To Establish Justice, to Ensure Domestic Tranquility: The Final Report of the National Commission on the Causes and Prevention of Violence* (Washington: Government Printing Ofiice, 1970).
58. Martin Luther King Jr., "Impasse in Race Relations," in King, *The Trumpet of Conscience* (New York: Harper and Row, 1968), 17. See Fredrick Sunnemark, *Ring Out Freedom! The Voice of Martin Luther King, Jr. and the Making of the Civil Rights Movement* (Bloomington: Indiana University Press, 2004), 195–232.
59. Burns, *To the Mountaintop,* 297–305, 309.
60. Ibid, 298, 318.
61. Martin Luther King Jr., "Where Do We Go from Here?" (address to the convention of Southern Christian Leadership Conference, Atlanta, August 1967), in James M. Washington, ed., *A Testament of Hope: The Essential Writings of Martin Luther King, Jr.* (San Francisco: Harper and Row, 1986), 250; Garrow, *The FBI and Martin Luther King Jr.,* 213–14.
62. McCartney, *Black Power Ideologies,* 116–19.

63. See Donald L. Horowitz, "Racial Violence in the United States," in *Ethnic Pluralism and Public Policy: Achieving Equality in the United States and Britain,* ed. Nathan Glazer and Ken Young (Lexington, MA: Lexington Books, 1983), 201–205.

64. Clayborne Carson, *In Struggle: SNCC and the Black Awakening of the 1960s* (Cambridge, MA: Harvard University Press, 1981), 259–60.

65. Ibid., 285.

66. Barone, *Our Country,* 425–26.

67. Quoted in Graham, *The Civil Rights Era,* 273.

68. Quoted in John T. Eliff, *Crime, Dissent, and the Attorney General: The Justice Department in the 1960s* (Beverly Hills, CA: Sage, 1971), 127.

69. Button, *Black Violence,* 136–38.

70. Fogelson, *Violence as Protest,* 123.

71. Barry Sussman, *What Americans Really Think: And Why Our Politicians Pay No Attention* (New York: Pantheon Books, 1988), 105.

Chapter 6

1. "Values: Generations Apart," *Public Opinion,* January 1984, 53.

2. Ronald Fraser et al., *1968: A Student Generation in Revolt* (New York: Pantheon, 1988), 354.

3. Landon Y. Jones, *Great Expectations: America and the Baby Boom Generation* (New York: Coward, McCann and Geoghegan, 1980), 80.

4. Lewis S. Feuer, *The Conflict of Generations: The Character and Significance of Student Movements* (New York: Basic Books, 1969).

5. C. Wright Mills, "The New Left" (1960), in *Power, Politics, and People,* ed. Irving Louis Horowitz (New York: Ballantine Books, 1963), 259, quoted in Peter Clecake, *Radical Paradoxes: Dilemmas of the American Left, 1945–1970* (New York: Harper and Row, 1973), 233.

6. Norman O. Brown, *Life against Death: The Psychoanalytic Meaning of History* (Middletown, CT: Wesleyan University Press, 1959); and Herbert Marcuse, *One Dimensional Man: Studies in the Ideology of Advanced Industrial Society* (Boston: Beacon Press, 1961).

7. C. Wright Mills, *White Collar: The American Middle Classes* (New York: Oxford University Press, 1951), and *The Power Elite* (New York: Oxford University Press, 1956); and William H. Whyte, *The Organization Man* (New York: Simon and Schuster, 1956).

8. Paul Goodman, *Growing Up Absurd: Problems of Youth in the Organized System* (New York: Random House, 1960).

9. William Appleman Williams, *The Tragedy of American Diplomacy* (Cleveland: World, 1959).

10. Regis Debray, *Revolution in the Revolution: Armed Struggle and Political Struggle in Latin America* (New York: MR Press, 1967).

11. Quoted in Maurice Isserman, "You Don't Need a Weatherman but a Postman Can Be Helpful," in *Give Peace a Chance: Exploring the Vietnam Antiwar Movement,* ed. Melvin Small and William D. Hoover (Syracuse: Syracuse University Press, 1992), 25.

12. Maurice Isserman, *If I Had a Hammer: The Death of the Old Left and the Birth of the New Left* (New York: Basic Books, 1987), 214.

13. Stanley Rothman and S. Robert Lichter, *Roots of Radicalism: Jews, Christians, and the New Left* (New York: Oxford University Press, 1983); cf. Robert Coles, "A Sixties Self," *The New Republic,* February 14, 1983, 36.

14. James Miller, *Democracy Is in the Streets: From Port Huron to the Siege of Chicago* (New York: Simon and Schuster, 1987), 94. See also Arnold S. Kaufman, *The Radical Liberal: New Man in American Politics* (New York: Atherton Press, 1968); and Kevin Mattson, "Re-reading *The Radical Liberal:* Revisiting Arnold Kaufman," *Dissent,* Summer 2000.

15. Diana Trilling, "On the Steps of Low Library: Liberalism and the Revolution of the Young," *Commentary,* November 1968, 30.

16. David Horowitz, *Radical Son: A Journey through Our Times* (New York: Free Press, 1996), 161–64. See also Abe Peck, *Uncovering the Sixties: The Life and Times of the Underground Press* (New York: Pantheon, 1985).

17. Annie Gottlieb, "What Was Blowing in the Wind," *New York Times Book Review,* July 7, 1985.

18. Isserman, *If I Had a Hammer,* 218.

19. Quoted in Fred Halstead, *Out Now! A Participant's Account of the American Movement against the Vietnam War* (New York: Monad Press, 1978), 43–44.

20. Text in Judith C. Albert and Stewart E. Albert, eds., *The Sixties Papers: Documents of a Rebellious Decade* (New York: Praeger, 1984), 176–96.

21. Paul Potter, *A Name for Ourselves: Feelings about Authenticity, Love, Intuitive Politics, Us* (Boston: Little, Brown, 1971), 152.

22. Miller, *Democracy Is in the Streets,* 216.

23. See Peter B. Levy, *The New Left and Labor in the 1960s* (Urbana: University of Illinois Press, 1994).

24. Maurice Isserman, "Hardhats and Longhairs," *Dissent,* Fall 1994, 570.

25. Irving Howe, "The Decade That Failed," *New York Times Magazine,* September 19, 1982, 83.

26. *Pravda,* May 30, 1968.

27. Charles DeBenedetti, *An American Ordeal: The Antiwar Movement of the Vietnam Era* (Syracuse: Syracuse University Press, 1990), 192.

28. See Max Weber, *Economy and Society: An Outline of Interpretive Sociology* (New York: Bedminster Press, 1968).

29. James Burnham, *The Managerial Revolution: What Is Happening in the World* (New York: John Day, 1941).

30. Sloan Wilson, *The Man in the Gray Flannel Suit* (New York: Simon and Schuster, 1955).

31. David Pichaske, *A Generation in Motion: Popular Music and Culture in the United States* (New York: Schirmer Books, 1979), 92–93.

32. Jean-François Revel, *Without Marx or Jesus: The New American Revolution Has Begun* (Garden City, NY: Doubleday, 1971), 242.

33. See Robert A. Rosenstone, "The Times They Are A-changin': The Music of Protest," *Annals of the American Academy of Political and Social Science* 382 (March 1969).

34. See Martin Torgoff, *Can't Find My Way Home: America in the Great Stoned Age, 1945–2000* (New York: Simon and Schuster, 2004).

35. Martin A. Lee and Bruce Shlain, *Acid Dreams: The CIA, LSD, and the Sixties Rebellion* (New York: Grove Press, 1985), 184.

36. See, for example, Alan Watts, *Zen and the Beat Way* (Boston: Charles E. Tuttle, 1997).

37. See Lewis Yablonsky, *The Hippie Trip* (New York: Pegasus, 1968), 36–37.

38. Keith Melville, *Communes in the Counterculture: Origins, Theories, Styles of Life* (New York: Morrow, 1972), 80.

39. Theodore Roszak, *The Making of a Counterculture* (New York: Doubleday, 1969), 208–209.

40. James F. Drane, *A New American Reformation: A Study of Youth Culture and Religion* (New York: Philosophical Library, 1973), 38.

41. Daniel Yankelovich, *New Rules: Searching for Self-Fulfillment in a World Turned Upside Down* (New York: Random House, 1981).

42. DeBenedetti, *American Ordeal,* 408.

43. Frances Fitzgerald, *America Revised: History Schoolbooks in the Twentieth Century* (Boston: Little, Brown, 1979), 11, 73.

44. Nancy Zarulis and Gerald Sullivan, *Who Spoke Up? American Protest against the War in Vietnam, 1963–1975* (New York: Holt, Rinehart and Winston, 1984), 42.

45. Carl Oglesby, "Trapped in a System," in *The New Left,* ed. Massimo Teodori (New York: Bobbs-Merrill, 1969), 182–88.

46. See James Tracy, *Direct Action: Radical Pacifism from the Union Eight to the Chicago Seven* (Chicago: University of Chicago Press, 1996).

47. Martin Luther King Jr., "Beyond Vietnam," in *Martin Luther King Jr. Speaks on the War in Vietnam* (New York: CALCAV, 1967), 11, 15.

48. Quoted in *The Washington Post,* September 3, 1967.

49. Quoted in Zaroulis and Sullivan, *Who Spoke Up?* 137.

50. Norman Mailer, *The Armies of the Night: History as a Novel, the Novel as History* (New York: New American Library, 1968).

51. Richard Helms with William Hood, *A Look over My Shoulder: A Life in the Central Intelligence Agency* (New York: Random House, 2003), 279–82.

52. Zaroulis and Sullivan, *Who Spoke Up?* 135.

53. See, for example, Anthony Summers and Robbyn Swan, *The Arrogance of Power: The Secret World of Richard Nixon* (New York: Viking, 2000), 298–305; and Richard Dallek, *Flawed Giant: Lyndon Johnson and His Times, 1961–1973* (New York: Oxford University Press, 1998), 584–88.
54. See Tom Bates, *Rads: The 1970 Bombing of the Army Math Research Center at the University of Wisconsin and Its Aftermath* (New York: HarperCollins, 1992).
55. Feuer, *Conflict of Generations,* 528–29.
56. See Reginald Zelnik and Robert Cohen, eds., *The Free Speech Movement: Reflections on Berkeley in the 1960s* (Berkeley: University of California Press, 2002).
57. Quoted in Max Heirich, *The Beginning: Berkeley 1964* (New York: Columbia University Press, 1971), 199–200.
58. Klaus Mehnert, *Twilight of the Young: The Radical Movements of the 1960s and Their Legacy* (New York: Holt, Rinehart and Winston, 1977), 29–30.
59. See Todd Gitlin, *The Whole World Is Watching: Mass Media in the Making and Unmaking of the New Left* (Berkeley: University of California Press, 1980), 129–32.
60. Ronald Fraser et al., *1968: A Student Generation in Revolt* (New York: Pantheon, 1988), 354.
61. Revel, *Without Marx or Jesus,* 242.
62. David L. Westby, *The Clouded Vision: The Student Movement in the United States in the 1960s* (Lewisburg, PA: Bucknell University Press, 1976), 163.
63. Tom Hayden, *Reunion: A Memoir* (New York: Random House, 1988), 278.
64. Quoted in Diana Trilling, "On the Steps of Low Library," 39.
65. *Newsweek,* May 13, 1968.
66. Ibid.
67. Quoted in Todd Gitlin, *The Sixties: Years of Hope, Days of Rage* (New York: Bantam Books, 1987), 308.
68. Trilling, "On the Steps of Low Library," 32.
69. Paul Berman, *A Tale of Two Utopias: The Political Journey of the Generation of 1968* (New York: Norton, 1996), 121–22.
70. Walter Laqueur, "Reflections on Youth Movements," *Commentary,* June 1969, 40.
71. Daniel Yankelovich, *The Changing Values on Campus: Political and Personal Attitudes of Today's College Students* (New York: Washington Square Press, 1972), 7.
72. Westby, *Clouded Vision,* 172.
73. *Griggs v. Duke Power Co.,* 401 U.S. 424 (March 18, 1971).

Chapter 7

1. Shulamith Firestone, *The Dialectic of Sex: The Case for Feminist Revolution* (New York: Morrow, 1970), 1.
2. Robert Chandler, *Public Opinion: Changing Attitudes on Contemporary Political and Social Issues* (New York: Bowker, 1972), 46.
3. Winifred D. Wandersee, *On the Move: American Women in the 1970s* (Boston: Twayne, 1988), xv.
4. See Joan Hoff, *Law, Gender, and Injustice: A Legal History of U.S. Women* (New York: NYU Press, 1991), 65.
5. "Declaration of Sentiments," adopted at the Women's Rights Convention, Seneca Falls, NY, 1848, text, ibid., appendix 2, p. 385.
6. Mary McDowell Papers, Chicago Historical Society, quoted in William Henry Chafe, *The American Woman: Her Changing Social, Economic, and Political Roles, 1920–1970* (New York: Oxford University Press, 1972), 15. See also Nancy F. Cott, *The Grounding of Modern Feminism* (New Haven, CT: Yale University Press, 1987), 3–4.
7. Woodrow Wilson, address to the U.S. Senate, fall 1918, quoted in Chafe, *American Woman,* 3.
8. See Peter Greidel, "The National Women's Party and the Origins of the Equal Rights Amendment, 1920–1923," in *History of Women in the United States,* vol. 20 of *Feminist Struggles for Sexual Equality,* ed. Nancy F. Cott (Munich: Saur, 1994).
9. Cott, *Grounding of Modern Feminism,* 6.
10. Jean Bethke Elshtain, "The Many Faces of Eve," *The New Republic,* January 18, 1988, 40.

11. Chafe, *American Woman,* 193–94.
12. Betty Friedan, *The Feminine Mystique* (New York: Norton, 1963), 18, 186, 336, 377.
13. Kate Millett, *Sexual Politics* (Garden City, NY: Doubleday, 1970), 157–233.
14. Sylvia Ann Hewlett, *A Lesser Life: The Myth of Women's Liberation in America* (New York: Morrow, 1986), 251.
15. Leila J. Rupp and Verta Taylor, *Survival in the Doldrums: The American Women's Rights Movement, 1945 to the 1960s* (New York: Oxford University Press, 1987), 22–23, 196.
16. Friedan, *Feminine Mystique,* 22.
17. Alessandra Stanley, "The Way It Was at Radcliffe," *The New York Times,* June 7, 1992.
18. Hoff, *Law, Gender, and Injustice,* 9–10.
19. Firestone, *Dialectic of Sex,* 33.
20. See Sara Evans, *Personal Politics: The Origins of Women's Liberation in the Civil Rights Movement and the New Left* (New York: Knopf, 1979), 212–13.
21. Wandersee, *On the Move,* xv.
22. William Henry Chafe, *Paradox of Change: American Women in the Twentieth Century* (New York: Oxford University Press, 1991), 126.
23. Barbara Ehrenreich, *Hearts of Men: American Dreams and the Flight from Commitment* (Garden City, NY: Anchor Press/Doubleday, 1983).
24. Ann Snitow, remark of 1970, requoted in review of Firestone, *The Dialectic of Sex, Dissent,* Fall 1994, 558.
25. Hoff, *Law, Gender, and Injustice,* 231.
26. Cynthia Harrison, *On Account of Sex: The Politics of Women's Issues, 1945–1968* (Berkeley: University of California Press, 1988), 75–80.
27. Jo Freeman, *The Politics of Women's Liberation: A Case Study of an Emerging Social Movement and Its Relation to the Policy Process* (New York: McKay, 1975), 52.
28. Judith Hole and Ellen Levine, *Rebirth of Feminism* (New York: Quadrangle Books, 1971), 19.
29. Cynthia E. Harrison, "A 'New Frontier' for Women: The Public Policy of the Kennedy Administration," in *Our American Sisters,* ed. Jean E. Friedman and William G. Stade, 3rd ed. (Lexington, MA: D.C. Heath, 1982), 553.
30. Text of recommendations ("American Women"), ibid., 435–38.
31. Hoff, *Law, Gender, and Injustice,* 234–36.
32. Alice S. Rossi, "Women—Terms of Liberation," in *The Seventies: Problems and Proposals,* ed. Irving Howe and Michael Harrington (New York: Harper and Row, 1972), 255. See also Freeman, *Politics of Women's Liberation,* 54–55.
33. Firestone, *Dialectic of Sex,* 36. Friedan had actually been encouraged by black moderates to take the NAACP as a model (Cynthia Fuchs Epstein, "The Major Myth of the Women's Movement," *Dissent,* Fall 1999, 85).
34. Ibid., 83–85.
35. NOW Statement of Purpose, October 29, 1966, text in Aileen Kraditor, ed., *Up from the Pedestal: Selected Writings in the History of American Feminism* (Chicago: Quadrangle Books, 1968), 363–69.
36. Nadine Brozan, "NOW at 20: Reassessment in a New Era," *The New York Times,* December 7, 1986.
37. Text in Robin Morgan, ed., *Sisterhood Is Powerful: An Anthology of Writings from the Women's Liberation Movement* (New York: Random House, 1970), 512–14.
38. Freeman, *Politics of Women's Liberation,* 75–76.
39. See especially Evans, *Personal Politics.*
40. Morgan, *Sisterhood Is Powerful,* xxxi.
41. Ross V. Speck et al., *The New Families: Youth, Communes, and the Politics of Drugs* (New York: Basic Books, 1972), 48–49, 89–90, 178–79.
42. Mary King and Casey Hayden, memorandum of 1964, published as "Sex and Caste," *Liberation,* April 1966, quoted in Marcia Cohen, *The Sisterhood: The True Story of the Women Who Changed the World* (New York: Simon and Schuster, 1988), 123.
43. Hole and Levine, *Rebirth of Feminism,* 111–12.
44. Ibid., 112.
45. Ibid., 113.

46. Wandersee, *On the Move*, 9–15.
47. Janet Mezzack, " 'Without Manners You Are Nothing': Lady Bird Johnson, Eartha Kitt, and the Women Doers' Luncheon of January 18, 1968," *Presidential Studies Quarterly* 10, no. 4 (Fall 1990).
48. Hole and Levine, *Rebirth of Feminism*, 117–19.
49. Ibid., 126–30.
50. Ibid., 123–24; Marcia Cohen, *The Sisterhood: The True Story of the Women Who Changed the World* (New York: Simon and Schuster, 1988), 149–53.
51. Ibid., 149.
52. Alice Echols, " 'Woman Power' and Women's Liberation: Explaining the Relation between the Antiwar Movement and the Women's Liberation Movement," in *Give Peace a Chance: Exploring the Antiwar Movement,* ed. Melvin Small and William D. Hoover (Syracuse, NY: Syracuse University Press, 1992), 172, 177–78.
53. Wandersee, *On the Move*, xiv–xv; see also Hole and Levine, *Rebirth of Feminism*, 116.
54. See Wandersee, *On the Move*, 6–7; Morgan, *Sisterhood Is Powerful*, xxvii–xxviii.
55. Redstockings Manifesto, text, ibid., 533–34.
56. Quoted in Wandersee, *On the Move*, 8.
57. Betty Friedan, "Up from the Kitchen Floor," *The New York Times Magazine*, March 4, 1973, 34.
58. Quoted in Wandersee, *On the Move*, 42–43.
59. Cohen, *Sisterhood*, 286–87.
60. Freeman, *Politics of Women's Liberation*, 84–88.
61. Wandersee, *On the Move*, 49–52.
62. See Daniel Horowitz, *Betty Friedan and the Making of the Feminine Mystique: The American Left, the Cold War, and Modern Feminism* (Amherst: University of Massachusetts Press, 1998), 102–52.
63. Carolyn Bird with Sara Welles Briller, *Born Female: The High Cost of Keeping Women Down* (New York: McKay, 1968), xiv.
64. Wandersee, *On the Move*, 66.
65. Cohen, *Sisterhood*, 243–44.
66. Millett, *Sexual Politics,* 178.
67. Ibid., 157.
68. Kate Millett, "Sexual Politics: A Manifesto for Revolution," in *Notes from the Second Year* (New York: Radical Feminism, 1970), 111.
69. Millett, *Sexual Politics,* 363.
70. Quoted in Cohen, *Sisterhood,* 246.
71. *Time,* August 31, 1970.
72. Betty Friedan, "Critique of Sexual Politics," *Social Policy* (November 1970), reprinted in Friedan, *It Changed My Life: Writings on the Women's Movement* (New York: Random House, 1976), 158–62; cf. Cohen, *Sisterhood,* 248–49.
73. Germaine Greer, *The Female Eunuch* (London: MacGibbon and Kee, 1970; New York: McGraw-Hill, 1971), 6, 8.
74. Greer, conversation of 1969 with Ajai Singh Mehta, editor of Paladin Books, quoted in Cohen, *Sisterhood,* 128.
75. Greer, *Female Eunuch,* 313–18, 320, 324.
76. William O'Neill, *Coming Apart: An Informal History of America in the 1960s* (New York: Times Books, 1971), 268.
77. Helen S. Perry, *The Human Be-In* (New York: Basic Books, 1970), 178.
78. Alfred C. Kinsey et al., *Sexual Behavior in the Human Male* (Philadelphia: Saunders, 1948); *Sexual Behavior in the Human Female* (Philadelphia: Saunders, 1953).
79. O'Neill, *Coming Apart,* 204–205.
80. Helen Gurley Brown, *Sex and the Single Girl* (New York: Pocket Books, 1962).
81. *The 1969 World Book Year Book* (Chicago: World Book, 1969), 340.
82. Perry, *Human Be-In,* 185–86.
83. Harrison Eddy, ed., *Sex and the College Student* (New York: Atheneum, 1966), 4–6.
84. *The New York Times,* March 15, May 13, 1968.
85. Charles Kuralt, *If You Would Be My POSSLQ* (New York: Holt, Rinehart and Winston, 1981).

86. Lawrence Lader, *Abortion II: Making the Revolution* (Boston: Beacon Press, 1973), 215.
87. *The New York Times*, April 18, May 1, 1968.
88. Morgan, *Sisterhood Is Powerful*, xxxi.
89. George A. Akerlof and Janet L. Yellin, "New Mothers, Not Married: Technology Shock, the Demise of Shotgun Marriage, and the Increase in Out-of-Wedlock Birth," *Brookings Review* 14, no. 4 (Fall 1996), 19. See also, by the same authors, "An Analysis of Out-of-Wedlock Childbearing in the United States," *Quarterly Journal of Economics* (May 1996).
90. Akerlof and Yellin, "New Mothers," 20–21.
91. Rosalind Pollack Petchesky, *Abortion and Woman's Choice: The State, Sexuality, and Reproductive Freedom*, rev. ed. (Boston: Northeastern University Press, 1990), 288.
92. Lader, *Abortion II*, viii.
93. *Griswold v. Connecticut*, 381 U.S. 479 (1965).
94. See David J. Garrow, *Liberty and Sexuality: The Right to Privacy and the Making of Roe v. Wade* (New York: Macmillan, 1994), 277.
95. Ibid., 297–323.
96. Text in Friedan, *It Changed My Life*, 102.
97. Petchesky, *Abortion*, 122–23.
98. Ibid., 124.
99. Lader, *Abortion II*, 81–82.
100. Petchesky, *Abortion*, 113.
101. Amy Kesselman, "Women vs. Connecticut: Conducting a Statewide Hearing on Abortion," in *Abortion Wars: A Half-Century of Struggle, 1950–2000*, ed. Rickie Solinger (Berkeley: University of California Press, 1998), 42.
102. Lader, *Abortion II*, 95–96; Petchesky, *Abortion*, 129.
103. Hoff, *Law, Gender, and Injustice*, 300–301.
104. Garrow, *Liberty and Sexuality*, 453–54.
105. *Roe v. Wade*, 910 U.S. 166.
106. Lader, *Abortion II*, 223.
107. Hole and Levine, *Rebirth of Feminism*, 54.
108. Wandersee, *On the Move*, 40, 46.
109. Jane J. Mansbridge, *Why We Lost the ERA* (Chicago: University of Chicago Press, 1986), 14.
110. Hugh Davis Graham, *The Civil Rights Era: Origins and Development of National Policy, 1960–1972* (New York: Oxford University Press, 1990), 418.
111. Ibid., 391, 393.
112. Hoff, *Law, Gender, and Injustice*, 232.
113. Mansbridge, *Why We Lost the ERA*, 13.
114. Hoff, *Law, Gender, and Injustice*, 245.
115. Mansbridge, *Why We Lost the ERA*, 2.
116. Joan Hoff-Wilson, ed., *Rights of Passage: The Past and Future of the ERA* (Bloomington: Indiana University Press, 1986), xvi.
117. Deborah L. Rhode, *Justice and Gender: Sex Discrimination and the Law* (Cambridge, MA: Harvard University Press, 1989), 30.
118. Barbara Ehrenreich, *Fear of Falling* (New York: Pantheon Books, 1989), 100.
119. Graham, *Civil Rights Era*, 232.
120. Wandersee, *On the Move*, 18–19.
121. Hoff, *Law, Gender, and Injustice*, 234, 245.
122. Rhode, *Justice and Gender*, 87.
123. Hoff, *Law, Gender, and Injustice*, 235–45.
124. Ibid., 229.

Chapter 8

1. William O'Neill, *Coming Apart: An Informal History of America in the 1960s* (New York: Times Books, 1971), 108.
2. Quoted, ibid.
3. See, for example, William Bennett, *The Book of Virtues: A Treasury of Great Moral Stories* (New York: Simon and Schuster, 1993).

4. See Peter Steinfels, *The Neo-Conservatives: The Men Who Are Changing America's Politics* (New York: Simon and Schuster, 1979), esp. 10–13.
5. Ibid., 294.
6. William Martin, *With God on Our Side: The Rise of the Religious Right in America* (New York: Broadway Books, 1996), 195.
7. *Christian Harvest Times,* June 1980, quoted, ibid., 196.
8. Stephen E. Ambrose, *Nixon,* vol. 2, *The Triumph of a Politician, 1962–1972* (New York: Simon and Schuster, 1989), 261.
9. Richard Reeves, *Nixon: Alone in the White House* (New York: Simon and Schuster, 2001), 14, 109–10.
10. Hugh Davis Graham, *The Civil Rights Era: Origins and Development of National Policy, 1960–1972* (New York: Oxford University Press, 1990), 302.
11. See Daniel P. Moynihan, *The Politics of a Guaranteed Income: The Nixon Administration and the Family Assistance Plan* (New York: Random House, 1973).
12. Ibid., 553.
13. See, for some recent appraisals, Adam Clymer, "Rethinking Reagan: Was He a Man of Ideals After All?" *The New York Times,* April 6, 2002.
14. See Elizabeth Drew, "A Reporter at Large: Legal Services," *The New Yorker,* March 1, 1982.
15. See Ken Auletta, *The Underclass* (New York: Random House, 1982); and Jonathan Freedman, "Cruel and Unusual Punishment," *The Washington Post,* October 22, 1995.
16. Herbert J. Gans, *The War against the Poor: The Underclass and Antipoverty Policy* (New York: Basic Books, 1995).
17. This shift is graphically illustrated in Samuel G. Freedman's account, *The Inheritance: How Three Families and America Moved from Roosevelt to Reagan and Beyond* (New York: Simon and Schuster, 1996).
18. See Jason DeParle, *American Dream: Three Women, Ten Kids, and a Nation's Drive to End Welfare* (New York: Viking, 2004).
19. Charles Murray, *Losing Ground: American Social Policy, 1950–1980* (New York: Basic Books, 1984).
20. Robert Greenstein, "Losing Faith in Losing Ground," *The New Republic,* March 25, 1985.
21. Quoted in Linda Greenhouse, "Church-State Issue to Be Sharpened," *The New York Times,* August 6, 1984.
22. Martin, *With God on Our Side,* 157.
23. Quoted, ibid., 189.
24. Described by Ann Banks, *Washington Post Book World,* October 17, 2004, 10.
25. Michael Lind, "Rev. Robertson's Grand International Conspiracy Theory," *New York Review of Books,* February 2, 1995, and correspondence April 20, 1995.
26. David Brooks, *Bobos in Paradise: The New Upper Class and How They Got There* (New York: Simon and Schuster, 2000), 10.

Chapter 9

1. Cited in Timothy Noah, "Birth of a New Idea," *The New Republic,* December 30, 1985, 20–22.
2. Arthur Marwick, *The Sixties: Cultural Revolution in Britain, France, Italy, and the US, c. 1958–c. 1972* (Oxford: Oxford University Press, 1998), 13.
3. "Radicals Keep '60s Ethos Alive," The Associated Press, October 20, 1990.
4. See Judith Hole and Ellen Levine, *Rebirth of Feminism* (New York: Quadrangle, 1971), 48–49, 55–57.
5. See Connie Threinen, "The National Women's Conference, Houston, November 1977," *The Stateswoman,* March 2001.
6. William Martin, *With God on Our Side: The Rise of the Religious Right in America* (New York: Broadway Books, 1996),163–65.
7. Winifred D. Wandersee, *On the Move: American Women in the 1970s* (Boston: Twayne, 1988), 195.
8. Ibid., 335.

9. Deborah Rhode, *Justice and Gender: Sex Discrimination and the Law* (Cambridge, MA: Harvard University Press, 1989), 209.
10. See Michele McKeegan, *Abortion Politics: Mutiny in the Ranks of the Right* (New York: Free Press, 1992), 23.
11. Quoted in Joan Hoff, *Law, Gender, and Injustice: A Legal History of U.S. Women* (New York: NYU Press, 1991), 303–304.
12. Karen O'Connor and Lee Epstein, "Abortion Policy," in *The Reagan Administration and Human Rights*, ed. Tinsley E. Yarborough (New York: Praeger, 1985), 205.
13. Hoff, *Law, Gender, and Injustice*, 310.
14. Quoted in David J. Garrow, *Liberty and Sexuality: The Right to Privacy and the Making of Roe v. Wade* (New York: Macmillan, 1994), 680.
15. Hoff, *Law, Gender, and Injustice*, 313.
16. John David Skrentny, *The Ironies of Affirmative Action: Politics, Culture, and Justice in America* (Chicago: University of Chicago Press, 1990), 224.
17. Hugh Graham, *The Civil Rights Era: Origins and Development of National Policy, 1960–1972* (New York: Oxford University Press, 1990), 33.
18. Ibid., 39.
19. Ibid., 475.
20. Nathan Glazer, "A Breakdown in Civil Rights Enforcement," *The Public Interest*, Winter 1971, 107–109, commenting on the 1970 report of the U.S. Commission on Civil Rights. Glazer elaborated his argument in *Affirmative Discrimination: Ethnic Inequality and Public Policy* (New York: Basic Books, 1975).
21. Daniel Patrick Moynihan, "The New Racialism," reprinted in Moynihan, *Coping: Essays on the Practice of Government* (New York: Random House, 1973), 204–205.
22. Graham, *Civil Rights Era*, 328.
23. Ibid., 383, 387.
24. Paul Craig Roberts and Lawrence M. Stratton, *The New Color Line: How Quotas and Privilege Destroy Democracy* (Washington: Regnery, 1995), 96.
25. Graham, *Civil Rights Era*, 389.
26. Skrentny, *Ironies of Affirmative Action*, 223–24.
27. Ibid., 227.
28. See Charles S. Bullock III, "Educational Opportunity," in *Implementation of Civil Rights Policy*, ed. Charles S. Bullock III and Charles M. Lamb (Monterey, CA: Brooks/Cole, 1984), 88.
29. See, for example, Bruce J. Schulman, *The Seventies: The Great Shift in American Culture, Society, and Politics* (New York: Free Press, 2001), 56–57.
30. Bullock, "Educational Opportunity," 82.
31. *University of California Regents v. Bakke*, 438 U.S. 265 (June 28, 1978).
32. Lawrence H. Fuchs, "The Changing Meaning of Civil Rights," in *Civil Rights and Social Wrongs: Black–White Relations since World War II*, ed. John Higham (University Park: Penn State University Press, 1997), 68.
33. See William G. Bowen, Martin A. Kurzweil, and Eugene M. Tobin, *Equity and Excellence in American Higher Education* (Charlottesville: University of Virginia Press, 2005).
34. See, for example, Randall Robinson, *The Debt: What America Owes to Blacks* (New York: Dutton, 2000) 'attacked as a perpetuation of segregation by the black linguist John McWhorter, "Against Reparations," *The New Republic*, July 23, 2001'.
35. For an impassioned defense of multiculturalism in its every aspect, see David T. Goldberg, ed., *Multiculturalism: A Liberal Reader* (Cambridge, MA: Blackwell, 1994).
36. Arthur M. Melzer, Jerry Weinberger, and M. Richard Zinman, eds., *Multiculturalism and American Democracy* (Lawrence: University Press of Kansas, 1998), editors' introduction, 4.
37. Nathan Glazer, *We Are All Multiculturalists Now* (Cambridge, MA: Harvard University Press, 1997), 94.
38. An early symposium on multiculturalism included Appalachians, Evangelicals, Jews, Italians, Irish, Gypsies, and even women, as well as blacks, Mexican Americans, and Chinese, but apart from the Hispanic anomaly, all Caucasian elements were thereafter generally lumped together in the white culture. Thomas R. Lopez Jr., ed., *No One Model America* (Toledo, Ohio: University of Toledo College of Education, 1979).
39. "Statement on Multicultural Education," ibid.

40. John T. Zepper, "Towards a New Unity," ibid., 110.

41. See, for example, Frances Fitzgerald, *America Revised: History Schoolbooks in the Twentieth Century* (Boston: Little, Brown, 1979). See also Walter A. McDougall, "What Johnny Still Won't Know about History," *Commentary* 102 (July 1996): 32–36, on controversies surrounding the "National History Standards."

Chapter 10

1. Alvin M. Josephy Jr. et al., eds., *Red Power: The American Indians' Fight for Freedom* (New York: American Heritage, 1971), 13–14.

2. Quoted in James Wilson, *The Earth Shall Weep: A History of Native Americans* (New York: Atlantic Monthly Press, 1999), 380.

3. Vine DeLoria Jr., remarks at the 23rd annual convention of the NCAI, quoted in Stan Steiner, *The New Indians* (New York: Harper and Row, 1968), 269.

4. Quoted in Guy B. Senese, *Self-Determination and the Social Education of Native Americans* (New York: Praeger, 1991), 144.

5. Paula Mitchell Marks, *In a Barren Land: American Indian Dispossession and Survival* (New York: Morrow, 1998), 321.

6. Quoted in Josephy, *Red Power,* rev. ed. (Lincoln: University of Nebraska Press, 1999), 31.

7. Troy R. Johnson, *The Occupation of Alcatraz Island: Indian Self-Determination and the Rise of Indian Activism* (Urbana: University of Illinois Press, 1996), 217.

8. President Richard M. Nixon, message to Congress, July 8, 1970, quoted, ibid.

9. Josephy, *Red Power,* rev. ed., 44.

10. James S. Olson and Raymond Wilson, *Native Americans in the Twentieth Century* (Provo,· UT: Brigham Young University Press, 1984), 171. The text of the "Twenty Points" is in Johnson, *Occupation,* 45–47.

11. Marks, *Barren Land,* 334.

12. Olson and Wilson, *Native Americans,* 167.

13. Statement by Russell Means, in Josephy, *Red Power,* rev. ed., 62.

14. Ibid.

15. See statement by Janet McCloud, ibid., 63.

16. Wilson, *The Earth Shall Weep,* 424.

17. See Michael F. Brown, *Who Owns Native Culture?* (Cambridge, MA: Harvard University Press, 2003).

18. Nathan Glazer, *Ethnic Dilemmas, 1964–1982* (Cambridge, MA: Harvard University Press, 1983), 159.

19. See, for example, Alvin J. Schmidt, *The Menace of Multiculturalism: Trojan Horse in America* (Westport, CT: Praeger, 1997), 29.

20. Richard Rodriguez, *Days of Obligation* (New York: Viking-Penguin, 1992), 69.

21. Juan Gonzalez, *Harvest of Empire: A History of Latinos in America* (New York: Viking, 2000), 173.

22. Ibid., 174.

23. Geoffrey Fox, *Hispanic Nation: Culture, Politics, and the Construction of Identity* (Secaucus, NJ: Birch Lane Press, 1996), 118–19.

24. Ibid., 128.

25. Ibid., 137–39.

26. Ibid., 143.

27. Michael Lind, "The Diversity Scam," *The New Leader,* July–August 2000, 29.

28. Desmond King, *Making Americans: Immigration, Race, and the Origins of the Diverse Democracy* (Cambridge, MA: Harvard University Press, 2000), 246.

29. National Research Council, *The New Americans: Economic, Demographic, and Fiscal Effects of Immigration,* ed. James P. Smith and Barry Edmonston (Washington: National Academy Press, 1997), 28; and Mark W. Nowak, "Debunking Immigration Myths," *Christian Science Monitor,* November 11, 1996.

30. Ibid.

31. See Roger Daniels, *Guarding the Golden Door: American Immigration Policy and Immigrants since 1882* (New York: Hill and Wang, 2003).

32. See, for example, John Cassidy, "The Melting-Pot Myth," *The New Yorker,* July 14, 1997; George Borjas, *Heaven's Door: Immigration Policy and American Economy* (Princeton, NJ: Princeton University Press, 2000).

33. Jeffrey Escoffier, *American Homo: Community and Perversity* (Berkeley: University of California Press, 1998), 36.

34. See Warren Johansson and William A. Percy, *Outing: Shattering the Conspiracy of Silence* (New York: Harrington Park Press, 1994), 81–88.

35. See, for example, Martin Duberman, *Stonewall* (New York: Dutton, 1993); and Charles Kaiser, *The Gay Metropolis, 1940–1996* (Boston: Houghton Mifflin, 1997). Both authors documented the cruelties suffered especially by gay men at the hands of the authorities.

36. Carl Wittman, "Refugees from Amerika: A Gay Manifesto," *San Francisco Free Press,* December 22–January 2, 1970, reprinted in Joseph McCaffrey, ed., *The Homosexual Dialectic* (Englewood Cliffs, NJ: Prentice Hall, 1972), 157, 167.

37. Duberman, *Stonewall,* xv.

38. Dudley Clendinen and Adam Nagourney, *Out for Good: The Struggle to Build a Gay Rights Movement in America* (New York: Simon and Schuster, 1999), 12.

39. Kaiser, *Gay Metropolis,* 205.

40. Escoffier, *American Homo,* 57.

41. Barry D. Adam, *The Rise of a Gay and Lesbian Movement,* rev. ed. (New York: Twayne, 1995), 82.

42. Wittman, "Refugees from Amerika," in *Homosexual Dialectic,* 168.

43. Laud Humphreys, *Out of the Closets: The Sociology of Homosexual Liberation* (Englewood Cliffs, NJ: Prentice Hall, 1972), 161.

44. See Toby Marotta, *The Politics of Homosexuality* (Boston: Houghton Mifflin, 1981), 312.

45. Ibid., 320–25.

46. Kaiser, *Gay Metropolis,* 275–77.

47. See *Diagnostic and Statistical Manual of Mental Disorders,* 2nd ed. (Washington: American Psychiatric Association, 1978).

48. Paul Berman, *A Tale of Two Utopias: The Political Journey of the Generation of 1968* (New York: Norton, 1996), 194.

49. See David Moats, *Civil Wars: A Battle for Gay Marriage* (New York: Harcourt, 2004).

50. Don Fersh and Peter W. Thomas, *Complying with the Americans with Disabilities Act* (Westport, CT: Quorum Books, 1993), 1.

51. Robert L. Bergdorf Jr. and Christopher Bell, "Eliminating Discrimination against Physically and Mentally Handicapped Persons: A Statutory Blueprint," *Mental and Physical Disability Law Reporter* 8, no. 1 (January–February 1984): 72.

52. Stephen L. Percy, *Disability, Civil Rights, and Public Policy: The Politics of Implementation* (Tuscaloosa: University of Alabama Press, 1989), 4–6.

53. *Equality of Opportunity: The Making of the Americans with Disabilities Act* (Washington: National Council on Disability, 1997), 12.

54. Willie V. Bryan, *In Search of Freedom: How Persons with Disabilities Have Been Disenfranchised from the Mainstream of American Society* (Springfield, IL: Charles C. Thomas, 1996), 28–30.

55. Joseph P. Shapiro, *No Pity: People with Disabilities Forging a New Civil Rights Movement* (New York: Times Books, 1993), 66–68.

56. National Council on Disability, "Toward Independence" (Report to the President and Congress) (Washington: Government Printing Office, 1986).

57. Shapiro, *No Pity,* 74.

58. *Equality of Opportunity,* 178.

59. Fersh and Thomas, *Complying,* 42, 129.

60. Quoted, ibid., 145.

61. See Douglas Martin, "Eager to Bite the Hands That Would Feed Them," *The New York Times,* June 1, 1997.

62. Shapiro, *No Pity,* 5.

63. See Thomas S. Szasz, *The Myth of Mental Illness: Foundations of a Theory of Personal Conduct* (New York: Harper and Row, 1961). Foucault's *Madness and Civilization* appeared in English translation in 1965 (New York: Pantheon Books).

258 • Notes

64. Ann Braden Johnson, *Out of Bedlam: The Truth about Deinstitutionalization* (New York: Basic Books, 1990), 53.
65. Ibid., 37.
66. Paul S. Appelbaum, *Almost a Revolution: Mental Health Law and the Limits of Change* (New York: Oxford, 1994), 50.
67. Rael Jean Isaac and Virginia C. Armat, *Madness in the Streets: How Psychiatry and the Law Abandoned the Mentally Ill* (New York: Free Press, 1990), 109–13.
68. Appelbaum, *Almost a Revolution*, 10, 12.
69. E. Fuller Torrey, *Out of the Shadows: Confronting America's Mental Health Crisis* (New York: Wiley, 1997), 143.
70. Appelbaum, *Almost a Revolution*, 146.
71. Torrey, *Out of the Shadows*, 144.
72. Robert H. Felix, quoted in *The New York Times*, October 30, 1984.
73. Appelbaum, *Almost a Revolution*, 50.
74. Torrey, *Out of the Shadows*, 147.
75. G.E. Zuriff, "Medicalizing Character," *The Public Interest*, Spring 1996.
76. Johnson, *Out of Bedlam*, 55, 69.
77. Jean B. Crockett and James M. Kauffman, *The Least Restrictive Environment: Its Origins and Interpretations in Special Education* (Rahway, NJ: Lawrence Erlbaum, 1999), 32.
78. Stanley S. Herr, *Rights and Advocacy for Retarded People* (Lexington, MA: D.C. Heath, 1983), 4.
79. Thomas K. Gilhool, "Education: An Inalienable Right," in *Public Policy and the Education of Exceptional Children*, ed. Frederick J. Weintraub et al. (Reston, VA: Council for Exceptional Children, 1976), 18.
80. Crockett and Kauffman, *Least Restrictive Environment*, 18–19.
81. As reported and criticized, ibid., 64–65.
82. National Council on Disability, "Toward Independence."
83. U.S. Court of Appeals for the First Circuit, quoted in *The New York Times*, May 28, 1989.
84. Quoted in *The New York Times*, September 28, 2001.
85. William M. Cruickshank, foreword, in James L. Paul et al., eds, *Deinstitutionalization: Program and Policy Development* (Syracuse, NY: Syracuse University Press, 1977), vii.
86. J.M. Kauffman, "Why We Must Celebrate a Diversity of Restrictive Environments," *Learning Disabilities Research and Practice* 10 (1995): 225–32.
87. Michael A. Resnick, quoted in *The New York Times*, May 14, 1997.
88. C. Ronald Huff, "The Discovery of Prisoners' Rights: A Sociological Analysis," in *Legal Rights of Prisoners*, ed. Geoffrey P. Alpert (Beverly Hills: Sage, 1980), 61.
89. Alvin J. Bronstein, "Prisoners' Rights: A History," ibid., 22.
90. *The Nation*, September 27, 1971.
91. David J. Rothman, "History of Prisons, Asylums, and Other Decaying Institutions," in *Prisoners' Rights Sourcebook*, ed. Michelle G. Hermann and Marilyn G. Haft (New York: Clark Boardman, 1973), 15.
92. Ibid., 17–21.
93. Bronstein in Alpert, *Legal Rights*, 24.
94. Huff, ibid., 62.
95. Bronstein, ibid., 41.
96. Described by Peter Passell in "Economic Scene," *The New York Times*, January 27, 1994, and January 11, 1996.
97. *The New York Times*, May 9, 2000.
98. Steven Pinker, "The Game of the Name," *The New York Times*, April 5, 1994. See also Ruth W. Grant and Marion Orr, "Language, Race, and Politics: From 'Black' to 'African-American,'" *Politics and Society* (June 1996).
99. Associated Press, July 27, 1999.
100. *The New York Times*, January 3, 1994.
101. See Julia Malone, "On the Mses," *Christian Science Monitor*, January 14, 1972.
102. See Harvey C. Mansfield Jr., "The Underhandedness of Affirmative Action," *National Review*, May 4, 1984.
103. See John Simon, *Paradigms Lost: Reflections on Literacy and Its Decline* (New York: C.N. Potter, 1980); William Cran, "Do You Speak American?" (WNET/RESO, 2005).

104. See Arthur M. Schlesinger Jr., *The Disuniting of America: Reflections on a Multicultural Society* (New York: Norton, 1998), 69–70.

105. See Kenji Hakuta, *Mirror of Language: The Debate on Bilingualism* (New York: Basic Books, 1986).

Chapter 11

1. The British writer Michael Young warned about this outcome in his futurist sociology, *The Rise of the Meritocracy, 1870–2033: An Essay on Education and Equality* (Baltimore: Penguin Books, 1961).

2. Hugh Davis Graham, *The Civil Rights Era: Origins and Development of National Policy, 1960–1972* (New York: Oxford University Press, 1990), 321.

3. Roger Kimball, *Tenured Radicals: How Politics Has Corrupted Higher Education* (New York: Harper and Row, 1990).

4. See Norman Podhoretz, *Breaking Ranks: A Political Memoir* (New York: Harper and Row, 1980); and David Horowitz, *Radical Son: A Journey through Our Times* (New York: Free Press, 1995).

5. David Brooks, *Bobos in Paradise: The New Upper Class and How They Got There* (New York: Simon and Schuster, 2000).

6. Marvin Olasky, *The Tragedy of American Compassion* (Washington: Regnery Gateway, 1992).

7. Daniel Bell, unidentified source but confirmed by personal communication.

8. Friedrich Engels to Vera Zasulich, April 23, 1885, in Karl Marx and Friedrich Engels, *Selected Correspondence, 1846–1895* (New York: International Publishers, 1942), 437–38.

Chapter 12

1. Ilya Prigogine, *Order Out of Chaos: Man's New Dialogue with Nature* (New York: Bantam Books, 1984), 22, 312.

2. Robert V. Daniels, *Year of the Heroic Guerrilla: World Revolution and Counterrevolution in 1968* (New York: Basic Books, 1989), 247.

3. Lester C. Thurow, *The Zero-Sum Society: Distribution and the Possibilities for Economic Change* (New York: Basic Books, 1980).

4. See, for example, Murray Bookchin, *Toward an Ecological Society* (Montreal: Black Rose Books, 1980) and *The Philosophy of Social Ecology: Essays on Dialectical Naturalism*, rev. ed. (Montreal: Black Rose Books, 1995); Amitai Etzioni, *The Spirit of Community: The Reinvention of American Society* (New York: Simon and Schuster, 1994); and Nancy Rule Goldberger et al., eds., *Knowledge, Difference, and Power: Essays Inspired by Women's Ways of Knowing* (New York: Basic Books, 1996).

5. Margaret Atwood, *Oryx & Crake* (New York: Doubleday, 2003); and Ronald Wright, "All Hooked Up to Monkey Brains," *Times Literary Supplement*, May 16, 2003, 19.

6. Steven Post, "Chaos and Entropy: Metaphors in Postmodern Science and Social Theory," *Science and Culture*, 2, no. 11, pt. 2 (1991), 188, quoted in Paul R. Gross and Norman Levitt, *Higher Superstition: The Academic Left and Its Quarrels with Science* (Baltimore: Johns Hopkins University Press, 1994), 96.

7. Martin W. Lewis, *Green Delusions: An Environmentalist Critique of Radical Environmentalism* (Durham, NC: Duke University Press, 1992), 2.

8. Rachel Carson, *Silent Spring* (Boston: Houghton Mifflin, 1962); Charles A. Reich, *The Greening of America: How the Youth Revolution Is Trying to Make America Livable* (New York: Random House, 1970); and Barry Commoner, *The Closing Circle: Nature, Man, and Technology* (New York: Knopf, 1971).

9. See Lester R. Brown, *Building a Sustainable Society* (New York: Norton, 1981); and Donella H. Meadows, Jorgen Randers, and William H. Behrens III, *The Limits to Growth* (New York: Universe Books, 1972).

10. Sabrina Juarez, "David Brower's Legacy," www.Ecoworld.com, 2004.

11. John C. Whitaker, "Earth Day Recollections: What It Was Like When the Movement Took Off," *EPA Journal* (July–August 1988), quoted in Philip Shabecoff, *A Fierce Green Fire: The American Environmental Movement* (New York: Hill and Wang, 1993), 113.

12. See, for example, Edward O. Wilson, *The Future of Life* (New York: Knopf, 2002).

13. Petra Kelly, *Fighting for Hope* (London: Chetto and Windus, 1984); and Rudolf Bahro, *Building the Green Movement* (London: GNP, 1986), excerpted in Andrew Dobson, ed., *The Green Reader: Essays toward a Sustainable Society* (San Francisco: Mercury House, 1991), 192, 197.

14. *The New York Times*, April 22, 1990.

15. Kirkpatrick Sale, *The Green Revolution: The American Environmental Movement, 1962–1992* (New York: Hill and Wang, 1993), 8.

16. Barbara Epstein, *Political Protest and Cultural Revolution: Nonviolent Direct Action in the 1970s and 1980s* (Berkeley: University of California Press, 1991), 9–14, 18–19.

17. Dave Foreman and Bill Haywood, eds., *Ecodefense: A Field Guide to Monkeywrenching*, 2nd ed. (Tucson, AZ: Ned Ludd Books, 1989), 14. See Edward Abbey, *The Monkey Wrench Gang* (Philadelphia: Lippincott, 1975).

18. Trip Gabriel, "If a Tree Falls in the Forest, They Hear It," *The New York Times Magazine*, November 4, 1990.

19. Quoted in James Borman, "Spare That Tree or Else," *The New York Times Book Review*, July 29, 1990.

20. Associated Press, May 27, 1990.

21. Michael Crichton, *State of Fear* (New York: HarperCollins, 2004).

22. Paul Krugman, "Noonday in the Shade," *The New York Times*, June 22, 2004.

23. Shabecoff, *Fierce Green Fire*, 255.

24. See Brad Knickerbocker in *The Christian Science Monitor*, February 15 and September 26, 2002.

25. Quoted by Gannett News Service, August 16, 1990.

26. Bruce Barcott, "From Tree-Hugger to Terrorist," *The New York Times Magazine*, April 7, 2002.

27. "Industrial Society and Its Future," *The New York Times* and *The Washington Post*, September 19, 1995. An overwrought treatise on Kaczynski, blaming his murderous extremism on the philosophical relativism allegedly taught in Harvard's "General Education" curriculum, is Alston Chase, *Harvard and the Unabomber: The Education of an American Terrorist* (New York: Norton, 2004).

28. Quoted in Lawrence E. Joseph, "Britain's Whole Earth Guru," *The New York Times Magazine*, November 23, 1986, 67.

29. Vaclav Havel, "The New Measure of Man" (remarks on receiving the Philadelphia Liberty Medal), *The New York Times*, July 8, 1994.

30. Joseph, "Britain's Whole Earth Guru," 95.

31. *The Burlington Free Press* (Vermont), June 7, 1991.

32. Susan Griffin, *Women and Nature: The Roaring inside Her* (New York: Harper and Row, 1978); and Carolyn Merchant, *Death of Nature: Women, Ecology, and the Scientific Revolution* (San Francisco: Harper and Row, 1980).

33. Joni Seager, *Earth Follies: Coming to Feminist Terms with the Global Environmental Crisis* (New York: Routledge, 1993), 3, 5.

34. Ibid., 282.

35. Maria Mies and Vandana Shiva, *Ecofeminism* (Halifax: Fernwood Publications, 1993), 164–68.

36. Judith Plant, "Women and Nature," in *Green Line* [n.d.], excerpts in Dobson, *The Green Reader*, 101; see also Judith Plant, ed., *Healing the Wounds: The Promise of Ecofeminism* (Philadelphia: New Society Publications, 1989).

37. Seager, *Earth Follies*, 167–202.

38. Theodore Roszak, *Voice of the Earth* (New York: Simon and Schuster, 1992), 213, 319–20, 312, 156.

39. Quoted in Colman McCarthy, "Restoring the Natural Balance," *The Washington Post Book World*, November 17, 1996.

40. John Paul II, remarks at an audience with American bishops, quoted in *The New York Times*, July 3, 1993.

41. Arne Naess, "The Shallow and the Deep, Long-Range Ecology Movement: A Summary," *Inquiry* no. 16 (1973), excerpted in Dobson, *The Green Reader,* 242–43.

42. Bob Pepperman Taylor, *Our Limits Transgressed: Environmental Political Thought in America* (Lawrence: University Press of Kansas, 1992), 91.

43. Bill Devall and George Sessions, *Deep Ecology* (Salt Lake City: Gibbs M. Smith, 1985); Bill Devall, *Simple in Means, Rich in Ends* (Salt Lake City: Peregrine Smith Books, 1988); and Taylor, *Our Limits Transgressed,* 95–97.

44. Rupert Sheldrake, *The Rebirth of Nature: The Greening of Science and God* (London: Century Hutchinson, 1995), 260.

45. Tom Hayden, *The Lost Gospel of the Earth: A Call for Renewing Nature, Spirit, and Politics* (San Francisco: Sierra Club, 1996), 230.

46. Bookchin, *Toward an Ecological Society,* 15.

47. Peter Singer, *Animal Liberation: A New Ethics for Our Treatment of Animals* (New York: New York Review, 1975); Bernard E. Rollins, *Animal Rights and Human Morality* (Buffalo: Prometheus Books, 1981); and Tom Regan, *The Case for Animal Rights* (Berkeley: University of California Press, 1983 and 2004).

48. Peter Singer, "Animal Liberation at 30," *The New York Review of Books,* May 15, 2003. Cf. Michael Pollan, "An Animal's Place," *The New York Times Magazine,* November 10, 2002.

49. *Christian Science Monitor,* December 20, 2002.

50. *Christian Science Monitor,* October 9, 2001; *The New York Times,* November 27, 2004.

51. *The New York Times,* June 1, 2002.

52. PETA Media Center, www.peta.org.

53. Jeremy Rifkin, *Biosphere Politics: A New Consciousness for a New Century* (New York: Crown, 1991), 70.

54. Robert Grant, "Red in Tooth and Claw," *Times Literary Supplement,* January 13, 1995, 3–5.

55. Philip Green, *Retrieving Democracy: In Search of Civic Equality* (Totowa, NJ: Rowman and Allenfeld, 1985), 3.

56. See Leo Marx, *The Machine in the Garden: Technology and the Pastoral Ideal in America* (New York: Oxford University Press, 1964); and Nina Cobb, "Civilization and Its Discontents: Variations of the American Dream," *RF* [Rockefeller Foundation], March 1986.

57. Jimmy Carter, Speech to the Nation, July 15, 1979. *Public Papers of the President of the United States: Jimmy Carter 1979,* book 2 (Washington: Government Printing Office, 1980), 1235–41.

58. Hazel Henderson, *The Politics of the Solar Age: Alternatives to Economics* (New York: Anchor Press, 1981), 160–62.

59. Jeremy Rifkin, *The End of Work: The Decline of the Global Labor Force and the Dawn of the Post-Market Era* (New York: Putnam's, 1995), 239–40.

60. Ivan Illich, *Shadow Work* (Boston: Marion Boyars, 1981).

61. See, for example, Leslie Eaton, "Is There Life after Wall Street?" *The New York Times,* January 29, 1998.

62. See Carey Goldberg, " 'Buy Nothings' Discover a Cure for Affluenza," *The New York Times,* November 19, 1997.

63. Christopher Lasch, *The True and Only Heaven: Progress and Its Critics* (New York: Norton, 1991), 530.

64. E.F. Schumacher, *Small Is Beautiful: Economics as if People Mattered* (London: Blond and Briggs, 1973), 70, 281.

65. See, most recently, Amitai Etzioni, *The Common Good* (Malden, MA: Polity, 2004).

66. John L. Thomas, *Alternative America: Henry George, Edward Bellamy, Henry Demarest Lloyd, and the Adversary Tradition* (Cambridge, MA: Belknap Press, 1983), 365.

67. See, for example, Michael S. Goldstein, *Alternative Health Care: Medicine, Miracle, or Mirage?* (Philadelphia: Temple University Press, 1999).

68. Bill Moyers, public television series *Healing and the Mind* and introduction to the book of the same title, edited by Betty Sue Flowers (New York: Doubleday, 1993).

69. Andrew Weil, *Spontaneous Healing* (New York: Knopf, 1995), quoted in *The New York Times,* June 17, 1996.

70. Lance Morrow, "Irrational Medicine," *The New York Times Book Review,* March 3, 1996.

71. Gerald Weissmann, *Democracy and DNA: American Dreams and Medical Progress* (New York: Hill and Wang, 1996), xv.

72. Langdon Winner, *The Whale and the Reactor: A Search for Limits in an Age of High Technology* (Chicago: University of Chicago Press, 1986), 5, 10.
73. Jonathan Rowe, "Our Neglected Wealth," *Christian Science Monitor,* April 30, 2002. Cf. David Bollier, *Silent Theft: The Private Plunder of Our Common Wealth* (New York: Routledge, 2002).
74. Christopher Lasch, *The Minimal Self: Psychic Survival in Troubled Times* (New York: Norton, 1984).
75. Bill McKibben, *Enough: Staying Human in an Engineered Age* (New York: Times Books, 2003).
76. Brian Appleyard, *Understanding the Present: Science and the Soul of Modern Man* (New York: Doubleday, 1993), xvi.
77. Paul Gross and Norman Levitt, *Higher Superstition: The Academic Left and Its Quarrels with Science* (Baltimore: Johns Hopkins University Press, 1994), 2.
78. Havel, "The New Measure of Man."
79. See Carl Sagan, *The Demon-Haunted World: Science as a Candle in the Dark* (New York: Random House, 1996).
80. *The New York Times,* June 6, 1995.
81. Timothy Ferris, *The New York Times Book Review,* October 15, 1995.
82. Gross and Levitt, *Higher Superstition,* 245.
83. Sandra Harding, *The Scientific Question in Feminism* (Ithaca, NY: Cornell University Press, 1986), 43, 47.
84. Gross and Levitt, *Higher Superstition,* 131.
85. Theodore Roszak, *Cult of Information: A Neo-Luddite Treatise on High Technology, Artificial Intelligence, and the True Art of Thinking* (New York: Pantheon, 1986).
86. Kirkpatrick Sale, *Rebels against the Future: The Luddites and Their War on the Industrial Revolution—Lessons for the Computer Age* (Reading, MA: Addison-Wesley, 1995), 259.
87. Ibid., 269, 278.
88. Quoted in Dirk Johnson, "A Celebration of the Urge to Unplug," *The New York Times,* April 15, 1996.
89. "Industrial Society and Its Future," *The New York Times* and *The Washington Post,* September 19, 1995.
90. George Trevelyan, *A Vision of the Aquarian Age: The Emerging Spiritual World View* (London: Coventure, 1977), 5–6.
91. See Brendan Sweetman, *The Failure of Modernism: The Cartesian Legacy and Contemporary Pluralism* (Mishawak, IN: American Maritain Association, 1999).
92. Marilyn Ferguson, *The Aquarian Conspiracy: Personal and Social Transformation in the 1980s* (Los Angeles: J.P. Tarcher, 1980), 26, 18, 23.
93. See John E. Mack, *Abduction: Human Encounters with Aliens* (New York: Scribner's, 1994).
94. Michael Murphy, *The Kingdom of Shivas Irons* (New York: Broadway Books, 1997).
95. David Johnston, "Spiritual Seekers Borrow Indian Ways," *The New York Times,* December 27, 1993.
96. Vine Deloria Jr., *Red Earth, White Lies: Native Americans and the Myth of Scientific Fact* (New York: Scribner, 1989).
97. Quoted in George Johnson, "Indian Tribes' Creationists Thwart Archeologists," *The New York Times,* October 22, 1990.
98. Quoted in *The Christian Science Monitor,* February 17, 1998. See Robert Wuthnow, *After Heaven: Spirituality in America since the 1950s* (Berkeley: University of California Press, 1998).
99. *The New York Times* and Associated Press, February 4, 2003.
100. Brian Doherty, *This Is Burning Man: The Rise of a New American Underground* (Boston: Little, Brown, 2004).
101. Mary Lefkowitz, "The Age of the Goddess," *The New Republic,* August 3, 1992.
102. Mark C. Taylor, "Ye Shall Be as Goddesses," *New York Times Book Review,* June 28, 1992, commenting on Anne Baring and Jules Cashford, *The Myth of the Goddess: Evolution of an Image* (New York: Viking Arcana, 1992).
103. Rosemary Radford Ruether, *Womanguides: Readings toward a Feminist Theology* (Boston: Beacon Press, 1985).

104. See Judith Weintraub, "Women Find New Religions," *The Washington Post,* May 10, 1991; and Karen Lindsey, "The New Feminist Spirituality," *Ms.,* December 1985.

105. *The New York Times,* August 11, 1987; see José Argüelles, *The Mayan Factor: Path beyond Technology* (Santa Fe, NM: Bear, 1987).

106. See, for example, Kirkpatrick Sale, *The Conquest of Paradise: Christopher Columbus and the Columbian Legacy* (New York: Knopf, 1991).

107. Lawrence H. Keeley, *War before Civilization* (New York: Oxford University Press, 1996), 18, 22.

108. Mariya Gimbutas, *The Language of the Goddess: Unearthing the Hidden Symbols of Western Civilization* (San Francisco: Harper and Row, 1989), quoted in Jay Mathews, "Did Goddess Worship Mark Ancient Age of Peace?" *The Washington Post,* January 7, 1990.

109. See Michael Adas, *Machines as the Measure of Men: Science, Technology, and Ideologies of Western Dominance* (Ithaca, NY: Cornell University Press, 1990).

110. See Samuel P. Huntington, *The Clash of Civilizations and the Remaking of World Order* (New York: Simon and Schuster, 1996).

111. See, for example, Meera Nanda, "The Science Wars in India," *Dissent,* Winter 1997, and *Prophets Facing Backwards: Postmodern Critiques of Science and Hindu Nationalism in India* (New Brunswick, NJ: Rutgers University Press, 2005).

Index